WORKING
PART-TIME

WORKING PART-TIME

Risks and Opportunities

Edited by
Barbara D. Warme,
Katherina L. P. Lundy,
and Larry A. Lundy

New York
Westport, Connecticut
London

Library of Congress Cataloging-in-Publication Data

Working part-time : risks and opportunities / edited by Barbara D.
   Warme, Katherina L. P. Lundy, Larry A. Lundy.
      p.   cm.
   Includes bibliographical references and index.
   ISBN 0–275–93142–0 (alk. paper)
   1. Part-time employment.   2. Part-time employment—Case studies.
   I. Warme, Barbara.   II. Lundy, Katherina L. P.   III. Lundy, Larry A.
   HD5110.W67   1992
   331.25′72—dc20   91–32680

British Library Cataloguing in Publication Data is available.

Library of Congress Catalog Card Number: 91–32680
ISBN: 0–275–93142–0

First published in 1992

Praeger Publishers, One Madison Avenue, New York, NY 10010
An imprint of Greenwood Publishing Group, Inc.

Printed in the United States of America

The paper used in this book complies with the
Permanent Paper Standard issued by the National
Information Standards Organization (Z39.48–1984).

10 9 8 7 6 5 4 3 2 1

In memory of Kitty Lundy

Contents

Illustrations

List of Abbreviations

AAUP	American Association of University Professors
ACT	American College Testing
AEFO	L'Association des Enseignantes et des Enseignants Franco-Ontariens
ASHE	Association for the Study of Higher Education
BCBSO	Blue Cross Blue Shield of Ohio
BScN	Bachelor of Nursing Science
CACSW	Canadian Advisory Council on the Status of Women
CBI	Confederation of British Industry
CSO	Central Statistical Office, United Kingdom
CUEW	Canadian Union of Educational Workers
CUPE	Canadian Union of Public Employees
CUPW	Canadian Union of Postal Workers
DLM	dual labor market
EEC	European Economic Community
ERISA	Employment Retirement Income Security Act, United Kingdom
ESRC	Economic Social and Research Council, located in the United Kingdom, a data archive funding agency
FWTAO	Federation of Women Teachers' Associations of Ontario

ILO	International Labour Organization
JTPA	Job Training Partnership Act, United Kingdom
NES	New Earnings Survey, United Kingdom
OCOTA	Ontario Catholic Occasional Teachers' Association
OECD	Organization for Economic Cooperation and Development, Europe
OECTA	Ontario English Catholic Teachers' Association
OLRB	Ontario Labour Relations Board
ONA	Ontario Nurses Association
OPCS	Office of Population Censuses and Surveys in the Department of Labour, United Kingdom
OPSEU	Ontario Public Service Employees Union
OPSTF	Ontario Public School Teachers Federation
RN	Registered Nurse
RNAO	Registered Nurses Association of Ontario
RNA	Registered Nursing Assistant
SAT	Scholastic Aptitude Test
SIC	Standard Industrial Classification code
SRHE	Society for Research in Higher Education
STC	Short-Time Compensation programs in some U.S. states
STWCS	Short-Time Working Compensation Scheme
THS	temporary help supply services (temp workers)
U.I.	unemployment insurance
U.K.	of the United Kingdom of Great Britain and Northern Ireland
U.S.	American, i.e., of the United States of America
WIRS1	Workplace Industrial Relations Survey 1980, United Kingdom
WIRS2	Workplace Industrial Relations Survey 1984, United Kingdom
YOP	Youth Opportunities Programme, United Kingdom
YTS	Youth Training Scheme, United Kingdom
YUFA	York University Faculty Association

Acknowledgments

It seems obvious that our greatest debt of gratitude is owed to those colleagues in Canada, Great Britain, and the United States who accepted our invitation to write papers for this volume. We were favored with patient contributors who facilitated our work by responding to editorial suggestion with speed and good grace.

We are grateful to Ellen Baar, Leslie Sanders, and Sharon Thomas for their careful criticism of parts of the manuscript. We also appreciate the assistance of Alexander van Gent in rendering manageable a variety of computer tasks. To Brendan Murray, Richard King, and Donald Maxwell, our thanks for bending computers and lasers to tables and figures. To Albertine MacNair, appreciation for applying her librarian's expertise to all the references in the text as well as the citations in the bibliography and to the compilation of names in the index.

We are indebted to the staff at Praeger Publishers in New York and at the Greenwood Publishing Group in Westport for their guidance and efficiency. In particular, we want to acknowledge the contributions of Alison Bricken, Anne D. Kiefer, Nita Romer, and Elisabeth A. Bruno.

Bastiaan van Gent was extremely generous with his time and expertise. Iris Codnita Bent provided creature comforts and life support; Hazel and Burton Thomas, infinitely tolerant of disruption, created a congenial environment in which to work. Finally, we extend thanks to our children, no longer children, for being interested, encouraging and, from time to time, parental.

Introduction

In recent decades, there has been a remarkable expansion of part-time employment in advanced capitalist societies. It has occurred in conjunction with rapid technological change, heightened economic competition on an international scale, industrial restructuring, and a pronounced shift in the relative importance of the goods-producing and service sectors of the economy. It has also coincided with alterations in the gender and age composition of the work force, and changes in attitudes toward the appropriate division of time between paid work and other activities.

Improved statistical monitoring and research have provided an increasingly clear picture of the extent of part-time jobs, their sectoral and occupational distribution, their nature, and the characteristics of part-time workers. What is less clear is the way in which economic, social and political forces have interacted to produce so many marginal jobs, typically low-paid, with few or no fringe benefits, no security, and with few opportunities for advancement. Still less clear is how these forces have interacted to determine *who* hold these jobs. Why are women and minorities overrepresented among part-time workers? If the attributes of these jobs were to be improved, what would the part-time work force look like, and how would its size be affected?

The chapters in this volume confront the complex picture that part-time work presents and attempt to provide a better understanding of the risks and opportunities it entails for individuals and for specific populations. On the one hand, part-time work reflects and contributes to a polarization of the workforce, consigning growing numbers of people to a state of economic insecurity from which there are few avenues of escape. On the other hand, the recent emergence of better forms of part-time employment prompts the question: what is its potential as a positive vehicle for providing the flexibility in working life that people are increasingly seeking?

In the study of work, academic specialization and the conventions of scholarly communication have tended to inhibit both the growth of theory building and the refinement of methodologies. We sought to provide an opportunity for exploring the many facets of part-time work. We solicited contributions from specialists in labor economics and in industrial relations, and from a variety of social scientists who are interested in the transformation of work. As drafting of the papers proceeded, there were some exchanges of rough copies to address omissions and contradictions. Discrepancies that remain reflect honest differences between scholars, and data that are equivocal or difficult to reconcile. Some topics relevant to part-time work, such as the participation of racial and ethnic minorities, aboriginal peoples, and people with disabilities, do require more attention than they have received. To provide a comparative perspective, our contributors were drawn from Canada, the United States, and the United Kingdom, spanning the English-speaking industrial nations of the West.

The chapters reveal interesting similarities and differences in the role that part-time employment plays in the economies of the three countries we selected. As McKie's overview and Dex's discussion of British and American women's part-time employment demonstrate, a comparative approach enlarges the scope of questions that can be raised. The general characteristics shared by the countries of the Anglo-American triangle are useful in helping to explain the substantial convergence in their reliance on part-time work. Had we selected industrialized countries that differed more markedly in terms of culture, social, and political institutions and economic structures, it would have been reasonable to expect far less convergence. However, the similarities among the three countries with respect to part-time work render all the more striking the differences that do exist concerning its distribution across industrial sectors and occupations and the characteristics of those who fill the jobs. These differences provide ample evidence in support of Beechey's claim that there is not one "inevitable" pattern of part-time employment (1987a: 213).

THE WORK MISMATCH

In spite of signs that a small fissure in the work ethic has begun to appear, work places remain "greedy" localities. With earnings continuing to fall behind inflation, many workers have to run harder just to stay even. Some do this by working overtime, some by working at multiple jobs. Many others are working longer hours, but without over-time pay, out of fear that they might lose their positions.

At the same time, there is evidence that a significant number of people would prefer to reduce their hours of work and earn less, if they could find a satisfactory way to do so. The standard connection to the world of work, both in terms of time and the organization of that time, does not suit the needs and preferences of everyone. Professionals are more able than others to exercise some discretion over their working hours. Some female physicians, for example, are choosing to work fewer hours than their male colleagues in what is still a "full-time" career (Williams et al., 1990).

Part-time workers themselves, as the papers demonstrate, are a het-erogeneous lot, working less than full time for a great variety of reasons. Reduced hours may free them to study, train, or retrain, to meet family commitments, to pursue avocations, to ease into retirement, or to sup-plement income in old age. One cannot, however, simply assume that part-time jobs as presently constituted match their needs. The majority of part-time workers are classified as voluntary and one can only spec-ulate about the extent to which their numbers would swell if some of the disadvantages attached to part-time jobs were removed. Little is known about those who may elect not to work at all because decent part-time jobs are not available or because satisfactory and affordable child-care arrangements are lacking.

There has been a disturbing growth in the proportion of part-time workers who are classified as involuntary; that is, they are working part time due to slack work loads or because they cannot find full-time jobs. These workers are sometimes referred to as the "hidden unemployed" or the "underemployed." In fact, the increase in North American part-time employment in recent years can be accounted for almost fully by the growth in the involuntary category (Coates, 1988; Tilly, 1990).

In modern society, where time is commodified and one speaks of "saving," "spending," "losing," and "wasting" time, the term *part time* is not a neutral one. Rather, it is given negative connotations, implying weak commitment, lack of ambition, and relative indifference to the material rewards of working. However, the "mad money" image of part-time work is untenable today, laid to rest by the increase in the working poor, the expanding numbers of involuntary part-time workers, the growth of single-parent families, the insufficiency of family incomes, the failure of social security to provide adequately for those with disa-bilities, and the increasing economic vulnerability of women at all stages of their lives. Employment, then, is no less central to the lives of part-time workers than it is to their full-time counterparts. One must, how-ever, go beyond merely exposing the myths about part-time workers. What is needed is an understanding of how these myths are reproduced and sustained in employment practices, in state policies, in the family, and in the wider culture.

SHAPING AND RESHAPING PART-TIME WORK

The chapters in Section Two examine the important role played by employers, the state, and unions in shaping and reshaping part-time work.

Employers

While part-time employment has expanded within almost all industries, it has spread most rapidly in the trade and service industries that have traditionally been areas of low-wage employment. As the papers show, employers may create part-time jobs for a variety of reasons. In general, the shift to part-time employment reflects the priority assigned to achieving staffing flexibility in a way that is assumed to keep labor costs as low as possible. In their grim portrait of part-time workers in the United States, Levitan and Conway observe that "employers who view part-time employees as disposable cost-saving devices write the rules for most part-timers."

The persistence of Taylorist assumptions about the "one best way" to organize work has meant a continuing reliance on large-scale production processes, inflexible work practices, rigid hierarchies of control, and the segregation of "thinking" and "doing" described by Reich (1983). Such an orientation invites the creation of compartmentalized, routinized part-time jobs that require little commitment from employees and give little in return. From this perspective, the underdevelopment and misapplication of human resources are not viewed as impediments to economic growth.

New and more creative patterns in the use of part-time workers are more likely to emerge in organizations in which a constant quest for innovation is supported by flexible structures that elicit experimentation. In such organizations, there is a bottom-up approach to change, with employees being encouraged to contribute to the refinement of technological applications and the redesign of work processes. Investment in human resources is seen as a prerequisite of economic growth. It is an approach that relies on employees who are prepared to make long-term commitments, to assume wider responsibilities, and to work on an interactive basis. These organizations are more likely to be concerned with cultivating contented and productive employees, to be more responsive to their priorities, and to be more willing to accommodate the preference for a shortened work schedule.

The State

Canada, the United States, and, increasingly, the United Kingdom can be described as liberal, residualist, welfare-state regimes (Esping-Anderson, 1989), in which state intervention is intended to moderate market consequences without challenging the principles on which the market is organized. Few would argue, however, that the state in the Anglo-American democracies has not, through economic and regulatory policies, also played a strong role in the primary distribution of income. Mildly redistributive welfare efforts rely on modest universal transfers, modest social insurance plans, and income-tested assistance designed not to jeopardize the traditional work ethic. This approach promotes differentiation between the poor who are dependent on the state and the majority who turn to the market to meet their welfare needs, often encouraged by tax incentives to do so.

The policy emphasis on compensation rather than prevention is reflected in labor market policies that stress income maintenance rather than promoting training, improvement in the number and quality of jobs, and family supports for labor market work.[1] None of the three countries is actively committed to a full employment policy, nor have they supported part-time work as part of a comprehensive approach to increasing worker skills, to reducing social policy costs by raising lifetime incomes, and to protecting the interests of youth, women, the elderly, and the disabled. As arbiters of competing interests, governments have not been innocent of bias; rather, they have facilitated the development of institutional structures that leave part-time workers largely undefended. Protective employment legislation, although rarely explicitly excluding part-timers, has been designed with the full-time worker in mind. Despite recommendations from such bodies as the Commission of the European Communities (in its draft directive on voluntary part-time work) and the Commission of Inquiry into Part-Time Work in Canada, more inclusive legislation has not been forthcoming, and movement in that direction has met with unbudging resistance from business communities.

Briar describes and evaluates how the state in the United Kingdom participated in generating part-time work, in shaping its conditions, and in casting it as "women's work" from 1941 to 1987. From the beginning of the period, such work was explicitly defined as suitable for married women, a stance that represented a compromise between the urgent need for wartime workers and the concern that women should continue to fulfill their domestic duties. In the postwar era, the state contributed to the expansion of part-time work in its role as employer, as well as by enacting legislation that increased the flexibility of the labor market. Briar challenges the claim that this expansion has given women greater equality of opportunity and argues that, on the contrary, it has effectively served to undermine the legislation on equal pay and equal opportunities.

Drummond looks at the impact on part-time work of governments in the Canadian federal system. He analyzes the assumptions that have conditioned their approaches both to work in general and to part-time work in particular. Reviewing employment standards, labor relations, social welfare, and human rights, he identifies some of the ways in which the state's treatment of part-time work and workers has had discriminatory consequences. Employment standards establish floors of acceptability above which improvements are a matter for bargaining. Because entitlement to this protection usually hinges on the definition of "employee" and on stipulations concerning continuity of employment, many part-time workers are excluded. In matters of social welfare, Drummond describes the double bind that part-timers experience: on the one hand, they are unlikely to receive pension or insurance benefits from their employers and, on the other hand, they have difficulty qualifying for state benefits when these are conditional on continuous employment.

As employers, the federal and provincial governments have not served as exemplars. Pursuing the same labor market economies, they have taken an approach to part-time work not unlike that of employers in the private sector. The 1980 federal government initiative to formalize previously ad hoc arrangements for hiring part-timers established two classes of part-time employees: only those who worked on a permanent basis for more than one third of a full-time employee's hours were to receive prorated benefits. Provincial governments, insofar as they provide benefits to any part-timers, have tended to make a similar distinction, thereby exempting the majority of their employees who work less than full time. In the United States, the Federal Employees Part-Time Career Employment Act of 1978 was more far-reaching than the Canadian program.

Is the state's future role to be confined to mitigating the worst effects of the creation of a growing part-time work force? Or can it be used to alter institutional structures so that they are more responsive to the needs and interests of those men and women who do not wish to, or who cannot, work on a full-time basis?

Unions

Unions, too, have been instrumental in shaping part-time work, both in the actions they have taken and in the actions they have eschewed. In all three countries, rates of unionization for part-time workers are considerably lower than for full-time workers and growth has lagged well behind the growth in the part-time work force. However, as McKie shows, there are strong differences among the three countries in the proportion of part-timers who are unionized and in the direction of the trends.

Blanchflower uses data from two large-scale surveys of British work places and plants, carried out in 1980 and 1984, to identify the major changes that occurred in the environment in which part-time workers were employed. The period was characterized by a transformation in industrial relations, bringing greater managerial control, more compliant unions, and leaner work forces, particularly in the highly unionized manufacturing sector. At the same time, according to the reports of managers, there was a general deterioration in the relations between management and workers. In both 1980 and 1984, half of all part-timers worked in non-union plants, while the proportion of all workers in non-union plants grew from 29 percent to 37 percent. Blanchflower argues that the substantial decline in private sector unionization since 1980 has enhanced the overall flexibility of the British labor market, narrowing many of the traditional differences between the full-time and part-time labor markets.

Pupo and Duffy say that Canadian unions "bargain away, bargain about, and bargain on behalf of" part-timers. The ambivalence that they describe has also been well documented in the United Kingdom and the United States (for discussion and references see Ellis, 1988; Kahne, 1986: Chapter 8). On the one hand, unions have fought to curb the expansion of part-time employment, viewing it as placing in jeopardy their goal of a reduction in the hours of the standard workweek. They have also seen it as a threat to full-time jobs. A number of labor disputes in the 1980s centered on the issue of part-time work. A flyer handed out to the public by unionists during the 1988 dispute between the Toronto Transit Commission and the Amalgamated Transit Union, Local 113, stated explicitly: "The TTC is not looking to the future job security needs of the next generation and, in today's shrinking market of well-paying jobs, our union believes we must ensure that all present and future TTC employment is full-time and not part-time."

On the other hand, the logic of numbers dictates that unions cannot afford to overlook the expanding pool of part-time workers as a source of new recruits. Unions are beginning to recognize that part-time working and job sharing are, for many people, an important option. Consonant with their concern to limit the growth of cheap labor, some unions have sought to extend protections and benefits to part-time workers. It is generally true that unionized part-timers receive higher pay, more fringe benefits, and greater job security than those who are not unionized (Zeytinoglu, 1987b).

Pupo and Duffy examine the contradictory roles of unions in perpetuating the oppression of vulnerable workers and in serving as vehicles for progress. Their paper presents a very mixed record: uneven organization of part-timers and inconsistent policies on matters related both to hours of work and to working conditions. The authors argue that scarce resources, misperceptions concerning the motivation of part-timers, and an historical tradition of protecting men's full-time jobs in keeping with the traditional ideology of the family wage, combine to give part-time workers' needs a low priority. The diffidence of unions is buttressed by the very strategies used by employers to maintain a fragmented work force, and by partiality in labor legislation. Much has been written about how unions, both in their structures and in their cultures, have constituted an inhospitable environment for women and how, in fact, they have espoused policies inimical to the interests of women (see, for example, Cockburn, 1983). "Women's issues," however, are increasingly appearing among collective bargaining objectives. These issues include child care, parental leave, and employment equity. More recently, policies supportive of workers with elderly dependents have been proposed (*Globe and Mail*, July 4, 1990). While women's issues are not in all respects identical to those pertaining to part-time workers, there is inevitably a considerable overlap, given the predominance of females in the part-time labor force.

The perceived reluctance of female part-time workers to join unions is often explained in terms of their multiple commitments, and they have also been regarded as difficult to organize because of the discontinuity in their employment. Further, the poor employment conditions characterizing many non-union work places are the very conditions that, rather than engendering collective resistance, may induce individual alienation and apathy, increasing the likelihood that people will quit their jobs. Nevertheless, women have provided the main growth in union membership in recent years. The notion that female workers are quiescent workers has been challenged, as White shows with respect to nurses, by the militancy of female-dominated unions that seek not only material gains but also greater control over the labor process.

It is not the growth of part-time working in itself, but rather the societal changes that this growth represents, that will likely alter the perspective of unions. As Ellis notes:

The changes in the nature of the labor force represented by the growth of part-time working, the concept of the "flexible firm," the pace of technological change and the discontinuities in employment which that has brought means that many of the problems traditionally associated with "women's work" will affect men too. Unions will need to address the problems of continuing education, retraining, equal pro-rata terms and conditions for different working patterns, and the structuring of those working patterns to meet human as well as technological needs (1988: 156).

It is in the long-term interests of unions to gain some control over how flexible working patterns are introduced, how they are used, and how they are compensated.

PART-TIME WORK AND THE LIFE CYCLE

Section Three of the book focuses on the significance that part-time work has for different stages of the life cycle and draws attention to the unsuitability of a linear career model to describe the labor-force attachment of growing numbers of people. The papers show that generalizations about part-time work must be qualified with reference to specific groups—the young, the old, and women at several phases of their lives—and must also recognize national peculiarities in both labor supply and demand.

Youth: Starting Out

In all three countries under consideration, there have been mounting concerns about the failure of educational and vocational training to prepare the young for employment in a knowledge-based economy (Select Committee on the European Communities, 1990; U.S. Department of Labor. Commission on Achieving Necessary Skills, 1991; Yalnizyan and Wolfe, 1989). None of the three countries structures the transition from school to work in a systematic way, and in all three the problem of youth unemployment has proved intractable. Young people who do not pursue post-secondary education confront a bewildering variety of state-sponsored training and work-experience programs that have come under criticism because of their short-term nature and because they do not provide adequate skills for permanent full-time employment. Part-time work has not been widely used in combination with study programs to provide young people with opportunities that will pay off in better full-time careers.

Rothman assesses the social and economic factors that have given rise to the working student in the United States. He examines the ways in which labor force participation interacts with other dimensions of the lives of young people. He argues that, for middle-class students, working is not demonstrably beneficial, nor has it been proved harmful. Part-time work is not a springboard to a career and, in fact, is perceived by students themselves as largely irrelevant to their futures. For them, the advantage clearly lies in the here-and-now: working gives them the wherewithal to participate in a consumption-oriented teenage culture, one that is assiduously courted in the marketplace. Young people from poor and working-class families have a strong financial incentive to work, but have less access to jobs.

Lowe and Krahn's Canadian study of work attitudes and labor market outcomes after graduation from high school confirms Rothman's assessment that part-time work is a "mixed blessing." For those who work while in high school, the chief benefit is discretionary income. They found that student part-time employment—low-status and gender-segregated—confers few labor market advantages on those who do not continue their education after high school. It does increase the likelihood of holding a job during postsecondary studies. Lowe and Krahn recommend that, in view of the tendency of employers to recruit teenagers at an ever-earlier age, attention should be given to negative effects of such employment on the social and psychological development of these younger teenagers.

Dale compares the role played by part-time work in the lives of British school leavers, students over the age of 16, and younger teenagers who are still in school. Despite high youth unemployment in the United Kingdom, the expansion of part-time jobs has had a limited impact on young people. The two main factors affecting the youth labor market have been the increase in the number of those staying on at school after the age of 16, and the creation of government training schemes. The Youth Training Scheme (YTS) has replaced full-time employment as the major activity of sixteen-year-old school leavers, providing employers with a cheap supply of youth labor. Only a small percentage of school leavers take part-time work as a substitute for full-time work, a move that jeopardizes their opportunities in the future. Employers with part-time jobs to offer prefer to recruit married women, who are viewed as more reliable, or students, who are likely to be better qualified.

Women and the Part-Time Expedient

The dramatic increase in the participation of women in the paid labor force has occurred together with delayed marriage, a rising divorce rate, a decreasing birth rate, compression of the child-bearing years, and a growing emphasis on economic independence for women. In their study of what they term the "individualization" of women's lives, Jones et al. (1990) provide detailed evidence that contemporary women undertake a greater variety of roles, move more freely among those roles, and display more individual variations in their life patterns than did earlier generations. Is this development emancipatory? What are the cumulative effects of fragmentation?

In the distinctive punctuation of women's lives, part-time work has potential relevance for several phases, since it represents an adaptive strategy that permits women to work for pay while maintaining primary responsibility for the exigencies of family life. The attractiveness of this option is, however, mitigated by the risks it entails for job satisfaction, immediate and lifetime earnings, and career progression. Moreover, women are not always able to achieve even the flexibility they seek by working part time, because the jobs often involve highly unpredictable schedules and inconvenient hours.

It has been well documented that the expansion of part-time work has reinforced, if not increased, the occupational segregation of male and female employment, producing what Robinson (1988) has described as a form of resegregation. Gender also enters the social construction of what constitutes full-time and part-time employment. For instance, a senior male lawyer who maintains a partial connection to a law firm while serving on the boards of other organizations is likely to be defined differently from a woman who combines her part-time legal work with unpaid labor in the home or with voluntary service organizations.

Dex's paper explores the substantial differences between women's part-time employment in the United Kingdom and in the United States. Using cohort data on work histories from the two countries, she identifies a stronger life-cycle aspect to part-time working among British women, and less downward occupational mobility after childbirth among American women. These patterns, she argues, cannot be explained simply in terms of women's preferences; rather, they are heavily influenced by social policy, tax policy, employer practices, and cultural traditions, all of which provide British women with fewer incentives and opportunities to enter full-time employment.

Duffy and Pupo's analysis of the Canadian situation emphasizes the contradictory nature of part-time work. The authors conceptualize it as an arrangement that fits neatly into the niche between capitalism and patriarchy, helping to sustain the two systems by drawing women into paid work while leaving the traditional modus vivendi between men and women undisturbed. Their review of the costs and benefits of part-time employment reveals the complexity of the concept of "choice" and the inadequacy of voluntaristic explanations of women's labor-force status.

Older Workers

While the work force is becoming feminized, it is also aging in most industrialized countries, due to falling birth rates and improvements in life expectancy. It is clear, however, that older workers, like women, experience disproportional employment hazards. Will the trend to slower growth in the population of working age produce attitudinal and institutional changes that will check the present deterioration of the labor market position of older workers? Will it give pause for a reconceptualization of part-time work?

Retirement patterns are becoming less rigid, largely on the early side of the standard retirement age, but this development has more to do with the responses of employers and governments to economic conditions than with a deliberate attempt to widen the options available to older workers (Blyton, 1985). Of the various routes to ultimate withdrawal from the labor force, some form of phased retirement has perhaps the greatest potential to cushion the impact of a major life change. Yet, despite evidence that many workers would prefer a shortened workday or workweek in their later years, opportunities that protect occupational status, relative earnings, and pension entitlements are rare. The more common path is full retirement followed by part-time working, with a significant loss in both status and income. In these circumstances, that older workers are increasingly willing to accept the inferior conditions of part-time jobs in their post-retirement years attests to their financial straits.

Canadians aged 55 and over comprise a growing share of the total population, but a decreasing proportion is remaining in the labor force. For those who do remain, there is an increasing tendency to work part time, particularly after age of 65. To shed light on this trend, McDonald and Wanner construct socioeconomic profiles of older Canadian workers of both sexes. They find that part-time work after age 55 is generally at the periphery of the economy. Before age 65, the conditions of employment for part-time workers are distinctly inferior to those of full-time workers. After age 65, conditions are poor for both full- and part-time workers; however, part-time work is the overwhelming preference. The authors predict that the labor supplied by older workers will gain in importance and may prove essential for sustained economic growth. If this is so, then the obstacles to their participation will have to be eliminated. The obstacles include the attitudes of unions toward part-time work, the stipulations of pension plans that create disincentives to working, the lack of retraining opportunities, and the reluctance of employers to permit graduated retirement.

Golden's paper on the marginalization of older workers in the United States emphasizes the definitive role played by employers in creating contingent jobs and in reducing their work force by means of early retirement schemes.[2] He questions the desirability of the early retirement trend, in view of evidence that it is increasingly involuntary. His examination of the rehiring practices of corporations suggests that most are highly exploitative. Golden points to the alterations in corporate policies and in legislation that will have to occur if part-time work is to make a contribution to the income security of older persons while providing them with greater discretion over both the age of retirement and the pace at which it is effected.

A CLOSER LOOK AT INDUSTRIES AND OCCUPATIONS

Several empirical studies of part-time work in specific contexts are reported in Section Four of the book. This narrower focus reveals both the heterogeneity and the hierarchical nature of jobs that are less than full time. As Tilly notes, when one looks beyond an economistic profile of the average part-time job, "fascinating glimpses of diversity emerge." How do "good" part-time jobs differ from "bad" ones, and in what industries and occupations are they most likely to be found? Research on non-traditional part-time work is valuable because it expands conventional notions of the work places in which reduced-hour patterns can be adopted. Research can also help to identify the risks that confront even the most advantaged part-time workers.

Tilly's study of part-time employment in the retail and insurance industries leads him to argue that shortened hours per se are not what makes part-time jobs inferior. He identifies "retention" and "secondary" part-time jobs, distinguished by levels of skill and training, breadth of job description, compensation, and connection with promotion ladders. Tilly examines the ways in which the two types are linked to the organization's broader set of employment relationships. Firms have a repertoire of labor markets from which to choose in order to meet their objectives of cost minimization, labor market flexibility, and labor market predictability. Tilly finds that, while the insurance and retail industries offer both retention and secondary part-time jobs, there is a large difference in emphasis. Insurers, seeking a stable work force, locate most of their positions in a salaried labor market and thus tend to create retention part-time jobs, though on a small scale. Retailers, who place more emphasis on cheap labor and are less concerned about turnover, put most of their jobs into a secondary labor market, creating large numbers of inferior part-time jobs.

Retention part-time jobs are negotiated on an individual basis to accommodate the priorities of employees who, by virtue of their skills and experience, are more able to command flexibility on the part of their employers. However, long-term arrangements of this kind tend to take the employee no further than midpoint up the job ladder. Thus, even firms with a broad conception of part-time work are unlikely to view it as suitable for high-level positions. Part-timers with good jobs clearly face greater career risks than full-time employees doing comparable work.

Zeytinoglu's study of part-time and occasional teachers at the elementary school level provides an interesting opportunity for a closer look at how these two tiers stand in relation to the full-time tier. In the Ontario elementary school system, teachers in all three tiers have the same qualifications and, in the classroom, perform the same tasks. Nevertheless, pay, benefits, access to training, and promotion opportunities vary consistently.

Part-time teachers are more advantaged than most part-time workers, since they receive, on a pro rata basis, the same salary and benefits as their full-time colleagues. Occasional teachers, who may work in one classroom for only a few days or for almost a full year, receive lower per diem pay and no benefits. Part-time and full-time teachers hold two types of contracts: an individual one with a specific school board, and a collective agreement signed by the teachers' association, which serves double duty as a professional association and a labor union. Occasional teachers, in contrast, hold an "implicit" contract to provide services for a limited period of time set by the employer. Although most are legally qualified to teach in Ontario schools, they are not considered "teachers" under the definition of the Teaching Profession Act, since they are not formally under contract. Therefore, under the province's collective bargaining legislation, they cannot come under the umbrella of the collective agreements that protect full-time and part-time teachers. Legislation thus helps to create, and to entrench, their marginality.

In terms of access to training, full-time teachers capture the lion's share of employer-sponsored training opportunities even though, officially, part-timers have equal access to such opportunities. Because training is so closely associated with the possibility of promotion to supervisory positions, the three-tier system works in the expected way: full-timers are considered first, part-timers next, and occasional teachers as a last resort.

Since the pay and benefits of part-time teachers are prorated, employers do not hire them for purposes of cost containment. Zeytinoglu's findings show that they are hired because they permit flexibility in work schedules, because they prefer to work part time, and because, as women with dependent children, they are perceived by employers to be suitable for part-time employment. Zeytinoglu notes that these women, also perceiving part-time work as suiting their needs at a specific period in their lives, do not calculate the risks that such a decision entails for their future careers.

Historically, universities have always made use of a variety of professionals to teach on a part-time basis. This practice has enabled them to maintain staffing flexibility in times of expanding and contracting enrollments, and to enlarge the scope of the curriculum. However, universities are increasingly hiring part-timers while restricting the creation of tenure-stream (tenure track) positions as a cost-saving measure in the face of curtailed government funding. This strategy involves indirect costs for the organization and high risks for many individuals. The presence of a permanent cadre of part-time workers strains the ideal of the collegium and is also thought to depress a university's scholarly productivity. More and more expensively trained academics are involuntary part-timers with an abridged mandate (that is, to teach *or* to conduct research), a mandate that increases the likelihood that they will have a truncated career.

While most part-time school teachers begin their careers in a full-time position, women who hold part-time positions at the university are apt to regard part-time teaching as a means of entry to an academic career (Ainsberg and Harrington, 1988). Lundy and Warme examine the impact of gender on the career trajectories of part-time faculty. They argue that a combination of factors—values internalized in the socialization process, domestic responsibilities, and institutional reward structures based on the male life cycle—negatively affects the career patterns of academic women. Women are more likely than men to be steered into part-time positions. Once there, they are less likely than men to make the transition to full-time positions, even though there are more female "involuntary" part-timers.

While Zeytinoglu emphasizes the compatibility of employer needs and employee preferences, White's analysis of the "retreat" to part-time work assigns less weight to the work–family nexus, and locates the crisis in hospital nursing largely in the labor process itself. Escalating costs and tight funding have prompted a management drive for greater productivity with fewer staff and have encouraged reliance on part-time and casual personnel. Thus, the composition of the hospital work force has changed and workloads have been intensified, threatening the quality of health care. The changes have come just when nurses have become more militant in their demands for greater control over their work, more respect in the medical hierarchy, taller promotion ladders, more in-service training, and better material rewards. The effect is centrifugal. There is more impetus to fight but, at the same time, conditions have induced a flight from the profession.

Increasingly, individual nurses are electing to leave hospital nursing entirely or are turning to part-time work in the hospital in order to escape from an intolerable situation. Is the part-time solution satisfactory? White argues that it fails to improve the job satisfaction of those who opt for it, and lessens the power of the nursing profession to demand change. Moreover, the hospital's growing reliance on part-timers has had a negative impact on the working conditions of full-time nurses—thus, in a downward spiral, exacerbating the exodus.

ACCOMMODATING DIVERSITY IN THE WORK PLACE OF THE FUTURE

There is general agreement that part-time work has become a permanent feature of modern industrial economics that it will continue to expand, though perhaps at a slower pace. Whether its conditions will be substantially improved is a matter of less agreement, despite the emergence of pockets of innovation that have demonstrated the potential of part-time arrangements to benefit employers and employees alike.

Kahne claims that part-time work offers both "a hope and a peril." Her paper juxtaposes the traditional model of part-time work with what she calls the New Concept model. New Concept arrangements, such as permanent part-time work, job sharing, work sharing, and phased retirement, have emerged slowly in both the private and public sectors since the 1960s, but have received relatively scant attention in research. There is evidence, however, that they have been applied over a broad range of organizational settings and throughout the occupational hierarchy. This diversity shows that part-time opportunities can successfully be attached to work that has hitherto been deemed to require a full-time commitment.

One of the feature shared by the New Concept arrangements is that they reward employees with the benefits that are usually attached only to full-time positions. The financing of benefits raises complex issues, including allocation of responsibility for costs among individuals, employers, and government agencies. Kahne sets out some of the approaches that have been adopted in the United States; the list suggests that there is a rich fund of experience that can be tapped in developing policies to extend these advantages to the rest of the part-time work force.

Job sharing, in which employees share the tasks, pay, and benefits attached to a full-time position, gives new meaning to the term "flexibility" in the context of part-time work. The arrangement permits widely varying patterns in both the distribution of time and the distribution of responsibility between the two incumbents. It provides a means of designing jobs to fit the needs of employees. Initially, job sharing arrangements were made on an ad hoc basis. More recently, and most noticeably in the public sector, employers have instituted job-sharing policies and schemes. Monty compares job sharing with work sharing (short-time working). The two forms have different objectives, different time frames, and are implemented on different scales. Work sharing practices, sometimes subsidized by governments, involve a temporary reduction in the hours of full-time workers as an alternative to layoffs. Monty argues that job sharing and work sharing represent very different tradeoffs in the priorities of employers and employees.

The number of people engaged in the more inviting New Concept arrangements represent only a small fraction of the part-time work force. What of the future? Speculation about how the implementation of new technologies will affect the nature and organization of work in general is germane to the future of part-time work as well. The optimistic view stresses the job-creation effects of the micro-electronics revolution, more fulfilling opportunities in high-tech areas, the elimination of disaffecting, diminishing, and mind-numbing work and greater flexibility for both employers and employees. In this scenario, the fruits of economic growth will be widely distributed, and the distinctions between full-time and part-time work will be blurred.

The pessimistic view raises the specter of a greater polarization of the work force, with a small number of good opportunities in the dynamic high-tech sector being overshadowed by the spread of contingent work, rising unemployment, and the continuation of pernicious distinctions among workers on the basis of hours worked. In this scenario, the benefits of growth will be inequitably distributed, deepening societal cleavages, sharpening regional differences, and, in the worst case, producing a social order that is unsustainable. The trends documented in this book indicate that part-time work now points in both directions. The contradictions lend urgency to the call for more enlightened public policies, greater accountability on the part of employers, and a more inclusive perspective on the part of the unions.

NOTES

1. In 1987, the proportion of public expenditure on labor market programs that was devoted to income maintenance was 75 percent in Canada, 65.4 percent in the United Kingdom, and 71.1 percent in the United States, compared with 30.1 percent in Sweden (Economic Council of Canada, 1990: 21).

2. For a discussion of state early retirement schemes, including Britain's Job Release Scheme (JRS) and its part-time component, see Blyton, 1985, Chapter 8. These schemes are also a response to economic conditions but are designed to combat unemployment among younger workers rather than to reduce the size of the work force.

I OVERVIEW

1 Part-Time Work in the North Atlantic Triangle: The United States, the United Kingdom, and Canada[*]

Craig McKie

Paid employment has become a central feature of identity and self-worth in Western countries. Rising labor-force participation rates for women and a convergent marginal decline in participation rates for men[1] have combined to focus attention on the increasingly pivotal role of employment in the structuring of social life within the institutions associated with work.

Much of the additional work created has been of a part-time nature, which is to say that it occupies less than a full portion of the normal week of work hours, or lasts for less than a full year of employment (however "normal" and "full" may be statistically or socially defined in a given jurisdiction). Conventionally, part-time work was seen as less permanent, less stable (and thus more insecure), less career oriented, and, in sum, less desirable. This view has been subject to sustained criticism, since part-time work may, notwithstanding these conventional judgments, allow a blending of otherwise conflicting life activities for the individuals concerned (Kahne, 1985).

There is a balance of advantage and disadvantage to part-time work for both employers and employees. For employees, the advantages lie in flexibility and choice of available work (Canada. Commission of Inquiry into Part-Time Work, 1983: 34–35), while the disadvantages lie in reduced access to fringe benefits, lower rates of pay, reduced job security (Organization for European Cooperation and Development, 1987: 28), conflict with full-time co-workers, and scheduling vagaries (Canada.

[*]Responsibility for the analysis and interpretation of data is solely that of the author and not of Statistics Canada.

Commission of Inquiry into Part-Time Work, 1983). For employers, advantages include reduced wage costs, reduced overtime (Nollen, 1982: 17) and reduced turnover, higher productivity by virtue of less fatigued workers, and lower absenteeism (Canada. Commission of Inquiry into Part-Time Work, 1983). Among the disadvantages to employers are higher administrative and training costs, and the opposition of full-time employees due to loss of full-time positions or overtime.

In a review of the status of part-time work in Europe, de Neubourg (1985) suggests that there are four major reasons why persons decide to work part time:

1. pressure of family responsibilities,
2. low importance accorded to full-time work,
3. disability, and
4. taxation, which reduces the end value of additional hours of work to the point where they are unattractive.

He goes on to suggest that "in Europe part-time employment is sought especially by married women who wish to combine paid work with household responsibilities whereas in Canada and the United States it is popular among young people who wish to combine paid work with training or education" (de Neubourg, 1985: 575). The common element is the blending of dissimilar activities in a heterogeneous lifestyle.

At least in Britain, the advantages of part-time work to employers outweigh the disadvantages:

The research findings indicate that the patterns of employers' demand for labor are the principal reason for the sustained growth in part-time employment at a time when adequate numbers of full-time workers are available. . . . The only disadvantage concerning the utilization of part-time labor, expressed by some managers, was the greater expenditure incurred in recruiting and administering a larger labor force, although there was no evidence of attempts to estimate such additional costs, or to offset them against advantages obtained from part-time employment. An equally unquantified but strongly held belief was that productivity of part-time workers was higher than that of full-time labor (Robinson and Wallace, 1984: 396–397).

It is not possible to come to a definition of part-time work that would be portable across all developed countries, because of differences in both the legislated limits to paid employment and the operations of the various national statistical systems. However, part-time employment is recognized as a distinct phenomenon in all Western jurisdictions, though its measured prevalence is to some extent a function of the statistical definitions employed.

CONTEXT SETTING: PART-TIME WORK IN THE COMMUNITY OF DEVELOPED NATIONS

Notwithstanding the methodological difficulties in drawing international comparisons, a broad-brush view of part-time work in the developed countries has been published by the Organization for Economic Cooperation and Development (OECD). The annual *Employment Outlook* of 1987 contained the following assessment:

It is evident, first, that since 1979 part-time relative to total employment has increased everywhere except in Italy and Sweden. However, since 1983 the share of part-time in total employment has declined in several countries—Finland, Germany, Ireland, Norway, and the United States. Second, there are large country differences: the part-time share is highest in the Nordic countries other than Finland, a country [with] almost 24 percent or more of [part-time] employment, in comparison with around 5 percent in Italy, Ireland and Greece. . . . Third, most part-time workers are women, and the proportion of total female employment that is part-time ranges from over 50 percent in Norway and the Netherlands to as low as 10 percent in Italy. In France, there has been a particularly large increase in the proportion of women in part-time jobs. . . . Fourth, the proportion of men employed part-time is quite low, but since 1979 has increased virtually everywhere (1987: 30).

While part-time employment is mostly concentrated at the growing edge of the service sector, there are pronounced differences between developed countries. Academic interest is particularly sharp with respect to the apparent correlation between levels of part-time employment and service sector employment, over the range of developed Western countries (see Kettle, 1987). According to the OECD: "The proportion in the distributive trades, which [are] dominated by retail trade, ranges from 5 percent in Italy to around 30 percent or more in Norway, Sweden, the United Kingdom and the United States. Second, social, community and personal services tend to make heavy use of part-time workers in all countries. . . . In general, mass production and capital-intensive industries rely much more on full-time employees" (OECD, 1987: 30).

PART-TIME WORK: PROBLEMS IN DEFINING

Defining part-time work in a manner such that the operational definition is portable across many or all Western jurisdictions is a very difficult matter. Though the community of Western developed countries is growing more interconnected each year, there are still profound variations in institutions such as the labor force. Clearly, the empirical measures show great differences on the dimension of utilization of part-time workers. These differences are no doubt firmly rooted in particular national cultures and cannot be easily explained away. Accurate measurement is thus a problem of considerable importance.

Part-time work may be defined behaviorally according to the hours worked by an individual (either with reference to a particular calendar range of dates, or on an average annual basis) or alternatively, it may be defined subjectively according to the assessment of the individual concerned. The first type of data may be derived from administrative records such as those kept by employers or by unemployment benefit schemes, or they can be reported by respondents in labor-force surveys. On the other hand, self-assessed part-time status data may only be derived from a survey of workers. In some jurisdictions, respondents' judgments are subject to interpretation according to a fixed standard of hours worked.[2]

There is little consistency in the way countries approach the measurement and the contradictory aspects of part-time work. Even within a single country, restatement of data to an average annual basis from a reference-week basis may cause two widely discrepant figures to appear for the same year. Implicitly or explicitly there is, in each country, a norm in hours worked per week for full-time status in a given occupational role, even though there is a long-term secular trend towards a shorter workweek in most countries in comparison to that which was normal at the end of World War II. Part-time status involves a number of hours significantly less than the normal full-time total, recognizing that mandatory overtime work may habitually inflate the real statistical norm of hours worked. International comparisons published by the OECD are usually drawn from household survey sources "where the range of definitions possible is very wide indeed"(OECD, 1985: 130). Sometimes work hours and self-definition are used in combination.

Alternative definitions have been offered. The International Labour Organization (ILO) has used one in which part-time work is "regular, voluntary work carried out during working hours distinctly shorter than the norm" (ILO, 1962). On another tack, an OECD source suggests that in the absence of standards, one should "use working hours 75 percent or less of normal working hours" (OECD, 1982: 28–29). Another definition, offered by the Council of the European Communities, suggests that part-time work is "work performed on a regular basis in respect of which an employer and a worker agree to shorter hours of work" (1982). Particular measurement difficulties arise for persons who, in the reference period, were absent for non-economic reasons such as illness, vacation, or strike. Persons totally absent during a reference period are: "excluded from disaggregation into full- and part-time workers in Japan, Norway and the United States but are classified as full- or part-time workers according to their usual hours of work in Australia, Canada, Finland, New Zealand, Sweden and the European Economic Community (EEC) countries. . . . Most countries, with the exception of Norway, appear to define part-time work in terms of hours usually worked rather than actually worked" (OECD, 1985: 130). Reference-point data in general miss part-year work phenomena, and also miss persons who are in and out of the part-time work force on either a voluntary or involuntary basis. Another set of difficulties pertain to the self-employed and to multiple job-holders with two or more "part-time" jobs.

Thus when comparing the United States, the United Kingdom, and Canada, we are faced with three different definitions.

In the United States

Those who usually work fewer than 35 hours per week. Included are part-time workers who, for economic reasons, usually work part time (OECD, 1987:29), but up to and including 1983, those who usually worked less than 35 hours, and did so in the reference week because of economic reasons, were excluded from both full-time and part-time figures.

In the United Kingdom

"People normally working for not more than 30 hours per week except where otherwise stated" (United Kingdom. Department of Employment, 1988a: S67). A more extensive definition published in 1976 described the part-time employee as follows: "Generally, an employee expected to work not more than 30 hours, excluding all overtime and main meal breaks, in a normal week; that is with normal basic hours of 30 or less per week: but exceptionally, if a teacher or academic, with normal basic hours of under 25 per week or, if an employee without specific normal basic hours, or described as part-time by the employer" (United Kingdom. Central Statistical Office, 1976: 337).

A further major revision of British labor-force data series was carried out in the summer of 1988.[3]

In Canada

Those who usually work less than 30 hours per week (35 hours until 1974), but those who usually work less than 30 hours yet consider themselves to be employed full time (e.g., airline pilots) are classified as full-time workers (OECD, 1985: 131; Statistics Canada, 1986: 91).

In Canada, workers are classified as part time if they work between one and 30 hours in the survey reference week (and are not in occupations such as airline pilot, in which fewer than 30 hours of work is considered full-time employment). To maintain international consistency, persons who work even one hour a week must be included in this category even though the attachment of such persons to the work place is tenuous. In Canada, only 9,000 individuals in 1985 were reported as working only one hour a week. Overall in that year, about 5 percent of the labor force worked fewer than 10 hours per week and about 190,000 worked one to five hours. In the latter group, two-thirds were female and 42 percent were students working in out-of-class hours. Almost 14 percent of persons in the range of five hours or less part-time work were engaged in a search for alternative or additional employment (Canada. Statistics Canada, 1986b).[4]

In published statistical tables concerning part-time work, there are two major bases of comparison when one is seeking to compare the three countries that are the subject of this analysis: annual average labor-force survey figures, and reference period figures that pertain only to a short period of time chosen for survey purposes. In addition, it is possible to use decennial (or in Canada, quintennial) Census figures in all three countries, but definitions to be used with Census data tend to be different, most notably with respect to their reference periods. In some cases, however, it is necessary to resort to Census data (as it was in Table 1.3 in this chapter) in order to fashion a forced comparison, which in turn can show the underlying dynamic of differentiation between the three national societies.

The OECD employs reference-point figures while some national statistical agencies publish annual average figures, or indeed publish both. This can lead to confusion since the two sets of figures for a single country can diverge markedly. For example, Canada had 20.7 percent of all those employed working part time in 1986 on an annual average basis (Canada. Statistics Canada, 1988: 3.11). On a reference-period basis, however, the corresponding figure was 15.6 percent; this latter figure is employed in OECD publications and other international comparisons.

PERMANENT AND TEMPORARY PART-TIME WORK

If part-time employment carries with it the stigma of insecurity of tenure, part-time and temporary employment are doubly marked. While few North American data are available on temporary work (seasonal, casual, or fixed-term contracted employment), there are some useful data from the United Kingdom (see King, 1987: 238–247). These are drawn from the labor force sample survey of 1985, and indicate that only 3 percent of full-time employment was of a temporary nature (OECD, 1987: Table 1.10, p. 38) while 16 percent of all part-time employment was temporary (up from 15.2 percent two years earlier). Of all temporary workers, 51 percent were aged 15 to 24; 54.7 percent were women (OECD, 1987: Table 1.9, p. 37).

CROSS-NATIONAL DIFFERENCES IN RATES OF PART-TIME WORK

In the community of Western developed nations, single countries, though linked through financial ties and operating with a considerable degree of simultaneity with other member states, maintain substantial differences in their labor force cultures. One of these dimensions of variation is the extent to which part-time labor is used to operate the institutions of a given country. For example, more British workers are employed part time than are U.S. workers or Canadian workers, and the differences are not minor.

In 1986, OECD data drawn from the respective national statistics agencies indicated that 15.6 percent of all Canadian workers, 17.4 percent of U.S. workers, and fully 22 percent of workers in the United Kingdom were employed part time. These proportions have in each case risen consistently over time from 12.5 percent in Canada in 1979, and from 16.4 percent in both the United Kingdom and the United States in 1979. The comparison, however, may be slightly misleading. When Canadian data are restated to an annual average basis to more closely approximate U.S. definitions and procedures, the Canadian figure rises above the U.S. total to 20.7 percent for the year 1986 and for at least seven previous years (Gower, 1988: 3.11)[5], indicating a much more rapid expansion in the Canadian work place than is evident in OECD publications. The main point is not which country is marginally higher or lower in percentage of all workers who are employed part time at a particular moment on a given measure. Rather, the point is about the nature, components, and direction of the increase in part-time employment, and ultimately, about its significance as a social phenomenon.

In this pattern of increase, Canadian women have been prominent, but nowhere is the pivotal role of women in the expansion of part-time employment more graphic than in the United Kingdom. Figures in Table 1.1 show that women dominate part-time work in that country. In comparison to their counterparts, about one in four Canadian women in the labor force were employed part time in 1986 (as opposed to fully 44.3 percent in the United Kingdom and 26.4 percent in the United States). This difference is not reflected in rates for males. There are relatively few British males who work part time (only 4.3 percent in 1986 as opposed to 10.2 percent of U.S. males and 7.8 percent of Canadian males) and their age profile, as shown in Table 1.4, is significantly different. At the very least, therefore, we can conclude that the manner in which men and women are anchored to the labor force is different in each country.

The higher overall rate of part-time work in Canada than that in the United States (shown on the basis of special reconciled figures using annual averages: Gower, 1988) is a persistent one that parallels a con-

Table 1.1
Part-Time Employment in Canada, the United Kingdom, and the United States, 1979–1986*
(percentages)

	Total Employment			Male Employment			Female Employment			Women's Share in Part-Time Employment		
	1979	1983	1986	1979	1983	1986	1979	1983	1986	1979	1983	1986
Canada	12.5	15.4	15.6	5.7	7.6	7.8	23.3	26.2	25.9	72.1	71.3	71.2
United Kingdom**	16.4	19.1	21.2	1.9	3.3	4.2	39.0	42.4	44.9	92.8	89.6	88.5
United States	16.4	18.4	17.4	9.0	10.8	10.2	26.7	28.1	26.4	67.8	66.8	66.5

* Canada and United Kingdom, reference-point basis; United States, "usual activity" status.
**Data for United Kingdom refer to 1985.
Source: OECD, Employment Outlook, September 1987, Table 1.3, 29.

Table 1.2
Part-Time Employment by Industry in the United Kingdom, Canada, and the United States (Percentages)

Industrial Classification for the United Kingdom	United Kingdom 1985	Canada 1986	United States 1986	Industrial Classification for Canada and the United States
All Industries	21.2	15.6	16.3	All Industries
agriculture, forestry, fishing, and hunting	17.8	15.3	*	agriculture, forestry, fishing, and hunting
energy and water	2.9	-	-	not applicable
mineral extraction and chemicals	5.7	2.2	3.1	mining
metals and engineering manufacturing	5.1	-	-	not applicable
other manufacturing	13.8	3.6	4.5	manufacturing
construction	6.3	7.3	7.8	construction
distributive trades	35.5	23.5	29.7	distributive trades
transportation and communication	6.5	6.1	7.6	transportation and communication
finance, insurance, real estate, and business services	15.3	11.6	10.7	finance, insurance, and real estate
other services	38.8	24.4	22.4	social, community, and personal services (including business services)
public administration	10.3	7.0	6.2	public administration

*excluded: agriculture and private household workers.
Source: OECD, Employment Outlook, September 1987, Tables 1.4 and 1.5, 30–31.

sistently higher rate of unemployment in Canada.[6] One might wonder whether the higher rates of unemployment and thus the larger numbers of potential competitors for employment of any type might allow employers to take greater advantage of the lower direct and indirect costs of hiring part-time employees. This question is especially pertinent, given the higher rates of both unemployment and part-time employment in the United Kingdom and Canada.

Shown in Table 1.2 is a breakdown of part-time employment by industry, using rough categories and allowing for discrepancies among the industrial structures of the three countries. It is worth noting that forestry, for instance, is a qualitatively different industry in North America than it is in the United Kingdom. Discrepancies aside, the table reveals considerable sectoral differences among the three countries; the British figures are, however, consistently higher across all sectors of industry, with the exception of construction (which has a heavy seasonal component in North America).[7]

VOLUNTARY AND INVOLUNTARY PART-TIME EMPLOYMENT

Some proportion of part-time employment is involuntary in the sense that the persons so employed would prefer full-time work but cannot find suitable positions. Data for Canada and the United States shown in Table 1.3 indicates that substantial portions of all part-time employment fall into this category. Especially during the recession of the early 1980s, the proportion rose rapidly to a peak of 30.1 percent in Canada in 1984. A figure of 32.6 percent was attained in the United States in 1983 (Akyeampong, 1986; United States. Department of Labor. Bureau of Labor Statistics, 1985: 57–58).

These data suggest that if a large supply of new full-time positions were created, there would be an outflow of approximately one-third of part-time workers to full-time status in both Canada and the United States, all other factors being equal. There remains, however, a sizable majority of part-time workers whose status is one of choice or necessity, a majority that apparently would not evaporate under more favorable employment conditions. One reason for this finding may be that some portion of part-time workers really have no choice but to work part time, if they work at all. Among the many reasons cited for seeking voluntary part-time work are legislated limits to pensioner earnings and inflexible schooling commitments (Deutermann and Brown, 1978).

AGE OF WORKER AND PART-TIME WORK

In the last decade, rates of part-time work seem, on an annual average basis, to have been generally higher in Canada than in the United States,

Table 1.3
Voluntary and Involuntary Part-Time Employment in Canada and the United States

	Voluntary	Involuntary	Involuntary as Percent of Part-time
Canada			
1975	880	109	11.0
1980	1,147	245	17.6
1981	1,219	268	18.0
1982	1,153	381	24.8
1983	1,180	471	28.5
1984	1,181	508	30.1
1985	1,240	516	29.4
1986	1,296	514	28.4
1987	1,337	485	26.6
United States			
1970	9,392	2,199	19.0
1975	10,694	3,542	24.9
1980	12,555	4,063	24.4
1982	12,455	5,852	32.0
1983	12,417	5,997	32.6

Sources: Statistics Canada, Catalogues 71–529, Labour Force Annual Averages 1975–1983, and 71–001, The Labour Force; U.S. Department of Labor, Bureau of Labor Statistics, Handbook of Labor Statistics, 1985, 57–58.

and highest of all in the United Kingdom. Comparing Canada and the United States first, and considering the full adult civilian labor force over the period 1980–87, the percentage employed part time in Canada rose from 17.8 percent to 20.6 percent, while the proportion in the United States rose from 16.9 percent to 17.3 percent, after reaching a 1983 peak of 18.4 percent that was associated with the recession of 1981–83. The Canadian proportion remained at or near its 1983 recession peak of 20.8 percent. These gradual and general increases mask significant age and sex differences in both countries.

In North America, increases have been most noticeable among the young of both sexes, and among older men. Older women have always had high rates. In 1987, the highest rates of part-time employment were among those aged 16 to 24 years (35.6 percent in Canada: 34.8 percent

Table 1.4
Part-Time Employment by Age and Sex in Canada, Great Britain, and the United States (Percentages)

Age	Country	Males			Females		
		1980	1981	1986	1980	1981	1986
16-17	Canada	41.6		56.9	51.1		69.8
	United States	50.6		59.6	59.9		66.6
under 20	Great Britain		1.4			3.9	
20-24	Canada	8.4		15.9	20.4		28.2
	United States	13.3		16.8	22.2		25.6
	Great Britain		1.0			7.8	
25-34	Canada	4.3		5.5	28.3		27.8
	United States	3.8		5.0	20.7		20.5
	Great Britain		0.7			36.1	
35-44	Canada	3.1		4.1	32.3		31.4
	United States	2.2		3.2	23.8		21.6
	Great Britain		0.7			49.2	
45-54	Canada	3.7		4.8	34.4		33.0
	United States	2.5		3.4	22.7		21.2
	Great Britain		0.8			44.8	
55-64	Canada	7.1		10.0	35.4		39.8
	United States	6.7		8.5	25.1		27.4
55-59	Great Britain		1.4			45.4	
60-64	Great Britain		3.4			62.7	
65 and over	Canada	39.2		43.7	61.1		61.7
	United States	46.2		46.2	58.9		59.4
	Great Britain		59.7			69.8	

Sources: Canada and United States, special reconciled calculations. Canada, Statistics Canada, Labour Force Survey, annual average basis. Great Britain, figures calculated from: United Kingdom, Central Statistical Office, Annual Abstract of Statistics, 1990 Edition, Table 6.12, Economic Activity: 1981, based on census data (working part time as a percent).

in the United States, and particularly among young women). For Canadian women aged 16 to 24, the proportion working part time rose from 32.1 percent in 1980 to 42.3 percent in 1987. Similar figures for the United States were 35.6 and 39.3 percent. The faster increase in Canada may reflect the rapidly expanding proportion of successive cohorts of Canadian women who undertake post-secondary education. In recent years, the enrollment of women has exceeded that for men; as of the 1986 Census of Canada, there were significantly more female university degree holders than male in Canada.

However, in all age groups, rates of part-time employment among Canadian women were higher than those for U.S. women, in some cases by as much as one third. For example, in 1987, 36.4 percent of Canadian women aged 45 and over in the labor force were employed part time as opposed to only 26.75 percent in the United States. This difference was consistent over the period 1980–87. Generally, for all Canadian women in the labor force, about one third have been employed part time throughout the 1980s (and about 26 percent in the United States). The increase has been almost exclusively among women aged 16 to 24 years of age.

For male members of the labor force, much of the part-time increase is concentrated in the 16 to 24 age-group, rising from 20.7 to 29.6 percent in Canada, and from 26.4 to 30.7 percent in the United States. However, in contrast to the female rates, there have been small increases for middle-aged men (3.8 percent of Canadian men aged 25 to 44, rising to a peak of 5.3 percent, then falling back to 4.9 percent in 1987; the American figures are 3.1, 4.6, and 4.2 percent respectively). One can also detect a small but steady upward trend for those aged 45 or more in both Canada (from 7.5 percent in 1980 to 9.3 percent in 1987) and the United States (8.4 percent in 1980 and 9.6 percent in 1987).

For the United Kingdom, 1981 Census data indicate a markedly different picture from that seen in North America. Very few younger Britons worked part time, and very few males of any age held part-time work status. Rather, it was middle-aged women who held most part-time positions. For example, of employed women aged 35 and over, almost one half were employed part time. Later data from the 1985 Eurostat survey (1985: table 42, p. 121) show that almost exactly 50 percent of employed British women aged 25 to 49 worked part time in contrast to less than 1.5 percent of employed men in the same age group. Clearly, in contrast to the experience in Canada and the United States, part-time work is almost entirely a female phenomenon in the United Kingdom. At the same time, part-time student labor is virtually absent. These differences are of such magnitude that they can be viewed as basic differences in the culture of work on the two sides of the Atlantic Ocean.

PART-TIME WORK AND UNIONIZATION

Membership in trade unions is also a phenomenon that varies greatly from country to country, at least in part according to whether or not public sector employees are permitted to bargain collectively. As a percentage of all wage and salaried workers, rates in 1983 varied across OECD countries from a high of 91.4 percent in Sweden to a low of 20.7 percent in the United States, with the latter declining to 17.5 percent in 1986 (Wood, 1984).

If working part time means, in fact, less job security and fewer fringe benefits, one might also expect to find a lower degree of unionization and an absence of collective agreements. Further, as the proportion of all work that is part time increases, there should be a decreasing degree of unionization in a given jurisdiction. Data on union membership are not universally available in the developed countries. Where they exist, they are neither as comprehensive nor as timely as one might wish. Indeed, for the United Kingdom, the data appear to be derived almost entirely from administrative records.

In the United States, published survey figures tend to support the view that unionization of part-time workers is uncommon and decreasing in incidence. Between 1983 and 1986, while the number of part-time workers grew (excluding for analytical purposes the self-employed), the number of part-time workers who were members of a "labor union or an employee association similar to a labor union" decreased from 1,446,000 (8.4 percent of the total) to 1,277,000 (7 percent). The total of part-time workers represented by unions, a wider category that includes those who, while not members, were covered by a union or an employee association contract, decreased from 1,787,000 (10.3 percent) to 1,530,000 (8.4 percent)(United States. Bureau of the Census, 1988: Table 667, p. 402).

In general, both union memberships and the number of trade unions in the United Kingdom have declined gradually in the past two decades. The number of trade unions reached a peak of 519 in 1973 and had declined to 335 by 1986. Indeed, the decline in numbers of trade unions can be traced back to an historic high of 1,358 in 1896, suggesting a continuous decline over more than 90 years. Membership peaked at 13,289,000 in 1979 and has since declined to 10,539,000 in 1986 (United Kingdom. Central Statistical Office, 1988: Table 6.20; United Kingdom. Department of Employment, 1988b: 275–278).

It is therefore highly improbable that part-time workers are increasingly members of unions in the United Kingdom, though it is not possible to establish this finding directly. Survey data from 1980 do shed some light on the British situation:

There were significant differences in the proportions of part-time employees who belonged to a union (28 percent) or who did not belong but had a union at their place of work they could join (22 percent), compared to full-time workers (51 percent and 18 percent respectively). Part-timers with no union at their place of work were also much less likely to say they would like a union they could join (28 percent compared with 51 percent of full-timers). Though regular attendance at union meetings was rare overall, part-timers who were union members were much less likely to go than full-timers. Seventy-two percent of part-timers who were union members never attended a meeting compared with 49 percent of full-timers (Ballard, 1984: 414).

See also the discussion in the chapter by Blanchflower in this volume.

In Canada, the pattern has been very different, with union member-ship in general holding steady as a proportion of all paid workers at about 32 percent (Neill, 1988: 12–15). While unionization rates in the United States have dropped precipitously (from 30 percent in 1970 to just 17.5 percent in 1986), rates in Canada have been stable for two decades. Unionization rates for female workers have been increasing as well, contrary to findings in other countries, raising the possibility that organizing efforts in emerging service sector industries are bearing some fruit. Indeed, the percentage of service sector workers who were mem-bers of unions in Canada rose from 25.7 percent in 1973 to 28.2 percent in 1982, while the proportion of covered workers in the goods-producing sector fell from 45.7 to 44.3 percent. The striking difference between Canadian unionization rates and others appears to be partially attrib-utable to unionization of public sector employment. About three quarters of public administration workers were members of unions while very few (less than 10 percent) in trade and finance were members.

As for part-time workers, in 1986 18.3 percent of all persons working in Canada on a part-time basis were members of trade unions (in contrast to about 35.8 percent of all full-time workers, down from about 38 percent in 1984), according to unpublished data from the Survey of Trade Union Affiliation, a biennial supplement to the Labour Force Survey. This pro-portion is up from 12.7 percent in 1971, 15.7 percent in 1982, and 16.3 percent in 1984. Thus, Canadian figures show a consistent, slow increase in the proportion of the unionized part-time work-force, in direct con-trast to the experience of the United States both in the direction of the trend and in the proportion unionized.

ALTERED WORK PATTERNS AND FAMILY FINANCES

Part of the reason for interest in part-time work is the hope or prospect that it will alter traditional patterns of male and female income differ-entials. A major reason for rising rates of female labor force participation, much of it part time and much of it in the service sector, has been to augment family incomes and perhaps even to create a more equitable balance between mates as to their economic power. This was especially true during the recession of 1981–83, during which average family in-comes tended to decline in real terms. What kind of changes in family finances have these changes in labor force participation made? Some tentative answers can be found in data from the Survey of Consumer Finances conducted periodically by Statistics Canada.

While dual earner husband-and-wife families now represent the norm in Canada (they were 64 percent of all husband-and-wife families that had experienced no husband unemployment by 1982), the importance

Table 1.5
Family Income Earned by Wife in Canada in 1985* (Percentages)

		Husband:									
		Worked						Some Unemployment		Not in Labor Force	
			49 + weeks mostly		Less than 49 weeks mostly						
Labor Force Status of Wife	Total	No unem-ployment	Full time	Part time	Full time	Part time	Number		Number		Number
Experienced No Unemployment	30.3	29.2	28.8	35.7	39.6	42.5	2,858,230	38.2	361,800	39.9	113,730
worked 49+ weeks full time	36.0	34.7	34.2	43.7	48.0	63.8	1,825,930	44.2	248,480	49.4	67,480
worked 49+ weeks part time	21.6	20.9	20.7	24.9	36.4	24.4	562,940	27.6	53,970	28.0	20,830
worked <49 weeks full time	19.2	18.9	18.0	35.0	31.7	15.0	215,780	20.9	31,010	22.8	9,980
worked <49 weeks part time	9.7	9.7	9.4	10.0	17.3	10.2	253,580	9.5	28,340	10.2	15,440
Experienced Some Unemployment	15.5	14.4	14.3	144.3	19.2	29.5	758,830	19.0	215,650	17.3	31,530
Not in Labor Force	0.5	0.7	0.6	0.2	1.7	0.3	1,709,920	0.1	264,460	0.2	312,790
Grand Total	20.6	20.5	20.3	23.6	25.7	29.6	5,326,980	24.0	841,910	14.7	458,050
Number	5,326,980	4,027,020	3,801,240	78,270	122,610	24,900					

*Economic Families, couples only, both husband and wife <65.
Source: Special calculation, Survey of Consumer Finances, Statistics Canada.

of the husband's income remains preeminent in family finances. The data indicate the persistence of traditional family earning patterns. In husband-and-wife families in Canada in 1982, in which the husband experienced no unemployment, very few wives were the sole earner where only one partner worked. Only about one half of one percent of all families fell into this category (as opposed to 35.1 percent in which the husband was the sole earner). In dual-earner families in which the husband experienced no unemployment, families in which the husband earned more than the wife outnumbered those where the wife's earnings were higher by a ratio of 7 to 1. Only where the husband worked fewer than 49 weeks, mostly part time, did the wife's income tend to be the larger component of the family total.

Also in 1982, the share of family income attributable to the wife's earnings was directly related to the husband's labor force experience. Where the husband experienced no unemployment, the figure was 35.5 percent. Where the husband worked less than the full year, full time, the figure jumped to 47.4 percent. Where the husband experienced unemployment, the wife's earnings increased family income by 47.1 percent, but where the husband's unemployment period was 27 or more weeks long, the contribution made by the wife was 56.4 percent.

Later data from the 1985 Survey of Consumer Finances (and shown in Table 1.5) show the specific interaction between husbands' and wives' employment patterns and total family income. Over all employment patterns, wives tended to contribute 20.6 percent of total family income in 1985. However, only in the case where the husband worked part time less than 49 weeks of the year did the wife contribute more than 50 percent of family income, and then only when she was working full time throughout the year. Even where the husband worked part time on a continuous basis, and the wife full time, the wife's contribution to the family total income was only about 44 percent.

Thus, part-time work, whatever its significance and importance for individual workers, has not extinguished (by hypothetically lessening the necessity for high male earnings) either the much more powerful pattern of lower average earnings by women, or their concomitant lesser contribution to family finances. The pattern is so powerful that, in 1985, where the husband did experience unemployment, or indeed was not even in the labor force, the contribution of wives to total family income remained below 50 percent, no matter what employment pattern for wives (full year/part year; full time/part time) is considered.

PUSH AND PULL FACTORS AND THE INCREASE IN PART-TIME WORK

The most notable overall finding from the comparisons made here is the persistence of very significant differences between the United States, the United Kingdom, and Canada in the ways in which part-time work is being used in their respective national economies. However, it has not escaped attention that part-time work as a proportion of all work is increasing in all three economies, nor that it is qualitatively different from full-time work, both in the reward structures associated with each type and in the permanence of the arrangements. There are both push and pull factors associated with this increase.

On the pull side may be listed the pressure felt by employers to reduce labor costs, meet fluctuating workloads, and extend hours of business, particularly in the service sector where much part-time work is now being created. In addition, there are the considerable financial advantages in employing part-time workers to whom few commitments have been made to provide what might once have been called a "career" and for whom the non-wage component of total compensation is typically less costly.

On the push side, there are several factors that make part-time work attractive to persons of both sexes, and these factors are related to stages of the life cycle. The employment of students in off-school hours has often been cited as an example of this life-cycle effect but, as has been shown, it is of limited pertinence in the United Kingdom. More recently, the increasingly important role of women in the labor force has brought other factors into prominence. The obvious difficulties in blending child-rearing responsibilities with paid employment in terms of time and energy pressures have pushed many women in the direction of part-time employment. This permits them to maintain links with the labor market, to provide income, to transfer paid work to hours more consistent with a mate's hours of work, and to secure the civil and pension status associated with paid employment.[8]

CONTEXTUAL FACTORS AND PART-TIME WORK

The nature of modern social life in a thoroughly urbanized Western world, the role of work, and the organizations in which it occurs are changing together. Clearly, the increase in part-time work must be seen in the context of these global-scale changes. There are many general contextual imperatives that add to the difficulty of modern life and that are, in turn, reflected in some respects in employment decisions. One interactive factor to be found in major metropolitan centers is travel time. It is not uncommon to find workers traveling up to three hours a day to and from work. Few day-care facilities have hours that accommodate such extensions of the working day, nor are those additional hours attractive to parents or children, even if they are affordable. The increasing prevalence of lone parenthood, family breakdown, living alone, and geographical mobility is also problematic. The latter has tended to sever the connections between individuals and their traditional support networks, placing more responsibility on individuals for meeting their own requirements in relative isolation.

The recession of the early 1980s placed pressure on real family incomes in Western countries and in many cases forced a second earner into the work-force just to preserve the family standard of living. Work interruptions based on extended periods of unemployment increased this pressure. Dual-earner families in North America are now, if not the norm, at least a well-established alternative to traditional family models that once included a stay-at-home spouse.

In addition, the 1980s saw the introduction of microcomputer-based technology into the office, factory, retail store, and home. This technology has tended to blur the distinction between work and non-work hours, and to promote the dispersion of workers in geographically, temporally, and socially disparate locations. Work itself can be time-shifted onto privately-owned equipment in the home. Work outside of normal hours can be both a hidden subsidy to employers and a means of providing more congenial surroundings for workers, who are faced with competing household and employer claims on time. All of these factors, though uncertain in their effects, have increased the pressures for innovative solutions in order to balance the need for paid employment with the requirements of civilized existence.

PART-TIME WORK AND THE DEMOGRAPHIC TRANSITION

As if this range of factors were not sufficient, one must also consider the demographic transition of Western societies to a low-fertility, aging population model. Clearly the changing demographics of the labor force are creating new problems for employers. Consider the plight of the small employer in Canada or the United States who seeks out the increasingly scarce teenager to work part time after school and on weekends ten years, twenty years, or thirty years from now. As Pearson (1987) put it: "While reductions in youth unemployment will of course be welcome, many recruiters for both jobs and training courses will have to think long and hard about innovation and overturning tradition, if they are to continue to meet their employment needs during the next decade and beyond" (Pearson, 1987). Shortages show up in unlikely ways. In 1987, the New York Telephone company was reported as having to interview 90,000 candidates to fill 2,000 jobs requiring not even a secondary school graduation diploma. Of the applicants, 84 percent failed basic literacy testing and marginally literate candidates were hired (Copeland, 1987: 54–55).

In contrast to the situation in the United Kingdom, the proportion of North American young people pursuing higher education, and the length of their educational programs, are increasing. Employers are affected because these developments raise the average level of education in the population, and decrease the number of persons seeking permanent employment in their late teens and early twenties. Some youths who would have been available for full-time employment are only available on a part-time basis. Thus part-time employment, both voluntary and involuntary, has come to play an important gap-filling role in Canada, the United States, and the United Kingdom. There are indications that this role will continue to expand in the future in each of the three jurisdictions, if only because the advantages to employers are perceived as incontrovertible. Once conceived as incidental to the standard structure of career employment, part-time employment now stands front and center as the growing tip of service sector employment, the major source of new jobs in developed Western countries. Even so, important national differences persist, with the British pattern remaining clearly distinct from that observable in North America.

NOTES

1. Generally, labor force participation rates in the United Kingdom, Canada, and the United States have shown similarities both in magnitude and direction of change. The rate for women in Canada went from 51 percent in 1980 to 56.6 percent in 1987 (51.5 to 56 percent in the United States). According to the 1985 Eurostat Labor Force Survey, the labor force activity rate for British women was 47.9 percent (1985: 83). Male labor force participation rates have been gradually declining. In Canada, the rate was 77.4 percent in 1987 and 76.2 percent in the United States; the labor force activity rate for British men was 72.9 percent in 1985.

2. For a detailed discussion of the widely varying national standards, see "Technical Note A" to the Organization for Economic Cooperation and Development, *Employment Outlook*, 1985. A recent comparison between European Economic Community countries on percentage of employees working part-time may be found in Eurostat, *Employment and Unemployment, 1988*, Table VI/2, p. 223; and *Employment and Unemployment, 1974–1980*, published in 1981, Table VI/4, p. 211. These sources contain specific weekly hours data too detailed to be considered here.

3. British employment statistics were revised from an "employed labor force" basis to a wider "work-force in employment" basis in 1988, to include participants in subsidized training employment programs. See: United Kingdom. Department of Employment, "Employment Statistics: Revised Presentation," *Employment Gazette*, August 1988c, S6.

4. In Great Britain, females on "adult pay rates" working part-time worked an average of 21.5 hours in 1984 in "manufacturing and certain other industries" (United Kingdom. Central Statistical Office, *Annual Abstract of Statistics, 1988 edition*, Table 6.14, p. 121).

5. Canadian employment data usually include people aged 15 and over,

whereas U.S. coverage starts at age 16. For the article cited, Canadian data were retabulated to include only people aged 16 years and over. The limit of work hours per week was also adjusted to the U.S. level (35 hours).

6. Unemployment rates have generally been higher in the United Kingdom and in Canada than in the United States. Comparing Canada and the United States, annual average unemployment percentages were similar prior to the recession of the early 1980s (7.4 percent in Canada; 7.1 percent in the United States in 1980), but the effects of the recession were much more severe in Canada, producing a peak unemployment rate of 11.8 percent in 1983 (in contrast to 9.6 percent in the United States and 11.6 percent in the United Kingdom, in 1985 and 1986). In each country, rates were highest for young males 16 to 24 years of age. These rates reached a peak of 22.6 percent in Canada in 1983 (19.1 percent in the United States in 1982). Rates for young women were always lower throughout the 1980s. In 1987, they rested at 12.5 percent in Canada and 11.7 percent in the United States (for young males: 14.8 percent in Canada, 12.6 in the United States). Furthermore, the incidence of long-term unemployment (six or more months) has always been much higher in Canada (23.8 percent of all unemployed women in Canada in 1987, and 14 percent in the United States). In fact, 38 percent of unemployed Canadian men 45 or more years of age had been unemployed for more than six months in 1987 (United States 27.3 percent). For women 45 and over, the relationship was the same (30.1 percent versus 17.4 percent in the United States). In the United Kingdom, the unemployment rate in 1984 was 11 percent, rising to 11.6 percent in both 1985 and 1986 before falling slightly to 10.9 percent in 1987. The unemployment rate for young males less than 25 years of age reached a peak of 21.2 percent in 1984; rates for young women reached a peak of 17.8 percent in 1984, a percentage reached again in 1986 (Eurostat, 1988: Table IV/1, p. 181).

7. Very detailed breakdowns of part-time employment by sex and Standard Industrial Classification (SIC) code (1980) are available for Great Britain from 1977 to 1984. See United Kingdom. Department of Employment, 1985: Table 1.4, pp. 10–23.

8. Joshi (1987) has reported that the typical woman in Britain forgoes 20 times the salary she earned at age 24 in the process of giving up work for several years to rear two children. In part, the career damage is reflected in part-time work upon return to the labor force, and lower rates of pay because of loss of experience and career continuity. The loss is put at £48,000 due to ten years of part-time rather than full-time work, almost as great as the loss of £54,000 for eight years' absence from the work-force.

II SHAPING AND RESHAPING PART-TIME WORK

2 Part-Timers: Living on Half Rations

Sar A. Levitan and Elizabeth A. Conway

The term "part-time worker" evokes familiar images of teenagers flipping burgers, mothers arriving home from work in time to meet the school bus, and semi-retired men and women lending assistance and expertise at the office. Lurking behind these images, however, are the bleak economic realities of part-time employment:

1. part-timers comprise more than half of those working for minimum and subminimum wages;
2. one in five part-time workers heads a family;
3. eight in ten are not covered by their employers' pension plans; and
4. one in five has no health insurance.

A short schedule often means inferior compensation for America's 19 million part-time workers (a figure that excludes about 300,000 agricultural workers). The occasional ad for a part-time senior executive notwithstanding, the vast majority of part-timers hold the same types of positions they always have held—low-wage, dead-end jobs that offer few, if any, benefits or promotional opportunities. Managerial, professional, and technical positions, which account for about 31 percent of full-time jobs, make up only 17 percent of part-time jobs. Nearly 78 percent of part-time jobs, but only 55 percent of full-time jobs, are in sales, clerical, service, and unskilled labor occupations. Part-time employment has grown at a much faster rate than full-time employment during the past two decades, and now accounts for one of every five persons at work in the United States (see Figure 2.1).

A combination of social and economic factors underlies the prolifer-

Figure 2.1
Part-Time Non-agricultural Workers, 1970–1987

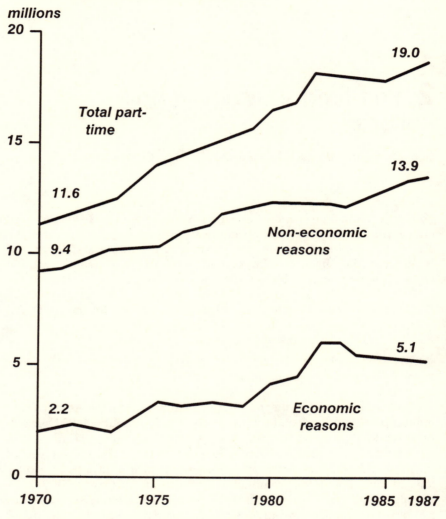

*Reprinted with permission of the publisher, M. E. Sharpe, Inc., 80 Business Park Drive, Armonk, New York 10504 U.S.A., from the *May/June 1988* issue of *Challenge*.

The authors are indebted to Professor Andrew Sum, director of the Center for Labor Market Studies, Northeastern University, and to Thomas Nardone of the Bureau of Labor Statistics, who provided labor force data and constructive criticism for this article.

ation of part-time employment in the United States. During the generation following World War II, workers enjoyed sustained increases in real earnings and fringe benefits. An exodus to suburbia accompanied this growing affluence, as automobiles and interstate highways made it possible for workers to live further from their jobs, and suburban developments made home ownership available to families across the income spectrum. Demographic shifts during this period created significant changes in family structure and economic roles. Women, both married and unmarried, entered the labor force and remained there throughout their child-rearing years. Independent young people, families split by divorce, and longer-lived senior citizens contributed to record numbers of households formed in the United States. Higher living standards and new households provided business with new markets and new employees.

As markets opened up, business catered to the new demographics, adjusting hours, product lines, and services to meet the changing lifestyles of customers. The rapid expansion of the service and retail sectors, which historically made use of shift-workers and part-timers, increased the economy's dependence on such workers. Since service and retail concerns, unlike factories, cannot stockpile their products, staffing adjustments may represent the most efficient way to handle business ebbs and flows.

FLEXIBILITY FOR WHOM?

The American economy has grown dependent upon a flexible work force, but society has not faced up to the consequences of this dependency. Workers look to part-time employment for a felicitous approach to balancing employment, family, and leisure time, while employers all too frequently see it as a means for achieving lower labor costs. The "bottom line" has been an expanded pool of low-wage contingent laborers unprotected by basic benefits. According to a national Chamber of Commerce official, traditional personnel practices "tend to handcuff the employer in a time when there is a revolution in the work-place." Part-time work and other alternative employment arrangements remove the handcuffs. As tradition or bargaining agreements dictate the minimum level of commitment a full-time, full-year worker can expect from an employer, employers unable or unwilling to break that commitment recruit temporary, part-time, or other contingent workers. "Disposable employees," as *Business Week* recently dubbed these contingent workers, provide employers a margin of flexibility. Those who choose to maintain a high level of commitment to a core of full-time, full-benefit employees may do so by adding to and subtracting from the peripheral work force as needed. Other employers, under the pretext of achieving flexibility, may use contingent workers to undermine unions, pay levels, or fringe benefits among full-time employees.

WHAT IS PART-TIME WORK?

The Bureau of Labor Statistics (BLS), the official arbiter in such matters, defines part-time as work of less than 35 hours per week. This category includes those who work less than 35 hours weekly but are considered full-time employees, and excludes full-time workers who have short hours due to noneconomic occurrences such as illness, industrial dispute, or holiday. Nearly one third of American nonfarm workers held a part-time job at some time during 1986, and one in five usually worked part time.

The BLS differentiates between part-time work for economic and noneconomic reasons, commonly referred to as "involuntary" and "voluntary" part-time work. Involuntary part-time employees work short hours due to slack work, the inability to find a full-time job, or other reasons pertaining to the demand for their labor. Those who choose part-time schedules because they do not want or are unavailable for full-time work, or for other reasons, are considered voluntary part-timers (see Table 2.1). The voluntary/involuntary distinction is not always clear-cut. An unknown number of those counted among the voluntary part-time work force are not unwilling, but rather unable, to secure full-time employment. For these workers, limited by physical or mental disability, a lack of affordable child care, inadequate transportation, or other difficulties, a part-time job may be the only feasible way to participate in the labor force.

Are Americans flocking to become part-time workers? Hardly. Involuntary part-time work represents the fastest-growing employment arrangement during the 1980s. Between 1979 and 1987, it increased about four times as fast as full-time or voluntary part-time employment (see Table 2.2). Slack work and the inability to find a full-time job account for nearly 94 percent of involuntary part-time employment. Victims of slack work often are full-time workers who face temporary reductions in hours due to an economic slump. In 1986, nearly 60 percent of this group usually worked full-time. In contrast, all of those who can find only part-time work and about one million with slack work will remain on reduced-hour schedules until they change jobs. These workers consequently remain involuntarily on part-time schedules for longer periods than those affected by slack work. In 1986, one in four of the former remained on reduced-hour schedules for longer than 15 weeks, compared with less than one in eight of the latter.

The differences between the two categories take on greater significance as those who can find only part-time work become the larger component

Table 2.1
Part-Time Workers, 1987

	Thousands
Economic reasons	5,122
Slack work	2,201
Could find only part-time work	2,587
Material shortages or repairs to plant and equipment	57
New job started during week	200
Job terminated during week	78
Non-economic reasons	13,928
Does not want or is unavailable for full-time work	11,689
Full-time for this job	1,549
Illness	137
All other reasons	554

Source: Employment and Earnings, January 1988, Table 31, p. 96, Bureau of Labor Statistics, United States Department of Labor.

Table 2.2
Growth of Involuntary Part-Timers (Millions)

	Full-time	*Part-time economic*	*Part-time non-economic*
1979	74.1	3.4	12.4
1987	84.3	5.1	13.9
Increase: 1979 to 1987	14%	52%	12%

Source: Employment and Earnings, various years, Bureau of Labor Statistics, United States Department of Labor.

of involuntary part-time workers. Until the 1980s, slack work caused most part-time work for economic reasons, but after the most recent recession, slack work declined much more sharply than the inability to find a full-time job. Since 1983, workers who could find only a part-time job have comprised more than half of those working part time involuntarily, a phenomenon that shows no sign of reversing despite con-

Table 2.3
Gender Differences (Percentage)

	Full-time	Part-time economic	Part-time non-economic
Female workers	73.0	6.1	20.9
Male workers	88.6	4.0	7.3

Source: Derived from Employment and Earnings, January 1988, Table 33, 197, Bureau of Labor Statistics, United States Department of Labor.

tinued improvement in business conditions. The expansion of part-time employment offers new flexibility to business, but it places a larger number of American workers at risk. In addition to semi-retired persons and teenagers attending school, the part-time work force includes a disproportionate number of females, minorities, and others who frequently encounter labor market difficulties. And for a majority of part-timers, whether voluntary or involuntary, a short schedule means low pay, few benefits, and minimal job security. Most, but not all, of those who choose to work part-time have other sources of income—a parent, spouse, pension, or another job—or view a short schedule as a means of acquiring some income while pursuing education, family responsibilities, or self-employment. In contrast, those who work short schedules for economic reasons often have no other source of financial support.

GENDER, RACE, AND PART-TIME WORK

Full-time workers have accounted for the vast majority of new women workers during the past two decades. Although most women are not part-time workers, most part-time workers are women. In 1987, women at work in nonagricultural industries remained nearly three times as likely as male workers to choose part-time work, and more likely to work part-time involuntarily (see Table 2.3). Married women frequently limit their paid employment during their child-rearing years. Women 25 to 44 years old are nearly eight times more likely than men in the same age bracket to choose part-time employment. But voluntary part-time employment is not growing in popularity among married women. Since the mid–1970s the number of employed wives has increased by more than one third, but the proportion of these women choosing part-time work actually has decreased slightly.

During the past few decades, black women have shown the greatest shift toward full-time schedules, as they moved from part-time domestic services into occupations offering standard work hours. This trend ap-

Table 2.4
Persons at Work Part-Time for Economic Reasons, 1987 (Non-agricultural Industries)

	Percent
Sex	
Female	6.1
Male	4.0
Race	
Black	7.9
White	4.6
Educational attainment	
Less than high school diploma	9.8
High school diploma	6.4
Four or more years college	2.6
Age	
16-24	8.5
25-44	4.2
45+	4.0

Source: Unpublished data from the Current Population Survey, Bureau of Labor Statistics, United States Department of Labor.

pears most clearly among married women. Since the 1970s, the rate of voluntary part-time employment among black working wives plummeted from 28 percent to 16 percent as these women entered full-time employment, while the rate among white married women remained virtually unchanged. While white wives continue to choose part-time work more often than white female family heads, black married women are as likely as black female family heads to work full time. Black and Hispanic men and women have historically experienced much higher rates of involuntary part-time employment than whites. Although part-time work for economic reasons is growing more rapidly among whites, it continues to increase and remains higher for minority workers than for whites. Educational background and age also affect involuntary part-time levels for workers of all races and genders. Teenagers and those who have not completed high school are particularly vulnerable. Nearly one in ten in those categories works part time involuntarily (see Table 2.4).

Cashiers, sales clerks, restaurant workers—many of them young or female—worked short schedules in earlier decades, much as they do today. In past years, however, service employment comprised a smaller segment of the United States economy. As industries dependent upon part-time workers came to employ a larger portion of the labor force, a larger proportion of jobs became part-time. Had the industrial distribution of jobs remained as it was in 1950, all other things being equal, today's economy would include at least three million fewer part-time jobs.

While the growth of the service and retail sectors undergirds the part-time employment boom, the increased use of part-timers within industries amplifies it. This is most notable in the area of wholesale and retail trade. Thirty years ago, 20 percent of workers in this industry held part-time jobs; by 1987 the rate was 30 percent.

LIVING ON HALF-RATIONS: WAGES, HOURS, AND BENEFITS

Part-time workers make up a majority of the five million Americans paid at or below the minimum wage. In 1987, women working part time comprised 44 percent of all such workers, and male part-timers accounted for another 22 percent. In the same year, part-time workers earned a median hourly wage of $4.42, compared with $7.43 for full-time workers. Much of the pay discrepancy between full-time and part-time workers can be attributed to who they are and what jobs they hold. Women, teenagers, and minorities often receive lower wages than others working in similar jobs. In addition, nearly one of every four part-timers holds a sales or food service job. In 1987, food service and retail sales workers comprised nearly half of all minimum-wage workers.

Although external factors account for most of the full-time/part-time wage gap, they do not explain all of it. A study conducted in the late 1970s found that after controlling for a wide variety of factors, including age, race, job classification, and education, women working short schedules still were paid 17 percent less and men 30 percent less than their full-time counterparts. Short hours combine with low wages, leading to low weekly earnings for part-time employees. Although they may work anywhere from 1 to 34 hours weekly, the average part-timer continues to work approximately half time.

Expanding the scope of compensation to include nonwage benefits exacerbates the discrepancy between part-time and full-time workers. Human resources consultants Hewitt Associates reported that less than half of 484 companies surveyed in 1985 provided benefits to part-time employees who worked fewer than 20 hours per week. The availability of benefits increased with hours worked, but remained significantly below that of full-time employees, even for those working more than

30 hours per week. The benefits employers most frequently offered to part-time workers were paid vacations and holidays.

In 1985, the most recent year for which data are available, nearly ten million Americans who worked part time at least part of the year had no health insurance. Almost 31 percent of those who experienced one or more weeks of involuntary part-time and 18 percent with some voluntary part-time work were uninsured. In the same year, only 8 percent of full-time, full-year workers lacked health insurance. Most part-time workers who do receive employer-provided health insurance are covered indirectly, as dependents under a spouse's or parent's policy. Although three quarters of full-time, full-year workers received health insurance through their own employers in 1985, only one third of involuntary part-timers and one quarter of voluntary part-timers had their own employer-provided policies (Figure 2.2).

Part-time workers are also much less likely than their full-time counterparts to be covered by a pension plan at work. In 1985, employers included over half of full-time, full-year workers, but less than 20 percent of those with some part-time work, in pension plans. Most part-timers without coverage work for employers who do not offer a pension plan, but many are excluded from coverage even when a plan exists (see Table 2.5). Since part-time workers are disproportionately young and pension coverage increases with age, low levels of coverage for this group may not be significant. The discrepancy remains across age groups, however. In all age groups, the rate of pension coverage among part-time workers is less than half of that for full-time workers (Figure 2.3).

Unemployment Insurance

Part-time workers are rarely as secure in their jobs as their full-time counterparts, but they are less likely to qualify for unemployment insurance in case of layoffs. In 12 states, a person working 20 hours per week at a minimum-wage job would not qualify for unemployment compensation, due to minimum earning requirements. Most states also prohibit beneficiaries of unemployment compensation from limiting their availability to part-time employment. Such policies deny unemployment compensation to those unable to accept full-time employment.

The Special Case of Moonlighters

Historically, most moonlighters were men working a second job to supplement income from a primary, full-time job. In 1970, for example, 7 percent of all male workers and only 2.2 percent of all female workers held a second job. Women are closing the moonlighting gap, however. According to recent data, 4.7 percent of employed women and 5.9 per-

Figure 2.2
Health Insurance as Fringe Benefit

Full-time, full-year workers

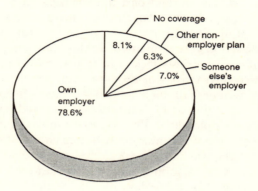

No coverage
8.1%

Other non-employer plan
6.3%

Someone else's employer
7.0%

Own employer
78.6%

Workers with one or more weeks part-time economic

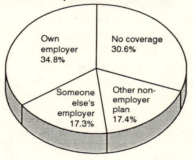

Own employer
34.8%

No coverage
30.6%

Someone else's employer
17.3%

Other non-employer plan
17.4%

Workers with one or more weeks part-time non-economic

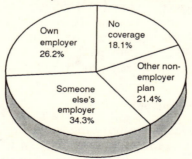

Own employer
26.2%

No coverage
18.1%

Other non-employer plan
21.4%

Someone else's employer
34.3%

Source: Unpublished data from the Current Population Survey, March 1986 Supplement. Tabulated by the Center for Labor Market Studies, Northeastern University.

Table 2.5
Part-Time Workers Covered by Their Employers' Pension Plans (Percentage)

	No plan	Plan exists, not included	Plan exists, included
Men			
Full-time, full-year	35.8	4.6	59.7
One or more weeks part-time economic	73.0	7.7	19.6
One or more weeks part-time non-economic	72.2	10.5	17.3
Women			
Full-time, full-year	34.4	7.7	57.9
One or more weeks part-time economic	69.6	12.5	17.9
One or more weeks part-time non-economic	71.3	13.2	15.5

Source: Unpublished data from the Current Population Survey, March 1986 Supplement. Tabulated by the Center for Labor Market Studies, Northeastern University.

cent of employed men held multiple jobs. The traditional picture of a moonlighter remains accurate for most men with multiple jobs—80 percent of them work full time on at least one job and hold a second full- or part-time job for extra earnings. In contrast, 40 percent of women who moonlight hold multiple part-time jobs. Although they work 50 hours per week on average, these multiple-job holders have part-time status, with its attendant risks of low wages and inadequate benefits.

POLICY ISSUES

Many workers desire alternatives to full-time, full-year work at various stages in their lives, and part-time employees may contribute to greater efficiency in the work place. Few would argue that such alternatives should be discouraged. Objections to part-time employment in its current form center on the treatment of part-time employees, and the spillover of this treatment onto other workers.

Employers often rationalize low wages for part-time workers, arguing that the wives and young people who accept the jobs are secondary earners lacking serious commitment to the work force. As the president of a large temporary-services agency told the *New York Times*: "You can't expect these people to have the same kind of work ethic that their fathers

Figure 2.3
Workers Covered by Employer's Pension Plan (Percentage)

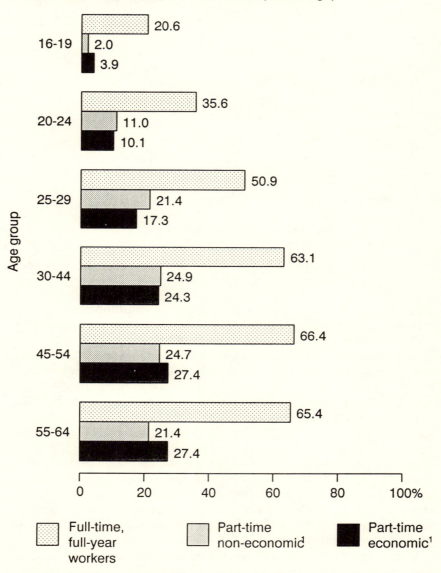

Source: Unpublished data from the Current Population Survey, March 1986 supplement. Tabulated by the Center for Labor Market Studies, Northeastern University.

Tabe 2.6
Families in Poverty (Percentage)

	Actual	*Without spouse's earnings*	*Percent difference*
Race/ethnic group of family head			
White	4.8	8.5	77
Black	16.7	25.9	55
Hispanic	13.6	21.4	57
Education of family head			
0-11 years	12.2	20.3	66
12 years	5.9	9.8	66
13-15 years	4.3	7.3	70
16+ years	1.4	4.2	300

Source: Unpublished data from the Current Population Survey, March 1986 supplement. Tabulated by the Center for Labor Market Studies, Northeastern University.

had, and their mothers didn't work." Such workers are not supporting families, the argument goes, but escaping household drudgery or earning pin money. Such a view obviously ignores more than five million Americans who are forced into part-time work by economic circumstances. Recent census data call it into question with regard to voluntary part-time workers as well. The three in ten working wives who hold part-time jobs contribute to their families' economic well-being, and in some cases keep them out of poverty. Recent data show that almost ten million American families have two employed spouses, one of whom works part time. Nearly one in ten of these has total earnings under 125 percent of the poverty line. If not for the supplementary earnings of the part-time employed spouse, an additional half million families would be poor or near poor.

A second source of income is essential to families in economically vulnerable groups, who frequently fall below the poverty line. Among two-earner families with a part-time employed spouse, one in five Hispanics and high school dropouts, and one in four blacks would be poor without the second earner's contribution (see Table 2.6). Although part-

Table 2.7
Employment Status and Poverty Rates

Employment status	Poverty rate
Full-time, full-year	2.7%
Unemployed	
1 to 14 weeks	15.3
15 or more weeks	29.6
Part-time for economic reasons	
1 to 14 weeks	16.5
15 weeks or more	22.3

Source: Linking Employment Problems to Economic Status, August 1987, various tables, Bureau of Labor Statistics, United States Department of Labor.

time work enables some families to escape poverty, more remain in poverty. More than three million part-time workers have a family income below the poverty line. Involuntary part-time workers fare worst, with poverty rates rivaling those of the unemployed. Of workers who experience 15 or more weeks of involuntary part-time employment, 22 percent live in families with incomes below the poverty line (see Table 2.7).

THE COST OF FLEXIBILITY: WHO FOOTS THE BILL?

Business often casts part-time employment as an accommodation of workers' desire for flexibility. Terms such as "mothers' hours" and "after-school work" reflect this representation of short schedules. While many employees clearly prefer the flexibility offered by part-time work, employers frequently reap the lion's share of the benefit. An employer faces certain fixed costs, such as payroll and supervision, for each employee regardless of the number of hours worked. However, the lower wages paid to part-time workers and foregone benefits offset or even exceed the fixed costs. A 1977 survey by the American Management Association found that 57 percent of managers using part-time workers reported that they produced savings in fringe-benefit costs. The survey also found lower wages and higher productivity associated with part-time employees.

Low compensation levels mean that part-time workers themselves bear many of the higher fixed costs associated with reduced hours.

Government and charity chip in, too, insofar as welfare payments, Medicaid, and other resources subsidize indigent part-time workers. The Bureau of Labor Statistics found that more than one in three Americans who had some involuntary part-time work between January and July of 1985 received some form of cash or in-kind government assistance.

The expansion of part-time employment also may affect pay and working conditions of full-time employees. In retail sales and other occupations, career full-time jobs continue to give way to less skilled, lower compensated, part-time positions. Companies may also use part-time or other contingent workers to undermine labor unions or to downgrade compensation standards for employees who remain on full-time schedules.

IMPROVE PART-TIMER COMPENSATION

Since taxpayers subsidize the cost of part-time work, the government has a strong financial interest, not to mention a moral responsibility, in correcting inequalities. In light of recent experience, reliance on the free market to make the necessary adjustments is hardly justified. Prescriptions for change include actions that would prevent employers from discarding their responsibility to provide employees with minimal compensation and working conditions. Some recent measures by states and the federal government have improved the situation of part-time workers. Provisions of the Tax Equity and Fiscal Responsibility Act of 1982 discourage employers from denying pension coverage to some part-time workers. New Hampshire recently passed a law, now under consideration in other states, which prohibits insurance companies from excluding part-time workers from coverage under group health plans. In addition to such specific remedies, many policy changes that would improve the wages, benefits, and working conditions of all low-wage workers apply to part-time workers as well. Among these are measures to raise the minimum wage, expand health insurance, and subsidize child care. A few employers are not waiting for government intervention, but are acting on their own. Several new approaches represent a revamping of part-time employment practices. These experiments offer promising alternatives for making part-time employment more equitable in the future.

"Job sharing" applies to two or more employees who fill one full-time job. Workers divide duties by time or project, to ensure that the entire job is done. Fringe benefits generally are included, although they often are prorated. Because job sharers contribute to a full-time job, they may face less danger of seeing the position deskilled than those in regular part-time work, and the provision of even partial benefits is an improvement over most part-time jobs. The Administrative Management Society found that 16 percent of responding American employers allowed job sharing in 1986. The prevalence of job sharing is increasing, albeit slowly, since some jobs may not be divisible, or may involve administrative difficulties or higher fringe benefit costs.

"Peak-time" programs are used primarily by some banking and financial firms to attract and retain permanent part-time employees. These firms face extreme variation in demand for their services and so rely heavily on part-time workers. Peak-time part-time workers receive higher hourly wages than their full-time counterparts, with the highest wages often paid to those with the fewest hours or the least convenient schedules. Current peak-time programs, however, tend to target suburban, middle-class housewives and other secondary wage earners and therefore offer no benefits. Nonetheless, they represent an improvement in pay for some part-time workers, and the addition of benefit packages could make them attractive to many others. "Work sharing" addresses the concerns of those affected by slack work. In the face of cyclical downturns, companies with work-sharing programs reduce work hours across the board instead of resorting to layoffs. Workers collect unemployment benefits for the hours or days spent idle, and the employer generally continues to provide health insurance and other benefits. Work-sharing programs, popular in West Germany, affect only a small number of U.S. workers. Twelve states have enacted voluntary work-sharing laws in recent years, and they appear to be gaining popularity slowly.

Part-time work could provide great opportunities to those who seek to balance work with family, education, or other priorities. For those who do not need to support themselves and their families solely on part-time earnings, and for those with valuable and highly demanded skills, such opportunities may be realized today. Employers who view part-time employees as disposable cost-saving devices write the rules for most part-timers. Until these rules are changed, by employers or by government fiat, a growing number of part-time jobs will represent a burden rather than an opportunity, imposing ever greater costs on public and private resources.

3 Governments and Part-Time Work in Canada

Robert J. Drummond

The scope and conditions of part-time employment in Canada are considerably affected by the actions of both federal and provincial governments, and the future of part-time employment will clearly be conditioned by the choices those governments make to take account of the growing phenomenon of part-time work. It represented 3.8 percent of all employment in Canada in 1953 and 15.6 percent in 1986 (Coates, 1988: 6). Indeed, the federal and provincial states, through the exercise of their responsibility for economic management, assist in developing the very conditions that make part-time work economically desirable and socially possible.

Tax policy, in particular, can be used to make part-time employment a more or less valuable strategy for firms, and a more or less lucrative opportunity for employees. Similarly, the provision of certain benefits out of the public purse may afford people the opportunity to accept part-time employment without a substantial diminution in their standard of living, and may allow firms to take advantage of the flexibility offered by a part-time work force. In the absence of such benefits, employees may be severely disadvantaged by acceptance of part-time employment, and firms may be pressured to improve total compensation to the point where no advantage accrues from work-force flexibility.

Commonly, the role of the state in relation to part-time work is described as twofold: governments as legislators and governments as employers (Canada. Commission of Inquiry into Part-Time Work, 1983: 133–144). As legislators, governments are seen as affecting part-time work in four main areas: employment standards, labor relations, social welfare, and human rights (Julie White, 1983: 97). As employers, governments affect a large proportion of the labor force directly. They also act to provide examples to other employers, not only in the private sector but perhaps most influentially in the broader public sector (such as universities and hospitals), where the conditions of work are more similar to those found in direct government employment.

In the Canadian federal system, the role of the state is complicated by the fact that its regulatory and legislative authority is divided between two levels of government. The regulation of the work force in the federal public service, and in certain federally regulated industries (such as railways, airlines, telecommunications, and banking), is a matter for the legislative authority of the national Parliament. Labor legislation governing all other industries, and that governing the public services of the various provinces, fall within the authority of provincial cabinets and legislatures. As a consequence, the legislation governing employment for most Canadians is locally diversified, although there are similarities in some provisions across provinces.

In seeking to understand the impact of government on the world of part-time work, it may be instructive to begin with an assessment of the presumably legitimate interests of the state (or of the community, though they are not necessarily identical) in the regulation of work in general, and of part-time work in particular. What are the rationales customarily provided for state intervention in the work place or the labor market, and what are the principles that are normally expected to guide the state when it embarks on that intervention? The most cursory observation reveals that the treatment of part-time work and workers by government, federal or provincial, is different in many areas from that accorded full-time employment and employees. It may be useful to inquire what factors account for the differences. Since the interests of firms and employees will often diverge with respect to conditions of work, it seems appropriate to investigate which set of interests is served best by the regulatory postures adopted by most Canadian governments. Finally, in view of the pattern of legislative regulation and employment practice displayed by Canadian governments, what can be said about the future prospects of part-time work in Canada?

EMPLOYMENT STANDARDS

Governments intervene to establish minimum standards for certain conditions of work, presumably because the community has an interest in the equitable treatment of all employees, even if those employees cannot command such treatment by means of their market scarcity or by recourse to union power. For employees, if the authority of the state can be brought to bear in support of a work-place benefit, the necessity for repeated and fragmentary conflict with employers is avoided. The resistance of employers will normally reduce the standard to a minimum, above which unions and individual employees must still seek to bargain for improvements. At the simplest level, to the extent that part-time workers can be excluded from the application of employment standards, to that extent the employer's costs for the maintenance of those standards can be reduced. Of course, the community interest in equitable treatment, and the part-time worker's interest in fair, not to say generous, conditions of work, will not be served if part-time workers are regularly excluded from minimum employment standards available to all full-time employees.

The norms implicit in the current application of employment standards in most Canadian jurisdictions are not conducive to the inclusion of part-time workers, particularly those who do not have continuous employment with one firm. Entitlement to the protection of employment standards is usually dependent on the definition of "employee" and on the nature of one's part-time association with the employer. People who work part of the week with the same employer throughout the year are more likely to qualify for protection than people who work seasonally or casually, or for a variety of employers on a temporary basis.

Employment standards can be grouped loosely into three categories: standards for work-place safety; standards governing the minimum level of monetary compensation; and standards governing the payment of wages for periods when no work is being performed, or when the employment might otherwise be terminated. The first category generally makes no distinction between full-time and part-time employees; the same standards of safety apply. The second category includes legislation establishing a minimum wage, regulations defining overtime, and provisions requiring a minimum number of hours to be paid for any day's shift. Part-time workers are sometimes denied the protection of such rules. The third category involves paid vacations and statutory holidays, maternity leave, and advance notice of termination. Again, part-time workers may be denied access to the protective standards applied to full-time employees.

There is general agreement with the proposition that the same standards of safety should be applied to workers, regardless of whether they are employed full time or part time. However, in some instances, casual employment with several different firms might expose a worker to hazards that would be more evident if that individual were continuously employed in the same location. For example, if exposure to a toxic substance had a cumulative detrimental effect, and if work-place standards limited total exposure at a job site in a particular time period, an employee who worked for several firms using the same substance might exceed tolerable limits of exposure without violating any one firm's standard of safety. A standard that had the employee, rather than the job site, as the focus would presumably avoid such a problem. However, it is not primarily in the area of safety standards that the differences between full-time and part-time workers may be seen.

No jurisdiction in Canada explicitly excepts part-time workers from the application of minimum wage standards, but most have provisions to deny minimum wage protection, or provide a lower minimum wage, to young workers or students, many of whom will be employed part time. Indeed, in Ontario the lower rate applies *only* to students working part time. The underlying premise of such restrictive legislation seems to be that younger workers (and especially students) are less in need of income because they are still somewhat dependent on parents or guardians, and, moreover, that they are not as productive as older, more experienced workers. Since many of the younger workers are employed in service and tourist industries, the lower minimum wage standard could be viewed as a sort of subsidy to those industries, but it is rarely defended on those grounds. Where a lower minimum is established for personal service workers in particular, the usual justification is that a portion of their total income will be provided in tips, and that a lower wage rate is therefore acceptable.

In defining overtime, the employer has an obvious interest in ensuring that the highest possible number of hours worked are defined as normal working hours, and that the portion identified as overtime is minimized. The employee, by contrast, has an interest in identifying the maximum possible hours worked as overtime and, therefore, eligible for extra compensation (usually time and a half or double time; that is, 1.5 or 2 times the normal hourly wage rate for each overtime hour worked). Part-time workers will be denied overtime compensation if the definition of overtime is derived from a full-time definition of a normal work week. For example, if overtime is defined as hours worked beyond eight in a 24 hour period, or beyond 40 in a seven day week, someone who regularly works 20 hours a week, or four hours a day, will rarely (if ever) qualify, even if they exceed their normal hours by 100 percent. Legislated standards of overtime are normally premised on the full-time definition of a workweek, so that part-time workers do not generally have a right to claim overtime pay for hours worked beyond their contracted normal work period. The implicit premise is that the hours of work and overtime employment standards were intended to discourage employers from forcing workers to put in more than (under most current standards) 40 or 48 hours a week, or eight hours a day.

The standards, it is presumed, are not intended to discourage employers from asking for eight hours of work from someone contracted to work four hours a day. However, for the voluntary part-timer, or for the part-time worker whose schedule is constrained by home and child-care responsibilities, the burden of taking on extra hours above, say, four, is no less than for the full-time worker who is asked to take on hours above the normal eight. By that reasoning, a government standard of overtime that was "prorated" would define as overtime, and hence as eligible for overtime rates of pay, those hours beyond the number contracted for or normally worked. Such a standard might put an onus on employers to contract for specific normal hours with casual or temporary employees, engendering additional administrative costs. Of course, such costs would be less for continuing employees who regularly worked a partial week. It should be noted that the definition of employee in most jurisdictions excludes some workers from the protection of hours and overtime legislation, while in some places (for example, British Columbia) the categories of employees excluded are numerous (Canada. Commission of Inquiry into Part-Time Work, 1983: 134). Many of these excluded categories will have a greater than average incidence of part-time employment.

Paid vacations and statutory holidays are widely accepted by employers and widely expected by employees. However, the employer's interest in minimizing payment for hours in which no work is done comes to the fore when entitlement of part-time workers to vacation is discussed. The underlying premise of legislation governing vacations and statutory holidays seems to be that employers should pay for such time off only for employees with whom they have a continuing relationship.

The link of paid vacation entitlement to time worked is enshrined in the widespread practice of providing longer vacations to workers with longer service records. In most Canadian jurisdictions, entitlement to paid vacation is limited to those who have worked the better part of a year with the same employer. Others are usually entitled to payment in lieu of vacation (except in Quebec, where paid vacation must be provided). There are only a few jurisdictions where an employee can become eligible for more than two weeks of vacation (as an employment standard), regardless of years of service with the same employer. In those cases, it seems likely that part-time workers would have to work many more years to attain the same benefit, since the accumulation of time worked is likely to be calculated on the basis of hours worked, rather than calendar years of full- or part-time employment. In this area, the interest of the state appears to have been to set a norm and to ensure minimum benefit to workers who have no recourse to other means of securing that benefit. Most jurisdictions have preferred to deal with the complication of part-time employment by providing for payment in lieu of vacation, as if the lesser hours worked by part-time employees provided the respite from work that vacation provides to full-time workers.

The model governing statutory holidays seems to envision an employee who is changing jobs just before or just after a holiday, and who is expecting both employers to pay. Consequently, employees must normally have worked some period for an employer before that employer is liable for statutory holiday payment. Thus, because they may not have established entitlement through hours worked prior to the holiday, part-time workers may often find themselves ineligible for even partial payment on holidays for which full-time workers are guaranteed compensation.

Advance notice of termination is a benefit to which one is not normally entitled unless one has established a period of employment with the same employer. This period ranges from two weeks to six months, depending on the jurisdiction. As a result, many part-time, seasonal, or casual workers are denied such notice, or pay in lieu of notice. From the perspective of employers, notice is an added cost, since they are compelled to employ or at least pay an employee for a certain period. The time is usually one or two weeks, although it may be more for long-service employees as a result of common law precedents in some jurisdictions, after concluding that they no longer require his or her services. Obviously, the fewer workers to whom notice must be given, the lower the cost to the employer. For the part-time employee, however, the lack of entitlement to notice adds another dimension of uncertainty to an already tenuous employment situation.

With regard to employment standards, most governments in Canada have not legislated explicitly to deny protection to part-time workers. However, the definition of employee (in some cases) and the requirements of time worked for entitlement to standard protection (in other cases) have operated to deny equal protection to part-time employees. Some indication of the varied pattern of part-time or seasonal work can be seen in figures derived by Coates from Statistics Canada (Coates, 1988: 11). Coates found that, in 1985, 52.7 percent of those who had worked at all during the year had worked 30 hours or more a week for all 52 weeks of the year (including vacation); 20.7 percent had worked full time for part of the year; 16.2 percent had worked part time for all or part of the year; and 10.4 percent had worked some full time, some part time, for all or part of the year. The costs of administering more complicated programs, or of extending standard protection to those currently uncovered, would ordinarily be borne by employers. By acting to preclude that necessity, governments in Canada have protected employers at the expense of part-time workers.

LABOR RELATIONS

The fact that the interests of labor and management frequently diverge creates an inevitable element of conflict in relations between them. At the same time, however, the mutually desired outcome of most negotiations between the parties is an agreement concerning the rules and procedures that will govern work-place relations. It is the presumably neutral interest of the community and the state that such agreement be facilitated, and that conflict between the parties be conducted in an orderly fashion. Of course, there are few members of the community who can maintain a genuine neutrality between labor and management, and critics on both sides will argue that the state's role is similarly not neutral. The laws established to govern labor relations are scrutinized by workers and managers alike to determine whose interests are mainly served by the current form of those rules. Governments become arenas for the struggle between management and labor or among different industrial sectors, and labor relations laws at any given time reflect the current "state of play" in the battle. The application of labor relations law to part-time work is no exception to that rule.

It is generally in the interest of employers to limit the extent of unionization. The organization of employees into trade unions is usually presumed to add to the employer's costs (indeed, one of the principal aims of unions is to direct more of a firm's earnings into the pockets of employees). From that perspective, part-time workers may be preferred in some settings because they are more difficult to organize. It is generally in the interest of employees to have the right to choose whether to organize themselves into a trade union in order to bargain collectively with their employer. To the extent that the laws governing unionization make that choice more difficult, or deny it entirely, the interests of employers are being served by the state, and those of employees are not.

Since one of the main strengths of organized labor is the threat to withdraw its services, the denial of the right to organize is, in some instances, defended by recourse to the need of the community for protection against the potential removal of essential services. However, in other cases it appears that the obstacles placed in the path of those who would organize to bargain collectively are intended to promote the convenience of regulators or the interests of employers. In most jurisdictions in Canada, governments do nothing to facilitate the organization of part-time workers; in some cases, they make such organization considerably more difficult; in a few instances, they make it entirely impossible.

The body of legislation governing labor relations in Canada is extensive. Julie White (1983: 109) counted some 200 pieces of legislation in Ontario alone affecting labor relations. It is not possible in this limited review to examine all of the provisions that particularly affect part-time workers. Suffice it to say that labor law in most Canadian provinces makes it particularly difficult to organize workers in small work places with high employee turnover, or in work places where employees are infrequently, irregularly, or seasonally present. Some jurisdictions forbid part-time employees in the public sector to unionize at all. In others, notably Ontario, the practice has developed of regularly certifying separate bargaining units for full-time and part-time workers, thereby denying to part-time workers the privilege of combination for bargaining purposes with their usually more powerful full-time colleagues.

In some industries where part-time employees are sufficiently numerous to constitute a powerful bargaining force, separate unions for part-time employees have been moderately successful (for example, the Canadian Union of Educational Workers, which has organized part-time faculty and teaching assistants on a number of Canadian university campuses). However, they remain exceptions that prove the rule. Union protection for part-time workers remains relatively rare.

SOCIAL WELFARE

The compensation package provided to full-time workers by most large employers in contemporary Canada is rarely restricted to wages or salary. Increasingly in the latter part of the twentieth century, workers and employers in such firms have agreed that part of compensation will be provided in the form of insurance protection (such as group life insurance, extended health care, and dental plans) or in-kind benefits (for example, fitness clubs, day-care centers, and subsidized lunchrooms). In smaller firms, or in industries where profit margins are less secure, the willingness, and perhaps even ability, to embark on long-term benefit programs have been much less. Employees in those settings have had to depend on personally purchased protection (even though their wages are lower and less secure), or on the social insurance programs established by the state. Indeed, it is partly the unwillingness or inability of private employers to provide such protection that has led the federal and provincial electorates to call upon their governments for social welfare programs that would provide at least minimum security against unforeseen hardship or would assist in saving against loss of income in retirement.

While some of the benefits provided by such programs are distributed universally, especially health insurance and income supports like the family allowance and the old-age security pension, others have been designed to reflect the work history of beneficiaries. In those instances, eligibility for the benefit, or its size, are related to the length of time employed or to the level of wages or salary earned. When a benefit is tied to employment history, its cost to government will be less than would be the same level of benefit provided on a universal basis. Any stigma that might then attach to a less than universal payment is mitigated by the notion that the payment derives from the contribution one has made as a member of the work force. Indeed, the costs to government may be defrayed in part by a sort of payroll tax or insurance premium drawn from employees or employers in relation to time worked or wages paid.

Part-time workers are thus placed in a sort of double bind. They are unlikely to have pension or insurance benefits as part of their compensation package from their employers, since the presumed administrative cost of maintaining prorated benefits for part-time workers usually discourages employers from including them in such benefit plans. A recent study of part-time work in federally regulated industries by Hay Management Consultants found that permanent part-time workers were likely to have some coverage in the six areas commonly provided almost universally to full-time workers. However, only about 20 percent of seasonal workers had coverage in most of those areas, and temporary or casual workers rarely had coverage in any of the areas, with the exception of short-term disability insurance (reported in Baker, 1987: 9). At the same time, part-time workers are less likely to qualify for government-provided benefits if those benefits are dependent on long-term or continuous employment. Benefits for which part-time workers have difficulty qualifying or are likely to pay premiums at a higher effective rate than that paid by full-time workers, or from which they are unlikely to achieve a reasonable level of protection, include Unemployment Insurance and Canada/Quebec Pensions (Julie White, 1983: 118–127). Since White's account was written, some improvements have been made in Unemployment Insurance provisions (see Coates, 1988: 95).

Governments have generally not compelled employers to provide benefits to part-time employees comparable to those they have provided to their full-time workers (exceptions are the Pension Benefits Acts of Ontario, Nova Scotia, and New Brunswick that require private pension plans to make provision for the inclusion of some part-time workers). By the same token, governments themselves have generally excluded or disadvantaged their part-time employees in undertaking the provision of benefits. The underlying premise of such legislation seems to be that part-time workers have only a tenuous connection or commitment to the labor force, and hence work-related benefits need not be provided to them. However, Statistics Canada reported in 1986 that 28 percent of part-time employees would have preferred full-time work (65 percent of male part-time workers between 25 and 54) (Baker, 1987: 2–3; Coates, 1988: 6–8). Even those who did not want full-time work included some who worked a regular part-time schedule and whose commitment to the labor force must be seen as a continuing one. A further argument often made is that prorating benefits for part-time workers would cost employers an unthinkable amount, and would reduce the availability of part-time work. However, the added cost is mainly direct (and, therefore, a part of negotiable compensation); the administrative costs appear negligible (Canada. Commission of Inquiry into Part-Time Work, 1983: 163–171).

Critics of government performance in this area are inclined to despair of compelling benefit payments by private sector employers, although some call for mandatory prorating of benefits already provided to full-time workers. For the most part, critics call upon government to modify its own benefit programs to provide greater universality or to include part-timers more meaningfully in work- or wage-related benefit programs. Employer-sponsored training or career development programs may be seen by workers as benefits that improve their earning power and potential for mobility. Such programs, however, are seen as investment in human capital, and employers will have an interest in reserving such opportunities for workers with whom they envision a continuing relationship. In some circumstances, of course, it would be to the employers' advantage to provide training to part-time workers as a means of preparing them to replace retiring full-time workers. Nevertheless, this training is normally provided only when a particular replacement has been identified. If employers can rely on some other firm or public agency to provide the bulk of general job training, they will reduce their own costs accordingly.

Government training programs are commonly justified as a state contribution to labor market development—improving the fit between labor supply and available labor demand. However, two other functions of such programs sometimes appear to take precedence. First, where governments contract with private sector firms to conduct the training, there is an element of political patronage in the selection of firms. Second, where training programs provide stipends or allowances, and are situated in areas of generally low or fluctuating labor demand, they serve primarily as income supplements for a reserve labor force of seasonal or casual workers. Therefore, neither private nor public training programs provide an unambiguous benefit to most part-time workers.

HUMAN RIGHTS

Most human rights legislation is directed at preventing discrimination, especially discrimination on the grounds of certain specified characteristics, such as race, religion, or sex. As such, it is generally applied in employment matters without differentiating between full- and part-time workers. However, some jurisdictions, such as Ontario, prohibit discrimination in employment on the grounds of age, but define age for these purposes as between 18 and 65. As a consequence, two categories with a high proportion of part-time employees—young students and retired persons—are not protected against discrimination in employment.

One effect of such legislation is to permit mandatory retirement, which discourages a phasing out of one's working life through transfer to part-time employment, possibly extending beyond normal pensionable age. The case that mandatory retirement is unconstitutional, since it denies equal protection under the law, has recently been argued and lost before the Supreme Court of Canada. The argument made for retaining the existing human rights code definition of age was that it provided a limit on protection from discrimination that was reasonable and demonstrably justified, owing to the need to provide employment opportunities for younger workers and to maintain the integrity of pension plans.

GOVERNMENTS AS EMPLOYERS

The Commission of Inquiry into Part-Time Work observed that the federal government was the largest employer in Canada, but that it employed the smallest proportion of part-time workers of any industry that presented briefs to the Commission (Canada. Commission of Inquiry into Part-Time Work, 1983: 136). In 1980, the federal Treasury Board undertook to provide some prorated benefits for one category of part-time worker in the federal public service. In so doing, they created two categories of part-time employee: those who worked more than one third of a full-time worker's hours on a permanent basis (and would receive all employee benefits on a prorated basis), and those who worked less than a third, or on a seasonal or short-term contract basis (and who would be denied any benefits and would be excluded from union membership). The bulk of part-time workers fell into the second category, although the total number of part-time workers in the federal public service remained small, at 1.1 percent of employees in 1981 (Canada. Commission of Inquiry into Part-Time Work, 1983: 136–137).

Provincial governments, to the extent that they made any provision for part-time employees at all, tended to make a similar distinction between continuing, long-term part-time workers and casual, seasonal, or temporary workers. Where there were any benefits for part-timers, they accrued generally to the former group. Governments as employers have apparently adopted much the same view of part-time work as employers in the private sector. The administrative inconvenience of providing benefits or protection to employees who are not committed to a single employer on a continuing basis over a long period has discouraged government employers as much as private ones. The recommendations of bodies like the Commission of Inquiry into Part-Time Work, who have argued that governments have a role to play as example setters for private sector employers, have largely fallen on deaf ears to date.

FUTURE PROSPECTS

The growth in part-time employment over the past decade can be attributed partly to economic downturn and the resulting underemployment—the availability only of part-time work for people who would prefer full-time work. However, part of the growth in part-time employment can be attributed to a fundamental social and economic change. It is government's response to that change that will determine how well we shall deal with part-time work and part-time workers in the succeeding decade.

The underemployment of human resources, represented by involuntary part-time work, undermines the productivity, and ultimately the wealth, of our society. To the extent that it is concentrated in particular industries or communities, it contributes to producing a segment of the labor force whose long-term employment experience is characterized by uncertainty, poverty, and despair. The creation of such a subclass must surely have a detrimental impact on the maintenance of civil society. However, to the extent that part-time work is voluntary and the benefits of that work are comparable, on a pro rata basis, with those from full-time employment, the above effects will be considerably mitigated.

The recently negotiated free-trade agreement between Canada and the United States has been attacked by some Canadians as being likely to reduce the availability in Canada of full-time, high-wage, skill-enhancing employment. Economic observers will presumably continue to debate this issue throughout the life of the agreement, and it will be difficult to disentangle the effects of the agreement from the effects of more general changes associated with a global restructuring of the international division of labor. However, if the agreement, or other forces, results in a decrease of full-time employment in manufacturing, with a concomitant increase in the relative importance of seasonal and part-time work in the resource and service sectors, the conditions associated with part-time employment become of increasing concern.

In view of the resistance by employers to the provision of prorated benefits, it seems likely that government will be pressed to expand its own work-related social welfare programs to make greater allowance for part-time employees. They will obviously do so only to the extent that revenues will permit, and probably to the extent that some sort of link can be maintained between work-force involvement and benefit eligibility. Reform in this area will probably aim at providing fairer measures of work-force involvement. Such measures would be for those who have a seasonal or irregular commitment to work, or who must work for multiple employers, so that they would not be disadvantaged relative to those who work approximately the same amount in a year, but who have a more regular part-time schedule or a continuing commitment to a single employer. In the meantime, if casual employees continue to be unprotected, either by employer benefits or work-related public benefits, there may be pressure for increased universal (or even income-targeted) benefits, unrelated to work history.

At present, it appears that governments have made little progress in responding to the growing phenomenon of part-time work, either as legislators or as employers. If the incidence of part-time employment continues to expand, however, governments will not long be able to resist the pressure to act. The increased efficiency promised by a flexible, part-time work force cannot be purchased indefinitely at the expense of equitable treatment of the part-time employees on whom one depends. If unions and individual employees cannot force firms to be accountable in this area, then governments will be compelled to do so.

4 Part-Time Work and the State in Britain, 1941–1987

Celia J. Briar

Part-time work, now understood in the United Kingdom as paid employment for less than 30 hours per week or, more commonly, for 16 hours or less, was virtually unknown in Britain before World War II.[1] By the 1980s, it had become the most typical working pattern for married women. Much of the expansion of part-time employment, together with the distinct conditions of part-time work in Britain, can be attributed to the policies of the state.[2] The purpose of this chapter is to describe and evaluate these policies and their results since 1941.

THE STATE AND THE EXPANSION OF PART-TIME WORK, 1941–1987

Part-time work was originally viewed as a compromise between a desperate need for war workers, and policy makers' concerns that women retain their domestic obligations.[3] This form of employment was actively promoted by the wartime government from 1941 on. At first, the means of promoting part-time work were low key, consisting chiefly of appeals to employers. Late in 1941, Winston Churchill proposed to Cabinet that: "Employers might well be encouraged, in suitable cases, to make further use of the services of married women in industry. This would often have to be on a part-time basis and means must be found to ease the dual burden on women who are prepared to play a dual role" (U.K. Proceedings of Cabinet, 65/20 Nov. 6th 1941: Memorandum by the Prime Minister). Similarly in 1942, the Ministry of Labour and National Service produced a booklet entitled "Mobilisation of Women-Power: Planning for Part-time Work," and, the same year, a Command Paper recommended that part-time workers be used to replace the 55 percent of male staff who had left banking (U.K. Parliament, 1942).

However, during the severe labor shortage of 1943, the state assumed power to conscript married women into part-time employment (except where they had children living with them).[4] Many employers were initially resistant to the notion of part-time women workers, although some soon recognized the advantages of workers who were less tired, more productive, less prone to absenteeism, and more tolerant of unpleasant working conditions. In 1943 there were 700,000 women in part-time employment,[5] and by 1951 the total had risen to 750,000, despite a temporary reduction in the overall numbers of women in employment in Britain at the end of the war (Klein, 1965).

In the postwar reconstruction period there was a labor shortage of sufficient severity for conscription of men into certain industries to be reintroduced. Once again, part-time employment was prescribed for married women in such a way as to allow women to continue to fulfill a "dual role": "Industries will need to adjust their conditions of work to suit, so far as possible, the convenience of women with household responsibilities and to accept, as they did in the war, the services of women on a part-time basis" (U.K. Parliament, 1946/7:28).

Policy makers were obliged to attempt to break down the resistance of employers to part-time workers, since many "seemed to regard part-time work of any sort as both complicated and uneconomic" (U.K. Parliament, 1955/6 xvii: 17). As late as 1960, a survey of personnel officers by Klein led her to the conclusion that "part-time workers will normally only be employed when all other means of recruiting full-time labor have been exhausted" (Klein, 1965: 131). Nevertheless, the employment of part-time workers continued to expand. Between 1948 and 1958 there was an increase of 37 percent in the numbers of women employed part-time; by 1959, part-time women workers had become 16 percent of the female labor force (U.K. Ministry of Labour Gazette. "Earnings and Hours of Part-time Women Workers in Manufacturing Industry." 1958: 453). Part of the increase, which continued more steeply in the 1960s, was accounted for by the state itself. In its role as an employer, the state recruited part-time teachers, nurses, and clerical workers. It would appear that, through a combination of propaganda and its own example, the state played a major role in persuading employers to test the advantages of employing female part-timers. When the postwar boom ended, part-time employment was still expanding. Between 1971 and 1978 almost one million part-time jobs were created for women, most of them in the service sector (U.K. Department of Employment. Employment Gazette, 1983: 173), as women's full-time employment was beginning to decline. As shown in Table 4.1, part-time employment accounted for 99 percent of the growth in women's paid work between 1978 and 1984.

Although, by 1984, part-time workers accounted for 44 percent of the

Table 4.1
Women's Full-Time and Part-Time Employment 1978–1984

	Full-time	Part-time
September 1978	5,624,000	3,611,000
September 1983	5,006,000	3,833,000
March 1984	4,945,000	4,103,000

Source: U.K. Hansard Parliamentary Debates (Commons), 6th ser. vol. 55, col. 141w.

female work force (excluding au pairs and outworkers or home workers), government departments were still expanding the provision of part-time jobs in the civil service (U.K. 1984, col. 166 w; 1985, col. 141w). State policies played a major role in the creation and expansion of part-time employment for married women, with the result that Britain has had a higher proportion of part-timers than the average for European Economic Community (EEC) countries (Walby, 1985). Likewise, the state has also been highly influential in establishing the distinct forms and patterns of part-time employment in the United Kingdom in terms of pay, job security, working conditions, and employment opportunities.

THE STATE AND THE SHAPING OF PART-TIME EMPLOYMENT IN BRITAIN SINCE 1941

Patterns of part-time employment in Britain were established at an early stage in its development. State policies have ensured that access to state benefits by part-timers, and their working conditions, pay, opportunities, and job security, have regularly been inferior to those of full-time employees. From the outset, part-time workers have been less likely than full-timers to qualify for state benefits. During World War II, employers realized substantial savings by not having to pay National Insurance contributions against unemployment and accidents in respect of part-timers (Summerfield, 1984: 145). In the 1980s these exemptions still applied in a high proportion of cases, saving some employers an estimated 15 percent of their wage bill (Clark 1982: 258).

In addition, there has been a policy of encouraging the recruitment of part-timers into the jobs with the least desirable working conditions. This was partly an automatic consequence of the policy of recruiting married women after all other available labor had been absorbed. However, in 1942, the Ministry of Labour specifically recommended that part-timers be allocated to the least pleasant jobs, characterized for example by "dirt, noise, heat and smell" (Summerfield, 1984: 145). It was further stated that: "women may tackle monotonous and heavy jobs better and with more energy than if they were working all day" (Ministry of Labour and National Service, 1942). During the postwar period, the state itself recruited part-time women workers into the least popular jobs. In 1969, a directive was sent from the Department of Health and Social Services to hospitals, requiring them to "actively encourage" women doctors to return to paid work on a part-time basis, and advising their placement in "posts which have proved difficult to fill on a whole time basis."

Women part-timers in the United Kingdom have tended to have lower rates of pay, compared with full-timers, than their EEC counterparts (Walby, 1985: 268). This appears to be due, on the one hand, to occupational segregation and the concentration of part-timers in the lowest pay grades, and, on the other hand, to the relative lack of overtime pay, occupational pensions, sick pay, paid holidays, and other fringe benefits. Hunt's 1965 survey found part-time women workers concentrated in a particularly narrow range of occupations, especially in the service sector; Martin and Roberts (1984) found that a higher proportion of women part-timers than full-timers worked only with other women.

The 1970 Equal Pay Act was, therefore, of little assistance to part-time women workers, who were obliged to compare themselves with an actual male in the same job in order to make a claim. Martin and Roberts (1984) found that women part-timers were earning only 79 percent of the hourly earnings of women full-timers, and only 58 percent of those of men full-timers. Moreover, the 1984 Equal Pay Amendment regulations, which allowed claims for equal pay for work of equal value, were made so difficult and complex that part-timers have been dissuaded from bringing cases. In addition, EEC recommendations such as the 1981 Draft Directive on Part-Time Work, which would have given part-timers the same fringe benefits as full-timers on a pro rata basis, have been firmly resisted by the U.K. government. The government has, in fact, attempted to veto its adoption for the entire European Economic Community (Beechey and Perkins, 1987: 158).

From the outset, part-time jobs in Britain have been chiefly "dead-end," having no promotional ladders or opportunities for training. Even in the part-time jobs created by the state, such as teaching and nursing, which required formal qualifications, women were expected to possess these qualifications already, and were confined to the lowest grades. In 1984, the U.K. government announced the creation of extra part-time jobs in the civil service. This was its contribution to adopting the recommendations of the EEC on positive discrimination toward women (U.K. 1984, col.166 w). By a curious piece of "doublethink," the government was promoting part-time work as "positive discrimination" designed to help women compete more effectively with men at work. In fact, this approach was simply helping more women to continue bearing the main responsibility for household labor and caring. Policy makers appeared to have overlooked the findings of Martin and Roberts (1984) and others, which showed that almost half of the women who entered part-time work after a career break experienced downward occupational mobility in that they entered into a lower occupational category. In fact, the government appeared to be undermining its own ostensible policies of promoting equality of opportunity for women at work.

FLEXIBILITY, JOB SECURITY, AND PART-TIME EMPLOYMENT

Arguably, the state in Britain has encouraged employers to view women part-timers as low-status, marginal, and disposable (Dex and Shaw, 1986: 128). Thus, although the state promoted the expansion of part-time employment for women, it did so in ways that made their position precarious. Part-time employees who worked less than 16 hours per week normally had no legal protection against unfair dismissal (for example, under the 1975 Employment Protection legislation). Employers availed themselves of this opportunity for a "flexible" work force. In 1982, one million female part-timers were excluded from the main provisions of protective legislation (Clark 1982). Martin and Roberts (1984) found that the number of hours worked by women part-timers peaked at just under 16 hours per week. In 1986, the government proposed to raise the threshold number of hours worked to qualify for employment protection or reinstatement after childbirth to 20 per week, and even this was restricted to employees with two years of uninterrupted service. It was clear that the great majority of part-timers would then not qualify for employment protection. However, the proposed changes were justified on the grounds that they would "reduce the restrictions which deter employers from creating new part-time jobs" (U.K. Parliament, 1986: 37).

During the late 1970s and the 1980s, the rapid expansion of women's part-time employment and the shrinkage of full-time jobs contributed to a belief that women part-timers were being used to substitute for full-time workers (Gardiner, 1976; Rubery, 1988). However, there appears to be very little evidence of this. Most of the expansion in part-time employment has been in the traditional "women's sphere" of the service sector (Milkman, 1976; Breugel, 1979), whereas in industries that have contracted, notably in manufacturing, part-time jobs have tended to be lost at a higher rate than full-time ones (Breugel, 1979). However, the alternative view that women are cushioned from labor market shrinkage by gender-based occupational segregation may also require some modification. It is true that sexual divisions were maintained intact (largely by state policies) from 1941 onwards, and it is also true that, even in a recession, most adult men would not be prepared to accept the pay and conditions prevalent in most of women's part-time jobs (Milkman, 1976). However, the boundaries between "women's jobs" and "men's jobs" can be shifted, as they were in wartime. There has been some evidence of attempts by the U.K. government in the 1980s to funnel unemployed young men and women into low-grade part-time employment, for example by the community program and the job-splitting scheme, both of which tend to exclude married women.

Women in Britain are widely regarded as having gained a firm and permanent foothold in the labor market. However, it can be argued that this view is exaggerated, and that women have been placed in an increasingly peripheral and vulnerable position in the labor market by state employment policies. The normal practice of aggregating full- and part-time employment statistics gives the impression that, in 1984, women constituted 41 percent of the paid work force. In fact, they constituted only 29 percent of the labor force, a proportion that had barely changed in 30 years. Instances of sacking part-timers first have been recognized as a form of sex discrimination which, in 1982, was declared unlawful by the Employment Appeals Tribunal. However, another tribunal of the same year ruled that it was a "case of business judgement whether to employ full- or part-timers and not the function of the tribunal to make such judgements." It was argued that: "Part-timers were dismissed first because it was considered more efficient to employ full-timers. Generally this is not unreasonable—a greater number of employees throws an additional burden on supervision and personnel functions." (Ojituku versus Manpower Services Commission cited in Earnshaw.) Given that efficiency criteria have been allowed to overrule the spirit of the 1975 Sex Discrimination Act, there appears to be some cause for concern for the security of part-time women workers.

CHILD CARE, "CARING," AND PART-TIME EMPLOYMENT

One reason why British women have been more likely to go into part-time, downgraded employment after childbearing has been the virtual lack of subsidized child care in Britain in "normal" times[6] (Dex and Shaw, 1986). Although there has been a degree of tension at times of severe labor shortage, between the Ministry of Labour and the Ministry of Health (and their successors), there has been a consistent overall policy regarding child-care provision. That is, state-subsidized child care has only been provided for a tiny (and stigmatized) minority of families unable to provide a "normal" family life. This service has also been made available to allow mothers to work during periods of exceptional labor shortages.

During World War II, despite a rapid expansion of working mothers, state nurseries did not cater for more than 6 percent of the preschool child population, and priority was given to "private arrangements made by the mother, that is the use of child minders" (Summerfield, 1984: 90). At the end of the war, the Ministry of Health quickly withdrew funding. Responsibility was transferred to local authorities, who raised the fees to cover costs. Since women were being moved back into low-paid "women's jobs," many could no longer afford to use the nurseries. The number of local authority day nurseries dropped, due to "lack of demand," from 785 in 1952 to only 453 in 1975 (U.K. 1947, vol. 444, col. 173; vol. 560, col. 700; Lewenhak, 1977: 292).

However, there were two instances in postwar Britain when nursery provision was expanded to allow women access to full-time employment. During the severe labor shortage in cotton and wool textiles between 1946 and 1950, the Ministry of Labour arranged for the supply of buildings and materials for special day nurseries (U.K. 1947, vol. 448, cols. 1860–61; U.K. Ministry of Labour Gazette, 1950: 192). Similarly, during the 1960s, special nursery classes were created to meet the shortage of trained teachers. By 1969, 236 nursery classes had been created for this purpose (House of Commons Hansard 5th Series vol. 745, col. 783; Mackie and Patullo, 1977: 116).

These kinds of measures were exceptional. Hunt's (1968) survey of women's employment commissioned by the Ministry of Labour found that there was a vast amount of unmet demand for state child care, since this was considered by mothers to be more reliable than private arrangements. The Ministry of Health interjected a policy statement into the report, to the effect that: "As far as day nurseries are concerned, these have been provided since 1945 primarily to meet the needs of certain children for day care on health and welfare grounds. *Their service is not intended to meet a demand from working women generally for subsidized day care facilities.* The number of places provided is therefore considerably less than the demand shown in the survey." (Emphasis added.) (Hunt, 1967: 94–95.) In 1973/74, following the recommendations of the 1967 Plowden committee, there was an expansion in the number of places in nursery schools; however, the majority of places in nursery schools and classes became part time, on the grounds that "young children should not be separated for long from their mothers" (Plowden, 1968: Vol.1: 121). It was, moreover, recommended that nursery schools, like day nurseries, should begin to give priority to hardship cases, that is: "children . . . who come from poor or unstable home conditions or whose mother is the sole parent and has to go out to work" (U.K. Parliament, 1974: 16).

In 1976/77—ironically, the year after the 1970 Equal Pay Act became legally enforceable—local authority day nurseries raised their fees considerably. Lancashire County Council, for example, increased their fees by 120 percent. Child care fees tend to be paid from the mother's earnings

(Land, 1981: 5). This escalation meant that a huge group of women were not seen as "hardship" cases but neither were they so well paid that they could afford full nursery fees. They could only hope—if they were fortunate—to obtain part-time places in nursery schools or classes for their children. Thus, these women were only available for short hours of part-time employment at the most. The Women and Employment Survey conducted by Martin and Roberts (1984) found that only 7 percent of mothers of children aged 0 to 4 were in full-time paid employment in the United Kingdom, and 20 percent were in part-time paid work. Moreover, women with school-age children are still constrained by the fact that the normal working day and year bear little relation to that of schools. Other than in wartime, state after-school care has not been provided on any significant scale. Its absence has also restricted women's hours of employment.

Policies of "community care" have had a considerable impact on the working hours of women over 40, especially since the 1970s. Unpaid caring, such as for the bedridden and the severely disabled, is over-whelmingly performed by women in the home.[7] In 1984, just over half of employed women in the Women and Employment Survey who provided care said that their hours of paid work were affected, and 79 percent of care givers were prevented from doing any paid work at all (Martin and Roberts, 1984; Beechey and Perkins, 1987: 15).

Finally, employment policies have ensured that men are normally unavailable to share the responsibilities of caring. Men have, with few exceptions, been expected to be available for full-time employment. Furthermore, the promotion of part-time work for older men and women during the 1950s envisaged shorter hours for men only as an alternative to retirement. According to the 1981 census, of the 9 percent of part-timers who were men, most were over the age of 60. Policy makers in the United Kingdom have also refrained from making shared parenthood easier, for example, by resisting the EEC's draft directive on Parental and Family Leave[8] (U.K. 1986, col. 623w).

THE BENEFITS OF PART-TIME EMPLOYMENT

The benefits of women's part-time work as perceived by statesmen have already been outlined. Married women in particular[9] have been viewed as flexible reserves of labor whose employment can be used at specific times and in specific areas without undermining the existing order of the labor market, yet whose unemployment—due mainly to benefit regulations—is largely invisible. However, the benefits of women's part-time employment to men require some comment.

Policy makers have been sensitive to the potential opposition of husbands to wives' employment in the period since 1941. During World

War II, the recruitment of wives was delayed, partly out of a fear that the men at the front would "lose their fighting spirit" if their wives were not waiting at home (U.K. 1942, col. 1070–7; 1941, col. 1481). The creation of part-time employment, though overriding the wishes of some husbands, meant that men's domestic comforts were preserved. Recruitment of women during the postwar labor shortage was done in such a way as "not to destroy home life, because that upsets the menfolk and the factories." The "wife's little job" added to household income without much altering the balance of power in the home. Men have also been spared women's competition for the better paid and more prestigious jobs in the labor market, and generally still experience upward occupational mobility over a lifetime, whereas married women's mobility is often downward.

For women, the benefits of part-time employment are less clear. While the value to women of at least partial independence and some participation in outside social life cannot be underestimated, part-time work should not be construed as promoting equality in either the home or the work force. Indeed, the use of part-time employment seems to have been used to minimize the effects of married women's mass entry into the work force in the long period of labor shortage from 1941 onwards. Currently, one effect of the continued expansion of part-time employment appears to be the undermining of the equal pay, equal opportunity, and employment protection legislation.

CONCLUSION

We have seen that, throughout the postwar years in Britain, the state has actively promoted and shaped part-time employment, aiming it predominantly at married women. The purpose of this concluding section is to assess, in light of the evidence presented, the view that part-time employment represents an opportunity for women, an opportunity that women themselves would freely choose.

Although part-time work has indeed been described by policy makers as creating new opportunities for women (U.K. 1984, col. 166w), this was, in fact, never the prime motivating force for its creation. Rather, part-time employment was designed initially to meet temporary labor shortages during wartime and the postwar years (with minimum disruption of the sexual division of labor in the work place and home). Later, it was intended to increase flexibility in the labor market.

Most recently, government concern to present part-time work as an opportunity for women appears to have stemmed from a wider concern to indicate that some positive action for women in employment was being enacted. This has occurred in the wake of the decision by the European Economic Community (of which Britain is a member) that the

British Sex Discrimination Act (1975) failed to meet the United Kingdom's obligations to the European Economic Community (EEC Directive 76/207/EEC Commission of European Communities versus United Kingdom of Great Britain and Ireland I.C.R.192, 1984). Arguably, a policy of promoting true equality of opportunity for women in the labor market should include intervention to address and dismantle discriminatory barriers on a systematic basis, to compensate for the effects of past discrimination, and to aim at equality of outcomes. However, in 1988, the Secretary of State for Employment argued that: "In general, terms and conditions of employment are matters best left for employers and employees or their representatives to determine" (United Kingdom, 1988, col. 165). Instead of promoting equality of opportunity in the work place, part-time employment, as it has been developed by the state in Britain, has tended to reinforce gender inequalities. Women part-time workers have been systematically recruited into the most menial positions within organizations. These positions are characterized by a high degree of occupational segregation, insecurity, low pay, low status, little autonomy, and few, if any, opportunities for formal training or advancement.

If part-time employment as it has been developed in Britain cannot be viewed as securing greater equality of opportunity for women in the labor market, can it at least be seen as preferable to full-time unemployment? After all, it was only at the end of World War II that the marriage bar (which meant the firing of women upon marriage from almost all public sector and many private sector jobs) was formally dismantled in Britain. While it may be conceded that part-time jobs, however dead-end, may have provided many women with a small income, some social contacts, and some relief from the isolation and frustrations of full-time housework and caring, there are several reasons why the gains should not be overstated.

First, because part-time employment was expressly designed to fit around women's domestic responsibilities from World War II onward, the view that housework and caring are the primary responsibility of women, not of men, has been reaffirmed. Acceptance of this view continues to limit women's availability for full-time employment. Second, the low pay characteristic of part-time jobs ensures that women remain in a state of semi-dependence upon male partners, with a limited bargaining position in the home. This dependence also makes it difficult for a woman to leave an unsatisfactory relationship, and to support herself and children with dignity. In addition, there has been a tendency for the rise in part-time employment, especially during the 1970s, to disguise a worrying shrinkage in permanent full-time jobs for women, particularly in the manufacturing sector. The move toward a higher proportion of part-time jobs tends to be accompanied by a reduction in women's leverage, as part-timers are less likely to be unionized. In summary, part-time employment represents a far more limited gain for women than is generally acknowledged, and one that is dependent upon the vagaries of an unstable market for labor.

It would be possible to create part-time employment in ways that do represent opportunities for real gains by women in the labor market. Permanent (rather than temporary or casual) part-time employment with full pro rata benefits and career paths would be a partial improvement. However, it would not provide the whole answer, because it would continue to support the domestic sexual division of labor (if such part-time work were still constructed almost entirely for married women), thus placing an automatic handicap on women workers. It is nevertheless possible to establish employment policies that give women more equal opportunities, such as job-sharing schemes for both men and women, or the option of a shorter working day for parents of both sexes.

In Britain, central government has been resistant to improving the position of part-time workers, although there have been attempts by a few authority employers to extend job-sharing schemes. It is difficult to explain this resistance simply in terms of the capitalist market's drive for profitability. If women part-timers are cheaper and more productive to employ than men, why should highly paid full-time male workers have been largely protected from their competition? It would appear that the creation of part-time employment in Britain has been shaped by, and continues to support, a particular form of patriarchy. Nonetheless, one way to challenge the legitimacy of this system is to expose the myth that part-time work in Britain has been constructed to create opportunities for women.

NOTES

1. However, other "flexible" working patterns were common; for example, "short-time" working during slack seasons, especially in clothing and textile trades; out-work, casual and seasonal work, laundry, and harvesting were also prevalent prior to World War II.

2. By "policies of the state" I am referring to those aspects of government policy toward women's employment which have remained essentially similar irrespective of which political party has been in office during the period since 1941.

3. Early in World War II, the Minister of Labour had expressed the erroneous view that women would not be required to any great extent as war workers. Thus, only young single women were initially conscripted into war work. Married women were not at any stage conscripted into full-time employment, and were exempt from conscription even into part-time work if they had children under 14 living with them. This policy proved almost disastrous to the war effort, as the labor shortage intensified (Summerfield, 1984).

4. This was done under the 1943 Control of Employment (Directed Persons) order (U.K. Ministry of Labour Gazette, 1943: 61).

5. This was the number stated by the Minister of Labour, Ernest Bevin (U.K. Hansard Parliamentary Debates (Commons). 5th ser. vol. 392 col. 460).

6. Dex and Shaw (1986) show that in the United States, where child-care expenses can be tax-deductible, the women are more likely than British women to remain in full-time employment and do not experience the same degree of downward occupational mobility.

7. Walker (1983) states that women provide twenty times as much unpaid care as men.

8. In addition, a Private Member's Bill on paternity leave, presented by Greville Jenner, M.P., in 1979, was defeated.

9. This applies particularly to white British women. Asian and West Indian women have, by contrast, tended to work long hours in employment at low rates of pay.

5 Part-Time Employment and Industrial Relations in Great Britain in the 1980s

David G. Blanchflower

> There is no clear evidence that part-time workers are being unjustly treated. Many of them enjoy a satisfactory degree of protection under our legislation, and in many cases there are sound economic or commercial reasons for applying different terms of employment to part-time workers as compared to full-time workers. This is a fact which part-time workers are ready to accept as a consequence of the nature of their work. In our view, arrangements between part-time workers and their employers are best left for voluntary agreements either individually or through collective bargaining where that is available (Letter from the Secretary of State for Employment).[1]

One of the major features of the British labor market in recent years has been both an absolute and a relative increase in the number of part-time workers. Between June 1971 and March 1988, the number of part-time employees grew by 55 percent, whereas the number of full-time employees fell by 18 percent. Recent forecasts suggest that the prime source of employment growth in the next few years will come from part-time jobs. It is particularly appropriate, therefore, to examine the characteristics of Britain's part-time labor market. A substantial body of literature already exists on why individuals choose to work part-time, and on the type of work they do (Elias and Main, 1982; Ballard, 1984; Martin and Roberts, 1984a; 1984b; Robinson and Wallace, 1984). However, relatively little is known either about the type of work places in which part-timers are employed or the industrial relations characteristics of such work places. To examine these issues, we make use of data from two large-scale representative surveys of establishments[2] undertaken in Great

Britain in 1980 and 1984. This builds upon earlier work using the 1980 data that were first reported in Blanchflower and Corry (1987). We concentrate here on identifying the major changes that occurred in the environment in which part-timers were employed during a unique period in the history of British industrial relations.[3]

We shall attempt to provide answers to the following kinds of questions:

1. What is the distribution of part-time workers by industrial sector and establishment size? How did this change between 1980 and 1984?
2. Is there a different system of industrial relations where part-time workers are employed? How did this change between 1980 and 1984?
3. Did the relative position of part-time workers improve over the period?
4. Does the employment of part-timers add a dimension of flexibility to the labor force that helps firms to meet unexpected changes in demand and production conditions?

WHY PART-TIME? AN ECONOMIST'S VIEW

It seems natural that an economist would look to the forces of supply and demand to explain the postwar rise in the number of part-time workers. What are the main supply and demand factors?

Supply

Employers sometimes allege that they are compelled to use part-time workers because of a shortage of full-time workers, which implies a supply constraint problem. Why are such constraints likely to occur? Suppliers of labor who seek part-time work presumably prefer to work for less than the full workweek.[4]

There are three groups in particular that might be expected to have strong preferences for part-time work:

Married women, especially those with children. They may wish to supply weekly hours below the full-time norm because they are also supplying labor in the home for child-rearing, cleaning, cooking, and other domestic responsibilities.

Young persons. Apart from market work they may also wish to supply hours for human capital formation in the form of education and training.

Older workers near or beyond retirement age. The reason may be an increased preference for leisure as family costs decline or health deteriorates. If these workers are receiving some type of pension, this is likely to reduce further the need for market work.

Demand

Why should an employer have a preference for employing part-time workers rather than full-timers? There may be several reasons:

Small Size of the Establishment. This is potentially important and involves a certain indivisibility in the employment of labor. A small establishment may simply not have enough work for a full-time secretary, bookkeeper, computer operator, or word processor. This indivisibility may be overcome as the size of the establishment grows (and vice versa if it declines).

Variability of Demand Combined with Storage Problems. Many products have variable demand, with periods of peak load alternating with periods of excess capacity. The variation may be seasonal, weekly, or even daily, but this in itself need not suggest a demand for part-time employment. For this we need to combine the existence of peaks and troughs in demand with the inability to store the product offered for sale. Bar service, for example, cannot be produced in slack times and stored for peak demand.

Utilization of Capital Equipment. Firms may employ part-time workers as a way of increasing capital utilization. The benefits to an employer arise out of either a higher output from a given stock of capital or a lower stock necessary to achieve the desired level of output. Capital savings are likely to be larger the more capital intensive production is, and the more susceptible the capital stock is to technological obsolescence.

Shortage of Full-Time Workers. This reason for the employment of part-time workers is sometimes given by employers. It is not of itself a specific demand factor, since it arises simply as a response to employee preference. It is likely to be primarily a short-term phenomenon.

Relative Cost of Part-Time Labor. Part-time labor may be cheap in comparison to full-time labor because wage rates per unit of labor are lower, because other costs associated with the employment of labor are less, or for both reasons.

Employer Attitudes toward the Structure of Industrial Relations. It seems to be the case that part-time workers are less likely than full-time workers to be members of trade unions. To the extent that employers have a preference for non-union workers, it is to be expected that they would favor part-time workers. There may then be a correlation between the use of part-time workers and informal, rather than formal, methods of industrial relations.

Unfortunately, it is very difficult to separate out and measure the relative importance of supply and demand. The number of part-time workers in employment at any one time will be the outcome of the interaction between the demand by employers and the supply of part-time labor by employees. This in turn may be related to the demand and supply of full-time employment. In certain circumstances, it may be possible to argue that the observed volume of employment is entirely demand-determined or entirely supply-determined. The former would be the case if we were confident that the labor market was in excess supply—hence, the quantity employed would be demand-constrained. The latter case would be true for markets in excess demand.

Although the two Workplace Industrial Relations Survey (WIRS) data sets contain detailed information on both the characteristics of the work places at which part-timers were employed and the overall structure of the establishments' work forces, the surveys were not specifically designed for an analysis of the part-time labor market. In particular, there is some information that, were it available, would have helped us in assessing the reasons why employers use part-timers. For example, employers were not asked why they did or did not use part-timers, or even about their relative cost.

The analysis undertaken in the following section cannot give complete answers to issues such as the causes of increased part-time working, including the relative importance of employer and employee demands, or whether increasing levels of part-time employment were at the expense of full-time employment. To distinguish the demand from the supply-side influences on observed employment would require a fully specified model and a wealth of individual and establishment data that have only recently begun to be available for Great Britain. (See Disney and Szyszczak [1984] for a very interesting attempt to do so, using time-series data). However, the WIRS surveys can provide important insights into the nature of this labor market. We are able to provide a nationally representative picture of the type of establishments in which part-timers are employed. The special novelty of this chapter is that we are able to examine changes not only in the industrial distribution of establishments and workers but also in the structure of their industrial relations environment.

THE DATA SOURCES

A study of this type is only as good as its statistical source. The data upon which the inquiry is based come from two large surveys of plants and work places in Great Britain, known as the Workplace Industrial Relations Surveys, conducted in 1980 (WIRS1) and 1984 (WIRS2). The samples for the surveys were drawn from the government's Census of Employment. To be included in the sample, an establishment had to have at least 25 employees (full- or part-time) at the time the sample was drawn (1977 in the case of WIRS1 and 1981 in the case of WIRS2). This limitation means that small work places, where approximately one half of all part-timers are employed,[5] are necessarily excluded from the analysis. For the study of changes in the industrial relations environments of part-time workers, the omission of the largely nonunion small business sector is unlikely to be a serious difficulty. Part-time workers employed in the sample of establishments from which the WIRS samples were drawn are more likely to be represented by unions, have better terms and conditions of employment, and be more highly paid than their counterparts in the excluded establishments.[6] Hence, the results reported here will understate such differences as do exist between full- and part-time employment.

The WIRS data cover the whole of England, Scotland, and Wales, and all of the manufacturing and service sectors of the British economy. Uniquely, both the public and private sectors are included in the sample. The major exclusions are agriculture, coal mining, and the armed forces. In 1980 and again in 1984, a nationally representative sample of approximately 2,000 establishments was achieved. Although these are multi-respondent surveys, we restrict ourselves to data provided by the senior managers who dealt with industrial relations. Large establishments were deliberately oversampled, because they were felt to be of special interest. The data sets provide information about more than one third of all the large work places in Great Britain. Such inequalities of selection necessitate the use of weights to maintain the overall representativeness of the surveys. A more detailed discussion of the WIRS sources is provided in Daniel and Millward (1983) and Millward and Stevens (1986).

EMPIRICAL EVIDENCE

Table 5.1 provides details of the changes in the distribution of employment by broad sector.[7] In most of the succeeding tables, we follow the same format as in Table 5.1. For both 1980 and 1984, we report the percent of the work force that were part-time, and the percentage of all part-timers. It is also possible to distinguish the percentage of establishments in a particular category. However, considerable care has to be taken with this measure because, first, average plant size differs between categories in any one year, and second, average plant size fell from 118 in 1980 to 108 in 1984.[8]

As can be seen from the third and fourth columns of Table 5.1, a higher proportion of workers in 1984 were employed in the service sector than was the case in 1980 (67 percent and 57 percent respectively). Changes in the structure of part-time employment were broadly in line with changes in total employment. By 1984, part-timers constituted 16 percent of the work force in establishments with at least 25 employees, compared with 14 percent in 1980. Table 5.2 presents the industrial

Table 5.1
Broad Classification of Part-Timers

	% Part-timers in Work force		% All Part-timers		% All Workers		Number of Establishments[1]	
	1980	1984	1980	1984	1980	1984	1980	1984
Private Sector	13	14	59	48	64	57	1,351 (1318)	1,266 (1186)
Private manufacturing	7	6	19	10	39	28	508 (750)	433 (600)
Private nonmanufacturing	22	21	40	38	25	29	843 (568)	833 (586)
Public Sector	16	14	41	52	36	43	633 (694)	731 (816)
Public manufacturing	2	3	–	–	4	5	35 (83)	39 (89)
Public nonmanufacturing	18	22	41	51	32	38	598 (611)	692 (727)
Manufacturing	6	5	20	10	43	33	542 (833)	472 (689)
Nonmanufacturing	20	21	80	90	57	67	1,441 (1,179)	1,525 (1,313)
Total Great Britain	14	16	100	100	100	100	1,984 (2,012)	1,997 (2,002)

1. Unweighted number of establishments in parentheses.

Table 5.2
Industrial Distribution of Part-Timers

Industry	% Part-timers in Work Force		% All Part-timers		% All Workers		Number of Establishments[1]	
	1980	1984	1980	1984	1980	1984	1980	1984
Energy and Water Supply	3	3	-	-	3	4	40 (63)	44 (67)
Other Minerals & Ore Extraction	4	4	2	1	6	6	67 (120)	81 (117)
Metal Goods, Engineering & Vehicles	5	3	6	2	18	12	203 (335)	152 (267)
Other Manufacturing Industries	10	10	11	6	16	11	233 (315)	194 (238)
Construction	3	3	1	-	4	3	117 (95)	84 (68)
Distribution, Hotels, Catering, Repairs	26	42	22	22	12	12	438 (274)	365 (247)
Transport & Communication	4	4	2	2	6	7	114 (134)	127 (165)
Banking, Finance, Insurance etc.	10	9	3	4	5	8	158 (103)	236 (169)
Other Services	24	36	52	61	30	37	612 (571)	713 (663)
Total Great Britain	14	16	100	100	100	100	1,984 (2012)	1,997 (2002)

1. Unweighted number of establishments in parentheses.

distribution of employment in establishments with at least 25 employees (full- or part-time) in Great Britain, using 1980 data from WIRS1 and, for 1984, using WIRS2. The decline in employment in the manufacturing sector that occurred over the period is particularly noticeable in Standard Industrial Classification (SIC) Orders 3 (Metal Goods, Engineering, and Vehicles) and 4 (Other manufacturing). For all workers, a higher proportion was employed in SIC Order 9 (Other Services) in 1984 than in 1980. By 1984, more than four out of ten employees in Distribution, Hotels, Catering, and Repairs were part-time.

The remainder of our discussion will concentrate on part-time employment in the *private sector* where the most pronounced differences in work-place characteristics exist between full and part-time workers. Table 5.3 presents distributions of employment by work-place size. Although a higher proportion of total employment in 1984 was in establishments with less than 100 employees than was the case in 1980 (38 percent and 33 percent respectively), *exactly* the opposite was true of part-time employment (33 percent and 38 percent respectively). This is, in part, because part-time employment fell relatively less rapidly than full-time employment in the largest establishments with at least 500 employees. These were the work places that experienced the most dramatic declines in employment over the period (Blanchflower, Millward, and Oswald, 1988).

Part-time employees were less likely to have been employed in establishments that experienced big declines in employment over the period, as Table 5.4 illustrates. We have grouped work places together into five categories in relation to their percent of change in employment. The elements in the table add vertically to 100 percent. For example, in 1980, 15 percent of all part-timers and 18 percent of all workers were employed at work places which declined by at least 20 percent between 1975 and 1980. Just under one in five of Britain's work places (184 out of a total of 1021) fell into this category. In 1980, 36 percent of part-timers were employed at private sector work places that had declined by at least 5 percent over the preceding five years, compared with 43 percent for total employment. Analogously, 42 percent of part-timers were employed in establishments in 1984 that had declined by at least 5 percent over the preceding *four* years, compared with 51 percent for total employment.

Now we turn specifically to changes in the industrial-relations environment in which part-time workers were employed. We have already shown (see endnote 6) that part-time workers were less likely than full-time workers to be members of a trade union. Table 5.5 shows that just over one half of part-timers in the private sector were employed in non-union establishments in both 1980 and 1984. In contrast, 29 percent of all private sector workers in the 1980 survey worked in non-union plants, compared with 37 percent in 1984.

Table 5.3
Distribution of Part-Timers by Establishment Size: Private Sector

Number of Employees	% Part-timers in Work Force		% All Part-timers		% All Workers		Number of Establishments[1]	
	1980	1984	1980	1984	1980	1984	1980	1984
25-49	22	17	29	24	17	19	704 (256)	663 (223)
50-99	15	14	19	19	16	19	349 (253)	338 (239)
100-199	14	15	17	20	15	17	164 (243)	156 (206)
200-499	12	13	18	18	19	19	92 (236)	80 (210)
500-999	7	10	6	8	11	11	25 (160)	20 (164)
1000-1999	7	10	6	6	11	8	11 (92)	7 (106)
2000+	8	9	6	5	11	8	6 (78)	3 (38)

1. Unweighted number of establishments in parentheses.

Table 5.4
Distribution of Part-Timers by Change in Establishment Size: Private Sector

	1975-1980 (WIRS1)			1980-1984 (WIRS2)		
	% All Part-timers	% All Workers	Number of Establishments[1]	% All Part-timers	% All Workers	Number of Establishments[1]
≤ -20%	15	18	184 (216)	17	28	227 (334)
> -20% and ≤ -5%	21	25	197 (258)	25	23	237 (242)
> -5% and ≤ +5%	14	15	147 (160)	20	14	153 (142)
> +5% and ≤ +20%	17	16	174 (162)	16	14	170 (130)
> +20%	33	27	319 (260)	22	20	257 (163)

1. Unweighted number of establishments in parentheses.

Table 5.5
Part-Timers and Industrial Relations: Private Sector

	% Part-timers in Work Force		% All Part-timers		% All Workers		Number of Establishments[1]	
	1980	1984	1980	1984	1980	1984	1980	1984
Non-union	21	19	51	52	29	37	677 (430)	663 (420)
Union recognition	9	10	49	48	71	63	674 (888)	604 (766)
Preentry shop	9	6	8	4	12	8	69 (134)	62 (100)
Postentry shop	8	9	18	15	30	23	208 (348)	159 (276)
Any union shop	8	9	22	15	35	24	259 (414)	175 (288)

1. Unweighted number of establishments in parentheses.

However, the proportion of establishments that were non-union only increased from 42 percent to 45 percent. This is probably explained by the closure of large (union) plants and the birth or growth of smaller non-union plants. Especially notable here is the decline in the number of individuals employed at work places where the closed shop existed. In such establishments, union membership is compulsory for one or more groups of workers to obtain (a preentry closed shop) or to keep (postentry closed shop) their jobs. Examples of the former are found in printing, dock working, and merchant shipping, and of the latter in mechanical engineering, vehicles, distribution, and transport. For further details, see Dunn and Gennard (1984) and Millward and Stevens (1986).

Although the evidence on the relationship between part-time employment and the nature of industrial relations is consistent with the earlier argument that part-time employment would be associated with informal rather than formal methods of industrial relations, it is not possible to infer the direction of causality of the observed relationship. It is not necessarily the pattern of industrial relations that "determines" the use of part-timers; the opposite causation is perfectly feasible, namely that the employment of part-timers "determines" the structure of industrial relations. However, over the period in which we are interested, it is often argued that there was an exceptional decline in the power of trade unions, and that the extent of this decline was so pronounced that the whole balance of power in negotiations altered in favor of management. The result, it is claimed, was a productivity miracle that generated record profits and rising real incomes for the "insiders" who kept their jobs at the expense of the "outsiders." For a version of this view and further details, see Blanchflower, Oswald, and Garrett (1988).

By 1984, the private sector work force was more adaptable and substantially smaller than it had been in 1980; this was especially true of the highly unionized manufacturing sector. The stark choice faced by many unions in the private sector had been to adapt or perish. They were forced to accept the new, demand-constrained situation and to operate new work practices that involved severe reductions in employment. The alternative they were faced with was work-place closure. Few surviving establishments, however, altered their union status over the period.[9] The growing importance of new, non-union, work places and the decline in the average size of surviving union plants are largely responsible for the changes in the industrial relations scene observed over the period. The extent to which the performance of the non-union work places was enhanced by their greater use of part-timers is still a matter of conjecture.

Despite the fact that the balance of power may have shifted in favor of managers, the general state of relations between management and workers seems to have deteriorated over the period from 1980 to 1984. Table 5.6 reports the views of managers. A relatively high proportion of part-timers in both years was employed at establishments where managers reported that industrial relations were "very good." However, the proportion of part-timers, full-timers, and establishments in this category fell significantly over the period. The state of industrial relations, as reported by managers, was generally better in the non-union sector than in the union sector.

Finally, Table 5.7 presents details of the performance of establishments in relation to others in the same industry. As this is a relative measure, it is not surprising to see little change in the distribution of work places across the three categories. However, we do observe a large relative increase between 1980 and 1984 in the proportion of full-timers in the non-union private sector work places that were performing "above average." Over this period, full-time non-union employment increased from 27 percent of total private sector employment in 1980 to 34 percent in 1984.

CONCLUSIONS

Our main findings are as follows:

1. Between 1980 and 1984, part-time employment grew from 14 percent to 16 percent of total employment in work places of at least 25 workers. This is less growth than is popularly supposed.

2. In 1980, approximately 80 percent of part-timers were employed in non-manufacturing; by 1984, this figure had risen to 90 percent.

3. Half of all part-time workers in the British economy are employed in establishments with fewer than 25 workers.

4. In 1984, one in six part-timers were employed in establishments that had declined in size by at least 20 percent between 1980 and 1984. This compares with two in seven overall.

5. In Great Britain in the 1980s, union membership of part-timers was approximately 30 percent compared with 50 percent for full-timers and 46 percent overall.

6. Half of all part-timers in Great Britain in both 1980 and 1984 worked in non-union plants. Overall, the proportion of all workers in such work places grew from 29 percent to 37 percent over the same period. For both full- and part-time workers, there were notable declines in the proportion of workers in closed shops.

7. Managers in the private sector reported that the state of industrial relations in their work places had deteriorated over the period 1980–1984.

8. In 1984, a substantially higher proportion of non-union workers was em-

Table 5.6
State of Industrial Relations: Private Sector

	% Part-timers in Work Force		% All Part-timers		% All Workers		Number of Establishments[1]	
	1980	1984	1980	1984	1980	1984	1980	1984
Union sector								
Very good	10	12	46	34	42	29	324 (365)	206 (233)
Good	10	10	32	46	31	47	209 (275)	285 (345)
Quite good	8	8	18	12	22	16	117 (197)	84 (124)
Other	8	9	4	7	5	8	24 (51)	29 (64)
Non-union sector								
Very good	22	20	56	49	55	48	373 (236)	319 (200)
Good	20	17	29	35	31	39	206 (132)	267 (163)
Quite good	27	22	12	9	9	8	64 (42)	47 (34)
Other	16	23	3	7	5	5	35 (20)	30 (21)
Private sector								
Very good	14	16	51	42	46	36	697 (601)	525 (433)
Good	13	13	30	40	31	44	415 (407)	552 (508)
Quite good	11	11	15	10	18	13	181 (239)	131 (158)
Other	10	13	4	8	5	7	59 (71)	59 (87)

1. Unweighted number of establishments in parentheses.

Table 5.7
Financial Performance and Employment: Private Sector

	1980			1984		
	% All Part-timers	% All Workers	Number of Establishments[1]	% All Part-timers	% All Workers	Number of Establishments[1]
Union sector						
Above average	53	56	234 (330)	49	48	222 (282)
Average	42	39	279 (358)	40	41	263 (305)
Below average	5	5	33 (57)	11	11	48 (67)
Non-union sector						
Above average	51	40	284 (185)	64	62	300 (208)
Average	43	53	232 (144)	33	35	243 (140)
Below average	6	7	31 (18)	3	2	26 (15)
Private sector						
Above average	52	49	518 (515)	56	53	522 (490)
Average	42	45	511 (502)	35	39	506 (445)
Below average	5	6	64 (75)	9	8	74 (82)

1. Unweighted number of establishments in parentheses.

ployed in work places with above average performance than had been the case in 1984.

The growth in part-time employment that occurred in the 1970s and 1980s seems to have conferred benefits on both employers and employees. Employers appear to have benefited from the flexibility that part-timers bring to their work forces. Employees have benefited because part-time work appears to fit in well with domestic commitments. The substantial decline in private sector unionization since 1980 seems to have enhanced the overall flexibility of the British labor market. As a result, many of the traditional differences between the full-time and part-time labor markets narrowed between 1980 and 1984.

NOTES

1. Reported in the Minutes of Evidence, House of Lords Select Committee on "Voluntary Part-time Work" Her Majesty's Stationery Office, July 1982: 131. (**Editors' note**: In this letter, the Secretary of State for Employment expresses the Government's reservations concerning the desirability of the European Economic Community's draft Directive on Voluntary Part-Time Working, issued in December 1981.)

2. Throughout this paper we define an establishment as an "individual place of employment at a single address or site." For further details, see Millward and Stevens (1986), Technical Appendix.

3. For a fuller discussion of the changes in British industrial relations over the period, see Metcalf (1988) and Blanchflower and Oswald (1988).

4. When female part-timers in the 1980 Women and Employment Survey were asked whether they wished to change the number of hours they worked, 83 percent said they were happy with their present hours, 6 percent expressed a preference for fewer hours, and 11 percent expressed a preference for more hours (Martin and Roberts, 1984a). It does appear, therefore, that the vast majority of female part-timers have a preference for part-time work and have not been forced into it because of a shortage of full-time jobs.

5. I calculate that, in Great Britain in the 1980s, 47 percent of part-time and 28 percent of full-time workers were employed in work places where there were fewer than 25 workers. This result is obtained from a major source of data on individuals undertaken every year from 1983 to 1987, known as the British Social Attitudes Surveys. For further details of these data sets, see Blanchflower (1989).

6. The British Social Attitudes Survey data for the period of 1983 to 1987 mentioned in note 5, permit the calculation that, on average, 29.6 percent of part-time workers were union members, compared with 49.9 percent for full-timers and 46.3 percent overall.

7. As background to the table, we should note that total employment over the period June 1980 to June 1984 fell by around 8 percent, while part-time employment remained more or less constant. Total manufacturing employment,

however, fell by approximately 20 percent (*Employment Gazette*, January 1985 and November 1988).

8. Average work-place size in the two surveys was as follows:

	WIRS1 (1980)	**WIRS2 (1984)**
Private sector	110	97
Private manufacturing	17	139
Private services	70	75
Public sector	134	127
Public manufacturing	294	266
Public services	126	120
Manufacturing	183	149
Services	93	96

For the distribution of establishments across these categories, see Table 5.2

9. Millward and Stevens (1986) report from a small panel element of the WIRS data that only 7 percent of work places altered their union status over the period. Similarly, a panel study of work places conducted by the Confederation of British Industry (CBI) reported that only 5 percent changed their union status (defined by the presence of collective bargaining agreements) over the period 1979 to 1986. In both cases, the proportion of plants changing their status from union to non-union was matched by a similar proportion moving in the other direction (Confederation of British Industry, 1987).

6 Ambivalence or Apprehension? The Labor Movement and the Part-Time Worker in Canada

Norene Pupo and Ann Duffy

Part-time workers present a complex set of issues for unions. Divergent short-term interests among different types of workers, historical precedents in which the introduction of part-timers was a management ploy, and a generally unsupportive collective bargaining structure together create an often unsatisfactory context for union efforts at organizing part-time workers. As a result, the organization of part-timers in Canada is uneven. Inconsistent policies among unionists on part-time and hours-of-work matters, and a myriad of other encumbrances, limit labor's unity on this issue. This paper discusses some of the complexities of the relationship between part-time workers and the Canadian labor movement.

ORGANIZED LABOR IN CANADA

In Canada, the percentage of unionized workers has been fairly constant for over a decade, at slightly over one third of the non-agricultural work force. In 1985, 34 percent of all paid workers, including 38 percent of males and 28 percent of females, were unionized (Neill, 1990: 202). In contrast, part-time workers in Canada, Britain, and elsewhere experience much lower rates of unionization (Coates, 1988; Martin and Roberts, 1984; Beechey and Perkins, 1987). In Canada, 18.8 percent of part-timers belonged to a union in 1984, including 13.6 percent of male part-timers and 20.9 percent of female part-time workers (Coates, 1988: 51).

Growth in union membership among part-time workers lags behind that of full-timers and does not reflect the recent growth in the part-time work force. If the part-time work force continues to grow without substantial increases in the degree of unionization, relative losses in overall rates of unionization will occur. Rates of unionization vary by sector, and the low rates in certain sectors, particularly in finance and trade, are related to high rates of part-time work. In these industries, managements are often inclined to employ part-timers because of their lower rates of unionization and labor's reported difficulties in organizing them, making union success unlikely without part-time representation.

Women's membership in unions more than doubled in two decades, increasing from 16.6 percent to 36.2 percent of union members between 1965 and 1985 (Canada. Statistics Canada, 1987: 11). Since 1980, female membership has experienced continuous growth, while male membership has leveled off (Canada. Statistics Canada, 1987: 29). This pattern may be explained by four interrelated factors:

1. the dramatic increases in women's labor force participation;
2. the trend toward deindustrialization and the demise of heavy industry;
3. the pattern of decline in international union membership, historically male dominated, along with gains in national and public sector unions; and
4. the organization of some female-dominated industries.

Women's increased labor force participation accounted for 94 percent of Canada's employment growth between 1981 and 1986 (*The Globe and Mail*, March 2, 1988: A1). At the same time, the recession in the early 1980s, plant closures, layoffs, technological change, and public sector cutbacks contributed to permanent declines in membership among males in heavy manufacturing industries (*The Financial Post*, April 28, 1984: 1). These losses were not recovered in subsequent years despite successful drives. While traditional sectors of male employment experienced declining growth rates (and declines in union membership) between 1975 and 1986, employment in female-dominated community, business and personal services increased by 50 percent (Lévesque, 1987: 89). Since 1970, increases in the degree of unionization have been recorded in areas of traditional female employment, such as among teachers, nurses, clerical workers, cashiers, and communications workers. The largest concentration of female union members is in the service sector, accounting for 56.7 percent of unionized women and 33.6 percent of total union membership in Canada (Canada. Statistics Canada, 1987: 40). It is precisely this sector of the economy that has boomed, accounting for 90 percent of job growth in Canada since 1967 (Economic Council of Canada, 1990: 4).

With the expansion of the female-dominated and increasingly unionized service sector, it would seem likely that many "good" jobs—well-paid, secure, and with benefits—would be created for women workers.

However, a significant portion of the work created in the service sector has been part-time or non-unionized. The community, business, and personal services sector accounts for about 50 percent of all part-time jobs (*The Financial Post*, June 25, 1983: 10). The rate of unionization among part-timers has not kept pace with the general growth in female union membership. As a result, two different kinds of work with qualitatively different conditions of employment are emerging. At present, about two thirds of service sector workers hold the "good" jobs—highly skilled, well-remunerated, and stable work that is often unionized—while one third have "bad" jobs that are poorly paid, insecure, frequently part-time, and generally non-unionized (Economic Council of Canada, 1990; Neill, 1990: 204). Part-time employment is an outstanding factor in this distinction between good and bad forms of work (Fine, 1990: A10; Lush, Heinzl, and Lakshman, 1990: A1, A2).

Although, in general, most women work in non-unionized female job ghettos (Armstrong and Armstrong, 1984), those in trade or commerce and finance, in particular, face a tremendous number of hindrances to acquiring the benefits of union protection. Management's willingness to hire part-time workers and their tendency to convert full-time jobs to part-time hours is related to the low rates of unionization and the lower wage costs associated with part-time workers. In relatively small work places, management's intimidation tactics and open hostility toward unions are frequently combined with paternalism and down-to-earth discussions on the exorbitant costs of unionization. These methods are often successful, especially in circumstances where divisions among workers, for example between full- and part-time employees, are already apparent (The Bank Book Collective, 1979).

These difficulties are compounded by the generalized perception, shared by union leaders, full-time workers, and management, that part-timers are temporary or only marginally committed to the work place, and that they are therefore not interested in union struggles for long-term protection and improvements in working conditions. Too frequently, it is these preconceptions about part-time workers which influence and deflect organizing efforts. However, this notion of temporariness is belied by the statistics on job tenure among part-timers (Canada. Commission of Inquiry into Part-Time Work, 1983). As long as union activists leave such attitudes unchallenged, they implicitly accept the notion that part-time jobs (as well as temporary and other non-traditional forms of work) should be left unprotected and marginalized.

THE LABOR MOVEMENT AND PART-TIME WORK: OFFENSIVE OR DEFENSIVE STRATEGY?

On the part-time work issue, unionists face two main courses of action (European Industrial Relations Review, 1985). One alternative is to reaffirm full-time job strategies by working to eliminate or restrict part-time work. This approach, however, would limit the availability of part-time work, disadvantaging people who prefer it. It would particularly affect women with young children who often prefer part-time work to either full-time unpaid work in the home or full-time paid work in the labor force (Pupo, 1989). The second option is to work toward the union-ization of part-timers, while adopting measures to safeguard full-time opportunities and options such as job sharing. Union leaders must con-tinually evaluate employers' reasons for offering part-time work, for converting full-time jobs to part-time hours, and for building a part-time work force made up largely of females, non-whites or others who have historically been vulnerable to marginalization within the paid labor force. This second course will present the greatest long-term protection for workers in an increasingly fragmented and deskilled work environ-ment.

A review of union activities in Canada over the past ten years suggests that union leaders have vacillated between these strategies, although the dominant thrust is toward limiting or eliminating part-time work. After interviewing several Canadian labor leaders, one commentator concluded: "The unions are committed to resist the tide toward part-time employment" (Benimadhu, 1986: 21). Within this context, the growth in part-time employment is seen as a management strategy that exploits workers while eroding the strength of organized labor.

Presumably, these negative attitudes toward part-time employment explain conflicts like the recent one between part-timers, the Canadian Union of Public Employees, and the Peel Board of Education. Part-time employees complained to the Ontario Human Rights Commission that the collective agreement negotiated by their Canadian Union of Public Employees (CUPE) locals 2544 and 2703 resulted in much better con-ditions of employment for full-time (mainly male) than part-time workers (mainly female). The settlement of the case acknowledged the disad-vantaged status of the part-timers and provided, among other improve-ments, for a 50 percent pay increase for the part-time employees (Jostman, 1990).

There is, however, no single platform, negative or positive, on part-time work in the labor movement. Labor negotiators inconsistently bar-gain away, bargain about, and bargain on behalf of, part-timers. Some identify part-time work as women's work and dismiss the possibility of organizing part-timers, because of inaccurate ideas about women's in-terest in unions or about the temporariness of these jobs. Others point to the difficulties and expense involved in organizing part-timers. As a result of such misperceptions, scarce resources, and an historical tra-dition of protecting men's full-time jobs and upholding the traditional ideology of the family wage, often at the expense of women's jobs, part-time workers' needs are not usually placed foremost on the bargaining table.

In short, a profound ambivalence exists within the labor movement regarding the part-time work issue. Labor's conflict is generated from a number of sources:

1. real or perceived disunity among part-timers;
2. tactics adopted by employers who use part-timers as a strike-breaking or union-eroding strategy;
3. the historical tradition within the movement to protect full-time jobs, and to embrace the family wage ideology and patriarchal family structure;
4. the nature of the collective bargaining structure (which generally places unions in a defensive stance);
5. state policy and the decisions of the labor boards; and
6. organized labor's long-term interest in reducing working time, without wage reductions, for all workers.

The resistance of many unionists to organizing part-timers must be examined in terms of the dynamics of structural forces and in the context of opposing factors both within and outside the labor movement. Locating this resistance to part-time work in the context of social structure by no means removes the responsibility from labor leaders for inaction or for discriminatory stands, nor does it excuse policies that are at best prosaic. Rather, it clarifies how exclusionary or non-progressive policies are developed, maintained, and supported.

Reactions: Part-Time Workers and Employers. Part-timers' reactions to unions are mixed (Duffy and Pupo, forthcoming). Among the pro-union faction, there is a strong desire for concrete proof of labor's support for part-time employment concerns. They want campaigns, for example, built upon the issue of prorated benefits, and evidence that negotiators strike deals for them that are at least equivalent to agreements for full-time workers. Some of the negative reactions to unions derive from the location of part-time work in service industries in which the ideology of professionalism and service is maintained at high costs to labor protection and justice. In some instances, particularly in small establishments, there is a strong attachment to employers who are described as often willing to accommodate family crises by maintaining a degree of flexibility in scheduling. Others feel betrayed by unions and have encountered unionists' disinterest in organizing part-timers. Overall, the range of part-timers' reactions toward unions is not dissimilar from that of full-timers. However, the degree of reluctance to support union campaigns reinforces the notion of disinterested part-timers.

Employers have resisted the unionization of part-time workers in a variety of ways. Some of their tactics include: using intimidation; sustaining divisiveness by employing students and temporary help; isolating part-time workers by means of scheduling, by job tasks, or by separating them spatially; offering part-timers incentives similar to those of full-time workers; fostering a climate of paternalism; and using high-tech performance evaluation techniques (Duffy and Weeks, 1981: 29–30; Julie White, 1983). The success of these measures rests on a number of factors:

1. the financial necessity of the part-time job;
2. the constraints on women part-timers' energy and time for unionizing;
3. the presumed temporariness of the part-time job; and
4. the relatively low level of commitment among trade unionists toward organizing the part-time labor force.

In employing part-time workers, managements point to their need for flexibility within their work forces to cover peak daily or weekly periods. By hiring part-timers, employers obtain the desired flexibility and also profit from a divided labor force, a labor force with differentiated interests regarding flexibility and hours of work. Canada Post's policies, for example, have effectively exacerbated tensions between full-time and part-time workers, and between part-timers and the Canadian Union of Postal Workers (CUPW). During the late 1970s, Canada Post often scheduled part-timers on the day shifts. Full-time workers interpreted this practice as a demonstration of preferential treatment for part-timers, since they initially had to build seniority with years of working night shifts before earning daytime schedules (Julie White, 1990: 121). Similar practices have been adopted at Bell Canada (Speck, 1988), in banking (Bank Book Collective, 1979; Baker, 1990), in the airline industry (Shalla, 1990), and in retail operations such as Eaton's and Simpson's (Currie and Sheedy, 1987).

In academe, part-time instructors are often hired to teach large undergraduate, summer, or evening session courses. These are usually the least desirable courses from the point of view of full-time faculty members. A large percentage of part-time instructors are unwilling part-timers waiting for full-time, tenure-stream appointments. Yet, teaching part-time rarely leads to a full-time academic career (Baker, 1985; Warme and Lundy, 1986 and 1988a; Lundy and Warme, 1989; Abel, 1985; Tuckman and Tuckman, 1980). Faculty associations condone this practice as a measure of protection for full-timers who, as a result, are free to pursue research activities that are more highly ranked by administrators when reviewing performance. The end result is a clear conflict between the interests of full-time and part-time workers.

The hiring of part-timers also extends the practice of intensifying labor, a practice initiated with the detailed division of labor and the process of deskilling. Both work relations and workers' ability to safeguard their skills are affected. This is the case in hospitals, where the increasing tendency to employ part-time nurses and floaters is related to the use of computerized patient monitoring and the subdivision of the professional nurse's role (Armstrong, 1988). The intensification of nurses' work also affects the jobs of nursing assistants, housekeeping staff, maintenance workers, and other semi- or non-professional employees. (J. P. White, 1990). Under such an arrangement, interactions with co-workers are reduced, isolation and division are reinforced, and union leaders, already skeptical about part-timers' commitment to unionization, become even more concerned about the proliferation of part-time employment.

Union leaders' commitment to protect full-time jobs, occasionally at the direct expense of part-time workers, may reflect their incorrect association of part-time workers with management, or their erroneous belief that part-timers have extremely dissimilar interests from those of full-time workers. Further, these attitudes (and attendant actions) do not take into account the large percentage of part-time work that is done involuntarily. In 1988, 24 percent of those working part-time did so because they could not find full-time work (derived from Canada. Statistics Canada, 1989). In the period between 1975 and 1986, involuntary part-time employment rose by 375.4 percent, while voluntary part-time work increased by 41 percent and full-time employment grew by only 15.2 percent (Akyeampong, 1986: 144). Significantly, the vast majority of unwilling part-timers are married women between the ages of 25 and 54 (derived from Canada. Statistics Canada, 1988) and these involuntary part-timers are largely found in the female job ghettos in the community, business, and personal service industries (Lévesque, 1987; Akyeampong, 1987).

Union leaders' ambivalence about part-time work and their resistance to organizing part-timers are manifestations of managements' tactical successes. The loyalty and paternalism developed between part-timers and managements (particularly in small work places) are sometimes enhanced by the immediate results of negotiations. In the short run, there are costs involved in unionizing. Related to both the union's full-time protectionist strategy and also to its principles of justice and equity, agreements may remove what are seen to be privileges with regard to the scheduling of hours, type of work, and seniority, while creating animosity with bosses and imposing costs through dues. Long-term protection provided by unions is difficult to assess in the worker's immediate context of having to juggle paid work around family schedules and, in general, of having to seek privatized solutions to personal and family arrangements.

Family Wage Ideology and Patriarchal Family Structures. Unions' bias in favor of full-time work is rooted in the historical practices of protecting males' wages and of lending ideological support to the notion of the family wage. Patriarchal family structure, the ideology of domesticity, and real family obligations have shaped women's work and their relationship to the labor movement (Julie White, 1980; Strong-Boag, 1979; McFarland, 1985; Klein and Roberts, 1974; Phillips and Phillips, 1983; McCallum, 1986). Societal pressures on women to marry and lead a "normal" domestic life may have dampened women's enthusiasm for organizing, while also undermining the labor movement's receptivity to women activists.

Women's reluctance and unionists' hesitations were supported by a number of structural and ideological factors:

1. the perception of a short paid working life for women;

2. the existence of the marriage bar;

3. the burden of an unequal division of domestic labor and child care; and

4. the ideology of women as secondary earners or as working for "pin" money.

All of these constraints historically combined with traditional stereotypical prescriptions of appropriate behavior for women, and contributed to common views about the futility of women's organizing. This long-standing tradition of employers' promoting competition between men and women workers, together with unions' response to protect the higher paid, higher status, more highly valued men's jobs, have affected unionists' contemporary stand on the part-time work issue. Unions' inconsistent support for women's work is intrinsically related to structural transformations within the labor market and the labor process, the tradition of craft unionism and control, the secondary stature of women's work, and the gender division of labor. Unions' degree of support varies as conditions change. Overall, unions demonstrate less support for women's causes when men's full-time jobs are threatened (Julie White, 1980; Frager, 1983; Baker and Robeson, 1986).

The Structure of Collective Bargaining. The structure under which unions operate necessitates the protection of one sector of workers from the encroachment of others. Unions do not succeed in challenging managerial power; rather they operate within the framework of that power (Rinehart, 1987; Briskin, 1983; Clarke, 1977). They have been unable (and have frequently refused) to shatter the dual labor market, or to change the structural conditions of women's work, job ghettoization, and women's marginalized position within the labor force. The structure recreates competition among sectors for position within the labor market and, more narrowly, within specific work organizations. The result is a fragmented working class, rife with divisions among occupations, craft groupings, racial and ethnic groups, between the skilled and the un- skilled, between men and women, and between full-time and part-time workers. Unions' defensive stance casts them in the position of scoring one small victory at a time. As a result, they operate to consolidate the resources of those already in the strongest position. Their individual victories, reflecting short-term needs and often won at the expense of other groups, contribute to the continued marginalization of part-time workers (Pupo and Duffy, 1988).

The current structure of collective bargaining necessitates the involve- ment of unions in day-to-day conflict management, leaving little time and few resources for more fundamental reform. Within this structure, campaigns are developed individually at the specific work place, and take into account the characteristics of a particular group of workers, the company's tactics, the level of commitment among the workers, and the degree of fragmentation. As a result, comprehensive policy on part- time work has not been developed within the labor movement. When organizers believe that part-timers are committed to the union, they will campaign for an all-inclusive bargaining unit. When they determine that part-timers are disinterested, or too difficult or too costly to reach, they may seek to exclude part-timers. Often, part-time workers and other marginalized groups are easily forfeited as a means of protecting more highly valued full-time work. Bargaining is often about part-timers rather than on behalf of them (England, 1987: 10–11). Sometimes, this has meant the acceptance of inferior agreements for part-timers (Duffy and Pupo, forthcoming; Weeks, 1980).

As a reaction to the tendency of employers to promote divisiveness within their work forces and to reduce costs through the use of part- time workers, unions have waged vigorous campaigns to limit part-time work. The question of the proportion of positions designated as part- time was central in disputes at Air Canada in 1985 (*The Financial Post*, March 9, 1985: 1) and at the Toronto Transit Commission in 1988 (Fine, 1988: E11; J. Armstrong, 1988: A6), as well as in contract negotiations with Canada Post in 1988 (Slotnick, 1988: A2). On labor's side, these actions are logical and justified by the need to challenge management strategies. However, labor's tactics for developing equity in the short- term lead to structural flaws that prevent equity over the long term. Winning limitations on part-time work defeats employers' schemes but, at the same time, may eliminate a paid work option, particularly for many women, students, and retirees. When seeking to limit part-time work, unionists should ask what is gambled in the process, and at whose expense. Promoting the unionization rather than the elimination or limitation of part-time work would minimize workers' losses by maintaining part-time work as an option.

The Role of the State. The union's defensive posture is further entrenched by the state's role in labor relations and by its part in maintaining the marginal position of part-time workers. The general tendency within the Ontario Labour Relations Board (OLRB), for example, is to separate full- and part-time workers. The rationale for this separation is that full- and part-time workers do not share a community of interest. The notion of different interests, however, may stem from inaccurate conceptions of the nature and structure of the labor force and from wrong assumptions concerning the orientations of part-timers or other "atypical" workers to work, unions, and job tenure. Ultimately, this logic limits the degree of unionization or its effectiveness for part-time workers (Pupo and Duffy, 1988). Separate bargaining units are often smaller, and lack both resources and clout. The majority of part-time workers in these separate units are women (Miller, 1988).

In another demonstration of the state's complex and contradictory role in balancing the short-term needs of labor against the long-term objectives of capital (Panitch, 1977; Cuneo, 1979), Cuneo (1990: 59–60) has analyzed business–state interaction around pay equity legislation and the part-time work issue. He found government support for the Canadian Manufacturers' Association's demand that pay equity legislation exempt casual part-time work, temporary training positions, and student jobs. This measure would effectively exclude the part-time work that employers might create to bypass the legislation. The labor movement fought such a measure as part of its general campaign against loss of income security, arguing:

1. that employers might convert regular part-time to casual or temporary work;
2. that training positions are often created for women entering non-traditional work and that the practice would divide their work from men's, perhaps cheapening all wages; and
3. that the practice might effectively establish differential pay rates for the same work.

In this campaign, labor's efforts have been restrained by the Canadian Human Rights Act and by the 1987 Ontario Pay Equity Act (Cuneo, 1990: 59).

THE ROAD TRAVELED AND THE ROAD AHEAD

The ambivalence of part-timers and the apprehension of unionists inadvertently strengthens employers' strategies in the work place. Employers' divide-and-rule tactics, combined with the state's inaccurate definition of communities of interest among full- and part-time workers and a degree of partiality in labor legislation produce a climate in which the unionization of the part-time work force is easily impeded. It is essential that unions revise their notion of part-time work and the part-time worker. In Sweden, Sundstrom (1982) found that when homogeneous groups of full- and part-time workers were compared, there was no difference in their commitment and orientation to the labor movement. Differences surface because part-timers generally work in industries in which there are lower overall rates of unionization. Other variations are explained by factors, particularly that of having preschool children, which influence the preference for shorter work hours in general. Restrictions on part-time work would limit women's (and especially, mothers') participation both in the labor force and in the political sphere, by restricting their union affiliation. Meanwhile, unions lose potential membership and bargaining power with the maintenance of women's secondary, marginalized labor market (Charles, 1986).

The policy of protecting full-time jobs operates at the expense of all women's jobs by maintaining labor-force segregation. Women's lower wages depress the wage scale (Fox and Fox, 1986) and, in turn, reinforce patriarchy and an unequal division of domestic labor. The primary purpose here is not to question the commitment to full-time work, but to seek an extension of policy and action to meet the needs of part-timers. It is important to understand how part-time work is shaped by family circumstances, and how it shapes political action.

The success of unions in attracting more female members in the future will depend on the readiness of unions to adopt an egalitarian ideology to replace their traditional familial ideology. They must recognize cultural differences between male and female workers, and particularly the contemporary constraints on women's time. Unions cannot afford to ignore either women's causes or their objections to unions' tactics. This is particularly true in light of the membership losses among males that have already occurred or are projected, with the decline of heavy industrial production, a recessionary economy, and free trade.

Women today are disproving notions about their complacency, passivity, and disinterest in organizing. Blue-collar, white-collar, professional and semi-professional groups, and full-time and part-time workers, are waging successful campaigns. They are transcending traditional union biases, confronting employers' intimidation schemes to protest the erosion of wages, job skills, health and safety concerns, and other conditions of their work (Sacks, 1988; Maroney, 1987; Briskin, 1983). The momentum of these workers, their numbers, and their demonstrated commitment are sending important signals to union leaders, especially within international unions and traditional male work spheres, to rewrite union policies so that they address women workers' concerns.

Labor's policies that discriminate overtly or covertly against part-time workers, simply because they work fewer hours, effectively maintain a divided labor force. Union complacency, together with problems with Unemployment Insurance provisions and other legislation that limit the benefits of short-term and part-time workers, contribute to the perpetuation of the lot of Canada's "bad jobs" as described by the Economic Council of Canada (Echenberg, 1990: A7). Unions should be at the forefront of action to eliminate incentives for employers to develop and maintain "bad jobs". The only solution is to work toward gaining all the privileges and compensation for part-timers that full-timers enjoy and to ensure that part-time work is voluntary and revocable. Addressing the part-time work issue in this way would be a step toward truly feminizing the labor movement and acknowledging the relation between paid work and family matters.

III PART-TIME WORK AND THE LIFE CYCLE

7 Working Youths in the United States

Robert A. Rothman

A large number of school-aged youths in the United States work on a part-time basis at least occasionally during the school year. This pattern is in some ways unique; youths in the United States are much more likely to be students and workers simultaneously than in any other industrial nation (Reubens, 1983). Moreover, the social and economic conditions that initially fostered student work seem likely to attract ever-increasing numbers of youths into part-time work in the future.

Social scientists, educators, and others concerned with the scholastic, developmental, and vocational implications of part-time work have produced a voluminous literature on the subject. Much of the literature is polemic, either championing the advantages or warning of the potential harm of part-time employment. Therefore, it is an opportune time to attempt to assess the factors that have converged to produce the working student, and to examine how work interacts with other dimensions of the lives of American youth.

This assessment will suggest that the working student has become a permanent feature of contemporary American society. Further, there is little support for either side in the debate over the merits of work. The common notion that working facilitates the transition to adulthood remains unsubstantiated; nor is there much indication that working is harmful. Actually, it has less impact, positive or negative, than might be expected. It would appear that many middle-class youths have been successful in adding part-time employment to their repertoire of activities without significant harm to the educational process and without disruption to their other social relationships. Less is known about the children of the less advantaged, especially the poor, but what is known is not as encouraging. They also work in significant numbers, but are pushed toward the labor market for different reasons, and their experiences there are perceived differently. Their part-time work experience is not all that different from what they anticipate in the future. For them, boundaries between youth and adulthood, and between part-time and full-time work, are blurred.

THE SOCIAL CONTEXT OF THE WORKING STUDENT

Most of American history was characterized by declining rates of labor-force participation by school-aged youths. Shrinking involvement in paid work was the outcome of the convergence of several broader social and economic trends (see, for example, Karabel and Halsey, 1977). The economy was changing, with the "unskilled" segment beginning to contract, reducing the number of entry-level opportunities for school-aged youth without skills. In addition, there was some pressure by labor unions to exclude younger workers from the labor force in order to protect the jobs of older workers. At the same time, there were developments within the educational sector that encouraged further exclusion of school-aged children from paid work. Recognition of the changing economy stimulated interest in equipping students with ever-higher levels of formal education. In addition, an awareness of the social and developmental problems of "adolescents" encouraged prolonging the transition period from youth to adult. Thus, the child labor laws of the 1930s and the extension of the age of compulsory school attendance reflected a number of developments in the larger society, all of which pointed in the direction of discouraging early exit from school.

This trend began to be reversed in the 1940s and 1950s. The reentry of school-aged youths as part-time workers who combine school and work has also occurred within the context of larger social and economic trends. Among the most important are the shifting role of youth and the shape of the economic structure, which interacted to produce a large number of working youths. The structure of the economy began to shift toward jobs that could be filled on a part-time basis. The shift to a service economy is well documented, with an increasing proportion of new jobs being generated in the service sector, at the expense of the manufacturing sector. These are the familiar food service, retail sales, clerical, and unskilled jobs that can be filled on a part-time basis. In addition, part-time schedules are consistent with the need of employers for a more flexible work force. Consequently, part-time work is becoming an ever-increasing segment of the labor force in the United States, not just for school-aged youth. Since the 1960s, part-time employment has grown at a faster rate than full-time employment (Nardone, 1986). In 1988, with a total labor force of 112.8 million, 20.1 million people (18 percent) were on part-time work schedules.[1] Official statistics suggest that approximately one third of high school students hold part-time jobs (Tooley, 1989). However, many work "off the books," and it is therefore widely estimated that between one half and two thirds of all 16- to 19-year-olds are actually working (for example, Rotchford and Roberts, 1982). In other words, 2.5 million high school students—males and females, wealthy and poor—have jobs.

WHY YOUTHS WORK

The availability of jobs creates the potential for employment, but does not explain why such large numbers of youths have moved into them. It is important at the outset not to overlook the simple fact that work for pay occupies a central place in the industrial societies. Paid work is a key element in defining income and life-styles, self-image, social identity, and one's place in the society (Renwick and Lawler, 1978). Children of school age will continue to be attracted into the work place as long as the society places such high value on work. For example, a child maturing in the United States is exposed to experiences that teach and reinforce the value of paid work. Many parents in the United States teach this lesson very early in the socialization process when they encourage, or even require, their children to perform routine tasks in the home in exchange for allowances (Goldstein and Oldham, 1979). Parental encouragement of paid employment is, in part, based on awareness that children will eventually have to enter the job market. It is also based on the widespread belief that paid employment helps to inculcate desirable skills and attributes. It is felt that work teaches tangible skills, and more intangible "work habits," such as responsibility and self-discipline, that are part of adult roles. Hard work is still believed to be the key to success in life (Kluegel and Smith, 1986: 44).

Perceptions of the value of work in American society were clearly demonstrated by the work-incentive programs of the 1970s. During that period, a number of government-backed plans were designed to integrate young people into the work place. Eventually, over three billion dollars were allocated to career education programs, often incorporating part-time work experiences. These programs need to be examined in the context in which they emerged, that is, as responses to what were perceived to be social problems (Steinberg, 1982). For one, there were the problems of minority youth in the labor market, evidenced by their extraordinarily high unemployment rates. There were also the hostile "countercultures" and the "generation gap" which seemed to signal the isolation of youth from the older generations. In the work place, employers encountered a restless and dissatisfied work force. Finally, there was increasing criticism of public education and the schools, underlined by declining test scores. What is most interesting from the perspective of the sociologist is that such diverse interest groups, concerned with vastly different social problems, could all agree that work experiences for school-aged youth would be *the solution* (or at least a vital part of the solution). It seems fair to conclude that parents, educators, social reformers, policy experts, business leaders, and politicians—an unlikely coalition—were united by the belief in the value of paid work. It was claimed that employment would foster healthy work habits, ease the transition from childhood to adulthood, narrow the gap between adults and children, deter delinquency, and revitalize interest in education. By the early 1980s, it became evident that work experiences could not deliver on their promises, and many have criticized the effort. However, it is important to understand this phase of our history in the context of the meaning of work. It was precisely because paid work was such a deeply ingrained feature of the culture that there was ready support for the program.

The more specific reasons why so many youths combine work and school is not all that well understood at this point, but at least two factors are important. One is the financial incentive, and the other is the declining attractiveness of formal education. Both factors would seem to be strongly influenced by social class considerations. It is clear that youths are drawn into part-time work for the wages they earn. This would lead us to expect to find higher levels of participation by the children of the poor and single-parent families. The available data do not generally reveal higher rates of part-time employment for disadvantaged youths. In 1981, Lewin-Epstein reported data that suggested that the highest rates of part-time employment among high school seniors were among the children of the most affluent parents. D'Amico (1984b) found somewhat higher involvement among the middle class (based on a measure of parents' socioeconomic status). McNeil (1984) found that 60 percent of those who had jobs came from families with family incomes over $25,000. Yet, field research consistently shows that the children of the poor are attached to part-time employment (Williams and Kornblum, 1985; MacLeod, 1987).

The failure to find a consistent relationship between income and part-time work does not mean that financial incentives are not relevant. One problem is methodological; most studies have counted employment rather than incentives to work. (Even measuring "looking for work" as Greenberger, Steinberg, Vaux, and McAuliffe (1980) did, will not capture the true picture, for there is the problem of "discouraged" workers.) The availability of work must be considered. Declining center-city areas may mean fewer after-school jobs in the areas where the poor are concentrated. In addition, lower-income youths in the market for employment may be at a disadvantage in competition for those jobs. A ready pool of middle- and upper-income youth, who might be perceived as more desirable workers, may depress the opportunities for the children of the poor.

Part of the financial incentive might more appropriately be referred to as the consumption incentive—the desire for discretionary income. For example, one analysis of spending patterns showed that most income derived from work is devoted to social activities and personal consumer goods like cars, concerts, clothing, music, and movies (Johnston, Bachman, and O'Malley, 1982). Greenberger and Steinberg (1986) trace the origins of this phenomenon to the post–World War II period. Relative affluence spread to the middle classes, accompanied by declining parental authority over teenage spending, giving teenagers more freedom to make their own choices. They suggest that consumer marketing expert Eugene Gilbert may have been the first to note the potentially vast pool of "free money" available to be tapped by adroit entrepreneurs. Certainly, the 1950s witnessed the explosion of marketing efforts directly aimed at this age group. The decline of family control over children's income was but one dimension of weakening parental influence, to be replaced by the social demands of the adolescent peer subculture. Spending patterns clearly revolve around participation and social status in the youth subculture.

Although a large share of young part-time workers' income is discretionary, some is set aside for long-term goals such as education. About 20 percent contribute money directly to the family (Greenberger et al., 1980: 196). Also, some income is used to replace or supplement parental responsibility for clothing. Thus, there is a strong financial incentive to part-time work, and there is no indication that it will decline.

Any consideration of the positive financial attraction of work must be balanced by an examination of the negative push of other factors, especially education. If schooling becomes less attractive, less rewarding, or less meaningful, then part-time work might seem a more attractive option. Some data suggest support for this interpretation. Employed students display lower levels of "academic self-esteem" and educational aspirations (Mortimer and Finch, 1986). McNeil's (1984: 32) predominantly middle-class students spoke of work as an escape from the boredom of the classroom. No definitive conclusion is possible, because of the unresolved issue of *causation* versus *selection*. At the risk of oversimplication, the question may be reduced to this form: does part-time employment (all other things being equal) cause "alienation" from school, or does alienation lead students to part-time employment?

However, the findings do point to a promising direction for further analysis. It would be useful to explore the possibility that schools are more alienating for working- and lower-class children, thus pushing them toward work that may further alienate them from school. Several current perspectives clearly point in that direction. For example, Rosenbaum (1976) focused on the process of "tracking," (streaming) which directs working-class youths into programs with relaxed grading requirements and fewer educational experiences that are less meaningful. Bourdieu and Passeron's (1977) more theoretical analysis builds upon the concept of "cultural capital." Bourdieu argues that families at the upper levels of the class system transmit a body of knowledge, ideas, and values to their children by exposing them to literature, the arts, and entertainment. This specific pattern of cultural capital places them at an advantage in the schools, which emphasize this same cultural capital, leading to superior academic performance. Children with more limited access to these socially valued aspects of the culture will be at a disadvantage and, in turn, will find the schools to be less congenial places.

Thus, two factors must be taken into account in understanding the influx of students into the work-force on a part-time basis: finances and consumption patterns, and dissatisfactions with the schools. Disaffection with the educational system and pressing economic incentives may well play a larger role in the lives of children of the poor and working class than among the middle and upper middle classes, where consumption incentives would seem to be more important. None of the factors, however, seems to be waning, and this suggests that youths will continue to work.

WORKING YOUTHS IN SCHOOL

Recognition that working has become such a common feature has led to attempts to assess the impact of work on other dimensions of adolescent life. Among the most important is the question of the implications of part-time employment for performance in the schools. There can be no debate over the value of educational credentials in long-term financial and occupational attainments. Thus, if part-time work interfered with education, youths would be sacrificing long-term advantages for short-term financial gains. A number of studies have compared part-time workers with non-workers on grade point average, and, less frequently, test scores on standardized achievement tests (Scholastic Aptitude Tests (SAT) or American College Testing (ACT).

Some studies point in the direction of a depressing effect on school performance, albeit a very moderate one, unless work takes up a large number of hours. In the extensive body of research that leads to this conclusion is Lewin-Epstein's 1981 study based on a national sample that reported lower grades among senior males who had worked at some point during their high school years, although there were no significant grade point differences among high school sophomores. McNeil's (1984) analysis is based on a more limited sample of Wisconsin students, but confirmed a negative relationship between working and grades. Finch and Mortimer (1985), and Mortimer and Finch (1986) followed a cohort of boys in public schools over an eight-year period, and showed a consistent pattern of academic disadvantage among student workers.

However, although there is some support for the conclusion that working has a negative impact on school performance, it is premature to generalize to all student workers because of sampling and methodological differences across the studies. Some studies were limited to males only, some were conducted in limited settings, and others depended on cross-sectional rather than longitudinal designs. Moreover, some of the differences are very modest. For example, grade point differences in the Mortimer and Finch study (1986: 74) amounted to less than two tenths of a point (2.76 for non-workers versus 2.60 for workers). There are also some studies that find no differences (Gade and Peterson, 1980; Hotchkiss, 1986; Green and Jaquess, 1987). At best, it is possible to conclude, with Greenberger and Steinberg (1986: 118), that no studies demonstrate that working has a positive effect on grades.

The assumption that working does have a depressing effect on grades for some students leads to the problem of explaining the process. The obvious answer focuses on the matter of time. On an absolute scale, student workers have less discretionary time; paid work consumes hours that cannot be devoted to scholastic work. Several studies have confirmed that student workers tend to curtail scholastic effort, taking fewer courses (McNeil, 1984) and spending less time on homework (D'Amico, 1984b). Such explanations are, at best, partial explanations, for students might sacrifice other activities (social, recreational) in favor of school. It is worth noting that all "time-use" studies must be interpreted with caution, for it is easy to draw the implicit assumption that time is simply a quantitative variable, ignoring the qualitative dimension that would require an exploration of the levels and intensity of effort expended during given blocks of time. There is some reallocation of time, showing up in about an hour less sleep, but the most dramatic change occurs among adolescent boys, who spend much less time in front of the television set (D'Amico, 1984b). Perhaps there is some threshold, some number of hours that students can devote to work without impairing their grades.

One final point must be considered in evaluating the impact of employment on grades. In an abstract sense, grades should be an absolute index of performance, but standards of grading do shift. Moreover, it is well documented in other contexts that non-academic factors impinge upon the process (for example, Vanfossen, Jones, and Spade, 1987). These factors may be behavioral (demeanor) or social (gender, race, social class). Applying that perspective to the student worker leads to a largely unexplored question: are working and non-working different social categories of students in the social structure of schools? More specifically, the research question is: do student workers behave differently, or are they perceived (or labeled) differentially, contributing to the observed variation in grades? Anecdotal evidence suggests that student workers may well exhibit distinctive behavior, and behavior that is negatively perceived. The popular press informs us that their conspicuous consumption patterns set them apart. A high school occupational specialist is quoted as saying, "You should see the student parking lot," a thinly disguised criticism of their expensive cars financed by part-time work (Meyers, 1986). There is also more systematic evidence of inattentiveness, disinterest, and lack of effort (McNeil, 1984). Such behaviors, considered alone, would contribute to lower performance. However, it is important to add the potential impact of the social identity of the student worker. If teachers resent the situation and feel they must compromise academic standards, as McNeil (1984) reports, it is possible that teachers' negative image of student workers is subtly and unintentionally translated into even lower grades for the working student.

It is appropriate to conclude that working students do not generally improve their scholastic performance, and that there may even be a depressing effect. Some students seem able to integrate at least a limited part-time schedule into their activities, while others may suffer academically, but it is not clear whether the variation can be explained by declining effort, by the role of the working student in the dynamics of the classroom, or by some interaction between the two. Of course, it may be that working students are more alienated from the schools and would not devote more hours to school work even if the time were available.

YOUTHS AT WORK

Part of the original impetus for youth employment programs was based on the assumption that work experiences would be beneficial, imparting useful skills and attitudes. There is very little indication that part-time work has the potential to offer useful skills, and this is dictated by the very nature of part-time work. Many jobs in the fast food industry, restaurants, and retail sales, are routine, repetitive, and highly specialized (Greenberger and Steinberg, 1986: 65–68). Very little time is spent on challenging and interesting tasks; a disproportionate amount of time is spent "cleaning things" and "carrying things." The accumulation of such skills prepare people only to assume other jobs of the same kind. There are some positive outcomes, but they are difficult to measure. Part-time experience can provide an introduction to the practical dimensions of work, like schedules, work-place rules, and authority. There are also more subtle benefits, such as a sense of self-reliance and the satisfaction that can be derived from completing tasks (Steinberg, 1982).

Balanced against the positive outcomes is the fact that working students also encounter an early introduction to occupational deviance and cynical attitudes toward work. The work place presents students with the opportunity to engage in a variety of forms of deviance (Ruggiero, Greenberger, and Steinberg, 1982). About one quarter were identified as relatively frequent offenders, and the incidence of deviance might even be higher because the research depended upon self-reported acts. Deviance was defined broadly to include both various forms of "employee theft" (stealing money and other things, giving away goods, and exaggerating hours worked) and "non-theft" deviance (lying to employers, deliberately damaging property, working under the influence of alcohol or drugs, and calling in sick). Since there is long-standing evidence that occupational deviance is a common feature of the world of work (Smigel and Ross, 1970), it must be assumed that part-time work merely accelerates exposure to these opportunities.

A different way of approaching part-time work experiences is to focus on how working students interpret them. More detailed investigation is required, but there are some suggestions in the literature. Among lower-income youths, part-time work seems to be perceived as a portent of the future. Some hold on to aspirations for upward mobility, but many others see only similar jobs in their future (MacLeod, 1987). Thus, the poor pay, unstable employment, and harsh working conditions of part-time employment have the potential to depress even further their occupational and educational aspirations. There is some indication that middle-class youths view their part-time work differently. For them, part-time work has little apparent relationship to their future in the world of work (Wijting, Arnold and Conrad, 1977; Mortimer and Finch, 1986). Their perceptions and aspirations, shaped by parental values and other early childhood experiences, are not significantly altered by the work experience. For them, it is simply and directly a source of income, and they continue to believe that they will embark on white-collar careers.

In general, there is not much indication that part-time work produces any major changes in behavior or attitudes. This is not an unexpected finding. Not only do part-time work experiences occur relatively late in the socialization process, thus having relatively less impact, but also it is unrealistic to expect them to overcome the continuing influence of social class, family, and school. However, it is important to note that working students, when compared to non-working students, do have somewhat higher incomes in the immediate post–high school years (Meyer and Wise, 1982; Mortimer and Finch, 1986). The reasons are not directly known, but some of the difference might be attributed to their early introduction to the expectations of employers, and the accumulation of job skills. Moreover, it is not known whether or not this economic advantage continues over the course of their working careers.

SOCIAL RELATIONSHIPS OF WORKING STUDENTS

Work and the classroom are but two dimensions of the lives of adolescents; they also have relations with peers and family. Unfortunately, not much is currently known about the wider implications of part-time work. The most exhaustive analysis of the impact that working has on social relations with peers and family members shows very little apparent change (Greenberger et al., 1980). Generally, workers spend no less time with their peers than do non-workers. Given the salience of peer relationships at this stage of the life cycle, it is not surprising to find that workers would be reluctant to sacrifice important social linkages. Moreover, there is no weakening of the intimacy of these friendships.

Extracurricular activities are also a form of peer activity, at least in part. The data here are less clear, ranging from no measurable impact (Greenberger and Steinberg, 1986: 249), to indications of systematically less involvement in extracurricular activities (D'Amico, 1984a; Green and Jaquess, 1987). As would be expected, the longer the hours worked, the greater the impact.

Working students do spend less time in family activities, suggesting that the time constraints imposed by employment are taken from time that might otherwise be spent with their families. Workers miss more family meals, spend fewer hours with the family in leisure pursuits, and devote less time to household chores than do the non-workers (Greenberger et al., 1980; D'Amico, 1984b). A reduction in the amount of time spent with the family does not have a corresponding impact on the quality of family relations. However, it may change the nature of some intrafamily relationships. There is, for example, a tendency for working males to discuss personal problems with their fathers. Perhaps a shared involvement in the world of work becomes the basis for this development.

This would seem to be the area that should demand the most attention in the future. Working has the potential to curtail or even alter some social relationships, but it also offers the opportunity to open new social avenues. Work may bring the student into contact with a new circle of people from different geographic and social origins.

CONCLUSION

It has frequently been pointed out that "youth" is a product of the industrial revolution (Kett, 1971). Youth became set apart in a transitional period between childhood and adulthood, a period often characterized as a period of ambiguity and confusion. During the 1970s, many argued that part-time work could facilitate the transition from child to adult. Not only would there be direct occupational benefits, but also more general traits such as maturity and responsibility would be fostered. A subsequent wave of scholarship challenged this approach, suggesting that part-time work had negative effects on educational attainments, and introduced youths to deviance and substance abuse. The most recent research tends toward claims that work is a "mixed blessing," having both positive and negative consequences.

In a broader context, the same research would also support a very different interpretation. In most instances, differences between working and non-working students are very modest; in other cases, they are statistically significant but substantively inconsequential. This suggests that many middle-class youths of school age have been able to integrate part-time work into their lives, without impairing their social lives, disrupting relations within the family, or sacrificing their grades. Part-time work does not seem to offer them any particular advantage in their later career development, but there is little indication that such rewards are expected. Many middle-class youths see it as largely irrelevant to adult roles; rather, it has become an almost "taken-for-granted" dimension of their lives, part of the life-style of their age group. In fact, scholars devote much more time and attention to the matter than these youths do. American youths seem to have accepted part-time work without overt objection. (It is impossible to locate evidence of such objections.) Perhaps youths have changed, almost unnoticed, with part-time work being just that—a part-time activity, one of the several parts of their social role.

In contrast, it is time to redirect the research agenda to a systematic exploration of the implications of part-time working for women, and for the children of the working class, the poor, and minorities. There are many unexamined questions. For example, we know that both males and females engage in part-time work, but we should investigate whether youth employment expands the career horizons of women, or merely reinforces the other social and economic forces that continue to channel women into less rewarding adult work (Greenberger, Steinberg, Vaux, and McAuliffe, 1983). Another question deserving attention is the role of part-time work in the lives of the less advantaged segments of the society. Middle-class youths can ignore the low pay and unrewarding conditions of most part-time work, but it might well further depress the educational and occupational aspirations of those who see it as a realistic preview of adult work.

NOTE

1. These data are from *Employment and Earnings* 35 (1): 18, of the United States Department of Labor, Bureau of Labor Statistics (1988). The Bureau defines part-time employment as less than 35 hours per week.

8 Do Part-Time Jobs Improve the Labor Market Chances of High School Graduates?

Graham S. Lowe and Harvey Krahn

Part-time employment has been steadily increasing among North American high school students. The service economy's demand for a cheap, flexible, and reliable pool of labor has fueled a huge growth in student employment during the past decade. Consequently, part-time employment has become the norm among older high school students. For many teenagers, a part-time job is the financial key to participation in an increasingly consumption-oriented youth culture.

Not surprisingly, the effects of part-time student employment are being questioned by educators, policy makers, and social scientists. There is little consensus about the long-term costs or benefits of this type of employment (Mortimer and Finch, 1986: 66; Rothman, in this volume; Coté, 1990: 12). Essentially there are two opposing views about the effects of student employment (Borman and Hopkins, 1987: 144). Some economists have claimed that a moderate amount of part-time work while in school leads to higher wages, a reduced risk of unemployment, and the chance of obtaining employment with the same employer. In contrast, psychologists and sociologists have identified negative social and psychological consequences, such as less time spent on homework and extracurricular activities, greater delinquency, and inhibition of the cognitive development necessary for identity formation.

The positive assessment of teenage part-time employment proposes that students who work while in high school, compared to those who do not, are better prepared to make the transition into the adult labor market. The evidence for this argument is, at best, fragmentary and dated. This paper attempts to clarify the effects of part-time student employment by addressing three issues central to previous debates.

Does a student's work experience increase the chances of finding a better job after graduation? In an increasingly polarized and competitive labor market, does a student's employment experience confer any post-graduation human capital advantages? Do student jobs assist the transition into adult jobs by inculcating work values and providing information about the labor market?

WORKING STUDENTS: RECENT TRENDS

Being a student and working part-time in low-wage, menial, service-sector jobs go hand in hand. Labor force participation rates among full-time students in Canada jumped from 32 percent in 1979 to 45 percent in 1989 (Coté, 1990: 12). At the same time, part-time employment (defined as less than 30 hours per week) among youth, especially females, was increasing, with a corresponding decline in their full-time employment. Between 1977 and 1987, the proportion of 15- to 24-year-olds in part-time employment rose from 21 percent to 32 percent (Cohen, 1989: 9).

Several larger socioeconomic changes provide the backdrop for this dramatic increase in student employment. Most important is the fact that 94 percent of Canada's employment growth in the 1980s was in service industries (Coté, 1990: 13). The greatest expansion has occurred in what the Economic Council of Canada (1990) calls *traditional* service industries—mainly retail trade and personal services—as opposed to *dynamic* services. The former have a much higher proportion of low-skilled, low-wage, temporary, and part-time jobs (Economic Council of Canada, 1990; Radwanski, 1986). Thus, 70 percent of all part-time youth workers are employed in retail trade; accommodation, food, and beverage services; and other traditional services such as amusement and recreation, and personal and household services (Cohen, 1989: 10).

While this paper focuses on the individual consequences of student employment, we must also be aware of the broader implications. Youth labor-force participation rates were soaring at a time when the relative size of this age cohort was shrinking. Service sector employers have come to depend on student workers just when this labor supply is dwindling. How will employers respond to these trends? In addition, because one quarter of labor-force participants aged 15 to 24 are students, concerns have been voiced that students are taking jobs that would otherwise go to their non-student, less qualified peers (Coté, 1990: 12). In light of these changing labor market and demographic realities, the implications of student employment for post-graduation labor market entry require careful investigation.

EFFECTS OF PART-TIME STUDENT EMPLOYMENT ON LABOR MARKET OUTCOMES

Part-time student work could affect initial employment after graduation in various ways. For example, student jobs may inculcate work attitudes and behaviors desired by employers. However, given the menial nature of most student jobs, it is difficult to extend this argument to specific job skills. Considering the importance of personal contacts in obtaining employment, having worked in high school may lead to a full-time job with the same employer. This could turn out to be a dubious advantage if, once graduated, young workers were unable to move out of low-status *student jobs*. Part-time work may also acquaint students with how the labor market operates, assisting in the job search process and perhaps creating "realistic" occupational expectations.

These potentially positive effects must be weighed against the possibility that students in part-time jobs may have less time for their studies and a weakened attachment to school. If lower academic achievement resulted, labor market chances would diminish due to the strong link between educational attainment and adult occupational status. The research literature provides only limited evidence of positive effects. Studies identifying the benefits of part-time work for students have tended to focus on short-term labor market outcomes. For example, several American studies found a positive relationship between hours worked in high school and post-graduation earnings and number of weeks employed (Meyer and Wise, 1982; also see Stephenson, 1979). Meyer and Wise (1982: 279) speculate that part-time student workers may acquire job-relevant personal attributes, although they lack data on what these attributes might be or how they are developed.

Other studies have examined whether part-time work experienced while in school improves one's chances of finding a job after graduating. Among Scottish school-leavers, work experience while in school improved the chances of finding a job, but a student's level and type of qualifications, age, gender, and family background, as well as local labor market conditions, were far more important in this regard (Raffe, 1988). Similar studies in Ireland (Breen, 1986) and England (Hoskins et al., 1989) found benefits only at times of high unemployment, or only for certain kinds of low-level jobs. However, higher youth unemployment during the 1980s, a low labor-force participation rate among students, and a different educational system in Great Britain make direct comparisons with Canada difficult (Ashton, 1988a).

Furthermore, there is no solid evidence that part-time employment socializes students to the adult work world, helping them to succeed in the post-graduation labor market. D'Amico (1984) reported that, in moderate amounts, part-time student employment fostered good work attitudes and behavior. Greenberger and Steinberg (1986) found that employed students were more self-reliant and had a stronger work ethic, but at the cost of lower academic performance. Some American analysts suggest that students from less privileged families may derive more benefit from part-time jobs than white middle-class students (who comprised Greenberger and Steinberg's sample) in that the former can thus acquire basic job skills that they otherwise would not obtain (Borman and Hopkins, 1987: 144–145).

While some student jobs may provide useful work experience, the vast majority involve routine tasks that require minimal skills (Krahn and Lowe, 1989; Radwanski, 1986). Most student workers spend little time talking with adult supervisors or co-workers (Hills and Reubens, 1983). This sort of interaction is a prerequisite for the kind of work-place socialization (as opposed to socialization into deviant behavior; see Greenberger and Steinberg, 1986) that would be useful to students after graduation. It is also important to consider why students seek employment. Part-time jobs are central to youth culture and therefore are more likely to be viewed by students as an immediate source of income rather than as a way of gaining useful work experience for the future.

Research identifying a negative impact of part-time student employment looks beyond immediate labor market outcomes to future disadvantages, in terms of psychological development and educational and occupational attainment. In one longitudinal study, students working long hours in demanding part-time jobs had lower grades, poorer academic self-concepts, and lower occupational aspirations in comparison with their non-working classmates (Mortimer and Finch, 1986). Another longitudinal study found that excessive amounts of part-time work increased the chance of dropping out of school (D'Amico, 1984). However, several subsequent studies failed to corroborate the negative influence of part-time work on school performance (Gottfredson, 1985; Green and Jaquess, 1987).

These inconsistent findings may stem from methodological and conceptual differences in previous research. For example, the longitudinal studies identifying labor market benefits were conducted in the early 1970s among males only (for example, Meyer and Wise, 1982). Generalizing from studies that document adverse long-term effects of part-time work is equally hazardous, but for different reasons. A major criticism of Greenberger and Steinberg's (1986) research is their reliance on a small, cross-sectional sample of white, middle-class students in four California high schools. Furthermore, labor market and social-psychological effects have not been examined simultaneously.

The limitations of existing studies underline the need for longitudinal research capable of systematically comparing working and non-working students on three key dimensions: education attainment, work socialization, and post-graduation labor market outcomes. Solid evidence on these issues is needed to help resolve the debate about the costs and benefits of student employment, especially in the context of the post-recession labor market. It is also useful to extend the discussion of part-time student employment beyond the United States, where most previous research has been conducted.[1] Our contribution, then, is to address the following questions, using data from a panel study of Canadian high school students who entered the labor market in 1985:

1. How do employed students differ in sociodemographic and educational characteristics from their peers who do not have part-time jobs during the final year of high school?
2. Why do students take part-time jobs, where do they work, and what do they earn?
3. Do working and non-working students have different work attitudes?
4. Among those students who leave school completely upon graduation, does part-time work experience make it easier to find a job?
5. Finally, do employment outcomes two years after graduation differ significantly on the basis of work experience acquired in the last year of high school?

DATA AND METHODS

Our data come from a longitudinal study of high school graduates in three Canadian cities. Baseline data (Year 1) were collected in the spring of 1985, just prior to graduation, in Edmonton, Toronto, and Sudbury. We believe that these three cities, while not representative of the country as a whole, reflect the basic variations in young people's school and work experiences in major urban centers. The average age of respondents in Year 1 was 18. The sample contains similar numbers of females and males.

Students were surveyed in a total of 25 high schools across the three cities. Because access to high schools and to classes within them had to be individually negotiated, we could not draw a random sample. However, schools in both middle-class and working-class neighborhoods were chosen. Within schools, we selected a diverse range of classes in both vocational and academic programs. Once permission had been obtained from parents of eligible students under the age of 18, researchers administered the questionnaire in classrooms during May of 1985.

The first major follow-up survey was completed in May, 1986 (Year 2), and a second took place in May, 1987 (Year 3). The data we analyze in this paper thus cover a 24-month period following graduation, as well as the final year of high school. The Year 2 and 3 questionnaires were administered through the mail. Prior to each of these follow-up surveys, newsletters were sent to respondents to keep them informed about the progress of the study and to report preliminary findings. Both the Year 2 and 3 surveys utilized a four-stage data collection procedure (Heberlein and Baumgartner, 1978; see Krahn, 1988, for details). We succeeded in contacting all but a few sample members by mail or telephone.

There were 2229 respondents in Year 1. Of these, 1906 (or 86 percent) gave their names and addresses so that we could contact them again in Year 2 and Year 3. By Year 3, attrition had reduced the sample to 54 percent (n = 1030) of those who gave contact information in 1985. It is this panel of 1030 individuals that we proceed to examine below.[2]

THE WORK EXPERIENCE OF HIGH SCHOOL SENIORS

Over two thirds (69 percent) of respondents were employed at some time during their last year in high school and a similar proportion (66 percent) had held a job during the previous summer. At the time of the Year 1 survey, in May, 1985, 57 percent were employed. Females were slightly more likely than males to hold part-time jobs, but this difference is not statistically significant. Respondents in Toronto were significantly more likely to be employed (74 percent) than were their peers in Edmonton (67 percent) or Sudbury (64 percent), reflecting the stronger economy in Toronto at the time.

With respect to those employed at the time of the Year 1 survey (n = 584), 91 percent of the females and 79 percent of the males reported clerical, sales, or service occupations. Those who had worked earlier in the term, but who were not employed when surveyed (n = 113), reported similar types of jobs. By comparison, about 40 percent of the Canadian labor force works in these three occupations (Krahn and Lowe, 1989: 45). Student workers, however, are concentrated at the bottom of these broad occupational categories. In fact, three specific jobs—sales clerk, food and beverage server, and cashier—accounted for 45 percent of the employment reported by our respondents. Only 7 percent of respondents held occupations in the managerial/professional category, and these typically were low-status (e.g., "manager" in a fast-food place). Gender differences were most evident in clerical occupations, where 29 percent of the females but only 13 percent of the males worked, and in blue-collar jobs (16 percent and 1 percent of males and females, respectively). In sum, student part-time employment is low-status and gender-segregated.

Those employed at the time of the Year 1 survey worked an average of 17 hours weekly. Males worked significantly more hours than females (weekly averages of 19 and 15 hours, respectively). Average weekly take-home pay (that is, after deductions) was $84, with Toronto students reporting somewhat higher pay ($91). Assuming that taxes and deductions amounted to 15 percent of total pay, we estimate gross earnings

Table 8.1

Work Experience During the School Term by Program of Study, Self-Reported Grades, Educational Expectations, and Parents' Education (Percentages)

	No job at all[1]	Employed now	Held job earlier		Total (Number)
High School Program:					
Academic	33	55	12		(652)
Non-academic	29	60	11		(378)
Self-reported grades past year:					
70% or better	37	51	12		(499)
Below 70%	27	62	11	*	(531)
Educational Expectations:					
University graduation	38	52	10		(451)
Other	27	60	13	*	(567)
Mother's education:					
University graduation	31	56	14		(140)
Some post-secondary	34	54	12		(155)
Other	29	60	11		(598)
Father's education:					
University graduation	34	54	12		(212)
Some post-secondary	30	60	10		(160)
Other	30	58	12		(481)
Total:	31	57	12		(1,030)

1. Four respondents, who did not answer this question, are included among those who did not report a job during the term

*Differences between means are statistically significant (p < .05)

of about $100 weekly, or just under $6.00 per hour for the total sample. Males had higher net earnings than females ($97 versus $71 weekly), largely due to their longer hours of work.

EDUCATIONAL AND SOCIOECONOMIC CHARACTERISTICS OF WORKING AND NON-WORKING STUDENTS

Table 8.1 examines the effects of educational and socioeconomic characteristics on employment during the final year of high school. Students in non-academic programs[3] were somewhat more likely to be employed, compared to those in academic programs, but the difference is not significant. However, respondents with lower grades and those not planning to complete university were significantly more likely to report employment.

Yet, these differences are not large. For example, 5 out of 10 students planning to graduate from university, compared with 6 out of 10 who did not have this goal, were employed just prior to the end of their senior year. A six-item school commitment index[4] (results not reported) correlates very weakly ($-.09$) with having worked at any time during the school term. In short, students with lower educational attainment and a less academic orientation tended to have a higher rate of participation in part-time employment, but we emphasize that this relationship is weak. Because having a part-time job is now so common, many academically motivated youth also worked while in high school.

By looking at students' socioeconomic backgrounds, we find additional support for the argument that part-time employment is a basic feature of contemporary high school culture. Respondents with better educated parents were not significantly more likely to be employed during their final year of high school. Other measures (not reported) of family socioeconomic status (parents' occupation, students' assessment of their families' financial situations) yield similar results. However, it is important to remember that family background operates indirectly through or streaming into academic and non-academic programs, with resulting class differences in educational and occupational aspirations and in educational attainment (Krahn and Lowe, 1990). Still, it is clear from these results that student employment cuts across social classes.

WHY STUDENTS TAKE JOBS

Figure 8.1 summarizes the reasons given by respondents in answer to an open-ended question about why they took their current or most recent job during the school term.[5] Money, or money along with another reason, accounted for over 70 percent of the reasons cited for working part time. Only 16 percent gave work experience, training, or other career-related reasons, or expressed interest in the job or the type of work performed. Male and female respondents gave similar answers, with the only significant difference being the greater propensity among females to cite money along with another reason.

Obviously, money is what motivated most of these teenagers to seek part-time jobs. Respondents were not asked why they needed this income. Yet, there is reason to believe that the money was not to live on, but to purchase the accoutrements of today's teenage life-style. Virtually all (96 percent) were living with their parents when surveyed. Moreover, reasons for taking a part-time job did not vary by socioeconomic background. Nor did they vary by educational orientation, with one exception: those planning to graduate from university were more likely, than were their classmates who did not have such plans, to take a job for the experience (10 percent and 5 percent, respectively, cited this reason).

Figure 8.1
Reasons for Employment During Senior High School Year, by Sex

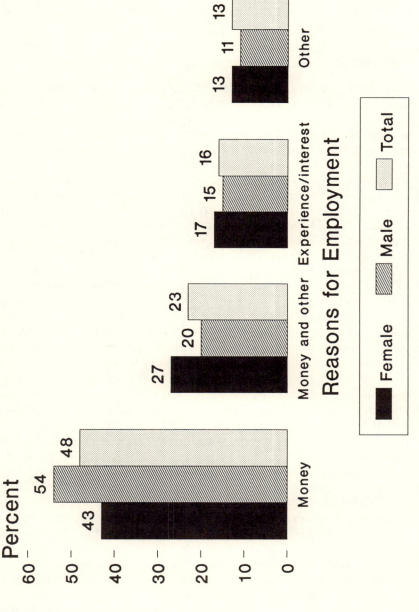

female number = 356   male number = 338

Thus, it appears that part-time employment in school is largely a phenomenon of youth culture, providing the immediate benefits of a disposable income. Very few students viewed their jobs in terms of future labor market payoffs.

PART-TIME JOBS AND WORK ATTITUDES

We now examine the proposition that one of the advantages of part-time employment for students is that it develops a strong "work ethic." For many employers, this would mean a willingness to work in low-wage jobs. Working while in school could acquaint students with labor market realities, particularly the limited job opportunities open to those with a high school diploma. By this reasoning, students with work experience would be more inclined to accept jobs at low wages. We investigated this hypothesis by asking respondents whether they would accept one of five common youth jobs at the minimum wage, when looking for full-time employment after leaving school: stocking supermarket shelves, cleaning restaurant tables, working at a hamburger place, working in a car wash, and doing telephone sales.[6]

Turning to Figure 8.2 we first observe a distinct hierarchy of student jobs, at least in the minds of the students themselves. Stocking supermarket shelves and cleaning restaurant tables were perceived as more desirable jobs than the three other kinds of work, especially telephone sales. It is even more interesting that work experience had exactly the opposite effect from that predicted. Indeed, presently or previously employed students were significantly less likely to be willing to accept any of these jobs. Rather than encouraging realistic (that is, lower) occupational expectations among students, exposure to low-wage menial jobs encouraged these students to aim for something better after graduation.

Part-time jobs also may shape students' general work values, along with their preferences for specific kinds of work, thus equipping them with a stronger work ethic. This greater motivation could give students with work experience in high school an edge over their non-working classmates when competing for jobs after graduating. Table 8.2 shows few differences between working and non-working students, in terms of their work values at the time of graduation. In general, these teenagers seemed highly motivated to work. Specifically, only about one in four did not feel ready for a long-term job commitment; there was virtually no difference between those with or without employment experience. Furthermore, there was little support for collecting unemployment insurance or welfare until a suitable job was available. Despite the importance of money as a reason for working while in school, the entire sample was evenly split on the merits of doing any job if it paid $15 an hour (about 2.5 times more than student jobs paid) after graduating.

Table 8.2
Work Values by Work Experience While in High School

Work Values	Average Score[1]		
	Worked earlier or now	Have not worked	Agree[1] (Percent)
I am not ready for a long-term commitment to a job	2.59	2.62	26
Everyone has the right to collect unemployment insurance until they find a job in their area of training	2.76	2.77	27
I'd rather collect welfare than work at a job I don't like	1.75	1.77	9
If I could earn $15 an hour, I would take any job	3.43	3.45	50
Having a job makes me feel I'm doing something useful with my life	4.28	4.26	85
If someone has worked hard in school, they are entitled to a good job	3.71 *	3.94	66
Everyone has the right to the kind of job that their education and training has prepared them for	4.05 *	4.23	76
(Approximate Number)[2]	(699)	(321)	(1020)

1. Respondents answered on a five-point scale with "1" representing "strongly disagree" and "5" representing "strongly agree." The percent in agreement combines scores of "4" and "5," and is calculated for the total sample.

2. Sub-sample sizes differed by 1 or 2 because of varying amounts of non-response.

*Differences between means are statistically significant ($p < .05$)

Instrumental work orientations[7] were more widespread among our respondents than in the adult labor force as a whole (Krahn and Lowe, 1988: 158), suggesting that age, rather than student employment status, is a key factor. There are no signs that part-time work experience makes students more concerned about this issue (Table 8.2). Generally speaking, paid employment was of central importance to these high school

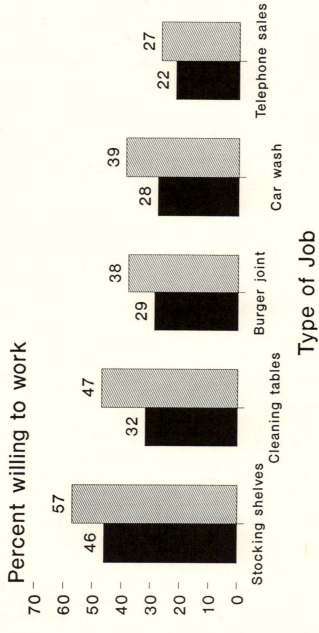

Figure 8.2
Willingness to Work in Minimum Wage Jobs, by Work Experience

Percent willing to work

	Stocking shelves	Cleaning tables	Burger joint	Car wash	Telephone sales
70					
60	57				
50	46	47			
40		32	38	39	
30			29	28	27
20					22
10					
0					

Type of Job

Work Experience

Worked   Didn't work

number=691 (worked)   number=318 (didn't)

graduates; 85 percent stated that having a job made them feel they were doing something useful with their lives. Again, there were no differences between working and non-working students.

The remaining two items in Table 8.2 tap job entitlement beliefs.[8] The first is an individualistic and meritocratic expression of entitlement: only those who work hard in school deserve a good job. The second is more universalistic: everyone who works hard in school is entitled to a good job. Both beliefs were quite widespread within the sample as a whole, but those who did not have a job during their graduating year in high school had significantly stronger entitlement beliefs. This finding could reflect a greater emphasis by non-working students on academic achievement. It is equally plausible that working students, having seen a wider range of factors influencing labor market success, realized that there are no guaranteed payoffs from education. Our analysis of similar beliefs among a sample of university graduates suggests that feelings of entitlement decline with age, as students develop a more pragmatic understanding of the labor market (Krahn and Lowe, 1990).

In sum, these differences in entitlement beliefs are the only evidence in Table 8.2 that teenagers who work part time during the school term developed greater realism about the labor market. Only in this limited way does work experience facilitate attitudinal adjustments to employment. For the rest of the items reported in the table, however, questions of causality (does part-time employment lead to changes in work attitudes among students, or do prior differences in attitudes lead some students to seek jobs and others to focus on their studies?) do not arise, given the identical work values among the two groups being compared.

PART-TIME JOBS, LABOR MARKET ENTRY, AND EMPLOYMENT OUTCOMES TWO YEARS AFTER GRADUATION

Do students who worked part time during their senior year move more easily out of student jobs and into adult jobs after graduating? This question is especially relevant to those not returning to school, but the majority of our sample had further education plans. In fact, three out of four (77 percent) of those who had worked during the school year planned to return to school in the fall of 1985, compared with 88 percent of non-working students. Among the small number not planning to return to school, 44 percent of the working students had already arranged a job, whereas only 23 percent of the non-working students had a prearranged job. This suggests that part-time student work may provide a stepping stone to a job after graduation. However, only 9 of the 65 respondents with a job arranged reported that it was obtained through a previous job. Most stated that they had obtained the job through "contacts." As for those who had not arranged a job, there were no differences between working and non-working students regarding job search plans. Most intended simply to "apply" for jobs, or to look through newspaper want ads.

Allowing that part-time work while in high school might provide a small advantage for entry to the labor market, are these better entry jobs than those obtained by students with no work experience in the final year of high school? Table 8.3 reports employment outcomes two years after graduation, and distinguishes between respondents who had left the educational system by the second year of the study (1986–87) and those who were still continuing their education full-time or part-time during the 1985–87 period. We have previously established (Krahn and Lowe, 1989; 1990) that students and non-students occupy different labor market locations. Thus, it is important to separate them for purposes of our present analysis. This separation also allows us to determine whether high school work experience improves subsequent part-time work opportunities for those students who continued in school.

Looking first at continuing students, we find no difference between those who had worked in their last year of high school and those who had not, in terms of average months of full-time employment or un-employment. However, those who had worked while in high school reported significantly more months of part-time employment in 1986–87. They also were more likely to have been employed at some point in the 1986–87 period and to have a job at the time of the May 1987 survey. In short, young people who worked while in high school were more likely to do so during their post-secondary education. Yet, the majority of students who had not worked during the 1984–85 high school year still reported labor market activity in 1986–87. This finding underscores our earlier point that combining employment and school has become the norm for youth.

The bottom panel of Table 8.3 shows that work experience gained in the final year of high school conferred no further advantages for those who remained in school. They were equally likely to be employed part time, and no more likely than those who had not worked in high school to have obtained higher-status jobs. Their pay was only slightly higher. Turning to respondents who had cut their ties with the educational system, the story line is far simpler. Other than having more months of full-time employment during 1986–87, having held a job during the last year of high school made no difference on any of the employment outcomes measured in Table 8.3. This one difference mirrors findings from earlier studies (for example, Meyer and Wise, 1982). However, these studies also found significant benefits in terms of higher wages, which we do not. Given our more comprehensive documentation of labor market outcomes, we feel confident in concluding that working

Table 8.3
Employment Outcomes (1987) by Work Experience While in High School by Educational Status in 1987

	Student		Non-student[1]	
	Worked	Did not work	Worked	Did not work
From May 1986 to April 1987:				
Average Months				
Part-time work	5.4 *	3.4	2.6	2.9
Full-time work	3.1	2.8	8.2 *	6.8
Unemployed	1.0	1.1	1.9	1.9
Percentage				
Employed at some time in 1986-87	97 *	90	98	95
Employed in May 1987	77 *	61	87	84
(number)	(457)	(246)	(246)	(77)
Of those employed in May 1987:				
Percentage				
Part-time	44	39	17	20
Managerial or Professional	13	15	7	3
Consumer Services Labor Market[2]	56	53	55	52
Weekly Average				
Take-home pay	$205	$196	$248	$238
(number)	(354)	(149)	(214)	(65)

1. Non-students: those who reported no full-time education and no more than two months of part-time education in 1986-87.

2. Consumer services labor market segment: clerical, sales, and service jobs in consumer services (retail trade, accommodation, food and beverage, entertainment and personal services).

*Differences between means are statistically significant (p < .05).

while in high school has negligible benefits for students who enter the labor market upon graduation.

CONCLUSION

Working at a part-time job while completing high school is widespread among teenagers. Indeed, two thirds of our respondents had worked at some point during their senior high school year. Socioeconomic background or gender had little bearing on who worked during the school term. What these students had in common was a singular motivation to work: money. Consistent with previous research, we did find variation in employment patterns by academic achievement. Perhaps having lower grades, lower educational aspirations, or being in a non-academic stream results from holding a job. The converse is equally plausible. Less academically inclined students, feeling more alienated from school, may place greater emphasis on non-school activities such as employment. While answers to these causal questions would be illuminating, they are beyond the scope of our data.

Proponents of student employment frequently promise the development of "better" work attitudes, but without supporting evidence. This study shows that employment experience in high school is not associated with differences in what we might loosely call a "work ethic." However, a job in high school may lead to a more realistic assessment of labor market opportunities. Students who did not have a job during their senior year felt a slightly stronger sense of job entitlement, but this group was also more willing to do a variety of menial student jobs at low wages. The latter finding refutes a key argument in favor of part-time student employment, namely, that work experience teaches students to be less choosy about the jobs they take.

As for labor market outcomes, among the small minority of graduates who did not return to school in the fall of 1985, those with high school work experience were somewhat more likely to have a job lined up at the time of graduation. Beyond this, there were few major differences between the working and non-working groups. In fact, working in high school seemed to have more of an effect for continuing students, increasing the probability of holding a job during post-secondary studies. For respondents who headed into the labor force after high school, having held a student job made one small difference: it increased the average months of full-time work.

On the whole, these results lead us to conclude that the real advantage of working while in high school is a disposable income. Post-graduation benefits—either in terms of a work attitude sought by employers, or a better job—are minimal. Some researchers have argued that a much longer follow-up period is necessary to draw such conclusions (Mortimer and Finch, 1986). We disagree, on the assumption that benefits would appear early rather than later in an individual's career. However, we might expect long-term *negative* effects of *excessive* student employment, given that previous studies have linked long hours of work by high school students to lower educational attainment (D'Amico, 1984; Mortimer and Finch, 1986). Indeed, more than ever before, higher educational credentials are needed to succeed in today's labor market.

In light of the above comments, the debate about the costs and benefits of student employment must be reassessed. We also need to examine employers in future investigations of part-time student work. Certainly, students work by choice, but it is the demand for their labor in the service sector that has fueled the trend. Fast-food outlets, convenience stores, gas stations, and a host of other low-wage service industries depend largely on teenaged student labor. However, the supply of student labor is dwindling. Shortages are already having an impact in the consumer service sector (Canada. Statistics Canada, 1989). Some of these employers have begun to tap other labor reserves, such as the elderly. It remains an open question as to how many seniors would be willing to work in jobs currently held by teenaged students.

The recent large increase in child labor law violations in the United States suggests that more younger teenagers are being recruited into the part-time work force (*Edmonton Journal*, 4 May 1990). Nilsen (1984) notes that in 1983, one in six American 14- and 15-year-olds were in the labor force, mainly in short-hour, unskilled jobs. This trend deserves close monitoring. If it increases, there will be good cause to reconsider how part-time student employment could be harmful to the social and psychological development of young teenagers. However, our findings regarding employment outcomes and work attitudes counsel against reexamining hypotheses about the positive labor market effects of part-time student work.

NOTES

Versions of this paper were presented at the Annual Meeting of the Canadian Sociology and Anthropology Association in a session on "Education and Social Inequality: I," May 30, 1990, Victoria, Canada, and at the World Congress of Sociology in a joint session of RC 30 and RC 34 on "Youth at Work," July 9, 1990, Madrid, Spain. The Major funders of this ongoing study include the Social Sciences and Humanities Research Council of Canada, the governments of the provinces of Alberta and Ontario, the Solicitor General of Canada, the cities of Edmonton and Toronto, the University of Alberta and Laurentian University, and the Royal Bank. We also wish to thank Alan Law for his research assistance.

1. Student employment during the school year is a significant labor market trend only in the United States, Sweden, Australia, and Canada (Reubens, 1983; ILO, 1987: 38).

2. A comparison of Year 1 respondents who subsequently dropped out of the study (in either Year 2 or Year 3) with those who participated in all three years, identified several possible sources of sample attrition bias (Krahn, 1988: 11–17). Response rates varied across the three cities, mainly due to different data collection strategies. Males, members of racial and ethnic minorities, and individuals with previous labor market experience had higher attrition rates. Academically-oriented youth and those from higher socioeconomic backgrounds were more likely to continue participating. Hence, the effects of gender and socioeconomic background are carefully examined in the following analyses.

3. Technical, vocational, and other streams which do not provide university entrance qualifications.

4. Respondents were asked how strongly they agreed or disagreed, on a five-point scale, to each of the following statements: continuing my education will help me get a good job; most of the classes at school are a complete waste of time; I (almost) always finish my homework; school is the same, day after day, week after week; most of the time in school they treat you like a child; overall, I have enjoyed my time in high school; for the sort of job I'm likely to get, you don't really need much education (alpha for the 6 items = .59).

5. In this and subsequent figures and tables we combine currently and previously employed students and compare them with students who did not work at all during their senior year, since there are no significant differences between the currently and previously employed groups regarding hours worked, types of occupations held, or the various dependent variables.

6. This question was adapted from one used by Borus (1982). The question also was asked with the hourly wage increased to $6.00. A similar pattern of results was observed for the $6.00-per-hour question, with somewhat more of the sample reporting willingness to take each job. This supports our earlier contention that money is a primary motivator for student workers.

7. Instrumentalism is an orientation to work as a means to an end. Thus, instrumental workers are motivated primarily by money (see Krahn and Lowe, 1988: 156–58).

8. These two items are modified from those originally developed by Derber (1978).

9 Part-Time Working among Young People in Britain

Angela M. Dale

Compared with those of many other industrialized Western nations, levels of part-time working in Britain are high. Exact levels vary with the data source used, but in 1987 part-timers formed about 24 percent of all employees. This percentage has risen slowly but steadily since the 1970s. In Britain, over 90 percent of part-time employees are female, and the great majority are also married. The 1980 Department of Employment's *Women and Employment* Survey (Martin and Roberts, 1984) found that having young children, particularly under ten years old, and being married, were the most important variables in predicting whether women worked part time or full time. However, for two other groups of the population, part-time work is also an important component. These are older men, particularly of post-retirement age, and young, unmarried men and women. Young people of 21 and under made up 10 percent of part-time workers in 1984. A radical transformation of the youth labor market has occurred in the past ten years.

PART-TIME WORK

From the early 1970s, there has been a steady rise in part-time work in the labor force at large, almost entirely due to an increase in the return to employment of mothers with young children. Britain is distinct from most of its Western neighbors, because British women are much more likely to leave the labor market when they have a child and resume working in a part-time capacity a few years later (Dex, 1984). By contrast, in North America and in much of Europe, women are considerably more likely to retain a full-time job, taking perhaps six or 12 months of maternity leave at the time of childbirth (Dex and Shaw, 1986).

The reasons for this British situation are complex and include a lack of child-care facilities, employment legislation that makes part-time workers an attractive proposition to employers, and an ideology that places the responsibility for child care firmly on the shoulders of mothers. For all these reasons, part-time work is usually performed by women who also have family responsibilities and who therefore seek convenient hours of work in a job that is near to home (Dale, 1987). The work is thus predominantly located in the service sector, usually requires few formal qualifications, and is low-paid.

Employers appear to assume that workers who do not provide a full week's work regard their work as secondary, that they are indifferent to promotion and career prospects, and that they find reduced rates of pay acceptable. However, employers also recognize that married women represent a stable and dependable work force, and this is a further reason underlying the recent expansion of part-time work. By using part-timers, employers can tailor the hours of work to suit the needs of the firm, thereby increasing flexibility while minimizing costs. In this situation, it is not surprising that the demand for part-time workers, as well as the supply, has risen, and there is some evidence of employers adopting strategies that enable them to increase the number of part-timers at the expense of full-time workers.

THE YOUTH LABOR MARKET

While the rate of unemployment in Britain increased gradually during the 1970s, the rate for young people rose consistently faster than for the labor force as a whole. In 1977, the unemployment level was 6 percent for the total work force but 8.8 percent for 16- to 18-year-olds. In 1982, it was 13.5 percent overall and 28 percent among 16- to 19-year-olds (Roberts, 1984). Reasons underlying this rise in youth unemployment are discussed in detail by a number of authors (Ashton, 1988a, 1988b; Finn, 1987; Roberts, 1984). One important reason is the demographic change in Britain, entailing an increase of 20 percent in the number of 16- to 18-year-olds between 1974 and 1984. During the same period, Britain experienced a massive recession, particularly in the manufacturing industry, with the result that, despite the increased number of 16- to 18-year-olds, 500,000 fewer young people held jobs in 1984 than in 1974 (Equal Opportunities Commission, 1986). Associated with the decline in manufacturing was a collapse of the apprenticeship system which, in the early 1970s, absorbed over a quarter of 16-year-old males but absorbed only 8 percent of them in 1984. Additional factors underlying the high rates of youth unemployment were the widespread policy of "last in, first out" when firms faced job losses, and the increasing number of married women seeking a return to the labor market in a part-time capacity.

Growing levels of unemployment among young people led to government fears that they would not become socialized into the world of work, would not conform to the norms of society and, as a result, would contribute to rising levels of crime and social unrest (Finn, 1987). At the same time, there were concerns that young people were receiving inadequate training for employment. The education system came under attack for producing school-leavers who were barely literate and numerate. Also, by comparison with other Western industrialized nations, the levels of job training given to young people in Britain were very low. It was in response to these demands and problems that the Youth Opportunities Programme (YOP) was introduced in 1978, with courses designed to "prepare young people for work and different kinds of work experience" (Finn, 1987: 111). The major dimension of the YOP provision was work experience provided by employers.

Until the late 1970s, it was still generally accepted that the majority of young people left school at 16 and moved into a full-time job. Indeed, in 1974 slightly over 60 percent of 16-year-old boys and just under 60 percent of 16-year-old girls went from school directly into employment; most of the remainder either stayed on at school or embarked on further education (Department of Education and Science, 1985). However, since the late 1970s, government training schemes have become increasingly important as a means of reducing high youth unemployment while also aiming to socialize young people into stable work habits and to provide some training for the needs of industry. The relative importance of the aims of social control and training is difficult to assess; it is probable that, for the young persons themselves, whichever seems dominant will depend upon whether the scheme leads to a permanent full-time job or whether it leads back to unemployment. The employment outcome, in turn, seems to depend very largely upon the job opportunities in the local labor market (Roberts et al., 1986; Ashton and Maguire, 1986).

The Youth Training Scheme (YTS) succeeded the YOP in 1983, and was intended as "a permanent bridge between school and work" (Cockburn, 1987: ix). By 1986, one in four people aged 16 were on YTS schemes and, in recognition of the difficulty that young people experienced in moving from YTS to paid work, the scheme was extended to cover two years rather than one. Ashton (1988) states that, in 1987, YTS served 27 percent of all 16-year-olds, with 31 percent staying on at school and 17 percent finding employment. In contrast with the period ten years earlier, the most significant change has been that YTS has replaced full-time work as the major activity of 16-year-old school-leavers. Concomitantly, there has been a marked increase in the number of young people who stay on at school beyond age 16, often taking vocational, one-year courses.

YOUNG PEOPLE AND PART-TIME WORK

Despite rising youth unemployment and increasing levels of part-time work, there is very little evidence of a significant increase in young people who take part-time work as a substitute for full-time work. The United Kingdom Labour Force Survey recorded economic activity for all adult members in a nationally representative sample of 85,000 households in 1979 and of 68,000 households in 1984. Table 9.1 shows that in 1979 about 1 percent of young men aged between 16 and 21 reported their "usual" economic activity as part-time work. For young women, this percentage rises with age, reaching 5 percent at age 21. In 1984 (Table 9.2), part-time work as the "usual" economic activity was still around 1 percent for young men, but for young women it had risen to about 6 percent by the age of 19. Because part-time work is associated with marriage and childbearing for women, it is important to establish whether the higher proportion of women in part-time work is likely to be accounted for in this way. For single men and women (that is, never married), part-time work in 1984 remains the same for those aged 16 to 19, but falls by one percent for those aged 20 and 21. It would seem, then, that young women are more likely than young men to take part-time work, irrespective of marital status. This difference may be related to the ways in which part-time jobs are constructed as "women's work."

It is perhaps surprising to find that the increase in part-time work has had such a limited impact upon young people. This will be discussed later in more detail. First, however, it is important to note the use of the term "usual" economic activity. The Labour Force Survey draws an important distinction between a respondent's "usual" situation regarding work, and whether the respondent did any paid work at all in the week preceding the survey. This distinction is of particular importance in understanding the work status of young people, many of whom are still at school or at college but do some part-time evening or weekend work.

The figures quoted refer to usual economic status, giving the category of "full-time student" precedence over "in employment." However, using the definition of any part-time work, irrespective of usual economic status, analysis of the Labour Force Survey shows that, in 1984, 12 percent of males and 17 percent of females aged 16 had a part-time job. For all those aged 16 to 21, 6 percent of men and 11 percent of women reported doing some part-time work in the week before the survey. The discrepancy between these figures and those shown in Table 9.2 is accounted for by young people who are classified as students in

Table 9.1
Usual Economic Activity by Age, 1979 (Percentage)

	16[1]	17	18	Age 19	20	21	All
Men							
Full-time employee	27	62	69	79	81	79	65
Part-time employee	1	0	0	1	1	0	0
Self-employed	0	0	1	1	2	3	1
Unemployed	8	5	6	6	5	7	6
Full-time student	63	33	23	13	10	10	27
Other	0	0	0	0	0	0	0
Inactive	1	1	1	1	1	2	1
Total Percentage	100	100	100	100	100	100	100
(Number)	(1,847)	(1,773)	(1,736)	(1,517)	(1,533)	(1,453)	(9,859)
Women							
Full-time employee	23	53	61	70	66	60	54
Part-time employee	1	1	2	2	2	5	2
Self-employed	0	0	0	0	1	1	0
Unemployed	6	5	4	6	5	5	5
Full-time student	69	38	26	10	9	8	28
Other	0	0	0	0	1	1	0
Inactive	2	4	7	11	17	21	10
Total Percentage	100	100	100	100	100	100	100
(Number)	(1,805)	(1,725)	(1,717)	(1,527)	(1,470)	(1,495)	(9,739)

1. The Labour Force Survey is conducted in the spring of each year. Those aged 16 at this time include both young people in the final year of compulsory schooling and young people from the previous school year.

their "usual" economic activity (mostly still at school) and, in a much smaller percentage of cases, young people who are taking a college-based YTS course.

It is, then, important to understand that, while a considerable amount of part-time work is done by young people, in the vast majority of cases part-time work represents an additional source of income and is not a substitute for a full-time job. However, as Ashton (1988a) has pointed

Table 9.2
Usual Economic Activity by Age, 1984 (Percentage)

	16[1]	17	18	Age 19	20	21	All
Men							
Full-time employee	10	31	47	59	58	58	43
Part-time employee	1	1	2	2	2	1	1
Self-employed	1	1	2	3	5	5	3
Government scheme	10	14	3	2	2	1	6
Unemployed	9	13	20	18	18	19	16
Full-time student	69	39	24	13	13	12	29
Other	0	0	0	0	1	0	0
Inactive	1	2	2	3	4	4	3
Total Percentage	100	100	100	100	100	100	100
(Number)	(1,366)	(1,434)	(1,298)	(1,277)	(1,255)	(1,272)	(7,902)
Women							
Full-time employee	9	31	42	51	53	53	39
Part-time employee	1	3	4	6	6	5	4
Self-employed	0	0	0	0	1	1	0
Government scheme	6	10	4	1	1	1	4
Unemployed	7	10	14	14	12	11	11
Full-time student	75	43	26	13	12	10	30
Other	0	0	0	0	0	1	0
Inactive	2	3	10	15	14	20	11
Total Percentage	100	100	100	100	100	100	100
(Number)	(1,282)	(1,341)	(1,269)	(1,221)	(1,236)	(1,229)	(7,578)

1. The Labour Force Survey is conducted in the spring of each year. Those aged 16 at this time include both young people in the final year of compulsory schooling and young people from the previous school year.

out, part-time work among students is much less frequent in Britain than in North America, and is largely confined to those still at school. The difference can, perhaps, be explained by the more elitist system of higher education in Britain, which provides government grants for those who obtain a place at a university or polytechnic with an intensive three-year course. These activities leave little time for paid work, except during the summer vacations. Because the interviews for the Labour Force Survey take place during May of each year, before the summer vacation begins, this major period of student employment is not recorded.

In 1984, of the 1 percent of young men and the 4 percent of young women aged 16 to 21 who recorded part-time work as their "usual" economic activity, the majority reported that they were working part time because they could not find a full-time job. Thus, for both men and women, there is a small number of those who take part-time work as a substitute for full-time work. However, for the vast majority of this age group, a YTS scheme provides the alternative to full-time work. It is, therefore, important to make a distinction between those young people who are working part time to supplement their income as students, and those who are working part time as a substitute for full-time work. They constitute two quite distinct types of part-time workers, with very different career trajectories, despite the fact that both may be doing similar kinds of work.

WHY SO FEW?

It is evident from the figures quoted that, despite the increase in part-time workers generally, and despite the high levels of youth unemployment, there has been only a limited increase in the percentage of young people who cite part-time work as their main employment status. Research carried out in 1985 by Roberts et al. (1987) in three contrasting areas of Britain (Liverpool, Chelmsford, and Walsall) found that those employers who were using more part-time labor at the expense of full-time workers were usually hiring women, with the effect that there were fewer jobs available for young people. Over half the employers in the study reported that they would not consider 16- to 17-year-olds for part-time work. Where part-time jobs for young people were available, Roberts et al. found that employers expressed a preference for students. They concluded: "In so far as any young people benefit from the division between core and peripheral work-forces, it seems likely to be those who continue at school or college beyond 16 . . . less qualified early leavers were more likely to have been squeezed out completely" (1987: 43). Ashton and Maguire (1983) have also argued that the growth of jobs in the service sector, which has accompanied the decline in manufacturing jobs over the last decade, has done little to provide work for young people. Rather, these jobs have been constructed on a part-time basis and recruit married women, thus accounting for the increase in part-time work among this section of the labor force.

Thus, there is evidence that where employers seek part-time workers, their preference is either for married women, who are seen by employers

as stable and hard-working, or for students, who are likely to be considerably better qualified and need less training than school-leavers. The
low levels of pay for women's part-time work (median gross hourly
earnings of £2.78 in 1988)[1] and the flexibility that employers achieve by
varying hours of work to meet fluctuating demand provide a considerable financial incentive to their employment. Where employers wish
to take on a school-leaver, government training schemes (YOP and YTS)
provide full-time school-leavers at a substantially subsidized rate of pay.
In 1988, YTS trainees were paid a flat rate of £28.50 per week at a time
when average gross weekly earnings were £88 for under 18 years of age
(New Earnings Survey, 1988). It is perhaps in recognition of the fact that
part-time work is usually constructed as unskilled, with few or no career
prospects and with levels of pay that are inadequate for a living wage,
that employers are reluctant to accept young people into part-time jobs.
Part-timers are invariably those who have another source of income,
such as women with working husbands or students who are working
on weekends or during vacations to supplement family support or stipends.

WHERE DO THEY WORK?

It is well established that part-timers are found predominantly in the
personal service sector, in sales work, and in clerical and secretarial jobs
(Martin and Roberts, 1984; Dale, 1987). A comparison from the 1984
Labour Force Survey of the occupational distribution of young people
working part-time with women over 21 working part time reveals that
these three occupational groups are of importance for all part-timers.
However, young people for whom part-time work does not form their
usual economic activity are mainly found in shop and other sales work
(44 percent), while 42 percent of all women over 21 in part-time work
are in personal service work, including catering, cleaning, and domestic
work. In terms of their occupational distribution, young people working
part time as their usual economic activity fall between these two groups.
This evidence lends support to the idea that, even within the part-time
labor market, there is some segmentation on the basis of age and gender.

THE EFFECT OF PART-TIME WORK ON THE CAREERS OF 16- TO 19-YEAR-OLDS

For the small percentage of young people who take part-time work
as a substitute for full-time work, there is evidence that it does, indeed,
have a depressing effect upon their employment prospects. The ESRC
16–19 Initiative provides some information on the effect of spells of part-

time work on the careers of young school leavers. This research program has studied the economic and political socialization of two age cohorts of young people over a three-year period. In four contrasting areas of Britain (Liverpool, Kirkaldy, Sheffield, and Swindon), a total of 6,000 young people have been surveyed at yearly intervals between 1987 and 1989. Work history data for the two years prior to the first survey in March 1987 show that, among the sample aged 17 to 18 at that time, those recording one or two spells of part-time work were more likely to be in full-time academic study at the time of the survey than those who had had no periods of part-time work. However, this contrast is quite simply explained by the fact that the former group is largely composed of young people remaining in education beyond 16 who took part-time work during the summer holidays.

Those for whom part-time work did not merely form a short interlude during a period of full-time study were much more likely to experience spells of unemployment and periods on a Youth Training Scheme. Only a very small number of young people (fewer than 2 percent of the sample) experienced periods of part-time work that extended continuously over more than six months out of the 27-month period. There is, then, little evidence of part-time work as a continuous employment status; rather, it is associated with marginal employment of short duration.

PART-TIME WORK AMONG THE UNDER 16s

The discussion so far has focused on young people who are past the permissible school-leaving age of 16. However, it is important to realize that much part-time work is done by younger schoolchildren for whom the income may form a very important supplement to pocket money. Evidence is again available from the ESRC 16–19 Initiative. The younger cohort (15 to 16 years old in 1987, and in their final year of compulsory schooling) were asked whether they were currently doing any part-time work or whether they had ever done any. Over 50 percent of youngsters in all four geographical areas had either current or past part-time jobs, although there was considerable variation by region, perhaps reflecting local levels of unemployment. Jobs recorded fell into a very narrow range, with shop work and paper routes accounting for about 60 percent of all jobs. The former was being done predominantly by girls and the latter by boys. For these young people, part-time work may actually improve job prospects, although evidence of this is not yet available. For example, a Saturday job at the hairdresser's may turn into a full-time apprenticeship.

SUMMARY

A radical transformation of the youth labor market has occurred in the past ten years. In contrast with the period ten years earlier, the most significant change has been that YTS has replaced full-time work as the major activity of 16-year-old school-leavers. Concomitantly, there has been a marked increase in the number of young people who stay on at school beyond age 16, often taking vocational, one-year courses. Despite rising youth unemployment and increasing levels of part-time work, there is very little evidence of a significant increase in young people who take part-time work as a substitute for full-time work. It is, therefore, important to make a distinction between those young people who are working part time to supplement their income as students, and those who are working part time as a substitute for full-time work. They constitute two quite distinct types of part-time workers, with very different career trajectories, despite the fact that both may be doing similar kinds of work.

It is perhaps in recognition of the fact that part-time work is usually constructed as unskilled, with few or no career prospects and with levels of pay that are inadequate for a living wage, that employers are reluctant to accept young people into part-time jobs. Part-timers are invariably those who have another source of income, such as women with working husbands or students who are working on weekends or during vacations to supplement family support or stipends.

Part-time work may provide young people with a welcome supplement to pocket money or to an educational grant. However, there is little evidence that it is forming a substitute for full-time work, despite the very high levels of youth unemployment in Britain during the 1980s. There are several reasons why this is so. Employers perceive part-time work as unsuitable for school-leavers, who are felt to need a "proper" job. The introduction of government training schemes (both YOP and YTS) represent, for young people, the promise of a channel into full-time work. At the same time, these schemes provide employers with a very inexpensive supply of youth labor.

NOTES

I would like to thank the Office of Population Censuses and Surveys (OPCS) for allowing the use of data from the Labour Force Survey, and the Economic and Social Research Council (ESRC) Data Archive for supplying these. The 16–18 Initiative has been funded by the ESRC and involves research teams from the Universities of Edinburgh, Dundee, Liverpool, Sheffield and Swindon.

1. The New Earnings Survey (NES) in the United Kingdom underestimates earnings of part-time workers as it omits about one third of all part-timers. Part-

timers omitted from the NES are those who do not earn enough to fall within the government's National Insurance payment scheme. Although earnings are based upon weekly totals, there is, nonetheless, a tendency for those with low hourly earnings to be excluded.

10 Women's Part-Time Work in Britain and the United States

Shirley Dex

INTRODUCTION

Part-time employment has been growing in industrialized countries over the past few decades, but far more in some countries than in others. What is common to all is that women constitute the bulk of the part-time work force. Why this should be so is an interesting question. A study by the Organization for Economic Cooperation and Development (OECD, 1983) reported that there is a close relationship between the overall participation rate of females and the evolution of part-time employment among industrialized countries. It is not a coincidence, therefore, that women are the new part-time work force, since it would appear that their increased participation in employment has occurred through part-time work.

One can gain some understanding of the growth of part-time women's employment by considering a single country. There are, however, richer data and wider issues to be explored when countries are compared. In particular, differences in socioeconomic policies between countries and their relative effects can be explored through comparative studies. This paper sets out to examine women's part-time work in Britain and the United States. The issues that will be explored through this framework are as follows: What influences the extent of part-time women's employment? What sort of jobs are part-time jobs? Why is it that women are filling these jobs? These issues will be explored through the literature on part-time work in Britain and the United States, and through comparisons between surveys of women in the two countries to which the author has had access: the Women and Employment Survey in Britain and the two women's cohorts of the National Longitudinal Surveys in the United States.[1]

Britain and the United States allow an interesting comparison on these issues because Britain has a particularly high incidence of part-time women's employment, whereas the United States has a much lower rate. This comparison will offer insights into the policy differences behind the extent of part-time employment in the two countries, and also into the role played by industrial structures and by supply and demand factors.

THE EXTENT OF PART-TIME EMPLOYMENT

In citing statistics on the extent of part-time work, one has to bear in mind that definitions of what counts as part time differ between countries. Official published statistics from Britain use a definition for most occupations of less than 31 hours per week. (Teachers are treated separately, and work part time if they work less than 22 hours per week.) In the United States, official statistics tend to use less than 35 hours per week as the definition. Some surveys allow the respondents to define themselves as either full or part time. The matter of which definition to use is not trivial. The conditions of work and the contractual positions of employees might be related to the contractual hours of work in the two countries, such that employees working less than 30 hours in Britain but less than 35 hours in the United States both have more vulnerable conditions of work. If this were the case, then to impose the same hours definition on the two countries would hide some of the extent of their similarities. False conclusions would arise, similarly, if the reverse occurred and employees working less than, say, 30 hours had similar conditions of work in both countries, even though the official definitions were different. This problem does not have a simple solution. Investigations of the conditions of work and statutory rights attached to part-time work in the two countries revealed that these were linked neither to 30 hours per week in Britain, nor to 35 hours per week in the United States. However, it is not possible to compare all the individual contractual positions that part-time employees have with their employers in the two countries. The evidence suggests that they vary enormously (Kamerman and Kahn, 1987). However, in the light of these differences, it seems to be reasonable to take a common 30-hours-per-week definition of part time for both countries, when comparing the survey data.

The OECD (1983) review reported that 42 percent of employed British women worked part time in 1981, and 24 percent of U.S. women. In 1983, these figures were largely unchanged. Both countries had experienced some growth in the extent of part-time work among women, but it was obviously greater in Britain than in the United States. Britain

Table 10.1
Usual Hours Worked per Week (Excludes Overtime)

Hours per Week	Younger Women (%) (26-36 in 1980)		Older Women (%) (44-58 in 1980)	
	Britain	U.S.A.	Britain	U.S.A.
0-9	9.6	3.5	6.6	2.3
10-19	21.4	5.9	16.0	5.8
20-30	25.8	13.6	27.4	16.5
31-34	4.6	2.5	5.7	2.7
35-39	21.5	11.8	22.8	13.1
40+	17.1	62.7	21.5	59.6
Total	100	100	100	100
(Number)	(809)	(2,254)	(1,114)	(2,027)

Sources: For Britain, The Women and Employment Survey of 1980 and, for the United States, the National Longitudinal Surveys, from Dex, Shirley, and Lois Shaw. British and American Women at Work. 1986, Basingstoke: Macmillan, page 25.

was among countries like Sweden and Norway with the highest rates, and the United States was among those, like France, with fairly low rates, although not the very lowest. Finland had only 8 percent of employed women in part-time work in 1981.

The surveys of women's employment in Britain and the United States provide some more detailed information about the extent of part-time work. It is not always possible to find surveys that use the same definitions, and this poses problems for comparative studies. We are able to make direct comparisons using similar categories from two surveys in 1980–81, for two similarly-aged cohorts of women. A breakdown of the usual hours worked by women in 1980 (Table 10.1) shows that 50 percent of British part-timers worked between 20 and 30 hours per week, whereas 60 percent or more of American part-timers fell into this category. Similarly, about 40 percent of British full-time workers worked 40 or more hours a week compared with 80 percent of American full-time workers. If the U.S. definition of part-time work were adopted (less than 35 hours), the differences between the two countries would still be great. The clusterings in the United States and Britain are very similar, with most women working part time for 20 to 30 hours per week and full time for over 35 hours per week. The results from surveys that used slightly different coding categories for hours of work are displayed in Table 10.2 using 1986 data. In the case of the U.S. figures, men and women are both included, but the majority of part-timers are women. U.S. part-timers tend to work longer hours than their British counter-parts.

Estimates of how these differences in the extent of part-time work translate into patterns of women's work history, from the 1980 work history data, are as follows: older British women (in their forties and fifties in 1980) had been employed for about 57 percent of the previous 13 years, compared with 52 percent of the time for U.S. women. More than one half of the employment time of these British women was spent in part-time jobs. An estimate for the American women suggests they spent only 20 to 25 per cent of their employment time in part-time work over these years.

There is also a strong life-cycle aspect to the choice of part-time em-ployment by British women. Very few British people work part-time when they first start work whereas in the United States part-time em-ployment is relatively common at this point, in conjunction with being a student. As many as two thirds of British women who take a break from work to have their first child return to a part-time job. The amount of part-time employment stays relatively constant thereafter, at an ag-gregate level, although individual British women may well be moving between part- and full-time jobs to some extent. In most countries, part-time employment becomes more common as retirement age approaches. The rates of part-time employment among U.S. women stay relatively constant over their life-cycle changes, after the initially higher incidence concurrent with education. These differences are visible in the figures in Table 10.3, where the proportions of women in different age groups who worked part time in 1983–84 are displayed.

OCCUPATIONS AND PART-TIME JOBS

It has become clear that part-time jobs are not distributed evenly across the occupational structure. They tend to be predominant in the lower levels of occupations. Women are already segregated into certain types of occupations. Part-time employment may well be augmenting this occupational segregation. The distribution of occupations, according to whether women defined themselves as working full or part time, is given in Table 10.4 for Britain and the United States, from 1983–84 data. It is evident from these figures that full-time jobs carry higher status (and presumably, greater rewards in pay) than part-time jobs in both coun-tries. The differences in status are more marked in Britain, and there are more U.S. part-time jobs at the top non-manual end of the occu-pational hierarchy than in Britain. In the United States, 24 percent of

Table 10.2
Hours of Work in 1986

Britain: Usual Hours Worked per Week (Married Women)	
Hours	*Percent*
0-10	9
11-15	9
16-30	36
31-35	4
36-40	29
41+	12
Total	100

United States: Hours of Work of Women in 1986	
Hours	*Percent*
< 30	19.5
30-34	9.4
35-39	9.7
40	42.1
41-48	8.9
49+	10.4
Total	100

Sources: For Britain, the Labour Force Survey of 1986, and for the United States, the Monthly Labor Review, April 1988.

Table 10.3
Women Working Part-Time in Britain and the U.S.A. by Age, 1983–84
(Percentage)

			Age Group		
	16-24[1]	25-34	35-44	45-54	55-64
Britain	16.0	39.4	54.5	50.5	54.1
U.S.A.	27.2	22.0	25.3	24.4	25.8

1. 18-24 in the U.S.A.

Source: Dale, Angela, and J. Glover. A Comparative Analysis of Women's Employment Patterns in the United Kingdom, France and the United States of America. Report to the Department of Employment, London, 1987.

Table 10.4
Occupational Distribution of Women in Britain and the U.S.A., 1983–84
(Percentage)

	Britain		U.S.A.	
	Full-time	Part-time	Full-time	Part-time
Professional & technical	20	13	22	18
Administrative & managerial	3	1	13	6
Clerical & related	38	21	37	35
Sales	10	16	5	6
Services	13	38	11	23
Agricultural	1	1	0	1
Production	15	9	12	11
Total	100	100	100	100
(Number)	(20,417)	(14,730)	(642)	(206)

Source: Based on the Labor Force Survey and the General Social Survey.

part-time jobs were in professional or administrative/managerial jobs, compared with only 14 percent of British part-time jobs. The latter are more heavily concentrated in services than are U.S. part-time jobs.

We can see more detail from the occupations of similar age groups of British and American women at the same point in their life cycle, from 1980 data in Table 10.5, showing their last job before having a first child.[2] There are similarities in the distributions of British and American women; in both, clerical work is the most common occupation, account-

CONCLUSIONS

Part-time work has a detrimental effect on women's status in both Britain and the United States. The employment position of British women with children is considerably worse than that of their American counterparts. This is partly because the extent of part-time employment is so much greater in Britain, and because part-time jobs in Britain are more likely than those in the United States to be in low-level occupations. Why this should be so is worth further consideration.

Much of the earliest British research traced the distribution of part-time employment through the structure of industrial employment, and particularly its predominance in service industries (G. Clark, 1982; D. Robinson, 1979; Elias and Main, 1982). A study by Owen (1979) of part-time work in the United States tested a number of hypotheses, and the results are similar to the early investigations of part-time work in Britain. Owen found that employers' preferences for part-time work were relatively weak in sectors where pay levels were high relative to the education of the work force, that employers were more likely to use part-time work where there was a technical need for it, and that employers tended to create part-time jobs where demographic factors were favorable. Given that part-time jobs are predominantly in services and also tend to be low-skilled, more recent research has focused on other questions, some of which arise from the particular distribution of part-time jobs. The recent research can be classified under a number of headings. Researchers have been concerned with the demand-side factors that have contributed to the growth of part-time employment (Beechey and Perkins, 1987; Robinson and Wallace, 1984b). The supply-side factors have also been examined, and some attempts have been made to sort out the relative importance of supply versus demand explanations of the growth (Dex, 1984; Dex, 1988).

In addition, consideration has been given to the role part-time work is playing in women's occupational segregation (Dex, 1987; Martin and Roberts, 1984). The legal and contractual positions of part-time women are being documented, as is the position that government has taken with respect to part-time work (Briar, 1987; see also Briar in this volume); this enables a comparison to be made between the de facto employment status of part-time workers and their actual position and conditions over business-cycle fluctuations. British sociologists are also now debating the theoretical and conceptual role that part-time employment is playing in the capitalist and patriarchal structuring of employment (Walby, 1987; Beechey and Perkins, 1987). These authors argue that the growth in women's part-time employment has arisen primarily because of employers' desire for flexibility. The desire for flexibility has grown alongside the restructuring of the British economy from the late 1970s onward, as manufacturing industries have declined markedly and service industries have grown. Women's part-time employment even continued to increase in the early 1980s in Britain during a period of severe recession. Part-time employment is a much more vulnerable type of employment in Britain, because employment protection and legislative rights are linked to hours of work according to criteria that often disqualify part-timers. Part-timers were not made redundant to any greater extent than full-timers in the 1980s recession of the British economy. This is probably because employers were busy restructuring their work forces away from full-time and toward part-time work over this period. In the future, part-timers will undoubtedly be vulnerable in the service industries, where costs are often predominantly labor costs, and where profit margins are under considerable pressure from competition.

The growth in part-time work also suits British women's preferences, to some extent, because it provides a way of combining paid work and child care. Part-time employment exploits women's position as child bearer and child rearer. In the face of a lack of provision for child care in Britain, or expensive child care without any ameliorating effects from the tax system, British women's choices are constrained. It has been argued, therefore, that part-time work is the latest form of patriarchal relations between men and women in the work place in Britain, allowing men to exploit women's position. While part-time work appears to satisfy women's preferences, it also exploits their position, at a certain time in their life cycle, in a way that often depreciates their skill, lowers their earnings, and reduces their capacity or desire to argue for improvements in working conditions, for the rest of their potential careers. These disadvantages of part-time work are not inherent in the work, but they are characteristic of the type of part-time work generated, certainly in Britain.

In seeking to understand why there is more part-time work in Britain than in the United States, a number of possible explanations are worth exploring. Supply-side factors could be operating through women's preferences and the constraints they face. Demand-side factors could be important, working through the structure of opportunities. Policies and legislation could also provide important clues. These are not necessarily mutually exclusive explanations. Indeed, it would be surprising if social policies did not affect both supply and demand sides.

On the supply side, British women may well have a greater preference for part-time work because of the child-care responsibilities that they face. It is likely, however, that British women's preference for part-time work is related to the child-care constraints they face. If a woman wants to work after childbirth, in a context where women are seen as having primary responsibility for child care, then taking a part-time job and relying on husbands or close relatives to look after the children while she is at work, as many British women do, is one way of achieving the two objectives. There are no provisions or policies in Britain that help to offset the costs of child care for the individual. In the United States, at least some child-care expense can be offset against taxes. Not surprisingly, more American women choose to pay for child care and to work full time. Part of the American women's apparently greater preference for full-time employment, therefore, is the result of the favorable tax provisions for child-care expenses that have been operating in the United States since the 1970s. It is also the case that American women receive benefits from working full time. The most important of these is that most employers pay for health insurance for full-time employees in the United States, but few provide insurance for part-time workers. The escalating costs of health care in the United States make this a valuable benefit. Clearly, it is not an incentive to British women to work full time, since they receive health care free. In this way, the social policy provisions in the two countries are having an indirect effect on women's occupational status. Since far more American women are single parents, there are also greater financial pressures on them, acting as an incentive to choose full-time work. The attitudes of British and American women toward work and home roles seem to be fairly similar. However, it could well be that British women think of part-time employment, but not full-time employment, as socially acceptable, whereas American women may find either part- or full-time employment acceptable.

However, British women's preference for part-time work cannot be the only reason for Britain's having more part-time jobs. There are favorable conditions for British employers who take on part-time workers, and this demand-side consideration has undoubtedly played some part in creating part-time opportunities in Britain. Martin and Roberts's analysis (1984) of the Women and Employment Survey found that the hours worked by part-time women peaked just below the 16 hours after which employees are eligible for greater employment protection in law and, probably, for more fringe benefits from their employers. Case studies of British firms and industries confirm that some employers have switched to employing more part-time employees to benefit from these provisions (Robinson and Wallace, 1984b), although there are additional overheads and recruitment costs involved in employing part-timers. Owen (1979) points out that these additional costs are extensive in the United States, especially if the nature of the work does not require part-time employees. In the United States, there are no offsetting employee insurance advantages, so that the additional costs are sufficient to dissuade U.S. employers from offering much part-time work. Nonetheless, part-time work has been increasing in the United States. Owen thinks part of the cause of the increase is that the structure of the U.S. economy has been changing and jobs in services have been on the increase. Also, employers have been more likely to create part-time jobs where there is a ready supply of labor, notably, female labor.

Far more of the part-time jobs in Britain are in low-skilled, often public sector jobs, where the nature of the work appears to demand a part-time commitment. Cleaners, dinner ladies in schools, and home helps are examples of this type of work. In these cases, the greater number of part-time jobs in Britain is partly linked to Britain's welfare state. There is no reason, however, to think that the United States has any less need for some of these jobs. Jobs like part-time cleaning and, to lesser extent, part-time clerical or secretarial jobs, are not part-time jobs to the same extent in the United States, possibly because contract agencies have proliferated more in the United States. These offer employers part-time services, but they offer workers full-time jobs. American researchers have started to document a growth in what they call "new concept part-time work" (Kahne, 1985). These newer part-time jobs are essentially those which have prorated fringe benefits attached, are more permanent, and have career structures. Their growth offers some explanation as to why U.S. part-time jobs are better than the British ones. However, it is not clear why U.S. employers should value part-time jobs at higher levels, whereas British employers are more reluctant to do so. Kahne's discussion of these new types of part-time work does not really resolve this question. Demographic factors, in particular the aging population, are the only reason offered for the increase in this sort of employment, since these sorts of jobs are thought to benefit older workers. Also, the United States had several short-lived policies to encourage their growth between 1978 and 1981; these stopped with the unfavorable economic climate of the 1980s, which brought changes in government policy. A set of demand considerations makes part-time work preferable in Britain. They are brought about by a mixture of policy measures and private initiatives, and they contribute, mostly indirectly, to British women's greater downward occupational mobility.

It is worth noting that the legislation outlawing discrimination against women in employment does not so obviously apply to part-time employment; the contractual position of part-time workers is often much weaker than for full-time workers, so that equal opportunities legislation offers few benefits to the former. Some recent British court cases have served to strengthen the position of part-time employees, particularly with respect to redundancy (Robinson and Wallace, 1984b). Since women are the predominant holders of part-time jobs, they are less likely to be discriminated against in recruitment to these jobs. Men are less likely to compete for what are predominantly lower-skilled jobs. Nonetheless, the potential benefits from equal opportunities legislation in Britain are much weaker than in the United States by virtue of British women's greater predominance in part-time work. An increase in the availability of part-time jobs in the higher-grade occupations in Britain would not necessarily improve women's security under law, although almost certainly it would improve their status, as it has done in the United States.

There might well be an environmental effect from the more aggressive pursuit of equal opportunities for American women. This environmental effect appears to have opened up more opportunities to them, and it has raised their overall status in the eyes of employers. By contrast, British employers probably see women much more as a part-time and marginal work force, suitable for lower-skilled "women's" jobs and, in fact, not protected by legislation to the same extent as full-time workers, especially if they work fewer than 16 hours. To the extent that part-time work continues to grow in both countries, the evidence suggests, on balance, that it will work against improving women's status and potential in the eyes of employers.

NOTES

1. A more extensive comparison of women's employment in the two countries, using these surveys, is contained in Dex and Shaw (1986), which also contains details about the two countries' surveys.

2. The original American occupational categories were recoded to be equivalent to the classification used in the British survey.

11 Part-Time Employment among Canadian Women: A Nexus between Capitalism and Patriarchy

Ann Duffy and Norene Pupo

Future commentators looking back on the twentieth century will no doubt see the massive movement of women into the paid labor force as one of the most significant sociological events of the century. In 1901, only one in seven Canadian women worked for pay and women made up a meager 13 percent of the total paid work force (Phillips and Phillips, 1983: 35). By 1988, more than half of all women worked for pay and women constituted 44 percent of the total labor force (Parliament, 1990: 100).

Not only has the female paid labor force increased phenomenally (women accounted for two thirds of the growth in employment between 1975 and 1988), but also its composition has been fundamentally altered (Parliament, 1990: 100). In 1900, the majority of female paid workers were single, aged 15 to 24, for whom marriage and children would mean withdrawal or expulsion from paid employment (Armstrong and Armstrong, 1988: 150). Even at mid-century (1951), only one in ten married women was employed, and married women made up less than one third of the female paid labor force (Phillips and Phillips, 1983: 36). Today, more than half of all married women work for pay (Canada. Labour Canada, 1987: 4). No longer does marriage or children necessarily exclude women from paid employment. Seventy percent of women with children aged 6 to 15 are employed; more than half of women with children 3 to 5 years of age, and slightly less than half of women with at least one child under 3, work in the paid labor force (Canada. Statistics Canada, 1985: 5). The relationship between gender, family, and paid employment is in the midst of fundamental alteration. In this process, new connections between capitalism and patriarchy are being forged.

A crucial element in this transformation of women's labor force participation has been the unprecedented expansion of part-time work. For increasing numbers of women, part-time work is the pivot in their relationship with capitalism and patriarchy. Part-time employment allows women to participate, albeit peripherally, in paid employment while not jeopardizing or straining the patriarchal structure of familial life. The part-time nurse, sales clerk, or cashier contributes to the family income, but still, presumably, has the time and energy to shoulder the lion's share of domestic and child-care work. Women's traditional role as economic dependent, secondary income earner, and family custodian is left intact by most forms of part-time work. Today, more than one in four (25.4 percent) of employed Canadian women work part time, and women make up over 71 percent of the over 2 million workers who are employed part-time (Canada. Statistics Canada, 1989: 87–88). This phenomenon is not restricted to Canada. In the United States, one in six workers was employed part time in 1989 and 75 percent of these workers were women (Thurman and Trah, 1990: 27).

In the 1970s and on into the 1980s, part-time work exploded in most industrialized nations. In Western countries more than 35 million people hold part-time jobs. In Norway, 25.6 percent, in the United Kingdom 24.7 percent, in Sweden 24.4 percent, in the Netherlands 21 percent, in Australia 20.1 percent, in the United States 17.3 percent, in Canada 15.2 percent, and in Japan 12 percent of all workers work part time (International Labour Office, 1989: 33). In Austria, Australia, France, and Switzerland, about one in 10 workers is a part-timer (ILO Information, 1986: 1; *The Economist*, 1984: 61). In many countries, part-time jobs have grown much faster than full-time employment opportunities. For example, Canadian part-time employment jumped 83.2 percent between 1975 and 1986, while total employment rose by only 25.3 percent (Lévesque, 1987: 88). Viewed from a slightly different perspective, between 1975 and 1985 part-time employment in Canada grew by 78 percent, while full-time employment grew by only 15 percent (Burke, 1986: 10). Similarly, between 1973 and 1983 in the Federal Republic of Germany, the Netherlands, Sweden, and the United Kingdom, while there was negative full-time growth, part-time jobs mushroomed by 65.4 percent, 45.3 percent, 37.2 percent, and 21.9 percent respectively (ILO Information, 1986: 1; see also Yamada, 1985). Throughout these countries, women comprise the overwhelming majority (from 60 to 90 percent) of part-time workers (ILO, 1989: 35).

The clear impression emerging from this statistical portrait is that part-time work is a significant component, particularly of women's employment, in most modern Western economies. While this overall conclusion is no doubt correct, it is important to point out that the term "part-time work" has not been employed in a consistent and clear fashion. For example, from 1953 to 1975, the Canadian Labour Force Survey defined part-time work as working less than 35 hours a week. In 1975, this was revised to 30 hours a week. However, other Canadian government agencies employ other standards. The Ontario Labour Relations Board, for example, defines a part-time employee as one who works less than 24 hours a week (Pupo and Duffy, 1988). The United States opted for a more flexible approach, defining part-time employment as "regularly recurring work performed on a schedule of from 16 to 32 hours per week" (Canada. Commission of Inquiry into Part-time Work, 1983: 39). In the European Labour Force Sample Surveys, respondents are asked to indicate "both the number of hours that are usually worked by their colleagues and the number they themselves actually worked during the reference week; if the actual hours are fewer than the usual hours, they are counted as part-time workers—even if they describe themselves as full-time workers" (de Neubourg, 1985: 559).

These various definitions may obscure the realities of part-time work schedules. For example, part-time female workers in Ontario average only 16.6 hours of work per week (Robb and Gunderson, 1987: 9). Other studies call attention to the widely varying hours (from no hours to 30 or more per week) that part-timers will work during any given period (Canada. Commission of Inquiry into Part-time Work, 1983: 60). Finally, statistics resulting from diverse definitions may or may not adequately differentiate between the many different types of part-time workers (Canada. Commission of Inquiry into Part-time Work, 1983: 37):

1. regular or permanent employees;
2. casual or contingent (on-call) employees;
3. temporary, short-term employees;
4. job sharers
5. part-timers who have temporarily accepted reduced worktime;
6. seasonal or part-year workers;
7. contract part-timers;
8. those engaged in phased retirement part-time work

Discussion of general trends in part-time work and of the overall characteristics of part-time workers should not obscure these important differences in the definitions, the realities of part-time work schedules, and the types of part-time work.

CANADIAN RESEARCH ON WOMEN AND PART-TIME WORK

Prior to 1970, Canadian women's participation in part-time work aroused relatively little discussion or research interest. *The Report of the*

Royal Commission on the Status of Women in Canada (Canada, 1970) serves as a useful signpost for the beginning of serious inquiries into the nature and implications of the growing female part-time labor force. The Report contained two contradictory themes, which today continue to echo through research and analysis. Although the Royal Commission recognized that part-time workers were subject to exploitation with the denial of fringe benefits, low wages, and exclusion from collective agreements (144,125), it ultimately recommended that the federal government explore the possibility of "greater use of part-time work in the Canadian economy" (399). Despite submissions to the contrary, the Royal Commission concluded that part-time work would alleviate some housewives' alienation from society by allowing them entry into employment, would permit women who wanted or needed to supplement their income to do so, and would ensure women up-to-date skills and experience when they returned to the full-time labor force (104–105). With some misgivings, the Royal Commission endorsed the part-time work alternative for women.

In the decades that followed, the pros and cons of part-time work for women were vigorously scrutinized. In the 1970s and early 1980s, a variety of government reports (for example, Pollack, 1981), union reports, and discussion papers concerning part-time work appeared. The most noteworthy and comprehensive review of the issue was Bossen's *Part-Time Work in the Canadian Economy* (1975). However, it was only in the late 1970s and early 1980s that academic and popular interest in the topic began to flourish. At the turn of the decade, Weeks published several seminal articles that focused on the exploitation of part-time workers (Weeks, 1978; 1980a; Duffy and Weeks, 1981). These articles examined the nature of employers' attitudes toward part-time women workers, identified some of the implications of government definitions and conceptions of part-time work for the unionization of part-timers, and attempted to develop an analysis of the relationship between the expansion of part-time work and the recurring crises of capitalism. A foundation was laid for further inquiry.

Finally, in 1983, the study of women's part-time employment came of age with the publication of two reports that irrevocably entrenched part-time work as a key issue in women's employment. White (1983) provided the first extensive and detailed discussion of women's employment as part-time workers. She focused first on the contradictory aspects of part-time schedules that simultaneously free women from some of the pressures of the double day while exploiting them in terms of benefits, pay, job security, and other extrinsic and intrinsic sources of job satisfaction. She went on to explore the relationship between part-time work and the economy in terms of the concentration of women part-time workers in the service and trade sectors, and the relationship between the expansion of part-time work and economic recession. White also examined the complexities of union issues surrounding part-time work, and discussed some of the implications of employment standards legislation, labor relations laws, social welfare legislation, and human rights laws for part-time workers. White concluded by arguing that women's part-time employment must be recognized as a long-term feature of the modern Canadian economy. Whether women (and men) part-timers were used or misused depended, in White's view, on unions' efforts to organize the majority of part-time workers who are not unionized, and on the introduction of protective government legislation.

Also in 1983, the *Report of the Commission of Inquiry into Part-time Work* was published. Although the authors of the Report did not focus exclusively on women part-timers, their wide-ranging examination and discussion of part-time work became the cornerstone for many subsequent investigations. The Commission reviewed the advantages and disadvantages of part-time work schedules, looked into the issue of definitions, described the characteristics of part-time workers and their jobs, reviewed diverse viewpoints on part-time work (unions, women's organizations, employers, governments, part-time employees), examined the issues of pensions and prorated benefits for part-time workers, and concluded with a discussion of job sharing as a new approach to part-time work. The countrywide public hearings that preceded publication, the publication itself, and its recommendations, permanently established part-time work as a fundamental employment issue.

Subsequent research on Canadian women's part-time work and related issues has increased exponentially. Analysts have studied the implications of part-time work for full-time employment (Jane Stinson, 1984), and the continued expansion of part-time work (Burke, 1986); they have considered part-time workers from a legal perspective (England, 1986) and have conducted research on the causes of part-time work growth (Lévesque, 1987), part-time unemployment rates (Clemenson, 1987), involuntary part-time work (Akyeampong, 1987), as well as the work satisfaction and job attitudes of part-time workers (Levanoni and Sales, 1988; DeHaney, 1988). They have examined part-time work as a strategy for balancing family and work responsibilities (Duffy and Pupo, 1986; Pupo, 1989). Analysts have also provided updated comprehensive examinations of part-time employment (Coates, 1988), and the mass media have identified part-time work as a significant public issue (*The Globe and Mail*, July 25, 1986; Cheney, 1988).

Following up on the 1983 Commission of Inquiry into Part-time Work, Labour Canada conducted a large-scale survey of federally regulated companies to determine the employment situation of their part-time workers, the numbers of part-time workers currently receiving fringe benefits, the cost of prorating all benefits, and the attitudes of part-time employees toward fringe benefit coverage (Canada. Labour Canada, 1985; 1986). The work conditions of specific kinds of part-time employees (nurses, teachers, academics) have also received research attention (Lundy and Warme in this volume; Warme and Lundy, 1986 and 1988a). Almost without exception, recent analyses of women's employment have included a discussion of part-time work as a central dimension of women's paid and unpaid labor (Lowe and Krahn, 1985; Armstrong, 1984; Armstrong and Armstrong, 1984; Michelson, 1985; Luxton, 1987; Armstrong and Armstrong, 1988). Women's part-time employment has been firmly and centrally established as a key women's issue.

From this emerging body of research and analysis, the basic dimensions of part-time work for Canadian women—who works part time, why they work part time, where they work, and how they feel about their part-time employment—are taking shape. In this process various perspectives on part-time work for women, are being clarified and refined. Some analysts, including many unionists are documenting the role of part-time work in the erosion of full-time employment and as a key component in the exploitation of peripheral workers. Others argue that the popularity of part-time work testifies to the necessity of alternative work schedules for women (and men). From this viewpoint, the expansion of part-time work, with complete prorated benefits, is to be applauded; it provides workers with a valuable alternative to the traditional full-time workweek without depriving employers of a more flexible work force. The future of part-time work for Canadian women depends both on the emerging patterns of part-time employment and on the policies toward part-time work that are currently being developed by government agencies, organized labor, employers, and women's groups.

THE DIMENSIONS OF WOMEN'S PART-TIME EMPLOYMENT

The most striking feature of part-time employment in Canada is the overrepresentation of women. Throughout the modern industrialized countries, women form the overwhelming majority of part-time workers. While 26.3 percent of employed Canadian women were working part time in 1988, only 8.4 percent of men were part-timers (Canada. Statistics Canada, 1988: 56). Between 1975 and 1985, the number of women employed part time increased by 84 percent, while full-time employment for women increased by only 31 percent (Burke, 1986: 10). Between 1975 and 1988, one third of all employment growth for women was in part-time work (Parliament, 1990: 102). Similarly, in the United States, 66 percent of all part-time employees in 1985 were women. While 27 percent of employed women were part-timers, only 10 percent of men had part-time employment (Nardone, 1986: 16). This pattern of female predominance in part-time work typifies industrialized countries (de Neubourg, 1985: 562, 564; Yamada, 1985: 706).

Typically, women who work part time are also married. In 1983, 79 percent or more of female part-timers in France, the Federal Republic of Germany, the Netherlands, and the United Kingdom were married (de Neubourg, 1985: 566; *Employment Gazette*, 1982: 479). In the United States, six of 10 women who work part time are married (Nardone, 1986: 16). In each country, significant numbers of unmarried young men (and women) also work part time. For example, in 1985, 80 percent of the 6.3 million Americans aged 16 to 24 who were in school and also employed were working part time (Nardone, 1986: 16). In Canada, 19.6 percent of all part-timers are men aged 15 to 24, and approximately 23 percent are women aged 15 to 24 (Canada. Statistics Canada, 1988: 56). It is this split in the North American part-time labor force between young, student part-time workers and older, married female part-timers that explains why Canadian part-timers are almost equally divided into married and single ranks, but 86.5 percent of all married part-time workers are women (Canada. Statistics Canada, 1988: 56). In general, it seems that the part-time worker is typically either young (student), disabled, female (often married), or older (ILO Information, 1986: 1). While single women may also find part-time work attractive, it is generally "very popular among *married* women in Sweden and the United Kingdom, fairly popular in Canada, the Federal Republic of Germany, and the United States, and only moderately popular in France and the Netherlands" (emphasis added) (de Neubourg, 1985: 569).

The part-time worker, frequently married and female, tends to work in the community, business, and personal services sector of the Canadian economy (Lévesque, 1987). The Commission of Inquiry into Part-time Work found that 75 percent of Canadian part-time workers were in the service industries of trade (wholesale and retail), and community, business, and personal services (Canada. Commission of Inquiry into Part-Time Work, 1983: 58). In 1988, 20.4 percent of all service sector workers were part time, while this was true of only 6 percent of goods-producing workers (Canada. Statistics Canada, 1988: 58). Throughout the industrialized countries, as these sectors of the economy grew, so too did part-time employment (de Neubourg, 1985: 569). Presently, three quarters of part-time workers are employed in the service sector (ILO, 1989: 37; de Neubourg, 1985: 569).

This pattern is reflected in the types of occupations part-time workers hold. In 1988, 86 percent of Canadian part-timers were in service, clerical, sales, or managerial/professional occupations (Canada. Statistics Canada, 1988: 58). A recent survey of 270 federally regulated Canadian companies found that 53 percent of all part-time employees were clerical or office workers such as bank tellers or bookkeepers. (Canada. Labour

Canada, 1985: 23). Research in Britain suggests a similar concentration in a narrow range of occupations (Beechey and Perkins, 1987: 32). Forty percent of British female part-time workers work in personal services occupations, such as catering, cleaning, and hairdressing (*Employment Gazette*, 1982: 481). Further, it seems that these part-time occupations, generally held by women, are even more sex-segregated than full-time female occupations. For example, one study found that 75 percent of part-time women workers worked only with women (Beechey and Perkins, 1987: 33). In many respects, part-time work is an important facet of the employment ghettoization of women workers.

THE COSTS AND BENEFITS OF PART-TIME EMPLOYMENT FOR WOMEN

Women's presence in the part-time labor force is generally accounted for in terms of their efforts to balance the conflicting demands of domestic labor and child care with the need to contribute to family income. Part-time work attracts women because it allows them to respond to strong ideological pressures to stay home with their children (White, 1983: 11), while also meeting the increasing need for two family-income earners (Armstrong and Armstrong, 1984: 174–175). The impact of the family's financial situation is borne out by a direct relationship between husband's income and wife's employment status. Husbands with high incomes are more likely to have wives who are not employed, and vice versa. Part-time women workers have husbands with a middling income (Michelson, 1985: 39).

The pressure of family responsibilities as part of the explanation of women's part-time work schedules is supported by the relationship between the age of children and the percentage of part-time women workers. Among women who are employed, more women (35 percent) with preschool children than women (31 percent) with children aged 6 to 15 work part time (Canada. Statistics Canada, 1985: 45; Michelson, 1985: 38). The impact of family responsibilities is also reflected in the fact that the majority of married women part-timers (54.7 percent) indicate that they do not want full-time work (Canada. Statistics Canada, 1988: 59). A 1986 survey of part-time workers found that the most common reason given for preferring part-time work was child-care responsibilities (Canada. Labour Canada, 1986: 20). In 1988, about 10 percent of female part-timers gave "family or personal responsibilities" as their reason for working part time. Finally, a rich variety of interview data also suggest that many women view part-time work as a useful strategy for coping with the role overload of domestic and paid work (Pupo, 1989: 93; Michelson, 1985: 43–50).

The explosion in part-time work for women must also be addressed in light of general socioeconomic conditions, including the growth in services and trade, the introduction of new technology, the growing recognition of cost savings from a flexible part-time work force, the general movement of women into the paid labor force, and as a response to recession and unemployment (White, 1983: 36–48). Some recent research suggests that since 1975 part-time work has increased in Canada, not because of a structural change in the economy, but primarily because all industries now "rely more on part-time work than they did in the past" (Lévesque, 1987: 101).

While individual women may understand their part-time work in personal, voluntaristic terms, economic conditions have created the possibilities of part-time employment. This work pattern is perfectly suited to the growing service sector of the economy with its deskilled tasks and its peaks and valleys of work activity (Garson, 1988). Fast-food restaurants, shops, and personal service outlets, for example, need a flexible work force that is quickly trained, easily replaced, and available on call for certain busy periods of the day, week, month, or year. Further, employers prefer not only the flexibility of part-time work scheduling but also the relative cost.

The part-time work that boomed in the 1970s and 1980s was frequently characterized by low wages and few, if any, benefits. Sick leave, vacation pay, statutory holidays, medical insurance, pensions, and other benefits were often not provided at all, or only in a limited fashion (Weeks, 1980b). As work-related benefits exceed 30 percent of employment costs, the denial of benefits to part-time workers represents a significant cost saving for employers. Today, many part-timers still receive few or no benefits. A survey of federally regulated industries found that 43 percent of part-time workers received paid vacations, 17 percent were given money instead of vacations, and 28 percent could choose time or money. Ten percent received neither vacations nor money. Of these workers, 33 percent received pensions, 62 percent had extended health care, 63 percent dental insurance, 64 percent life insurance, 59 percent short-term disability insurance, and 41 percent long-term disability insurance. In short, substantial numbers of these part-time workers continue not to receive benefits routinely offered to full-time employees (Canada. Labour Canada, 1986: 25). The situation is likely to be considerably worse for employees who fall outside of federal regulation.

From a business perspective, part-time workers continue to constitute a cheap, flexible work-force (Weeks, 1980a). For the employee, the costs attached to part-time employment often include reduced benefits, low wages, lack of job security, few opportunities for advancement or on-the-job training, little or no control over scheduling and monotonous, repetitive work (Duffy and Pupo, 1986).

It is these two views of part-time work—as a solution to the role overload of married women and as an exploited reserve army of labor—that capture the contradictory nature of part-time work. Many married women with young children in the home speak in positive terms of the flexibility, relaxed pace, time for themselves, and time for family that they are afforded by a part-time work schedule (Pupo, 1989: 91): "I work part-time because I want the best of both worlds. Financially, I don't have to work full-time. I like to balance the time between personal and professional growth, my growth as a mother, and to spend time with my children." Because of these positive aspects of part-time work, some analysts (Canada. Commission of Inquiry into Part-time Work, 1983; White, 1983) have called for the expansion of part-time work opportunities while also recommending prorated benefits and permanent status.

Other analysts, however, have pointed out that the increased use of part-time workers (women, students, the disabled, and the elderly) is simply a means to tap a cheap, often unorganized work force, and tends to reinforce the ghettoization of women as a peripheral labor force (Armstrong, 1984). "Yes [I would recommend part-time work] if they could get by on the income. If the income isn't a problem . . . and if they're just doing it to get out, to satisfy their needs but not financial needs." (Forty-two-year-old telemarketing representative.) Recent research supports this more critical stance on part-time employment. "The Board of Education treats us like second-class citizens. It pays us because it has to pay us, but it won't negotiate with us, it won't do anything that looks at our qualifications. We're not given any seniority. If they're going to do hiring, they'll hire the supply teachers last" (Pupo, 1989: 93). De-Haney (1988: 22) found that women part-time employees derived a lower level of intrinsic satisfaction from their jobs than those who were full-time employees. Given that part-time jobs typically are monotonous and "lacking . . . [in] opportunities for advancement and adequate utilization of . . . job skills," the lack of job satisfaction appears as a predictable cost attached to much part-time employment (DeHaney, 1988: 22–23). Levanoni and Sales' research similarly suggests that part-time workers (mostly female) are less satisfied with job security, pay, and scope of job than full-time workers. The net result may be a distinctly disgruntled worker. This focus on the costs of part-time employment is also reflected in newspaper articles that refer to part-time workers as part of the "economic underclass" (Cheney, 1988). However, it is organized labor that has been particularly vigorous in pointing out the drawbacks to part-time work and the exploitation of part-time workers (see Pupo and Duffy in this volume).

WOMEN'S PART-TIME WORK IN THE FUTURE

There are four main themes that are likely to figure prominently in any future discussion of part-time work for women. First, it appears that the enormous growth in part-time employment is, since 1983, leveling off (ILO, 1989: 43; Lévesque, 1987). It remains to be seen whether another recession will trigger increased use of the part-time labor force in the midst of negligible or negative full-time growth. Such a pattern would confirm the widespread belief that part-time employment is being used by employers as a cheap, flexible alternative to offering full-time employment to workers. Second, analysts are exploring whether legislative changes will slow the growth of part-time work opportunities. Pay-equity legislation, along with prorated work benefits, may reduce the economic advantages of hiring part-time workers. For example, as of January 1, 1987, all federally regulated industries were required to extend their pension plans to part-time workers who met specified eligibility criteria (Canada. Labour Canada, 1986: 23). As part-time employment becomes more expensive, it may become increasingly unattractive to employers, encouraging them to seek alternative means to reduce labor costs. In this scenario, casuals and other non-permanent contingent workers may grow in numbers.

Third, involuntary part-time employment has expanded rapidly in recent years. Between 1975 and 1986, there was a 375 percent increase in the number of Canadians working part-time only "because they were unable to find full-time jobs" (Akyeampong, 1987: 26). The proportion of involuntary part-time workers has similarly grown. Although, in 1975, only 11 percent of part-time workers were classified as involuntary, by 1984 30 percent were unable to find full-time work. The rate dropped slightly in 1986 to 28 percent (Akyeampong, 1987: 26). The highest percentage (41 percent) of these involuntary part-timers are women aged 25 to 54 (Akyeampong, 1987: 27). It is anticipated that any future downturn in the economy will further increase the rates of involuntary part-time employment. Increased application of microtechnology may similarly result in the increased availability of part-time jobs and the reduction of full-time opportunities (Garson, 1988).

Finally, it remains to be seen whether more radical demands for a greater range of work-sharing options (Handy, 1985), for reduction of the full-time workweek (Armstrong, 1984), and for the elimination of the misleading distinctions between non-work (domestic labor and child care), full-time, and part-time employment (Luxton, 1987) will be effectively mobilized in the 1990s. At present, part-time work fits neatly into the niche between capitalism and patriarchy. Individual women may lead more manageable family lives, but continue to be penalized by low-wage, dead-end jobs. The traditional patriarchal family, with its male breadwinner and female support staff, is left unruffled. Employers are provided with a flexible, inexpensive work force. Whether women's part-time employment will continue to sustain capitalism and patriarchy or, instead, will germinate a resistance to both, depends in large measure on the actions of women and labor activists in the coming years.

12 Part-Time Work and the Older Worker in Canada

P. Lynn McDonald and Richard A. Wanner

The study of older workers in Canada has largely neglected the fact that an increasing proportion of workers over 55 years of age are in some form of part-time employment. As a consequence, the study of part-time work has not been linked to long-term developments in the labor force, particularly the decline of employment in the primary and manufacturing sectors and its concomitant increase in the service sector, the rising tide of early retirement, and the shrinking size of the birth cohorts that will be entering the labor force in coming decades. The objective of this paper is twofold: conceptually, to anchor the study of part-time work in the late career within the framework of the extensive research available on retirement, both at the individual level and at the social structural level; and, to provide a socioeconomic profile of older Canadian part-time and full-time workers in order to facilitate an understanding of the process by which people are channeled into part-time employment. What are the consequences for the future of both work and retirement?

Canada's population is aging, primarily as a result of rising life expectancy, low birthrates, and the maturing of the postwar baby boom generation. Canadians aged 55 years or more comprised 17 percent of the total population in 1976, but by 1986 the proportion had risen to approximately 20 percent (Akyeampong, 1987b). Yet, a shrinking proportion of people in this age group are remaining in the labor force. For those aged 55 to 64, the proportion in the labor force decreased from 53.5 percent in 1976 to 50.3 percent in 1986; for those 65 years of age and over, the proportion declined from 9.5 percent in 1976 to 7.1 percent in 1986 (Akyeampong, 1987b).

Of those older Canadians who remain in the labor force, the trend is toward part-time employment as the worker grows older. Among employed workers aged 55 to 64, 12.8 percent worked part time compared to 10.5 percent of their 25- to 54-year-old counterparts. Those most likely to hold part-time jobs are 65 and over. Nearly 35 percent of employed persons in this age group work part time. At the same time, there has been an increase in the proportion of older workers in part-time jobs. In 1986, 12.8 percent of all employed 55- to 64-year-olds were in part-time jobs, compared to 8.2 percent in 1976. Among those 65 years of age and over, the proportion increased from 26.9 percent in 1971 to 34.7 percent in 1986 (Akyeampong, 1987b; Coates, 1988). As is the case for other age groups, it has been women who are more likely to work part time in the older age groups. While only 5 percent of all employed men aged 55 to 64 were part-time workers in 1986, 27.8 percent of employed women of the same age were part-timers. In 1986, 30 percent of employed men and 45 percent of employed women 65 and over worked part time (Méthot, 1987).

While these older Canadians represent a small share of the total labor force—9 percent for those aged 55 to 64 and 1.5 percent for those aged 65 and over—they still represent a force that will have to be reckoned with by governments, employing organizations, and unions. It is clear that older workers will have a significant effect on the size and composition of the future labor force. As Foot (1987) observes, the baby boom generation has now been completely absorbed into the labor force, and the smaller birth cohorts following it will provide increasingly smaller numbers of new workers. Although women continue to enter the labor force in greater numbers, older women appear to be retiring earlier, so this source of labor-force growth is unlikely to be sustained in the long run. The labor supplied by persons over 55 years of age will gain importance, indeed may be required to sustain the continued growth of the economy (McDonald and Wanner, 1989).

Part-time work, especially among those over 65 years of age, may hold the key to what is required to retain the older worker in the labor force in the immediate future. If this is the case, governments, out of necessity, will have to rethink pension policies so that they encourage continued full-time and part-time work rather than serving as incentives for early retirement (Stryckman, 1987; McDonald and Wanner, 1989). At the firm or organization level, the presence of older workers who desire part-time work will place pressure on the work organization to increase part-time work opportunities, to create new employment arrangements (job redesign, job sharing, graduated retirement schemes), to implement new performance appraisal systems, to modify benefit packages, and to provide retraining opportunities. Unions will be forced to reevaluate their view that part-time work is a threat to employment (Canada. Commission of Inquiry into Part-Time Work, 1983; Coates, 1988), and many workers may have to abandon their belief that working part time into old age represents the "breaking of the social contract," a contract that has been established in our society to give the older worker "the right" to retire (Myles, 1984; Stryckman, 1987).

If part-time employment continues to grow among older workers, a scenario that may be highly plausible (Lévesque, 1987), then we need to know who these older part-time workers are and what characteristics distinguish them both from those older workers who work full time and from those workers who are out of the labor force. In this paper, we construct a profile of these older part-time workers in Canada on the basis of data from the January 1986 Labour Force Survey conducted by Statistics Canada, and from The Displaced Workers Supplement to the Labour Force Survey sponsored by Employment and Immigration Canada. In keeping with the aim of this volume, we examine part-time work from the perspective of whether or not it constitutes an opportunity or a risk for older workers.

THE OLDER CANADIAN WORKER

Most Canadian research pertaining to older workers has been conceptually anchored within the study of retirement. Despite recent challenges to mandatory retirement and the arbitrariness of age 65 as a universal retirement age, it remained the pensionable age for 88 percent of Canada's private pension plans in 1980 (Canada. Statistics Canada, 1982a). It also remained the age of eligibility under the Canada and Quebec Pension Plans and Old Age Security programs. Some programs do provide full or partial pensions at an earlier age (e.g., the Canada and Quebec Pension Plans), but the norm stands at 65. As a result, most research has focused on labor-force participation rates of those aged 55 to 64 (the early retirees), those aged 65 (the on-time retirees), and those who retire after age 65 (the late retirees). All of these workers have usually been labeled "older worker," if Canadian government and business publications are any indication (Canada. Commission of Inquiry into Part-Time Work, 1983). Here we simply point out that this chronological definition is less than satisfactory, especially from a gerontological perspective, and that there is little agreement in the research literature as to what constitutes an older worker (Ashbaugh and Fay, 1987).

The plummet in labor-force participation rates of younger workers has spawned a number of studies attempting to explain why older workers retire early. This research has shown clearly that Canadians want to retire, and that they want to retire early. In 1984, a Gallup survey found that 47 percent of the workers aged 18 and over intended to leave the labor force before age 65 (Canadian Institute of Public Opinion, 1984). Numerous studies have shown that perceived health, unearned income (pensions and assets), attachment to work, and attributes of the marital unit are important predictors of retirement. Those in poor health tend to retire early (Ciffin and Martin, 1977; Baillargeon, 1982), as do those who can afford it (Ciffin and Martin, 1977; Kapsalis, 1979; McDonald and Wanner, 1984). Once these factors are taken into account, those workers who are less attached to their work (McDonald and Wanner, 1989) are also more likely to retire early, as are single men and married women (McDonald and Wanner, 1984).

These individual preferences have been reinforced by structural factors that have encouraged early retirement. The transformation of Canadian society from an agrarian period, in which most workers were either farmers or self-employed, to a "post-industrial" period (Bell, 1973), in which a majority of workers are now employees of large bureaucratic firms or government agencies with orderly career lines and mandatory retirement policies, accounts for part of the trend toward earlier retirement (Pampel and Weiss, 1983; Wanner and McDonald, 1987). The growth of both government and private pension plans that replace workers' lost earnings after retirement has also been linked to the trend toward early retirement. It is important to note that, while changes in industrial structure influence the labor-force participation patterns of older men (65 and over), and changes in pension benefits influence the patterns of the younger men (those 55 to 64), neither set of influences accounts for the patterns of labor-force participation observed among older Canadian women (Wanner and McDonald, 1987). There is also recent evidence to suggest that men working in the core of the economy (durable manufacturing, the construction trades, and the extraction industries) tend to retire earlier than those in the periphery of the economy (agriculture, non-durable manufacturing, retail trade, and subprofessional services). Again, the pattern does not apply to women (McDonald and Wanner, 1987).

Understanding why people retire at age 65 has become significant only in light of the legal assault on mandatory retirement under the Canadian Charter of Rights and Freedoms and provincial human rights legislation. There are a number of issues at the heart of the mandatory retirement debate, but they can be reduced to two major concerns usually voiced by governments, business, and organized labor. If mandatory retirement is eliminated, older workers will not retire, and this will increase the tax burden on future generations of workers, increase costs to the employer in terms of salary levels and benefits, prevent the career advancement of middle-aged workers, produce an obsolete work force, and exacerbate the unemployment problem (Conference Board of Canada, 1980; McPherson, 1983). The second major concern is that older workers are unproductive as a result of the aging process. According to the research on these matters, neither concern is justified (Gunderson and Pesando, 1980; McPherson, 1983).

The extent of *involuntary* mandatory retirement in Canada is small (Ciffin and Martin, Economic Council of Canada, 1979; Gunderson and Pesando, 1980). Based on the retirement survey of Health and Welfare Canada, Gunderson and Pesando (1980) report that mandatory retirement as a reason for retirement is given by less than 1 percent of those under 65 years of age, 17 percent of those aged 65 and about 27 percent of those over 65 years of age (1980: 354). Of all the men and women in this Canadian study, over 60 percent of those who retired because of mandatory retirement *retired at the ages they preferred* (Canada. Health and Welfare, 1977: 22). In other words, a small proportion of Canadians retire specifically because of mandatory retirement, and well over half of them prefer to do so. If mandatory retirement is completely abandoned, it is not likely that the labor-force participation rates of this group will appreciably change, making most of the above-mentioned issues a matter of academic speculation.

The notion that older workers are not productive as a result of the decrements associated with aging is equally erroneous. There is a large body of recent research, particularly in the United States, which shows that older workers are just as productive as their younger counterparts on most measures (Rosen and Jerdee, 1985; Conference Board of Canada, 1980; Doering, Rhodes and Schuster, 1983). Extended absences from work due to illness are slightly more prevalent among older workers than among younger workers, but absences due to injury are higher for younger workers than for older workers (Akyeampong, 1987). By and large, the unhealthy tend to select themselves out for early retirement.

Without mandatory retirement, it is important to know who will work past the normal retirement age of 65, and why they continue to work. In 1986, for the 175,000 Canadians aged 65 and over who continued to work or who retired and went back to work, the employment levels were highest for those 65 to 69, compared to those 70 years of age and over (Méthot, 1987: 7–9). As noted earlier, the majority of these worked part time and did so by choice. In 1986, 85 percent of the men and 79 percent of the women did not want full-time work. About 27 percent of the men and 12 percent of the women were employed in agriculture, and of all employed older persons in 1986, 21 percent of the men and 18 percent of the women were self-employed (Méthot, 1987).

The evidence explaining late retirement and work after retirement is meager relative to explanations of early retirement. Canadian studies of persons working past 65 years of age have shown that these older workers tend to be well educated, with upper occupational status; they are married men and single women who enjoy reasonably good health and who are attached to their work (Canada. Census, 1976; Canada. Health and Welfare, 1977, 1982; McDonald and Wanner, 1982; Nishio and Lank, 1987). Despite the apparent contradiction with the finding that it is upper occupational status individuals who work into old age, a number of recent studies have indicated that financial reasons motivate these workers (Palmore et al., 1985; McDonald and Wanner, 1982; Boaz, 1987; Nishio and Lank, 1987), but the need is greater for women than for men. One study has shown that these late retirees are better educated and more likely to be self-employed in small businesses and farming, where they are less likely to receive substantial rewards from working. That women are more motivated to work out of financial need is most likely a reflection of early career contingencies, lower overall earnings, less stable careers, and a lower likelihood of receiving private pensions. Underlying these explanations is the fact that women have been concentrated in industries in which few firms offer pension benefits (retail trade, business, and personal service industries), and that they have tended to work part time (Canada. Statistics Canada, 1985).

Some advocates of mandatory retirement have argued that, given high levels of unemployment among the younger population, older workers should retire to create opportunities for younger workers. Aside from the fundamental injustice of such observations, there is little available evidence to support or refute this view. In the U.S. context, it has been argued that older workers will not take away jobs from the currently unemployed, because the unemployed will find jobs that are vacant due to a lack of skilled workers to fill them (Robinson, 1982). In Canada, Baillargeon and Bélanger (1982) report that many of the jobs created by retirement will simply disappear, because some employers want to reduce the size of their labor force but cannot do so easily due to union contracts. The 1982 report of the Manitoba Commission on Compulsory Retirement also concluded, tentatively, that job opportunities for the young would not be affected by the abolition of mandatory retirement.

The difference in unemployment between older and younger workers decreased between 1982 and 1986. The unemployment rate for younger workers fell from 8.8 percent to 8.2 percent while the rate for those 55 to 65 years of age actually increased from its level of 6.9 percent in 1982 to 7.3 percent in 1986 (Akyeampong, 1987). Some researchers have argued that older workers tend to become discouraged during unemployment and this prompts them to retire early (Akyeampong, 1987; McDonald and Wanner, 1989). Finally, the trend toward part-time work on the part of older workers has been interpreted as evidence for the gradual transition of older workers from full-time work to no work, that is, to retirement (Canada. Commission of Inquiry into Part-Time Work, 1983). Regrettably, there is no precise Canadian evidence to support this view. There is little information on what motivates older part-time workers (Canada. Commission of Inquiry into Part-time Work, 1983). One Canadian study did find that about 35 percent of men and 47 percent of women still working would prefer part-time work as a transition to retirement (Canada. Health and Welfare, 1977: 25). However, the extent of the practice of "graduated" retirement in Canada is unknown. Several factors militate against its practice. Many pension plans explicitly forbid continued employment in the same organization once an employee reaches retirement, the amount of the reduced pension to be paid is often inadequate, and participation in statutory plans can sometimes be too expensive because ceilings are not prorated for part-time workers (Canada. Commission of Inquiry into Part-Time Work, 1983). One of the rare Canadian studies that directly surveyed older workers solicited their views on several of these issues. Older workers wanted mandatory retirement abolished. They wanted more opportunities for part-time work, and they noted that phased retirement should be considered as a serious option for older workers (Canada. Commission of Inquiry into Part-Time Work, 1983: 109).

OLDER PART-TIME WORKERS

The study of retirement has generated a limited amount of information about Canada's older workers, but little of it has pertained directly to older part-time workers. Indeed, there are few Canadian studies that directly address the older part-time worker. The information that does exist is scattered across various government documents and usually warrants no more attention than a few fleeting paragraphs. For these reasons, we reanalyze data from the Statistics Canada's January, 1986 Labour Force Survey and its Displaced Workers Supplement, focusing specifically on the older part-time worker. Because older persons do not constitute a homogeneous group, and because the labor-force patterns of women, particularly older women, are very different from those of men, we look at those persons aged 55 to 64 and 65 to 69 according to gender and full or part-time employment. We also compare those part-time workers who are in the labor force with those not in the labor force. These data are less than adequate because they do not include health, attitudinal, or pertinent financial variables, but they do provide a more detailed picture of Canada's older part-time workers than is currently available.

Part-Time Workers Aged 55 to 64

At the outset, it is important to recall that only 5 percent of all employed men aged 55 to 64 were part-time workers in 1986, compared to 27.8 percent of employed women of the same age group. While one government report has argued that men are disproportionately under-represented among part-time workers, because our society has tradi-tionally dictated that men work and that they work full time (Canada. Commission of Inquiry into Part-Time Work, 1983: 52), we would sug-gest another explanation. Canadian research has shown that a higher anticipated retirement income is likely to lead to early retirement among male workers between 60 and 62 years of age (Kapsalis, 1979; McDonald and Wanner, 1984). It is quite likely that the men in this age group continue to work full time until at least 60 years of age so that they can qualify for pension benefits that normally would not be as substantial if they had worked part time. In contrast, women often do not belong to a pension plan—about 31.2 percent do, compared to 45.1 percent of males—and if they do belong, they probably do not qualify for the pension (Canada. Statistics Canada, 1982a :15). In short, women may not be as constrained by pension eligibility to work full-time as are men. There are other reasons for women's concentration in part-time em-ployment that will become apparent from the data in Table 12.1.

Table 12.1 reports percentage distributions for the socioeconomic char-acteristics of those aged 55 to 64 by sex and employment status in 1986. It is immediately obvious that married women are more likely to work part time than full time, although there is no distinction for the men. There is some suggestion that marriage may provide opportunities for women to work part time because of the increased economic resources that result from the marital union. That the single women and those widowed, separated, or divorced (other) are working full time rather than part time would support this observation. Single men may work part time rather than full time because they have fewer family respon-sibilities and can afford to work part time. Those men who are divorced, widowed, or separated are more likely to work full time, perhaps because of the financial demands associated with these statuses.

As can be seen in Table 12.1, there is little difference in the educational attainments of part-time and full-time workers, suggesting that educa-tion has little to do with who works full time or part time. However, a larger proportion of part-time workers are found in the tertiary industries (trade, community, business, and personal service), while full-time workers are more in evidence in the secondary industries (manufactur-ing, construction). The concentration of part-time workers in tertiary industries is reflected in the occupational distribution. Both male and female part-time workers are overrepresented in sales and services, the women more so than the men. This is to be expected, given the overall concentration of women in these occupations. The high percentage of both male and female part-time workers in service industries is attrib-utable to the fact that the service sector has traditionally offered more part-time employment and, from a relative perspective, is the fastest

Table 12.1
Socioeconomic Characteristics of Workers Aged 55 to 64, by Sex and Employment Status, 1986

Characteristics	Men Full-time	Men Part-time	Women Full-time	Women Part-time
Marital Status				
Married	87.7%	87.0%	55.9%	76.3%
Single	5.0	7.6	10.4	4.3
Other	7.3	5.4	33.7	19.4
Education				
None or elementary	33.2	29.6	24.2	25.2
High school	41.4	46.0	48.6	51.0
Some post-secondary	5.4	6.7	7.1	6.7
Post-secondary certificate	7.9	9.2	10.5	10.9
University	12.0	8.4	9.5	6.2
Industry				
Primary	10.5	12.0	4.1	8.4
Secondary	31.3	18.0	14.9	6.8
Tertiary	58.2	70.0	81.0	84.7
Occupation				
Professional	9.6	8.5	16.0	13.8
Managers	16.1	12.0	12.4	5.6
Clerical	5.6	5.3	30.4	22.5
Sales	8.7	11.5	7.3	17.4
Crafts and operatives	39.6	32.1	10.0	3.6
Services	12.3	20.6	20.4	30.2
Farming	8.1	10.0	3.5	6.9
Class of Worker				
Paid, private	63.6	59.8	68.1	68.8
Paid, government	21.0	12.9	22.8	14.7
Employer	5.3	3.7	1.6	2.0
Own account	10.0	23.2	8.5	10.9
Unpaid family	0.0	0.4	2.0	3.6
Industrial Sector				
Core	52.5	39.1	48.0	34.5
Periphery	47.5	60.9	52.0	65.5
Job Tenure				
1-6 months	4.6	24.3	5.1	13.6
7-12 months	2.2	2.9	3.0	5.0
1-5 years	10.9	30.8	14.8	17.8
6-10 years	11.6	12.7	18.6	20.9
11-20 years	24.5	9.7	32.9	26.6
Over 20 years	46.2	19.6	25.6	16.1
Work Status				
Displaced	6.9	13.4	4.4	7.2
Not displaced	93.1	86.6	95.6	92.8
Unionized				
Yes	34.9	24.2	28.6	14.4
No	65.1	75.8	71.4	85.6
Reason for Part-time Work				
Personal/family responsibilities	—	9.4	—	15.2
Could only find part-time work	—	30.2	—	21.9
Did not want full-time work	—	58.4	—	62.8
Other	—	2.0	—	0.1
(Number)[1]	(735,374)	(31,240)	(2,797,252)	(117,302)

1. Weighted to population totals.

Sources: Canada. Statistics Canada. The Labour Force Survey. January, 1986, and Canada. Employment and Immigration Canada. The Displaced Workers Supplement to the Labour Force Survey. 1986.

growing sector of the Canadian economy (Akyeampong, 1987; Lévesque, 1987). What is of interest is that part-time workers are located in lower-status occupations to a greater extent than full-time workers, notwithstanding the similarities in their educational attainment.

Older part-time workers are also more likely to be employed in one primary industry, agriculture, and in the occupation of farming. Farming is an "older" occupation and one characterized by self-employment, a feature that would make part-time work easier to achieve (Akyeampong, 1987). Overall, there are more part-time workers who are self-employed than full-time workers. This largely reflects the preponderance of the former in agriculture (Akyeampong, 1987).

Part-time workers are more likely to be displaced by permanent layoff or plant closure than are full-time workers, and men are more likely to be displaced than women. These findings are good indicators of who is carrying the burden of unemployment, which was higher than usual for this age group in 1986 (Akyeampong, 1987). The part-time older worker, like every other age group of part-time workers, is less likely to be unionized and is characterized by much shorter job tenure than the full-time worker.

Lastly, the breakdown by economic sector offers another way of viewing the worker's position in the economy, and must be included as a rough indicator of the quality of the worker's job. Firms in the core of the economy (durable manufacturing, construction trades, extractive industries) tend to have higher wages, better working conditions, and fringe benefits, and are more likely to be unionized. The jobs within core firms tend to be organized into orderly career tracks wherein earnings and occupational prestige increase steadily over time (Spilerman, 1977). In contrast, firms in the peripheral economy (agriculture, nondurable manufacturing, retail trade, subprofessional services) are noted for low wages and fringe benefits, high worker turnover, little unionization, and "chaotic" career lines that exhibit no regularity in earnings or prestige increments.

As can be seen in Table 12.1, 60.9 percent of the men and 65.5 percent of the women working part time are found in the periphery of the economy, compared to 47.5 percent of the full-time male workers and 52 percent of the female full-time workers. Assuming that the dual-economy perspective is correct, we can only conclude that the part-time workers in this age group are sorely disadvantaged compared to their fellow full-time workers. Although there were no financial variables readily available in this data set, we do know from other studies that those older workers in the periphery have lower wages and fewer pension benefits than those in the core of the economy (McDonald and Wanner, 1987). The findings here that part-time workers are more likely to have lower occupational prestige, shorter job tenure, are more likely to be displaced, and are less likely to be unionized, suggest that this group experiences *financial outcomes* that are similarly unfavorable. Notwithstanding these observations, 58.4 percent of the part-time men and 62.8 percent of the women did not want full-time work. Obviously, part-time work is an important option for these workers, so important that they are willing to tolerate less than optimal working conditions to achieve their ends.

If we compare this group of employed part-time workers aged 55 to 64 to those former part-time workers in the same age group out of the labor force at the time of the survey, we have a better picture of their relative circumstances. Former part-time workers outside of the labor force are those workers who were neither employed nor actively seeking a job in 1986, but whose previous job was a part-time job. Of Canadians in this age group, well over half were out of the labor force because of retirement following job loss or illness (Akyeampong, 1987: 110). As seen in Table 12.2, those part-time men aged 55 to 64 in the labor force tend not to be married, have a better education and higher occupational status, and are more likely to be in tertiary industries and self-employed. Compared to those out of the labor force, these part-time men are less likely to have been displaced, more likely to be unionized, but are over-represented in the periphery of the economy.

At first glance, the argument could be made that these part-time workers are relatively disadvantaged compared to those out of the labor force because they, apparently, could not retire early or leave the labor force even if in poor health. Those part-time workers in the core industrial sector may have had this opportunity due to orderly career lines that resulted in their early retirement, an affordable option because they had a better chance of receiving a pension. Although it is a compelling argument, one could also suggest that those out of the labor force were forced out prematurely through lack of education, more displacement, or less unionization. Whatever the interpretation, it is clear that the majority of the part-time men fared better on most variables, and that working in the peripheral sector at least allowed them to pursue their desired form of employment.

The women of this age group who are still in the labor force are clearly better off than those who are out of the labor force. They are better educated, have about the same occupational status, are less likely to have been displaced, are more likely to belong to a union, and are more likely to be employed in the core sector of the economy. It is conceivable that the women out of the labor force could have been pushed out because of their sectoral location and their lower levels on the status-attainment variables. Considering that a majority of the part-time women in the labor force preferred this form of work, we can safely argue that part-time employment, compared to no employment, is a favorable work option for these women. Finally, when we look at part-time work as part of the continuum from full-time work to no work, we have some indirect evidence that part-time work may be a bridge to early retirement. Single men and married women with lower occupational status, low attachment to their work, but with an adequate income, tend to retire early. The pattern is fairly similar for the part-time workers in these data.

In brief, it would seem that older part-time workers are less advantaged on most socioeconomic variables than those who work full time, and that they are more likely to work at the periphery of the economy than in the core. As a result, the quality of their work life is probably not as favorable in terms of orderly career development and the concomitant increments in earnings and occupational status. Compared to those part-time workers out of the labor force, however, they appear to be more advantaged on most variables, giving them an edge in securing part-time work. That a majority of both men and women prefer to work part time, perhaps as a transition to retirement, underscores the importance of this form of employment, implying that part-time work is an opportunity, albeit a palliative one, given the location of much of this work in the peripheral industrial sector.

When the part-time workers in the age group of 65 to 69 years are considered, the proportions are dramatically higher. In 1986, 30 percent of employed men and 45 percent of employed women worked part time. As was noted earlier, men who work past the "normal" retirement age of 65 years are more likely to be selfemployed in peripheral industries, and are working to enhance their income. These conditions would allow them to skirt the regulations governing retirement and pension eligibility and would explain why they work to improve their income. This would also explain why there is such a large surge in the proportion of older men working part time. It has been well documented that those Canadian women who work past 65 years of age are compelled to do so out of economic necessity. That their proportions increase only bespeaks their precarious financial situation.

Table 12.3 presents the percentages for the socioeconomic characteristics among those aged 65 to 69 by gender and employment status. Many of the trends are the same as for the slightly younger group, but there are some notable differences. Both married men and women tend to be more likely to work part time. What is remarkable is the overall increase in the single men and women working part time, compared to the younger group just reviewed. The greatest growth in part-time employment has been among single persons and may account for these increases (Coates, 1988: 13), but this is not the whole story. The majority of these older single persons must be working part time to survive economically. In 1986, the poverty rate for unattached elderly women was over 46 percent, compared to 32 percent for men (Canada. National

Table 12.2

Socioeconomic Characteristics of Part-Time Workers Aged 55 to 64 and 65 to 69, by Sex and Labor Force Status

| | Aged 55 to 64 | | | | Aged 65 to 69 | | | |
| | Men | | Women | | Men | | Women | |
Characteristics	In Labor Force	Not in Labor Force	In Labor Force	Not in Labor Force	In Labor Force	Not in Labor Force	In Labor Force	Not in Labor Force
Marital Status								
Married	87.0%	91.1%	76.3%	76.6%	88.9%	78.9%	66.4%	80.5%
Single	7.6	4.3	4.3	3.2	11.1	3.4	11.1	0.5
Other	5.4	4.6	19.4	20.2	*	17.7	22.5	18.0
Industry								
Primary	12.0	7.6	8.4	6.6	24.5	17.6	6.6	10.3
Secondary	18.0	31.2	6.8	6.7	13.6	1.5	10.3	4.8
Tertiary	70.0	61.2	84.7	86.7	61.9	80.9	83.1	84.9
Class of Worker†								
Paid	72.8	79.1	83.5	83.5	58.1	61.1	88.4	65.8
Own account	26.8	13.9	12.9	9.0	41.9	19.2	7.0	29.7
Unpaid family	0.4	0.0	3.6	3.9	*	4.8	4.6	2.5
Industrial Sector								
Core	39.1	61.0	34.5	32.3	35.6	30.6	37.9	18.5
Periphery	60.9	39.0	65.5	67.7	64.4	69.4	62.1	81.5
Unionized								
Yes	24.2	8.1	14.4	12.8	*	*	13.5	6.2
No	75.8	91.9	85.6	87.2	*	*	86.5	93.8
Work Status								
Displaced	13.4	14.1	7.2	8.3	*	1.4	12.8	7.9
Not displaced	85.6	85.9	92.8	91.7	100.0	98.6	87.2	92.1
Education								
None or elementary	29.6	41.9	25.2	35.7	38.1	34.4	10.7	51.3
High school	46.0	39.3	51.0	47.3	14.6	51.7	51.2	37.7
Some post-secondary	6.7	3.6	6.7	3.9	*	3.6	20.8	*
Post-secondary certificate	9.3	3.7	10.9	8.0	37.6	*	5.8	11.0
University	8.4	11.3	6.1	5.0	9.8	10.3	11.4	*
(Number)■	(31,240)	(16,045)	(117,302)	(4,383)	(3,521)	(4,383)	(6,101)	(11,002)

†May not add to 100% because those "never in the labour force" were not included.

*Too few cases for accurate estimates or no cases.

■Weighted to population totals.

Sources: Canada. Statistics Canada. The Labour Force Survey. January, 1986, and Canada. Employment and Immigration Canada. The Displaced Workers Supplement to the Labour Force Survey. 1986.

Table 12.3
Socioeconomic Characteristics of Workers Aged 65 to 69, by Sex and Employment Status, 1986

Characteristics	Men		Women	
	Full-time	*Part-time*	*Full-time*	*Part-time*
Marital Status				
Married	86.3%	88.9%	49.1%	66.4%
Single	2.8	11.1	12.7	11.1
Other	10.9	—	38.2	22.5
Education				
None or elementary	45.2	38.1	10.3	10.7
High school	30.6	14.5	73.9	51.3
Some post-secondary	3.2	—	2.5	20.8
Post-secondary certificate	9.8	37.6	4.3	5.8
University	11.2	9.8	9.0	11.4
Industry				
Primary	25.7	24.5	5.4	6.6
Secondary	15.6	13.6	7.4	10.3
Tertiary	58.7	61.9	87.2	83.1
Occupation				
Professional	8.2	9.8	10.3	5.0
Managers	9.8	0.0	9.2	6.0
Clerical	3.0	—	26.1	22.6
Sales	11.8	1.6	30.1	13.8
Crafts and operatives	31.4	29.9	6.3	3.0
Services	14.2	48.7	12.7	43.0
Farming	21.6	9.9	5.3	6.6
Class of Worker				
Paid, private	62.4	56.4	65.4	67.9
Paid, government	8.4	1.8	4.5	20.5
Employer	5.3	25.0	1.2	—
Own account	23.9	16.9	16.8	7.0
Unpaid family	—	—	12.1	4.7
Industrial Sector				
Core	33.8	35.6	21.5	37.9
Periphery	66.2	64.4	78.5	62.1
Job Tenure				
1-6 months	4.5	15.9	2.8	17.4
7-12 months	0.4	17.4	—	3.1
1-5 years	12.6	7.4	—	22.9
6-10 years	16.6	20.2	24.8	1.9
11-20 years	20.5	22.7	34.8	31.3
Over 20 years	45.4	16.4	37.6	23.4
Work Status				
Displaced	8.2	—	0.7	12.8
Not displaced	91.8	100.0	99.3	87.2
Unionized				
Yes	100.0	—	—	13.5
No	—	—	100.0	86.5
Reason for Part-time Work				
Personal/family responsibilities	—	19.3	—	20.4
Could only find part-time work	—	—	—	15.3
Did not want full-time work	—	80.7	—	62.0
Other	—	—	—	2.3
(Number)[1]	(735,374)	(31,240)	(2,797,252)	(117,302)

1. Weighted to population totals.

Sources: Canada. Statistics Canada. The Labour Force Survey. January, 1986, and Canada. Employment and Immigration Canada. The Displaced Workers Supplement to the Labour Force Survey. 1986.

Council of Welfare, 1988: 67). Part-time work is undoubtedly critical to these older single persons.

For men, there is little difference between part-time and full-time workers in terms of level of education, while the older part-time women are slightly better educated than the full-time women, most noticeably at the upper end of the educational scale. It may be that this higher educational level allows them to choose better-paying part-time jobs that make full-time work unnecessary.

The part-time men are more likely to be found in tertiary industries than the full-time men, are more likely to be concentrated in service occupations, and are more likely to be self-employed, although farming is dominated by full-time workers. As Table 12.3 indicates, part-time women are less in evidence in tertiary industries, but continue to be concentrated in the service occupations when compared to full-time women. The part-time women in this age group, more than full-time women, are more likely to be paid workers than self-employed. The men working part time are not displaced workers, but neither are they unionized, as are the full-time workers. Both men and women exhibit shorter job tenure than full-time workers.

On average, it seems that the full-time workers in this older group are only slightly superior on most of the status attainment variables. The reason may be that there has been a huge influx of full and part-time workers into the peripheral sector of the economy. Whereas 47.3 percent of full-time men aged 55 to 64 were in the periphery, the figure is 66.2 percent for those men aged 64 to 69. For women, the figure jumps from 52.0 percent to 78.5 percent for the full-time workers. The part-time men's and women's share of peripheral work is actually less than that of full-time workers. There has been a considerable leveling effect to the extent that all the workers in this age group become more equally disadvantaged through working in the periphery. This is not an unexpected trend. Older workers tend to gravitate to the periphery of the economy, where they are more likely to find work, because employers usually do not reward their employees according to level of skill, they do not pay benefits, and they are not constrained by mandatory retirement policies (Hodson, 1978). What is of note is that the part-time workers, both male and female, are more likely to be employed in the core sector than are the full-time workers. Although we have no evidence, we would suspect that the larger proportion of part-time workers than full-time workers in the core of the economy are workers who have retired and are now working on a contract basis. This is an attractive arrangement for employers because they secure experienced workers at lower cost (no benefits), compared to maintaining full-time employees with all the attendant costs of fringe benefits and pensions. Again, the preference is for part-time work, especially among the men. Few workers were engaged in part-time work involuntarily.

As Table 12.2 indicates, these older part-time workers are generally in a more favorable position than those part-time workers out of the labor force, which would lead us to conclude that part-time work is a definite opportunity, especially if the worker is located in the core of the economy. Those part-time workers at the periphery, who constitute the majority of part-time workers, are no better off than the full-time workers, and both groups could be considered disadvantaged.

CONCLUSIONS

We have attempted to provide an initial profile of older part-time workers in Canada from the perspective of whether or not part-time work represents an opportunity or a risk for these workers. Based on a somewhat crude analysis carried out against the backdrop of the existing retirement research, we have argued that part-time work constitutes an opportunity for those workers aged 55 to 64, insofar as they desire part-time work, and that it may represent an attempt to withdraw gradually from the labor force into full retirement. The quality of the opportunity is, however, somewhat dubious. Although these workers have no less education than their full-time colleagues, they are concentrated in those industries that offer part-time work at the periphery of the economy where working conditions are less optimal than those encountered by full-time workers. Workers who are part time are not likely to be rewarded with increments in earnings and occupational prestige, are not likely to develop their skills, and probably forego any fringe benefits. These part-time workers rank higher on the status-attainment variables than those out of the labor force. This would suggest that part-time work is an opportunity, but that it is not open to all older workers.

The situation of those aged 65 to 69 is distinct from the younger age group and is characterized by a concentration of both full- and part-time workers in the peripheral sector of the economy, but with larger proportions of full-time workers being located at the periphery. All these aged workers are, therefore, somewhat disadvantaged in their working conditions, whether they are part time or full time. If anything, the part-time workers may have a slight advantage in obtaining work in the core industrial sector, because they would ultimately be a cheaper source of labor. This group of older workers overwhelmingly prefers to work part time, even more so than the younger cohort. In light of the large proportions of older workers who desire part-time work, and their willingness to work under adverse conditions, it is clear that part-time work is a crucial work option for older workers, and one that shows signs of permanence. Governments, employing organizations, and unions will have to come to terms with this reality, to make part-time work an equitable rather than an inequitable opportunity.

13 Employment and the Marginalization of Older Workers in the United States[*]

Lonnie Golden

THE SETTING: NEW EMPLOYER PERSONNEL STRATEGIES

Business firms in the 1980s increasingly turned to short-run payroll cost-reduction to become more flexible and cost-competitive in international and domestic markets, to avoid hostile takeover attempts and to enhance quarterly profit reports. Many firms are relying more on human-resource departments to cut or contain labor costs, rather than concentrating their efforts on enhancing productivity. This paper looks at the impact on older workers' economic status of the two increasingly prevalent employer strategies, contingent work and early retirement, and explores the relationship between older worker employment and part-time work.

CONTINGENT WORK

One of the strategies used by employers is the expansion of contingent work, including temporary and part-time jobs. It is especially common in retail trade and services industries, and in clerical and service occupations. The creation by personnel policy of a contingent work force has gradually been replacing the full-time, permanent work force combined with a layoff recall system (Way, 1988). An enlarged "periphery" at the expense of "core" jobs has been partly the result of a general shift in relative bargaining power toward employers in both non-union and unionized industries. This shift has allowed most employers unilaterally to implement these short-run, profit-maximizing personnel strategies

[*]This chapter draws heavily on *Social Insecurity: Economic Marginalization of Older Workers*, 9to5, National Association of Working Women (September, 1987), for which Golden was the primary author. It is used with permission of the Association.

without much resistance or threat of immediately harmful consequences. Virtually all of the increase in part-time employment since 1979 is in the "involuntary part-time" category, while temporary jobs constitute an increasing share, now one in 13, of new jobs created. Older workers have not been immune to these developments. Ten percent of "temps" hired through temporary help supply (THS) services are aged 55 and over. While this is roughly proportional to their presence in the labor force, temps are usually thought of as youths and mothers who are seeking to gain some job experience.

The core work force itself has been absorbing much of the impact of employer cost and flexibility goals. Real hourly earnings have been dropping since 1979 (U.S. Bureau of Labor Statistics), while average weekly hours of work became more unstable in the 1980s than they had been in the previous four decades.[1] Older workers in the core are particularly vulnerable due to their relatively higher wage and salary costs; their higher non-wage costs of employment, such as retirement and health plan contributions and paid vacations; the absence of graduated scales in severance pay systems;[2] and age discrimination in hiring, promotion, and training decisions (Herz and Rones, 1989).

EARLY RETIREMENT

Workers in the core jobs, particularly in relatively large firms, have also been at risk because of a growing tendency on the part of employers to pursue a second strategy, staff downsizing. The use of early retirement schemes to achieve this downsizing has been increasingly popular, primarily because it is seen, relative to across-the-board layoffs, as less disruptive and less damaging to the morale of the remaining employees. This view is shared by a variety of observers:

There appears to be a considerable increase in the use of retirement inducements as a means of reducing labor costs. (Rones, 1988: 42).

An often used technique [of work-force reduction] is the early retirement incentive program usually aimed at highly paid employees aged 50 and over. . . . (Meier, 1988: 168).

Many organizations have used [early retirement incentives] to reduce both the size of the work force and cost. (American Management Association, 1987: 13).

Early retirement schemes have recently been used by 40 percent of the *Fortune* 500 companies. A 1986 survey found one third of employers using "early retirement windows," with 40 percent of these using the scheme repeatedly.[3] This is an increase from the one quarter of companies reporting early retirement offers in 1982 (Popa, 1983). An American Management Association (AMA) survey found that 44 percent of organizations attempting downsizing would likely use early retirement incentives for their salaried work force, and 31 percent for their hourly workers. Corporations such as RJR Nabisco, ITT, and even International Business Machines (IBM), which was reputed to be a "no layoff" employer, made extensive use of early retirement packages to reduce staff in the 1980s. The Bureau of Labor Statistics (BLS) reports that since 1974 many private pension plans at large companies have reduced the normal retirement age. Almost all permit early retirement at 55 years of age with smaller penalties for doing so (Belous and Appelbaum, 1988: 6). While some companies have made efforts to retain and recruit older workers, they remain the exception; most move older workers out earlier. Norwood (1986: 89) has predicted, "As the huge baby boom generation grows older, there is probably no other labor market issue that will incite such forceful policy debate and such intense political pressure as early retirement."

There is ample evidence that the age of retirement has been declining significantly in recent years. For example, an estimated 70 percent of those reaching 65 years of age are already retired (*Business Week*, August 10, 1987), and less than 20 percent of those aged 65 to 69 are employed. The fraction of the population aged 60 to 64 electing early retirement under social security benefit provisions rose from 14.1 percent in 1970 to 23.2 percent in 1984 (Belous and Appelbaum, 1988: 6). In 1986, the number of employees in large companies with pension plans, who retired before 65 years of age, soared to 84 percent of all retirees, up from 62 percent in 1978. The controversy predicted by Norwood stems in part from the concern that the decision regarding early retirement will be increasingly involuntary, and is therefore not desirable. Indeed, there is indirect evidence that, even now, earlier retirement is not primarily voluntary. The bulk of existing economic research on retirement behavior typically treats all retirements not due to health factors or adverse labor market conditions as voluntary retirement. This approach gives the impression that retirement is purely the result of worker choice, and that the trend toward earlier retirement is welfare-enhancing and universally desirable. It is questionable whether the trend is economically or socially desirable if it is increasingly induced by financial incentives and if it is not targeted solely at those workers who envisage work as less agreeable, less rewarding, or less affordable than retirement.[4]

THE INVOLUNTARY NATURE OF EARLIER RETIREMENT'S

The fact that a majority of early retirement incentive programs are not accepted attests to the often involuntary nature of retirement. Of workers aged 40 and older surveyed by the American Association of Retired

Persons (AARP), only 41 percent responded that they would accept a financially sweetened early retirement offer (1986). Another study found that one in three eligible workers accept such offers (Herz and Rones, 1989: 18).[5] In 40 percent of the early retirement incentives offered by the largest corporations, less than one half elected the option. Offers are often accepted because employees perceive the threat of layoff as the alternative, risking the forfeiture of extra pension benefits.[6] Not surprisingly, acceptance rates are much lower for relatively low-income and poorly educated workers. In addition, offers are often only available for a relatively short specified period, such as two months, which U.S. courts have deemed to be ample time.[7]

Early retirement incentives are both a cause and a symptom of the declining retirement age for all workers. Such schemes are typically available only at the management level. Clerical workers, for example, are often nudged or pushed out of their jobs, not induced:

California Federal Savings and Loan notified Rhoda, 55, that she was being transferred, in the hope that she would quit or retire. When she accepted the offer, the company reneged and offered her a position at a more distant branch that, for health reasons, she couldn't move to. She knows the company wants younger workers but she wants to work another 6 years. (9to5 member, June, 1987.)

I've never heard of inducements to go. Clericals have enough trouble getting inducements to stay. (9to5 member, June, 1987.)

Some are pushed to contingent worker status, a fate to which older aged workers are particularly vulnerable:

A relatively older worker in Dallas was called into the office one day. After waiting four hours in the waiting room without pay, she was told to make up her mind right then and there between layoff with severance pay without recall or going to part-time status. She was not given time even to call her husband. She said, "I have a family and need the money, so I took the part-time work. I went right back to work just shaking. I was so upset I couldn't even write." (Former data entry agent with over 11 years of service: 9to5, 1988: 133.)

The trend to earlier retirement is certainly welcome if it is a function of wealth or the dual-income family, the nature of jobs, and worker health factors. It may also plausibly reflect workers' reallocation of leisure time toward the end of their working lives. However, early retirement is voluntary only if it is chosen over existing alternatives. Whether voluntary or not, the falling retirement age will produce a growing pool of potential workers outside the labor force.[8] In the 1980s, it appeared that it was mainly the demand side of the labor market that was creating the growth in the share of part-time and contingent jobs and the expanding pool of older workers outside the labor force.[9] Whether the structure of jobs and labor markets will be transformed to accommodate the needs of older workers thus depends mainly on the future actions of employers.

APPLICATION OF THE DUAL LABOR MARKET FRAMEWORK

To analyze labor market trends toward earlier retirement and the growth of temporary and involuntary part-time jobs, the dual labor market (DLM) framework may be useful. The DLM approach assumes that the actions of employers dominate labor market developments, whereas the standard neoclassical model of labor market attributes retirement and part-time employment trends primarily to the preferences of suppliers of labor. DLM analysis assumes that labor markets can be characteristically different in nature. In its simplest form, it divides labor markets into primary and secondary labor markets, usually distinguished along occupational lines. A primary sector job possesses features such as relatively high pay, an array of non-wage benefits, and job security, as well as opportunities for promotion and for skill and career development. Secondary jobs, in contrast, typically have low compensation, no benefits, and are intermittent or unstable. They also have limited opportunity for advancement, and provide little reward for skill development. Over time, workers gradually adapt and take on the characteristics of the jobs they maintain.[10]

In the last decade, there has been some erosion of primary-type jobs, a result of both the increased substitution of part-time for full-time staff and the declining share of total employment in relatively large-sized firms.[11] In addition, not only are there distinctive labor markets for secondary workers, but the dichotomy is increasingly appearing within the same firm and even within the same occupational category in the same firm. Temporary workers, for example, are often placed in jobs peripheral to the establishment, with less compensation and employer commitment than that bestowed on similar core jobs. Nearly identical jobs within a firm may systematically receive tasks that differ markedly by skill requirement and responsibility. Occupations in which jobs are being divided into core and contingent range anywhere from fast-food clerks, cashiers, secretaries, and billing clerks, to librarians, tax accountants, and university professors.[12]

A simultaneous countertrend occurred with the reasonably strong growth of employment in the 1980s: the rise of the "contingent economy." There are three aspects to this contingency. The first is contingent jobs: temporary jobs and part-time jobs dependent, for example, on peak demand periods or store hours. Second, there is contingent work: jobs that are fairly secure, but with hours that can vary widely. Workers with part-time status may have hours ranging from, say, 15 to over 40 hours per week.[13] The third aspect is contingent pay: per-hour compensation that is increasingly based on establishment performance (Belous and Appelbaum, 1988: 1). Part-time workers fall into either of the first two categories.

LABOR MARKET SUPPLY AND DEMAND FORCES

Demographic trends point to a potentially growing pool of older workers. The share of the U.S. population that is aged 55 and older is expected to remain at 22 percent through the year 2000 but will rise to 31 percent by 2020 and to 34 percent by 2050. These population trends will partially determine the future age character of the labor force, but that character hinges on future participation patterns as well. The BLS expects the median age of the work force to rise from its current level of 35 to 39 by the year 2000. The BLS also predicts that the 55-and-over share of the total labor force will shrink to 11 percent from its 1983 fraction of 14 percent, while the 65-and-over share will shrink to 2 percent from its current 2.6 percent level.[14]

Currently, 80 percent of men aged 55 to 59, 56 percent of men aged 60 to 64, and 16 percent of men 65 and over participate in the labor force. The comparable figures for women are 50 percent, 13 percent, and 7 percent, respectively. Labor force participation by the year 2000 is projected to fall to 63 percent for the entire aged 55 to 64 group of men and to 10 percent for men 65 and over. Participation of women aged 55 to 64 is expected to rise to almost 46 percent and to fall to almost 5 percent for those 65 and over (Fullerton, 1987).

These projections are, of course, purely speculative. They depend heavily upon private employer actions, such as corporate early retirement campaigns, age discrimination, and misperceptions about older workers.[15] Public policies with respect to social security, pensions, and the duration of unemployment insurance benefits also affect the propensity to retire. Finally, the older workers' subjective preferences for leisure and work, as well as their response to real earnings attainable through labor market work will affect their decision to continue workforce participation. Only significant institutional change on the demand side of the labor market will prevent a mass exodus of older labor suppliers from the labor force.

Demand for Older Workers in the Labor Market

While the accepted use of early retirement incentives may reduce demand for older workers, the reduction may be offset by the growth of contingent work. As one human resource executive remarked: "Older workers represent a gold mine to us. They are just what we want [in terms of contingent workers]" (Belous and Appelbaum, 1988: 2). Since 62 percent of all employed women 65 and over and 46 percent of employed men 65 and over hold part-time jobs, defined as entailing less than 35 hours per week, there is some indication that older workers wishing to remain employed may actually prefer the shorter than full-time work schedules. The growth in temporary jobs may also accommodate the preference of some workers for part-year work, although there is much evidence that temporary workers in general would prefer permanent positions.[16]

LABOR MARKET HARDSHIP AND THE EROSION OF INCOME SECURITY

> An awful lot more people–especially skilled people—are being let go to be replaced by younger workers, in recent years. (Administrator, Cleveland Heights Skills Available.)

Aside from the declining retirement age and the marginalization of many jobs, the increased specter of job displacement has been the most prominent threat to the security of the incomes of older workers. Between 1983 and 1988, workers 55 and over accounted for 20 percent of all displaced workers (defined as workers 20 and over with at least three years' job tenure who have permanently lost their jobs due to plant closing or relocation, slack work, or abolition of position or shift). This represents a proportion higher than their 13 percent segment of the total labor force. When an industry, occupation, or firm is declining, seniority clearly offers less protection than is commonly presumed.[17]

Three adverse consequences suffered by displaced older workers are long spells of unemployment, substantial pay loss upon reemployment, and possible withdrawal from the labor force. Average and median durations of unemployment after displacement are significantly longer for workers aged 55 to 64 than for the rest of the labor force; in 1986, the durations were 24 and 11 weeks respectively, compared to 15 and 7 weeks for all ages. Average earning losses endured with displacement for all workers are estimated at about 13 percent for men and 16 percent for women; yet it is about 18 percent for male workers, about 20 percent for females, aged 50 to 61. The income drop stemming from displacement is substantial for women:

When women's plants shut down, they wind up taking jobs cleaning homes, [as] home health-care aides, or low-paid clerks. (Director, Cleveland Council of Unemployed, 1987.)

A woman manager in her 50s from Milwaukee who was dismissed from her $36,000-a-year job has been unemployed for so long, she's now interviewing for clerical work at half her previous pay. (9to5 Field Organizer.)

For older workers, the most serious problem with displacement is that it frequently results in their complete withdrawal from the labor force. Thirty-five percent of all 55- to 64-year-olds displaced over the 1981–85 period, for example, were no longer in the labor force by January 1986. This percentage is over twice the average for workers of all ages. This is actually somewhat higher for women, even though two out of three displaced workers are men. For workers 65 and over, it is almost five times the all-age average—69 percent for men and 76 percent for women. Clearly, a permanent layoff is likely to push the older workers out of the labor force entirely.[18]

In 1985, median annual labor market income for men and women aged 55 to 64 who worked full time was approximately $28,400 and $16,800, respectively. For those aged 65 and over, it was $26,100 and $14,500 (U.S. Bureau of the Census, Consumer Income Series, P–60, no. 154). Labor market work as a source of income for the typical worker who was 65 and over is restricted, because two thirds of this group work either part time or part year, and one fifth of these older workers earn the minimum wage or less (compared with less than one tenth of the overall labor force).

Pension coverage has slipped to about 43 percent of the labor force from its peak of 45 percent in 1981. Employers are shifting the burden of retirement contributions more toward workers by switching from defined-benefit to defined-contribution and shared funding schemes, which also tend to produce smaller eventual benefits. While social security benefits rise only 3 percent for each year that retirement is delayed, a rise in the retirement age to 67 is slated to occur from 2002 to 2027. Thus, even for those near retirement who have non–labor-market income, more income insecurity, rather than less, seems to be on the horizon. Recent job creation trends hold little promise as a means of improving future income security, due to a dramatic decline in the share of new jobs held by workers aged 35 and older, jobs that are located in the relatively highest stratum of pay (Bluestone and Harrison, 1986). Part-time opportunities will grow with the rise of employment in smaller enterprises, but pay there is traditionally lower.

Special Problems of Older Women

The gap in pay between females and males—the ratio of income earned by full-time, year-round women workers to that of men workers—widens with age. Although the average ratio is approximately 70 percent for all female workers, it is only about 61 percent for those over 45 years of age. The small improvements seen in the pay ratio in the last two decades have registered mainly in the younger age brackets, and only slightly in the 45 to 54 bracket.

Pension coverage is less common for women than for men, with only 21 percent of women collecting earnings from their own or their husband's pension, even though 42 percent of women in 1985 participated in some pension plan. Also, the extent of vesting is lower, and benefits are smaller where women receive coverage. This is partly because of their somewhat shorter average job tenure. However, it is mainly because of occupational segregation of women into lower-paying jobs that lack pension provision, such as part-time jobs and jobs in small firms (Shaw, 1988: 73–77). The persistence of sex and age discrimination helps the gap between female and male wages to continue as an income gap after retirement.

Women's labor force participation is characterized by repeated exits and reentries. Many female workers are "displaced homemakers" returning to the labor force after a long absence.[19] It is questionable whether the problems of intermittent participation, low pay, and pension inadequacy will be alleviated by an expansion of part-time jobs as they are now structured.

"Rehirees": Employers Increasingly Hire Retirees

We see more and more interest in hiring retirees. (Executive Director, National Council on Aging.)

A large number of lower-paying jobs will be filled . . . by workers 65 and over who require extra money to supplement Social Security payments, small pensions or savings. Their ranks might include some of the thousands who have lost their jobs through corporate cutbacks or mergers. Older workers who have retired or dropped out of the job market in recent years are the lost battalion, a force that has drawn the interest of company managements. (*New York Times,* December 31, 1985.)

Employers are increasingly hiring or rehiring retirees to reduce costs by tapping into a potentially productive, yet cheap, source of labor. To assess the desirability of these programs, one must distinguish between programs designed to retain or rehire workers at the highest status possible and those aimed at cost-cutting by hiring older workers at the lowest possible level of compensation and training commitment. The former simultaneously achieve cost savings for employers and increased earning opportunity for older workers. The latter only increase the presence of older workers in contingent jobs. If what employers gain often translates into a sacrifice on the part of rehired workers, then older workers are enlisted to subsidize their own employment.

To cite some examples of the transformation toward more formal rehiring practices:

1. Digital Equipment Company in Massachusetts realized cost savings in the form of reduced training and absenteeism by hiring retirees when extra workers were needed on the shop floor.
2. Omni Communications in Lynn, Massachusetts, recruited older workers to the point where 60 percent of its telemarketers are now aged 55 and over.
3. Zayre, claiming productivity benefits and cost savings through the Job Training Partnership Act (JTPA) and senior employment service subsidies, set up a booth in a local shopping mall to recruit older-aged workers.

Cost savings are a major driving force behind the rehiring, but the rehiree often loses seniority status, severance pay rights, previous hourly pay, job status, paid vacation, sick leave, or additional health and pension plan contributions:

Usually the retirees return to much lower status work. (Administrator, Cleveland Heights Skills Available.)

A woman I know in her late 70s came out of retirement to become a full-time secretary at a bank, through a THS. She remained a temporary employee for over three years. (9to5 member.)

The Cuyahoga County Library System in Ohio has each branch maintain a list of retirees available on call, as needed, as the "most organized manner of filling in without causing disruption," superior to the previous practice of using transfers from other branches to fill temporary vacancies. The rate of hiring is "erratic," and there are no additional pension contributions if the retiree works less than an average of 20 hours per week. The hourly pay rate is linked to the position being filled, and is in no way connected to previous pay, skill level, or length of service.[20]

The group audit processing department of Blue Cross Blue Shield of Ohio (BCBSO) calls back former employees during peak work-load periods or special projects. Since there is no formal pay policy, a clerical worker could have retired at the top of the grade's pay range of $18,000, yet the rehiree could conceivably be paid at or near the entry-level wage of about $13,265. The "job bank" at the Travelers Corporation, the largest and most often acclaimed rehiring program, allows pension credits to be collected for up to 960 annual hours of work,[21] but the pay of these employees is set at the midpoint of the pay scale for the particular job rather than being commensurate with experience, skill, or previous pay. To recruit retirees from outside the firm, Travelers threw an "unretirement party" complete with refreshments and "I'm unretired" buttons for recruits (*New England Business*, October 6, 1986).

Some employers have established in-house or outside employment agencies designed specifically to facilitate or administer the rehiring of retirees and other temporary workers. Grumman Aircraft maintains a retiree pool referred to as "job shoppers." Workers are hired through a separate firm called "Procurement" and earn their previous pay but no additional benefits (Bureau of National Affairs, 1987). Union Carbide rehired its own retirees through "Mature Temps," a THS agency almost exclusively placing older clerical workers. Continental Illinois Bank and Trust maintains an older worker crew through its own THS agency, "Ready Workforce."

The formal rehiring pool is a mixed blessing for older workers, since the benefits of reemployment are restricted by the often exploitative nature of this new employment relationship. Innovative retention and recruiting practices that are beneficial are too scarce.[22] It is thus not a reliable way to improve older workers' economic status, and threatens to add retirement-age workers to the already growing pool of marginalized workers.

Formal rehiring schemes were often started as more informal practices, and thus informal rehiring is likewise questionable in its ability to raise the economic status of older workers. Kentucky Fried Chicken boasts a 55-and-over work force of about 3,500, and announced formal plans to raise that number by 1,500 in one year. Burger King (in Solon, Ohio) employed a 58-year-old woman who recently picketed her own employer when they rejected her request for a $0.70-an-hour raise. The firm offered her a $0.10 raise instead. She declared, "I have these four years of experience and here I am getting $3.80—only $.30 an hour more than the new hires" (Cleveland Plain Dealer, July 16, 1987). Laying off and then rehiring the same older individual is not an uncommon abuse of the rehiring system. A man who worked 34 years for Owens-Corning Fiberglass Corporation found his position eliminated in a company restructuring, but was hired back as a subcontractor at less than half his former annual pay of $80,000, with no benefits, and he now pays rent for his office.

Both demand- and supply-side forces in the labor market may serve to continue or intensify the use of rehirees in the future. Employers may increasingly discover the cost-effectiveness of older workers. On the supply side, there is the maturing of the baby boom, fewer younger workers, and continued income insecurity. A survey showed that 31 percent of the retired heads of households returned to work (Coplan, 1986), suggesting that the insecurity in retirement is widespread.

Older Workers and Part-Time Work

Part-time work opportunities constitute an obvious vehicle to help improve the economic status of older workers by means of labor market income. A significant proportion of older workers is already working part-time hours (defined as less than 35 hours a week). One third of men and one half of women aged 62 to 64 are still in the labor force, and 53 percent of workers who are 65 and over work part time. One in five employed men who are 55 and over, and one in three employed women who are 55 and over, were on part-time schedules in the late 1980s.[23] However, workers 55 and over still represent a smaller proportion of the part-time labor force (7 percent) than their share (8.1 percent) of the full-time labor force (Belous and Appelbaum, 1988).[24]

Among older workers, the desire for part-time work is high. Well-publicized polls taken for the American Association of Retired Persons (AARP) demonstrate that almost 80 percent of workers aged 55 to 64 expressed interest in working part time, or in retiring gradually as a way to postpone full retirement. Only 18 percent *planned* to retire prior to 65 years of age, and the desire to stay in the work force steadily increased as workers approached 65 years of age. Furthermore, 73 percent of those still working past 65 years of age said that they would postpone full retirement if given the gradual retirement or part-time opportunity.[25] There is indirect evidence of the wish to work part time as a transition: 19 percent of unemployed men and 41 percent of unemployed women aged 60 to 64 were seeking part-time work. For those 65 and over and unemployed, 54 percent of men and 62 percent of women were seeking part-time work.[26] In 1986, in the age group 55 and over, there were more than 30 men unemployed for every hundred who were seeking work; for women 55 and over, there were 51 unemployed to every 100 who were seeking work.

Despite the preference of older workers for part-time work, only 15 percent of them worked part time in the year before full retirement, excepting those retiring after 68 years of age (Kahne, 1985: 37). A principal obstacle is the minimum-hours constraint faced by the majority of workers. The absence of downward flexibility in weekly hours of scheduled work for 63 percent of workers leaves one with a discrete rather than continuous labor supply choice: full-time job, part-time job, or complete retirement.[27] Older workers are also constrained by the fact that so few employers encourage working beyond retirement age.

Work After Retirement

Over 40 percent of retirees in the AARP survey indicated that they would prefer to be working (1986). A survey of retired labor union members under 65 years of age showed that 25 percent are working again (6 percent full time, 8 percent part time, and 10 percent in temporary jobs). Another 15 percent conveyed that they want work. Of this 40 percent of retirees, 61 percent prefer less than an eight-hour day and 70 percent favor a shorter than 5-day week (Belous and Appelbaum, 1988: 7–8). Post-retirement work currently entails a significant downgrading in occupational status and in average hourly earnings, and is thus less common than it could be. The key problem is the scarcity of viable part-time options for retired or retiring workers.[28] One survey of 800 retirees from three large firms showed that 42 percent of retirees not working during retirement indicated that the job opportunities available to them paid so little they had opted against searching for jobs (Rones, 1983). One half of union retirees surveyed cited low pay and lack of suitable opportunities as obstacles to post-retirement work, while one third cited unsuitable hours (Belous and Appelbaum, 1988: 8–9).

Women's Experience

Twenty percent of men and women are working one year after retirement, mainly because of income insecurity and in spite of receiving social security benefits. Downward occupational mobility is less common in women, who are more likely to remain in the same occupation in post-retirement work; their jobs, however, are already low-status or low-paying (Shaw, 1988: 78–79). Two of five unmarried women, and one of four married women, who do not receive pensions, are employed; by contrast, only 10 percent of all women who are receiving pension benefits are employed. Also, women typically receive a lower monthly social security benefit. If trends toward later average ages of child bearing and greater longevity continue, then older women workers may face more family responsibilities and intensified economic pressures to continue working.

IMPROVING PART-TIME OPTIONS, AND OTHER POLICY REMEDIES

Demographic changes and a coming shortage of skilled labor require policies that promote labor force attachment and high-quality employment opportunities for older-aged workers. Market failure, combined with institutional constraints in the labor market, make activist policy all the more necessary to achieve the general social welfare policy objective, which is to preserve and broaden individual options (Parnes and Sandell, 1988: 18, 19). Two principal constraints are the low quality of available part-time jobs and the limited opportunity for older workers to reduce their work hours as a transition to retirement.

The creation of more part-time jobs will not in itself improve the economic status of older workers and promote longer labor force attachment. Job creation must be accompanied by four additional developments:

1. *Upgrading the quality of contingent, part-time jobs currently being created, including more job sharing.* Private and public employers must begin *redesigning part-time jobs* for older workers who are nearing retirement. Only 9 percent of employers are currently doing this. Only 13 percent offer training or retraining options to older workers for the skill upgrading that is required to increase mutual attachment between older workers and firms (Root and Zarrugh, 1985). Training investment in employees declines after 40 years of age, yet 90 percent of surveyed workers between 50 and 62 years of age expressed interest in additional training.[29] Age discrimination is an obstacle:

The company wouldn't train Fran, (only) 50 years old, because they thought she wouldn't stay long enough. (Director, Cleveland Council of Unemployed, June, 1987.)

Many older workers at a large health insurer were denied training or were moved to another department when a new computer claims processing system was installed. (Organizer for Service Employees International Union, August, 1987.)

Reduced hours for older workers or more flexibility in hours—weekly, annual, or lifetime hours—would be beneficial. An AARP survey found that 44 percent of workers over 40 years of age, and 32 percent of those over 62, rank opportunity for reduced hours as a major consideration in delaying retirement (Meier, 1988: 183). Yet, less than one in twelve employers offers some form of reduced work load for older workers (Root and Zarrugh, 1985).[30] Work sharing (reducing work-force hours per week to avoid layoffs) can be targeted toward workers nearing retirement. "V-Time" goes further by allowing workers to volunteer for an extended period of hours reduction anytime, which employees can choose to use as a transition to retirement.[31]

2. *Spreading the use of phased retirement programs to provide a smoother transition to retirement.* Only 2 percent of older workers now benefit, formally or informally, from such programs.[32] Seventy-five percent of older-worker respondents to a 1983 Canadian government survey (Canada. Commission of Inquiry into Part-Time Work, 1983) favored an option of part-time work if it could be combined with prorated pension benefits. Sweden's national pension plan allows partial pensions to those aged 60 to 64, with demonstrated past labor-force attachment, if work hours are reduced toward the minimum of 17 per week. Part of Sweden's high percentage (57 percent) of workers aged 60 to 64 remaining in the work force can be attributed to this program. Partial retirement has been instituted with success at a few selected companies, mainly for salaried professionals with long length of service (Meier, 1988: 181–182; 9to5, 1987: 115–118).[33]

3. *Expanding self-employment opportunities for older workers and retirees.* This strategy offers a part-time hours option and a relatively high degree of flexibility in work schedules (Rones, 1988: 33).[34]

4. *Signing into law certain federal legislative initiatives.* Social security laws can be

amended to limit the discouragement of post-retirement part-time work. Legislation raising the earnings-test ceilings ($6,120 under 65 years of age and $8,160 for those aged 65 to 69) without distorting equity, and increasing the delayed retirement credit from 3 percent to 8 percent added to the benefits of those who postpone retirement, should be implemented as soon as possible rather than waiting until its scheduled date of 2007.

The Employment Retirement Income Security Act (ERISA) should be amended to encourage continued, part-time work by prohibiting caps on years of service that are counted toward future pension benefit, making rates of accrual at least actuarially neutral for those who delay retirement, and encouraging employers to make *full* pension contributions during the years of reduced hours. Quicker vesting and more pension portability between jobs would expand coverage to women in particular and ease the economic strain of retirement.

The Part-Time and Temporary Worker Protection Act should be adopted. This would amend ERISA by reducing the number of hours required for pension eligibility from 1000 to 500 per year, where a pension plan exists. It would also secure pay, benefit, and job rights parity. Thus, it might help to curb the excessive creation of contingent jobs and reduce the threat of dichotomy into a two-tier labor market. In addition, the Act mandates prorated benefit coverage for part-timers where a plan exists for full-timers.

The Family and Medical Leave Act should also be adopted. The Act includes a provision that requires firms with over 50 employees to grant unpaid leaves of absence, with job protection, to workers who are caring for aging relatives—an informal "eldercare" program.[35]

The Fair Labor Standards Act should be amended to require an overtime pay premium for older-aged workers (and all part-timers) past a reduced work-week limit of, for example, 25 hours.

Unemployment Insurance (UI) taxes can be used to penalize employers who are inducing labor-force withdrawal through early retirement schemes. They can also be used to reward (with reduced tax rates or exemptions) employers who are, for example, hiring women over 45 years of age, hiring and training displaced homemakers, or instituting job sharing. Short-Time Compensation UI benefits should be expanded to supplement the incomes of workers who are temporarily on reduced-hour schedules.

Funding for and participation in displaced homemaker networks and for the 3 percent set-aside under the JTPA for workers 55 and older should also be expanded.

Minimum-wage increases would help to make low-skill part-time jobs a more viable option for those older workers and retirees who are seeking part-time schedules in new jobs.

Finally, it is important that the public sector itself take the lead in experimenting with innovative alternatives to the standard, fixed 40-hour workweek.

To summarize, an expanding pool of potential workers outside the labor force is being created by the maturing of the population, the increasing popularity of staff downsizing through early retirement schemes, and persistent age discrimination in the labor market. At the same time, employers are creating more contingent jobs, which may absorb many of these older workers. If older workers are hired as part-time employees, and if the majority of part-time positions retain their secondary labor market status, then the erosion of income security for older workers will continue. Developments such as the hiring or rehiring of retirees by firms as a cost-reduction strategy effectively make these employees subsidize their own employment.

Although only 7 percent of the total part-time work force consists of workers aged 55 and over, there is substantial interest in part-time work in this age category. One in five men and one in three women aged 55 and over, and over half of those employed who are aged 65 and over, are already working part-time hours. Three in four of those working past 65 years of age would prefer a gradual transition toward retirement, and a substantial share of retirees are interested in working part time. However, they are limited by the scarcity of viable opportunities. More innovative corporate policies to expand the availability of phased retirement and quality positions with reduced hours, and the enactment of legislation to protect or upgrade the economic status of part-time and temporary jobs, would allow workers to maintain their desired partial connection to the work force without having to join the growing ranks of workers in substandard, marginalized employment.

NOTES

1. This is so, though average hours for full-timers remain at the same level. See Owen (1988). Instability in hours has grown from month to month in the 1980s to its highest rate since the Great Depression (Golden, 1989).

2. Only 15 percent of employers use age in the computation of severance pay, for example, whereas the percent is much higher in Sweden (American Management Association, 1988: 40).

3. Hewitt and Associates survey cited in Herz and Rones (1989: 18).

4. Several surveys in the early 1980s found that inflation was a major reason behind the preference to postpone planned retirement. Presumably, this preference to continue working was to avoid erosion in real income levels. Yet, inflation has remained ahead of the growth of hourly earnings in the 1980s, which should similarly produce a desire to prolong work life. Other surveys have found that older workers searching for work tend to be those who cannot afford to retire. See Rones (1988: 44).

5. The American Association of Retired Persons states that early retirement incentive schemes are used as "older worker termination" programs.

6. Hogarth (1988: 29, 30) finds that a higher perceived probability of layoff heightens the acceptance rates of early retirement bonus offers.

7. IBM followed up its 1986 early retirement campaign by offering the package again in 1987 to anyone who had previously rejected it, albeit with trimmed-down incentives. (*Wall Street Journal,* July 23, 1987).

8. One concern with earlier retirement ages will be the increasing pressure placed on social security and pension funds to sustain older workers.

9. For empirical evidence that the employer side of the labor market is the force responsible for the rapid rise in temporary jobs, see Golden and Appelbaum (1990).

10. For example, primary sector workers develop marketable skills and require little supervision, while secondary workers exhibit high job turnover and frequent absenteeism just low enough to avoid being discharged.

Osterman (1988) divides the primary sector into three submodels of employment: salaried, craft, and industrial. The first is comprised of highly paid, white-collar jobs with mutual long-term commitments between employees and employers. The second contains highly skilled workers tied to their particular craft rather than to a single employer, and the last features blue-collar jobs along well-defined promotion ladders, with work rules such as those found in unionized manufacturing establishments. (See the Tilly article in this volume for concrete examples of occupations in each category.)

11. For evidence of the former, see "The Dun's 5000 Survey on Part-Time and Temporary Employment: 1986 and 1987 Results" (Dun and Bradstreet Corporation, 1987). Large firms tend to exhibit sizable "internal labor markets" within the organization that are conducive to primary-type jobs.

12. Part-time jobs can be either primary or secondary. Tilly refers to the dichotomy as "retention" and "secondary" jobs, while Kahne (1985) labels them as "New Concept" and "Old Concept." In essence, the distinction is based on whether the part-time position enjoys equal status or receives lower status than comparable full-time positions. A significant hourly pay, benefit, and job security difference from full-time jobs is created because the vast majority of part-time positions are of the secondary variety; managerial and professional occupations are an exception. (See Tilly and Kahne in this volume.)

A difference between Kahne's and Tilly's analysis is that Kahne seems to suggest that "New Concept" part-time jobs have been growing over time, at least until they stalled in the mid–1980s.

13. For evidence of the wide range of variation in part-time workers' hours, see Kahne and Tilly in this volume.

14. This stems from the expectation of a continuation in the dramatic drop in labor force participation of males aged 62 to 64 (from 69 percent to 48 percent, between 1970 and 1983) and in the stagnation of 55- to 64-year-old women, despite increased participation of women under 55. [See Morrison (1983)].

The aging of the European population over the last two decades may offer the United States a glimpse of its own future (Norwood, 1986).

15. Older workers perform as well or better, on average, than relatively younger workers in terms of productivity, turnover, sick days and absenteeism,

health, accident rates, decision-making ability, learning, and intellectual functioning (American Association of Retired Persons, 1986). For evidence of age discrimination, see Rones (1988: 20, 21).

16. A national survey of temporaries in Great Britain found that 73 percent preferred permanent jobs (Standing, 1986). An extensive Canadian survey of temporary clerical workers revealed that at least 41 percent were in temporary jobs involuntarily.

17. Part of the erosion of seniority protection in work-place decisions, such as the allocation of promotions, training, and layoffs—where 89 percent of labor contracts use seniority as a criterion—can be traced to the decline of unionization (see Bureau of National Affairs, 1984).

18. While the 1981 unemployment rate was 2.8 and 3.2 percent for women and men who were aged 65 and over, the unemployment-plus-discouragement rate was 8.3 and 5.9 percent respectively (Rones 1988: 44).

The longer average unemployment durations of older workers give them a higher probability of exhausting their unemployment insurance benefits. This increases the likelihood of withdrawal into retirement, since withdrawal may be the only economically viable option.

19. Seventy-nine percent of displaced homemakers are over 45 years of age, and almost 40 percent of these women have poverty level incomes (Shaw, 1988: 71, 72). Of women between 45 and 64 years of age, 76 percent of the divorced, 69 percent of the never married, and 50 percent of the widows now participate in the labor force.

20. Interview with Cuyahoga County Library personnel director, July 1987.

21. Allowing these employees to work beyond the 960-hour limit would require vesting in the company's pension plan. See Meier (1988: 186).

22. See Root and Zarrugh (1985) for evidence of the paucity of innovative personnel practices that benefit workers nearing retirement.

23. Since 1976, the proportion of both older groups working part-time hours has grown by 3 percent. The number of women 45 years of age and over employed part-time involuntarily shot up 51 percent between 1979 to 1986.

24. Belous and Appelbaum use BLS data. By industry, the 55-to-64 age group roughly mirrors the pattern for all workers, while 63 percent of workers who are 65 years of age and over are concentrated in the trade and services industry. There is a substantial amount of occupational shifting around the retirement age. For example, 14 percent of workers aged 55 to 64 are in service occupations; this rises to 19 percent for the group aged 65 and over.

25. A survey of adults aged 18 to 80 by Louis Harris and Associates for the National Council on Aging (1981). Over half the group aged 55 to 64, and 80 percent of the group aged 65 and over, preferred to continue to work on a part-time basis in the same kind of job.

26. BLS 1986 data. See Rones (1988: 44).

27. For evidence see Gustman and Steinmeier (1983: 78–81). Those 55 years of age and over who do partially retire usually do not do so in the jobs that they held full time.

28. One vital characteristic of part-time jobs that renders them a non-viable option is low pay. Herz and Rones (1989: 18, 26, 28) estimate that when the

average hours of work fall from 35 to 20, average hourly earnings decline by 30 to 40 percent.

29. Forty-four percent were interested in obtaining training for their current job (including computer training), 22 percent for a similar job, and 11 percent for a totally different job, according to Meier's summary of unpublished results of the 1985 survey of the American Association of Retired Persons (1988: 178–179).

30. A Conference Board survey in 1983 found that only about 14 percent of all firms have redesigned jobs or work hours for workers 65 years of age and over. See 9to5 (1987: 115, 116) for non-U.S. innovations to reduce the work-loads of older workers.

In general, hours are primarily employer-determined; thus, weekly hours are much too rigid. Cyclical downturns, at least in the post–Great Depression era, have produced widespread layoffs rather than work sharing and, recently, an expansion of contingent work-forces in part to absorb downturns in product or service demand. Although average weekly hours have become slightly more variable in the 1980s this is most likely due to the increased share of part-time jobs and the substitution of mandatory overtime for additional employment in industries.

Flextime policies are beneficial to older workers but not wholly useful as a transition to retirement since flextime usually involves a fixed, rather than reduced, length of the workweek.

31. U.S. Labor Department surveys find that many working adults actually prefer more weekly hours. Thus there is a potential social welfare gain if hours could be redistributed toward them and away from workers nearing or past retirement who would prefer shorter hours at their customary job. Early labor force withdrawal, absenteeism, and quitting would most likely decline as a result.

32. See Rones (1988: 26) for indirect evidence of the scarcity of gradual retirement. Phased retirement plans can be implemented through reduced weekly hours, work scheduled for alternate weeks or months, extended vacation weeks, or "rehearsal retirement" periods.

Only one in five workers who are eligible for a phased retirement plan opt for it, a sign that employee fears and lack of knowledge in a program lacking precedent are fairly strong obstacles. See 9to5 (1988: 116, 117) for successful corporate examples.

33. See Meier (1988: 184) for obstacles to inducing workers to opt for part-time work at their current job, even with partial pensions.

34. Christiansen asserts that self-employed older workers have an enhanced ability to sustain their careers after 65 years of age, and claims that many older Americans already work "off the books" to avoid the social security earnings test.

35. Seventy-eight percent of informal caregivers are over 45 years of age, and 72 percent of these are women. Studies have found that from 8 to 28 percent of female caregivers have quit their jobs to provide care.

IV A CLOSER LOOK: INDUSTRIAL AND OCCUPATIONAL CASES

14 Two Faces of Part-Time Work: Good and Bad Part-Time Jobs in U.S. Service Industries

Chris Tilly

Are part-time jobs in American service industries good jobs or bad jobs? More specifically, do part-time employees in these industries tend to be in high-skill or low-skill jobs? Two managers respond:

It would have to be a routine job that we can break up . . . we don't want people at higher grades to be part-time [because] for these higher grades, there's quite a bit of training. (Personnel director at an insurance company, II.A.)[1]

You're going to find our more-skilled, higher-level people in this [part-time status]. Our senior analysts and above as opposed to just the programmer who's just producing code where the skill level is just technical. (Data processing manager at an insurance company, IX.E.)

What are the advantages and disadvantages of hiring a part-time worker? Once more, two managers have different answers:

The pluses of hiring part-time people are the [low] rate of pay that you're able to pay them, the increased [schedule] flexibility that it will allow you, particularly if you have a varying business, varying volume. . . . And also the benefits that are available to a full-time person are not available to a part-timer. . . . [The minuses are] the abilities, experience and work level that they achieve. Their loyalty to the position and the company. . . . I'm talking about absenteeism, I'm talking about tardiness, shrinkage, attitude. . . . [And] the part-time ratio . . . turn[s] over much faster than the full-time ratio. (Supermarket manager, VII.D.)

You probably will not find more committed employees than your part-time population. . . . Part-time people will tell you they work much harder than full-time people. . . . They want to hold onto their position. They want to do it all. They're driven. . . . [But] lack of availability is an issue. You're not as available.

It slows things down. It's hard to schedule meetings. . . . [Part-time employment is] also expensive in terms of benefits. (Employee services director at an insurance company, IX.A.)

What do the contradictory responses of these managers reveal? The answer is that there are two distinct types of part-time employment in the service industries. The first manager in each case is talking about *secondary* part-time jobs. Secondary part-time workers have low skill and compensation compared to their full-time counterparts, and are immersed in a secondary labor market with little prospect of advancement. Employers use secondary part-time employment to attract workers, such as housewives and students, who will accept minimal compensation. Secondary part-time jobs are "bad" part-time jobs.

The second manager answering each question is describing a completely different type of part-time employment: *retention* part-time jobs. Retention part-time workers have skill and compensation levels comparable to, or above, those of full-timers. Their part-time schedules are special arrangements negotiated to retain or attract valued employees, typically women with young children. Retention part-time jobs are "good" part-time jobs. The distinction between secondary and retention part-time jobs proves a useful prism for understanding the utilization of part-time employment in the service industries. We shall develop the distinction and then apply it to the shape of part-time employment in the U.S. retail and insurance industries.

The notion that there is more than one type of part-time work is perhaps not a startling one; after all, most of us have come into contact both with part-time sales clerks and with part-time professionals. However, most economic analysis of part-time employment has overlooked this idea. Instead, economists have tended to focus on the *average* part-time worker. Thus, we know that the mean hourly wage of part-time workers is roughly 40 percent below the mean for full-timers. Only about one half of this wage differential can be explained by the fact that part-time workers have different observed characteristics (sex, race, education, experience) than full-timers, and are concentrated in industries and occupations with below-average wages (Owen, 1979).[2] In addition, on average, part-time workers are less likely to be covered by fringe benefits. For example, Ichniowski and Preston (1985) find that the probabilities of having sick leave, paid vacation, pension, or health insurance are significantly decreased for part-time employees. Part-timers are from 11 percent to 33 percent less likely to receive these benefits, depending on the specific benefit and on the source of data used for estimation.

The average part-time job is also characterized by short duration and little opportunity for promotion. A part-time worker has been on the job an average of 3.4 years, well below the average of 5.7 years for full-time women and 8.1 years for full-time men (Rebitzer and Taylor, 1988). Nollen, Eddy, and Martin (1978), who surveyed unit managers and personnel officers at 39 companies that employ part-time workers, found that both groups tended to consider part-timers "less promotable" than full-time workers.

Behind these averages, fascinating glimpses of diversity emerge. Blank (1986) finds that after controlling for other worker and job characteristics, part-time women earn lower hourly wages than comparable full-time women in most occupations—but that part-time women earn *higher* hourly wages than full-timers in managerial and professional occupations. Nollen et al. report that, although half the companies surveyed give part-time workers no health insurance at all, one third offer part-timers the full benefit, not prorated. The latter companies, in effect, offer more health benefits on a per-hour basis to part-timers than to full-timers. Even more interesting, although 36 percent of the unit managers and 35 percent of the personnel officers surveyed by Nollen et al. described part-time workers as having higher turnover rates than full-timers, another 21 percent of unit managers and 35 percent of personnel officers reported that part-timers had *lower* turnover rates. The survey also yielded split opinions on the relative productivity of part-time and full-time workers.

Kahne (1985), in contrast to most economists who examine part-time work, identifies two categories of part-time employment: "Old Concept" and "New Concept" part-time jobs. According to Kahne, New Concept part-time workers are viewed by employers as being permanent workers with career potential, rather than as temporary or intermittent workers. The New Concept part-time job also generally provides fringe benefits, unlike the Old Concept part-time job. The Old Concept/New Concept distinction is a helpful start in thinking about "good" and "bad" part-time jobs.

INTERNAL LABOR MARKET THEORY

To build on Kahne's insight, it is necessary to explore why there may be more than one type of part-time employment, and how these types are linked to the firm's broader set of employment relationships. The theory of internal labor markets offers tools to do just that. Internal labor markets are sets of jobs within the firm, linked by common features: breadth of job definition, level of skill and responsibility, connection with job ladders, level of compensation, and expected tenure (Doeringer and Piore, 1971).

Osterman, in a recent systematization of internal labor market theory (1988), argues that firms choose combinations of internal labor markets to pursue objectives of cost minimization, labor flexibility, and labor predictability. To attain these three objectives, a firm fashions a particular labor market structure or set of structures. Doeringer and Piore (1971), among others, emphasize the differences between the labor markets of different firms—particularly between primary labor market firms that offer steady jobs with promotion ladders and secondary labor market firms that offer high-turnover jobs with no prospect for advancement. However, Osterman (1982) points out that, in fact, many firms combine a number of different labor markets. A firm's markets for managers, clerical workers, and skilled and unskilled production workers may be quite distinct.

What is the repertoire of labor markets from which firms can choose? Osterman (1988) proposes a typology of industrial, salaried, craft, and secondary labor markets. The *industrial* labor market was, until a few years ago, the standard model for manufacturing production workers: long tenure and job ladders, on-the-job skill acquisition, narrow job definitions, little decision-making power, and job security tempered by layoffs. The *salaried* labor market, on the other hand, corresponds to that of managers or actuaries, again featuring long tenure, job ladders, and on-the-job training, but with broad and flexible job definitions, substantial decision-making power and discretion, and an implicit life-time employment guarantee. The *craft* labor market is composed of work-ers like the skilled carpenter or computer programmer. It is characterized by short job tenure, loyalty to craft rather than to a particular firm, advancement by shifting from one firm to another or by accumulating skill rather than by climbing a ladder in a particular firm, and skills acquired off the job (through apprenticeship or education). Finally, the *secondary* labor market is characteristic of a typing pool or custodial staff: short tenure, no job ladder, little skill, and low pay. Borrowing a term from Doeringer and Piore (1971), we can refer to the industrial, salaried, and craft labor markets as primary labor markets. At a first approxi-mation, the distinction between good and bad jobs is the distinction between primary and secondary labor markets.

TWO TYPES OF PART-TIME JOBS

The research reported here draws primarily on a set of 82 open-ended interviews conducted during 1987/88 with managers, union officials, and workers. The companies and unions represented are almost all located in the retail and insurance industries—a high and a low part-time em-ployment sector, respectively. They are drawn from the Boston and Pittsburgh areas—a labor-shortage and a labor-surplus area, respec-tively. Two service industries were chosen for scrutiny because an over-whelming 86 percent of part-timers work in service industries; 35 percent are in wholesale and retail trade alone (United States Bureau of Labor

Statistics, 1988). The interviews include a total of 31 companies, and 15 unions and other labor organizations. Although the companies and unions are anonymous, claims based on interviews are referenced with the relevant interview index number.

In the retail and insurance industries, as noted, part-time jobs break down into two categories: secondary and retention.[3] The key characteristics that distinguish secondary from retention part-time employment are skill and training, compensation, turnover, and connection with promotion ladders.

Skill, Training, Responsibility

Secondary part-time jobs involve low levels of skill, training, and responsibility. In retail stores, the more skilled and responsible tasks tend to be covered by full-timers, while low-skill tasks are handled by part-time workers. For example, most supermarkets use only full-time workers in meat-cutting jobs, which are skilled jobs.[4] On the other hand, a supermarket manager stated that front-end employees—cashiers and baggers, both relatively unskilled jobs—represent "the bulk of the part-time work force" (VII.C).

Even within low-level job categories like stock clerk in a supermarket, or sales clerk in a convenience store or department store, different tasks are assigned to part-timers and full-timers. Full-time employees are more likely to be given responsibilities such as ordering, receiving goods, taking inventory, or doing paperwork. Part-time workers are more likely just to stock the display cases or ring the register. A supermarket store manager reported: "[The full-timers] come in the morning and get things set up, do the prep. The part-time employees then just maintain it for the rest of the day. It's different to set up and do ordering than to just dump more fruit out there" (VII.C).

The distinction between part-time and full-time tasks may be formal or informal. In one convenience store chain, "They [full-timers] might even do some paperwork, some smaller duty that the manager would delegate to a full-time clerk. . . . It's not in their job description, it's just something they're assigned, or they can do it, and they want to do it. But really, as far as the job description, no, there's no difference between a full-time or a part-time" (III.I). In a fast-food company (I.G), similarly, full-timers do meal preparation and recovery (cleanup), a somewhat more varied and complex set of tasks, while part-timers come in during peak mealtimes to cook and serve. In insurance, secondary part-timers are found in unskilled service jobs (cafeteria, building service) and in lower-skilled clerical jobs with more discrete, less integrative tasks. Part-time clerical jobs were described as "not crucial" (IX.E), "[located in] your production departments" (VIII.A.2), "[jobs where] somebody can put down their work and somebody else can pick it up" (II.D), "a routine job that we can break up" (II.A), and "usually just one job, duty—a repeated task," especially "when there are certain times of day that need service" (II.). Typical part-time clerical jobs include data entry, filing, mail sorting, direct mail stuffing, and typing in a typing pool. There is some evidence of an inverse correlation between training time and use of part-time employment in claims processing at insurance companies. An insurance company manager commented: "Part-timers are in jobs that require a shorter length of training and normally have a faster learning curve or shorter learning curve" (VIII.F).

All of this, however, is only half the story. The other half pertains to *retention* part-time jobs, concentrated in technical and professional occupations with *high* levels of skill, training, and responsibility. For example, the manager of an insurance company's pension systems area stated about his part-time employees: "The fact that they're part-timers . . . really serves two purposes. One, they're still raising their children. . . . But the most important thing is that they have a wealth of knowledge and are very critical resources in the area that is very difficult to find replacements [for]. . . . It takes three to five years [for a new person] to develop to the level of expertise where they could contribute very heavily to the pension world" (IX.D). He emphasized that in order for him to consider granting someone a part-time job, "It has to be someone who is critical to my goals." The same reasoning applies to certain jobs in retail as well, although these jobs are a small minority of retail's part-time workforce. The personnel director of a supermarket chain noted: "In the [computer] system's area, we have tried to customize the job to fit the job seeker. It's a very tight labor market. . . . A lot of computer people like to work part-time" (I.A). A neat summary of the twofold character of part-time jobs was provided by an insurance company's personnel director: "Training costs are . . . minimal for support jobs. Routine jobs—collating, printing, shipping, typing. That's one reason we don't want people at higher grades to be part time. For these higher grades, there's quite a bit of training: there's a mix of classroom, formal, and on-the-job training. So, usually, if someone is part time in these grades, it's formerly full-time, already trained employees—people who requested part-time hours" (II.A).

Pay and Benefits

Secondary part-time workers receive reduced fringe benefits and in some cases lower hourly pay than full-timers. As a fast food company's personnel director observed, "traditionally, American business doesn't provide fringe benefits to part-time workers" (I.G). Every retail company surveyed pays lower fringe benefits to part-timers. Retailers commonly exclude part-time employees from one or more of the insurance benefits (health, life, disability). One supermarket chain estimates that it spends 20 percent of base pay for benefits for part-timers, compared to 36 to 41 percent for full-timers. Since the chain also offers part-timers a lower rate of pay, this means that the costs of part-time benefits are roughly one quarter as great on a per-hour basis. In Pittsburgh area supermarkets, the lowest rung of part-timers, "customer service clerks," better known as baggers, receive no benefits at all.

In fact, informants from six of the 17 retail companies surveyed reported that they even have employees working 40 hours who are considered part-time employees and who receive lower fringe benefits (I.D, III.A.1, III.E, III.H, III.J, VII.D). One of them explained, "I do have people working 40 hours a week in baggers' jobs. But they are not considered full-time people.... The difference is the rate of pay that they're able to get. And also, the benefits that are available to a full-time person are not available to a part-timer. It's really just a job title more so than the work performed ... " (VII.D). The majority of insurance companies also reduce benefits for part-timers. Two of the companies offer part-timers only prorated vacation and holidays (as compared with sick pay, health, life, and accident insurance for full-timers in one case) (II.A, IV.E). The insurance companies offering reduced benefits include the insurers in which secondary part-time employment is most common. Notable among the latter are three health insurers (VIII, II.F, IV.F.1), the only insurance companies in the survey to adopt deliberate strategies of expanding part-time employment.

At supermarkets, it is standard for part-timers to receive both reduced benefits and lower hourly wages (II.B, III.B). One chain's personnel director estimates that the company pays part-timers, on average, half the hourly wage of full-timers (VII.A.1). Nationwide, supermarket chains surveyed by *Progressive Grocer* magazine reported an hourly wage of $4.80 for a part-time clerk in 1987, roughly 80 percent of the average hourly wage of $5.92 for a full-time clerk (*Progressive Grocer*, 1988).

Once more, there is another side to the coin. Where *retention* part-time employment is a major form of part-time work, a part-time job generally comes with full benefits and pay. The insurance companies, in which there are substantial numbers of retention part-timers (II.E, IV.A, IV.D, IX), provide full benefits to all employees working above some cutoff in the range of 18 to 24 hours per week. This criterion covers the bulk of part-timers. In these cases "full benefits" means full insurance benefits and other benefits that are prorated.

In contrast with the retailers who have "part-timers" working 40 hours, at least one insurance company had a "full-timer" working 20 hours:

Manager: When Carol ... was ill, did she work part-time for a while?

Executive Secretary: The one that had the heart condition? Yes. She worked half days but she was still considered a full-timer.

Manager: She was a full-time, regular employee (IV.D).

Setting benefit levels for part-time workers is something of a blunt instrument: it is not practicable to offer full benefits to some (retention) part-time workers, and partial benefits to other (secondary) part-timers. Thus, it is not surprising to find generous fringe benefit provisions for part-timers at the *companies* that use the most retention part-time employment, and reduced fringe benefits at the companies where secondary part-time employment is most common.

Turnover

High turnover is the bane of managers who employ *secondary* part-timers. Retailers universally report higher turnover among part-timers than among full-timers. In most settings, part-time turnover is overwhelmingly attributable to quitting—"easily 90 percent or more," according to a supermarket manager (VII.B). The high turnover of retail part-timers stands in striking contrast to the remarkable stability of full-timers in retail, especially in companies where a union contract improves wages and working conditions:

They *marry* those jobs (III.B).

The turnover rate with the full-timers is very, very slim, almost nil. You know, we're talking a full-timer leaving probably only because of retirement, and some chance of them finding a higher-paid job (III.A.1).

Insurers also commented on higher turnover among part-timers (II.A, IV.E). Managers at two health insurance companies that employ large numbers of secondary part-timers were particularly emphatic:

Part-time[rs] have a much higher rate of turnover (II.F).

My guess . . . based on my experience is I'd run a 15 to 20 percent turnover rate in the full-timers annually and I'd run closer to a 40 to 50 percent turnover on part-timers (VIII.F).

Among retention part-timers, on the other hand, part-time employment is an *alternative* to turnover:

Interviewer: What's your sense of what would happen if you said to these women: "No, you can't have part-time hours"?

Manager: I think in every case they would terminate their employment. And that . . . comes from the fact that their skills are very marketable. . . . I suppose the trade-off that's mentally taking place by me and by other managers when these situations are coming up is that . . . here are my choices: [if I say yes] I get less work for the same position; if I say no, how am I going to replace the skill set? (IX.E)

In many cases, retention part-timers eventually move back to full-time hours, sometimes as a result of company pressure: "We don't like people to stay on part time forever. . . . Some departments will tolerate part-time employees for six to 12 months. Then they'll look at them again after a year. The vast majority of employees who go part time return to full time after a year" (II.B).

Promotion Ladders

Secondary part-time jobs tend to be both entry level and dead-end. *Retention* part-time jobs, however, are generally located partway up a promotion path. In both cases, promotion beyond a certain limited span means moving to a full-time job. In all kinds of retail establishments, for example, secondary part-time jobs form the bottom of a ladder that extends upward to full-time jobs, and ultimately into management. Some food retailers (I.D, III.A, III.D, III.I, VII) have a formal requirement that full-timers be hired exclusively from the part-time ranks, not from outside the company, and still others (III.J) apply this policy de facto. However, although most full-timers in retail food were once part-time workers, few part-time workers become full-timers (I.A, I.G, III.B, VI.C, VII.A). The explanation for this paradox is that there are very few full-time jobs—less than 20 percent of the jobs in the store, in some cases (I.B, III.A.2, III.B, III.G, III.H)—and that full-timers turn over slowly.

At insurance companies, secondary part-time jobs are often isolated from the rest of the work force by non-standard shifts (IV.E, IX.C) or because they are concentrated in geographically remote locations. In a suburban part-time facility run by one of the health insurers, 93 percent of the workers are part-time (VIII.C). This operation is more segregated than any of the supermarkets surveyed. Thus, moving to full-time work from a secondary part-time job may involve a change in shift or job location. Some companies have additional rules designed to minimize such mobility. For example, a Pittsburgh insurer requires part-timers to stay at least one year before moving to a full-time job (IV.F.1).

Retention part-time workers, on the other hand, perch in the middle of job ladders. As noted, retention part-time arrangements are usually worked out for employees who have substantial company-specific training, such as underwriters, or for workers with very marketable skills, such as systems analysts. However, working a part-time schedule at this level generally means foregoing further promotion, at least until the worker returns to full-time hours. A life insurer's director of employee services noted succinctly: "We don't hire part-time people and run them up these ladders as part-timers" (IX.A.2). Part-timers are also generally barred from management positions at the top of the job ladder. In the words of the data processing manager of a life insurance company, part-time schedules are only tolerated among "individual contributors," not "team leaders" (IX.E).

THE LINK WITH INTERNAL LABOR MARKETS

A picture of secondary and retention part-time employment is emerging. The former is marked by minimal skill, training, and responsibility, low benefits or hourly wages, high turnover, and little connection to promotion ladders. The latter exhibits an opposite set of characteristics. This is precisely the distinction between secondary and primary labor markets. Secondary and retention part-time jobs are the way they are because they occur in particular internal labor markets; a secondary labor market in the case of retail clerks and insurance claim coders, a salaried labor market in the case of technical and professional workers, and a craft labor market in the case of computer programmers. In other words, part-time jobs are good or bad for the same reasons that full-time jobs are. There is nothing inherent in part-time jobs that dictates that they must have low productivity and compensation. Even in a retail food store, where the boundary between high- and low-compensation jobs is the line between full- and part-time status, it is the secondary labor market embodied in the part-time jobs, not their shortened hours, that brands them as inferior. A part-time systems analyst who works for the same retail food company has a productive, high-paid job.

All this is not to say that jobs in any type of labor market are equally likely to be part time. Jobs in secondary labor markets are more likely to be part time than those in primary labor markets. Retention part-time employment is by its nature exceptional, extended to one employee at a time on a negotiated basis. Secondary part-time employment, on the other hand, is applied to entire job categories. The differentiation between secondary and retention part-time employment, coupled with the notion that firms choose their internal labor markets, helps to understand the striking difference in the amount of part-time employment used in retail and insurance. In March 1985, retail and insurance workers sampled in the Current Population Survey (conducted monthly by the U.S. Census Bureau) had rates of part-time employment of 38 percent and 11 percent, respectively. The retail and insurance companies surveyed in this study had even more divergent average part-time rates of 60 percent and 5 percent.

This contrast between retail and insurance, though partly the result of different time patterns of product demand in the two industries, is due in large part to the fact that insurers and retailers have chosen very different labor markets. Insurers have chosen to arrange most of their labor force in a salaried labor market. This labor market is characterized by job designs that entail responsibility, broad job definitions—hence, continuous rather than discrete tasks—and substantial training ladders. To secure a stable work force, insurers aim for primary earners. All of these features of the salaried labor market make it difficult to accommodate part-time work. To the extent that a company using this labor market employs part-timers, it will create *retention* part-time jobs. As noted, however, retention part-time jobs are exceptional arrangements, and remain small in number.

Retailers, on the other hand, have chosen to place most of their jobs in a secondary labor market. This means breaking down jobs to units that entail little skill or responsibility. The work force need not be especially stable or committed, but must be cheap. Secondary part-time employment is consistent with this labor market. In fact, creating part-time jobs is a way to attract a secondary work force and to legitimize a lower standard of pay. For retailers, creating large numbers of secondary part-time jobs is a key labor market strategy.

Although retailers and insurers are constrained by the shape of the product markets that each of them confronts, there is also an element of employer discretion in these labor market arrangements. This element is highlighted by *exceptions* to the rule, companies that have shifted the boundaries between primary and secondary labor markets away from their usual positions in each industry. Some insurance companies run many of their clerical functions as a secondary labor market, staffed with part-timers (II.F, VIII). Some retailers organize their work forces as a primary labor market, and use far fewer part-timers (VI). A comparison of labor-surplus Pittsburgh and labor-shortage Boston documents the pervasiveness of the secondary/retention distinction. There *are* significant differences in part-time employment between the two cities. Pittsburgh, for example, has a higher rate of involuntary part-time employment, due to labor market slack, and a lower rate of voluntary part-time employment, due to low rates of labor-force participation among women and teens. Nevertheless, both cities have secondary and retention part-timers. In both cities, retail employment is dominated by a secondary labor market made up of part-time jobs, whereas insurance employment is primarily a salaried labor market of full-timers, with only a few retention part-timers. In short, the basic structure of part-time employment in service industries appears to be identical in the two cities.

In the United States economy as a whole, not surprisingly, the evidence suggests that secondary part-timers outnumber their retention counterparts. Most part-timers are concentrated in low-wage service industries more akin to retail than to insurance. Their lower average wage, lower probability of obtaining fringe benefits, and shorter average job tenure reflect the fact that, in these industries, large numbers of secondary part-timers outweigh small numbers of retention part-timers.

In conclusion, the answer to the question posed at the beginning of this paper—"Are part-time jobs in United States' service industries good jobs or bad jobs?"—is that they are both. Two opposite types of part-time jobs, secondary and retention, coexist. This is so because part-time employment has different uses in different labor markets. The retention part-time model gives cause for optimism. Indeed, part-time jobs need not be poorly compensated, low-skill, dead-end jobs. However, the optimism must necessarily be limited since, unless there is a major transformation of U.S. employment, retention part-timers are likely to remain a small minority in the part-time work force.

NOTES

This research was funded in part by the Cuddahy Foundation, the United States Department of Education's Javits Fellowship, and the Economic Policy Institute. Opinions expressed are the author's alone.

1. The interviews that form the basis for this paper are indexed by numbers beginning with Roman numerals, to identify companies while preserving anonymity.

2. Although Owen's research was conducted ten years ago, unpublished data from the U.S. Bureau of Labor Statistics provided by Nardone indicated that the differential in *median* hourly wages has remained roughly constant at 40 percent from 1973 to 1987.

3. In other industries, there are other types of part-time employment. For example, work sharing (temporary hours reductions during downturns) in manufacturing and construction is distinct from both secondary and retention part-time employment. However, since most part-timers work in service industries, these two types are of particular interest.

4. Five companies specifically discussed the staffing of their meat department. Four of them use only full-time cutters (III.A.1, III.H, III.G, I.A), while the fifth (VII) uses part-timers as well.

15 Part-Time and Occasional Teachers in Ontario's Elementary School System

Isik Urla Zeytinoglu

New types of employment structures are emerging in public and private sector organizations, as a solution to the employer's demand for flexibility and low labor costs. Full-time employment, once the "norm," is being replaced by part-time and other types of temporary employment structures. The academic and popular media have been predominantly interested in part-time employment in the private sector; yet increasingly, similar shifts in employment structures are emerging in public and semi-public organizations, such as federal ministries, hospitals, and schools.

Contrary to the general opinion that part-time work exists only in unskilled, low-valued, and low-paying jobs, in both private and public sector organizations there are a substantial number of highly skilled and well-paying professional part-time jobs held by teachers, nurses, engineers, consultants and managers. Why are these highly skilled professionals employed on a part-time basis? What are the typical characteristics of the professionals working part time? What are the employment conditions in these jobs? This study will examine these issues by focusing on one of the most enduring part-time professions, elementary school teaching.

Part-time teaching is a practice long established among elementary school teachers in Ontario. It has existed since the kindergarten programs were included in the elementary schools' curricula. Now, part-time employment is no longer the sole preserve of the kindergarten teachers but is instead becoming common throughout the elementary school system; this trend warrants close examination. There are two additional reasons for choosing the elementary school teachers as the focus of analysis in this study. First, teaching at the elementary school level is a profession that is substantially the same throughout the school boards. Because it is not subject oriented like secondary school teaching, it does not have those discrepancies in the employment conditions, responsibilities, or workload that stem from perceived or real differences in the subject taught. Thus, focusing on a narrowly defined occupation will help us to avoid comparing full-time and part-time employees who perform quite different jobs within the same occupational group.

Second, part-time teaching is predominantly a unionized profession. With the exception of some occasional teachers, all the full-time and part-time teachers are members of the teachers' associations, organizations that function both as professional associations and as labor unions. In comparison to most part-time employees, who are not unionized (Canada. Commission of Inquiry into Part-Time Work, 1983; Zeytinoglu, 1987c), part-time teachers seem to be unique within the part-time labor force because of their high percentage of unionization. They are, therefore, worthy of further study.

TEACHERS' CONTRACTS, THEIR ASSOCIATIONS, AND EMPLOYERS

In the Ontario elementary school system, there are three types of teachers: full-time, part-time, and occasional. They are classified according to the type of employment, the type of contract they hold, and the type of legislative coverage. In terms of the type of employment, full-time teachers are employed by a school board for a consecutive period and on a full-time schedule for at least a year. Part-time teachers are also employed for a consecutive period and on a regular basis, but for a fraction of the full-time teachers' schedule. A part-time teacher may teach from one third to more than one half the workload of a full-time teacher. An occasional teacher—also referred to as a substitute teacher—is employed to fill a vacancy on a temporary basis if, during the school year, a teacher is absent from regular duties due to sickness or death. An occasional teacher may teach for a few days or for almost a full school year, depending on the vacancy.

The education sector is unique in terms of the teachers' employment contract. Most teachers have two types of contracts: an individual (written or implicit) contract, and a collective agreement signed by the association (union). Full-time and part-time teachers all have individual contracts with the school boards to provide services on a full-time or part-time basis. Occasional teachers, although considered non-contract by the school boards and government, do, according to common law, hold an implicit contract to provide services only for the time period required by the employers. Consequently, in theory if not necessarily in practice, an occasional teacher has the freedom to decide to work whenever called in. Full-time and part-time teachers, on the other hand, are obliged to work for the duration of their contract.

If they are unionized, teachers have an additional contract, which is a collective agreement covering the salary and overall employment conditions for the one-year or two-year period, depending on the time period for which the agreement is negotiated. In terms of the coverage of a collective agreement, there is another distinction made among the three types of teachers. According to the Teaching Profession Act,[1] a teacher is a person legally qualified to teach in an elementary school and is under contract. Full-time and part-time teachers fall within the jurisdiction of the Act. Although occasional teachers may be (and most are) legally qualified to teach in Ontario schools, they are not considered as "teachers" within the definition of the Act, since they are not under contract. Therefore, under the education sector's collective bargaining legislation,[2] occasional teachers cannot be covered by the same agreement as full-time and part-time teachers, but instead are required to negotiate a separate agreement. Furthermore, occasional teachers are statutorily restricted from joining the full-time and part-time teachers' unions, although some unions have in practice been able to circumvent this restriction by creating sister associations.

Teachers' Associations

In Ontario, full-time, part-time and occasional teachers are organized under four associations and a public sector union. With the exception of the occasional teachers, all elementary school teachers in Ontario are required by legislation to join one of the associations, based on their sex, language, or the type of school board for which they teach. Male elementary school teachers, employed by a public school board and under contract, are members of the Ontario Public School Teachers Federation (OPSTF), which has approximately 14,000 statutory members.[3] Female elementary school teachers, employed under contract in public school boards, are members of the Federation of Women Teachers' Associations of Ontario (FWTAO), which has approximately 33,000 members. In schools in which French is the first language, L'Association des Enseignantes et des Enseignants Franco-Ontariens (AEFO) is organized. It has approximately 5,500 members. In Catholic school boards, both male and female teachers are organized under the Ontario English Catholic Teachers' Association (OECTA). The Association currently has a membership of 25,000 elementary and secondary school teachers.

Occasional teachers are not organized along the same lines as full-time and part-time teachers; instead, they are separated according to the school board. Occasional teachers employed in separate schools are organized by the Ontario Catholic Occasional Teachers' Association

(OCOTA), which is a sister organization of OECTA. Occasional teachers in public schools are organized as separate bargaining units of either the OPSTF or the Ontario Public Service Employees Union (OPSEU). Still, the majority of occasional teachers remain unorganized.

School Boards

As mentioned above, there are two types of school boards in Ontario: public school boards and separate school boards. The immediate employer of the teachers is a school board, although the ultimate employer is the provincial government. In terms of collective bargaining, the associations negotiate with the school boards. In Ontario, there are 182 school boards, with 3,742 elementary schools, employing 60,118 elementary school teachers (Ontario Ministry of Education, 1987).

Negotiations for Part-Time and Occasional Teachers

Negotiations for full-time and part-time teachers are held together, since both types of teachers are in the same bargaining unit. Furthermore, in public elementary schools the OPSTF and the FWTAO's local branches (local unions) negotiate jointly in all jurisdiction across the province to reach one agreement per school board. OECTA's units (local unions) negotiate with the separate school boards and sign agreements for both full-time and part-time teachers employed at the elementary school level. The AEFO locals and the group with which they are associated, either the OPSTF and FWTAO or OECTA, negotiate together and reach a single agreement. Occasional teachers are a totally separate group in terms of negotiations. They fall under the jurisdiction of a separate act, the Ontario Labour Relations Act, and therefore negotiate separately from the full-time and part-time teachers.

Studying the Part-Time Professional

Part-time work has been a topic of interest for many researchers; yet only a handful of studies exist of part-time professionals. Macro-level studies on part-time employment present significant differences in employment conditions for full-time and part-time workers, particularly in terms of pay and benefits (Canada. Commission of Inquiry into Part-Time Work, 1983; Zeytinoglu, 1987c; White, 1983). While these studies provide invaluable information on the part-time work force, they do not focus on skilled part-time workers. A few studies on part-time professionals, such as part-time university faculty (Lundy and Warme in this volume; Warme and Lundy, 1988a; Zeytinoglu and Ahmed, 1988) or nurses (Dixon, 1987; Pilkington and Wood, 1986), conclude that, relative to their full-time counterparts, part-time professionals are employed as marginal workers. Their status and employment conditions, however, have improved through unionization and the standardized scheduling of part-time work. In addition to studies on the marginality of part-time workers in their work place (Beechey, 1987; Beechey and Perkins, 1987; White, 1983), and the segregation of part-time workers into female-dominated jobs (Holden and Hansen, 1987; Weeks, 1984; Spencer, 1988), there is Kahne's (1985) discussion of the possibility of a "new concept" of part-time work in which full-time earnings are prorated, fringe benefits are paid, and a career progression is possible.

Focusing primarily on part-time workers in non-professional occupations, others (Dombois and Osterland, 1987; Osterman, 1987; Evans and Bell, 1986) attempt to explain part-time employment within the overall framework of economic recession, international competition, and the restructuring of work. These studies approach part-time work as a new form of flexible utilization of labor whereby firms segment their operations in such a way that they create a well-developed employment system for a certain group of permanent workers and a secondary system for a clearly differentiated group of temporary workers.

While their approaches and methods of studying the part-time phenomenon are different, researchers nonetheless assume that a dichotomous employment structure exists in the work place. There is one structure for the "core" group, consisting of full-time employees, and another for the "peripheral" (secondary) group, which comprises part-time employees. Applying this dichotomous model to the elementary school system, one finds that full-time teachers are the "core" workers, and part-time and occasional teachers are the "peripherals." The core group tends to be characterized as one in which employees with permanent status are central to the long-term future of the organization. The training and development resources of the organization are mainly devoted to these employees, and they are more likely to enjoy good career and promotion prospects. The "peripheral" group has little access to career opportunities, receives little training from the organization, and tends to have high turnover and less secure jobs (Evans and Bell, 1986).

THE ONTARIO STUDY

To examine the employment conditions for full-time, part-time, and occasional teachers, I conducted interviews in the summers of 1987 and 1988 with three teachers' associations representing the English speaking teachers, and two school boards, one representing the public school board and the other representing the separate school board. In addition, a survey was sent to a sample of boards and teachers associations' locals that were located in Ontario. The interviews and the survey contained similar questions, designed to reveal the following: the profile of part-time teachers, why part-time teachers are hired, and the promotion, training, and layoff policies for part-time and occasional teachers in comparison to full-time teachers.

To select the survey sample, I obtained in October 1986, on request from the Ontario Ministry of Labour, a listing of collective agreements, specifically covering full-time and part-time teachers in Ontario. The list contained a total of 97 agreements pertaining to full-time and part-time teachers. Of those agreements, the ones expiring in 1988 were eliminated. Since the questionnaires were to be mailed in 1988, I did not expect the parties to respond at a time when they could possibly be in negotiations. In addition, agreements that covered less than 100 teachers were eliminated because I wanted to focus on larger school boards. Because of the nature of the study, secondary school teachers or other groups of workers employed by the school boards were also eliminated. After these eliminations, the survey sample consisted of 51 collective agreements covering 51 school boards and 83 association locals.[4]

The procedure for mailing the questionnaires was different for the school boards and the associations. For the school boards, a letter informing them of the survey was mailed to the Director of Education and to the highest-ranking human resources manager. After the initial mailing of the questionnaire, we telephoned those school boards that did not respond and offered another copy of the questionnaire. A reminder letter and a second mailing of the original questionnaire were sent to those boards that did not respond to the initial requests. This procedure resulted in an 80 percent response rate from the school boards.

For the associations, we contacted the presidents or the research staff, explained the purposes of the questionnaire, and requested their assistance. After the associations' approval of the contents of the questionnaire, we made arrangements for the mailing process. The questionnaires were mailed by the two associations to their local union representatives. Upon our request, a letter of acknowledgement was included with each questionnaire. Through our contact person in the association, we followed up with a second mailing. The third association provided the mailing list of its local union representatives. In that case, we followed the same procedure as for the school boards. This procedure resulted in an average response rate of 52 percent from the three associations. Participation in the study was based on the understanding that the identity of the organizations would be kept confidential and anonymous. Interviews provided an overview of the part-time and occasional teachers and their employment conditions. These qualitative data were supported by the quantitative data obtained from the questionnaires.

Interviews with Associations and School Boards

Interviews supported the typical employment characteristics generally associated with part-time work: low-valued jobs, little prospects for promotion, insecurity and, where not unionized, low pay. At the same time, interviews illustrated the diversity in employment policies based on the continuity and regularity of the teaching assignments. Interviews indicated that full-time and part-time teachers earn the same salary and benefits, prorated for part-time teachers. Occasional teachers, on the other hand, are paid prorated salary only if they are unionized. The majority of the occasional teachers are not members of a union and are generally paid lower salaries per day than their full-time and part-time counterparts. Furthermore, many do not receive benefits.

In the interviews, the typical part-time teacher emerged as female with dependent children, and working part time on a voluntary basis. Most part-time teachers began their careers in full-time positions. Occasional teachers, however, were a mixed group. Some were working in occasional teaching jobs on a voluntary basis, while others were working on an involuntary basis because they were unable to obtain a full-time contract with a school board, yet wanted access to those full-time jobs through part-time or occasional positions.

From the interviews, it was learned that the major factors influencing a school board's decision to hire part-time or occasional teachers were the following: the board's demand for flexibility in scheduling work, the teacher's preference to work part time, and the gender of the teacher, since female teachers are considered more suitable for part-time work. Teachers' associations and school boards did not consider low labor costs an important factor in employment decisions for the unionized teachers, since collective agreements provide for an equivalent compensation package. They did, however, indicate that low costs may be a factor in hiring unorganized occasional teachers.

In terms of the promotion of teachers to full time above entry-level positions, interviews indicated limited career ladders. Although, according to the collective agreements, there is a yearly movement on the salary grid, the parties do not consider it as a promotion. Promotion in an elementary school environment means a move to a supervisory level, such as a vice-principal position. Representatives of the associations and the school boards said that, if there were equally qualified full-time, part-time, and occasional teachers as candidates, full-time teachers were generally considered first. If a full-time teacher were not available, then a part-time teacher would be considered, followed by an occasional teacher as a last resort. Nonetheless, occasional teachers have a relatively good chance to be considered because not all part-time teachers would want to fill a full-time vacancy. The representatives stated that since many female part-time teachers are voluntarily part time, they would turn down a promotion offering full-time employment.

One of the association representatives indicated that there have been cases where a part-time supervisory position, such as that of vice-principal, was given to a full-time teacher rather than to a part-time teacher. In such cases, the full-time teacher would be responsible for the part-time vice-principal position and would teach half time. The school board would hire another part-time teacher to fill in the second half of the teaching position. This strategy clearly eliminated the promotion possibilities of any existing part-time teachers. According to school boards, however, part-time teachers could not be promoted to a part-time supervisory position because the position required full-time commitment: 50 percent in a managerial capacity and 50 percent as a teacher. In addition, interviews suggested that personal qualifications, such as ability and responsibility, are considered to be more important for promotion than the teacher's seniority.

In reply to the training questions, both the teachers' associations and the school boards indicated the existence of extensive training programs for competency on the job. However, in order to be considered for promotion, individuals had to take outside courses on their own time and at their own expense. In terms of access to training, the interviews suggested that full-time and part-time teachers had equal access to employer-sponsored on-the-job training programs. In practice, however, part-time teachers, because of their fewer hours of work, had limited access to such programs. Occasional teachers generally had even less access to training programs. Layoffs are not common among teachers. Should they be necessary, then according to the collective agreement, they would be in the order of reverse seniority. Consequently, occasional teachers would be laid off first, followed by regular part-time, and lastly by full-time, teachers.

Survey Findings

Following interviews with unions and employers, we surveyed a larger sample on the same issues.

Why Do School Boards Hire Part-Time and Occasional Teachers? Analysis of the questionnaire data suggests that certain factors are important in hiring decisions, and that others are less important or not applicable to the education sector. As Table 15.1 shows, school boards do not consider low wages or benefits as factors influencing their hiring decisions. This is because their collective agreements already cover both groups of teachers and provide prorated salary and benefits to part-time teachers. In the case of occasional teachers, school boards hire them not necessarily because they are cheaper to employ, but because someone has to fill in

Table 15.1
School Boards' Reasons to Hire Part-Time Teachers and Associations' Views

| | Responses from School Boards | | | | Responses from Teachers' Associations | | | |
| | Responses with NA† excluded | | | | Responses with NA† excluded | | | |
	% NA†	Number of Responses	Rank	% in Rank	% NA†	Number of Responses	Rank	% in Rank
Low wages	83	7	8	72	66	13	3	23
Low benefits	78	9	8	44	55	17	2	29
Flexibility in scheduling	31	27	1	44	31	27	1	52
Flexibility in layoff	71	12	4	42	58	16	1	31
Employee prefers to work part-time	12	36	1	44	18	32	1	38
Employee is suitable for part-time work	41	24	2	46	32	18	2	32
(Number)	(41)				(41)			

†Not Applicable (NA).

an unexpected vacancy when a full-time or part-time teacher is absent from work.

The other factor that seems to be inapplicable to the elementary school teachers is flexibility in layoff decisions. Education is not a sector that can be easily influenced by fluctuations in the economy and by the layoffs that often result from such fluctuations. It is a service-producing sector that requires continuity. Changes in the number of teachers constitute a gradual fluctuation that depends on the demographics of the population rather than on market forces. Furthermore, when part-time and occasional teachers are hired, they agree to provide services for the school year or until the replaced person is available for work. The individual contract, whether written or implicit, binds both the teacher and the employers, and thus eliminates flexibility in layoffs as a factor in the decisions to employ part-time teachers.

If we exclude the "not applicable" responses from the data and analyze the ranking of the factors for the school boards, the individual's preference to work part time and the school boards' demand for flexibility in scheduling work are ranked as the most important factors (see Table 15.1). As one respondent from the school boards makes clear:

The teaching contracts make no distinction between full time and part time re: rate of salary, benefits, or working conditions. The part-time teacher, in general terms, does not contribute to the total school program in as complete a way as does a full-time teacher. This is a consideration for staffing a school, as the extracurricular program of a school is of significant importance. All teachers need to become involved in this aspect of the school's program. However, a part-time teacher does provide flexibility to in-class programming and therefore has significant potential for a school board in its attempts to be as efficient as possible with the allocation of teaching staff.

Data indicate that stereotyping also influences the hiring decisions. As Table 15.1 shows, among those respondents from the school boards that provided a ranking, 46 percent would consider hiring a part-time or an occasional teacher if, in their opinion, the employee were suitable for part-time employment. Often suitability for part-time teaching consisted of being female with dependent children.

The responses from the teachers' associations and school boards are comparable, although the percentage support for "not applicable" responses is lower for the representatives of the teachers' associations. Teachers' associations consider low labor costs and flexibility in layoffs as insignificant factors in hiring decisions (see Table 15.1). A majority of the associations' respondents are of the opinion that school boards hire part-time teachers for the flexibility they provide in scheduling work. They also indicate that employers hire part-time teachers because the teachers themselves, particularly female teachers, want to work part time. A female respondent supports this view by saying: "In my opinion, part-time employment opportunities are the perfect arrangement for many families. Part-timers tend to work more than their specified percent (just as many full-timers work more than 100 percent), so I see them as a bargain. Job sharing is a way of accommodating part-time workers. Unfortunately, our administration tends to look upon this specific arrangement unfavorably." While female teachers are seen as wanting to work part time, they are also, as the responses illustrated, becoming increasingly concerned that if they convert to part time, they may find it difficult to revert to full-time employment once they are ready to do so. In addition, the associations' respondents consider that the stereotyping of females as "suitable for part-time employment because of their child-care responsibilities" plays a significant role in influencing the employers' hiring decisions (ranked as second).

While the majority of the respondents from the associations consider low labor costs as not applicable to the education sector, those who responded seem to rank low benefits and wages as relatively important in hiring decisions, particularly for occasional teachers (see Table 15.1). One of the association respondents elaborated on this issue:

Our occasional teachers have no bargaining unit. They are a small group which changes regularly and, in addition, they are geographically spread out. They are at the mercy of the school board. Occasional teachers who fill in for extended periods of time really have the worst situation. They have *no* benefits. If they are sick one day they lose salary, but they may find themselves teaching eight or nine months continuously. Classroom assistants and teachers' aides have little or no security but when they are hired full time they do have benefits which beat the occasional teachers' situation.

Overall, the data support the interviewees' claim that part-time and occasional teachers are hired because they provide flexibility in scheduling work, they are suitable for part-time work, and employees prefer to work part time. Low labor costs and flexibility in layoffs do not seem to be important factors for hiring part-time and occasional teachers.

Promotion Possibilities for Part-Time and Occasional Teachers. In promotion decisions, the school boards indicate a clear preference for full-time teachers (see Table 15.2). However, they also indicate that if a full-time teacher is not available or is unwilling to fill the full-time position, they would consider promoting a part-time teacher, and lastly, an occasional teacher. Table 15.3 shows that the majority of the respondents from the school boards consider education and experience as the most important factors in promotion decisions, followed by personal qualifications and seniority. As one of the employer respondents says: "The only promotion is to principal, vice-principal, co-ordinator, or consultant position

Table 15.2
Promotion, Training, and Layoff Policies by Type of Teacher

	School Boards					Associations				
	Rank	Number of Responses†	%†	Number of Responses*	%*	Rank	Number of Responses†	%†	Number of Responses*	%*
Promotion										
Full-time	1	41	73	33	91	1	41	90	39	95
Part-time	2	40	65	31	84	2	40	73	36	81
Occasional	3	40	40	23	70	3	39	46	24	75
Access to training										
Full-time	1	41	66	28	96	1	41	73	30	100
Part-time	1	41	54	27	81	2	41	44	28	74
Occasional	9 ■	39	75	10	50	9 ■	40	55	18	61
Layoffs										
Full-time	3	41	39	29	55	3	41	46	27	70
Part-time	2	41	63	30	87	2	41	46	26	73
Occasional	1	41	66	27	100	1	41	46	20	95

†Majority ranking, *including* not applicable answers.
*Majority ranking, *excluding* not applicable answers.
■9 means not applicable.

Table 15.3
Factors Influencing Employment Decisions

	School Boards					Associations				
	Rank	Number of Responses†	%†	Number of Responses*	%*	Rank	Number of Responses†	%†	Number of Responses*	%*
Promotion										
Personal qualifications	2	41	59	37	65	2	39	56	38	58
Education and experience	1	41	73	39	77	1	39	64	39	64
Seniority	3	40	60	35	69	3	39	67	36	72
Layoffs										
Personal qualifications	3	40	40	28	57	3	41	49	29	69
Education and experience	2	40	48	31	61	2	41	61	33	76
Seniority	1	41	61	37	68	1	40	76	40	78

†Majority ranking, *including* not applicable answers.
*Majority ranking, *excluding* not applicable answers.

which is generally full time. We would promote the best qualified applicant who has the education, experience, and the personal skills to perform the job." Although the respondents from the teachers' associations concur with the employers' ranking of factors, a few respondents from the associations also state that other factors, such as political reasons, affirmative action programs, or interview ability, play an influential role in promotion decisions. For example, an association respondent said that "there is no consistent or coherent policy on promotions but it is pure whim," and another stated, "in the public sector (that is, in education), jobs are given to friends or relatives. Hiring procedures are loose and can be overruled by supervisory personnel."

Training Programs for Part-Time and Occasional Teachers. In the education sector, training for proficiency on the job is important. In this study, however, the focus is on a different type of training—the one that prepares employees for advancement to supervisory-level job opportunities. The responses to our survey show that at least 71 percent of the school boards provide training to full-time and part-time teachers, but only 8 percent indicate that the same training programs are available for occasional teachers. In terms of priority in access to training programs (see Table 15.2), the majority of the employers claim that they provide equal access to full-time and part-time teachers. A substantial majority, however, reply that the question is not applicable to occasional teachers, indicating that, because of their intermittent work schedules, occasional teachers do not attend or are not encouraged to attend the training programs. In addition to training for career advancement, there are professional development days sponsored by the teachers' federation. On such days, occasional teachers who are working at that time, perhaps covering a maternity leave, then attend the training session. However, they do not have access to management and supervisory training programs sponsored by the employer. An employer representative responded to this question as follows: "Training programs for teachers are basically Ministry Course/University Course. In most cases, teachers pay their own tuition. However, the board does assist persons who are requalifying to retain a position by providing financial assistance where possible. Supply [occasional] teachers aren't covered by the collective agreement and therefore do not get the benefit or the promotional opportunities until internal posting is completed."

In terms of the availability of training programs, the majority of the association representatives indicate that training programs are available for full-time teachers (63 percent). More than half (54 percent) consider training to be available for part-time and occasional teachers. However, in reply to the question of who gets the priority in access to training programs, respondents from the teachers' associations rank full-time teachers first, followed by part-time teachers. For the occasional teachers, more than half of the respondents indicated that this question did not apply, either because they are not covered by the agreement or because they are not provided with the opportunity to attend training programs (see Table 15.2).

Layoff Policies. Employer responses to layoff questions revealed that a large percentage do not consider layoffs as applicable to their sector, and prefer not to answer the question. Of those who replied, a substantial majority ranked occasionals as the first to be laid off, followed by regular part-time teachers and then by full-time teachers (Table 15.2). In terms of the factors influencing layoff decisions, employers consider seniority the most important factor, followed by education and personal qualifications (Table 15.3). An employer respondent explained: "Teachers have a transfer surplus process which considers seniority and qualifications. The least senior with the least skill or qualifications is required to be the first to be laid off." With respect to layoff decisions and the factors that influence those decisions, similar rankings were produced by teachers' associations and employers, suggesting the secondary status of part-time and occasional teachers in comparison to full-time teachers.

CONCLUSIONS

School boards hire part-time and occasional teachers for three major reasons: the flexibility they provide in scheduling the teaching assignments, the employee's preference to work part time, and the employer's perception of the employee as suitable for part-time employment. Our findings also indicate that low labor costs and flexibility in layoff decisions are insignificant factors in hiring decisions. There appear to be three distinct applications of employment policies with respect to full-time, part-time, and occasional teachers. While full-time teachers enjoy preferential treatment in employment policies, part-time and occasional teachers are employed as peripherals. However, school boards also differentiate within the peripheral group. Specifically, in the application of employment policies, school boards indicate that there is a definite preference for part-time teachers who have regular employment contracts with the school boards over occasional teachers who are employed on a temporary basis.

Our results reveal some similarities to, and some differences from, the overall part-time working population. In common with part-time workers in the labor force, the part-time and occasional teachers in our study are also predominantly female. Although the secondary school profession has some male teachers, these male teachers all work full time. It is not surprising for us to find that males are not in the part-time or occasional teaching labor force. In our patriarchal society women work only part time so that they may raise their children, while men

enjoy uninterrupted full-time work with minimum child-care responsibilities. The teachers, their associations, and employers are a reflection
of the society. Although both female and male teachers perform the
same job and have the same qualifications, society expects female teachers to take time off or to work part time, raising children, while it expects
male teachers, who might be in exactly the same circumstances as
women, to work full time and be the breadwinner of the family. Not
surprisingly, imbued with these societal values and norms, both female
and male teachers and their unions unquestioningly accept these norms
and values and conform to these expectations. Their employers, influenced by the society's attitudes toward women, make decisions according to the expected norms and values.

An ultimate result of these attitudes is the slow career progression, if
any, of female teachers who choose to work in part-time or occasional
teaching schedules. Like their sisters in the part-time work force, these
part-time and occasional teachers join the ranks of the peripheral work
force. Since they do not receive priority in access to training for advancement, and since they have low seniority because of their intermittent careers, these teachers, like most part-time workers, do not get
the chance to be promoted to supervisory positions. Regrettably, many
part-time or occasional teachers who voluntarily choose to work part
time do not realize that this unfair treatment will occur until they actually
seek career progression or full-time employment.

Part-time and occasional teachers in this study, however, are advantaged over most other part-time workers by having unionization and a
skilled occupation. The interaction of these two factors positively influences the wages and benefits of part-time and occasional teachers. Unlike
most part-time workers in the labor force who are not unionized, these
unionized part-time teachers earn the same, but prorated, salary and
benefits as full-time teachers. Although occasional teachers are the worst
off within the education sector, in comparison to most casual part-time
workers in the labor force they enjoy a relatively good standard of living,
particularly if they have been unionized.

NOTES

The author would like to thank school boards and teachers' associations for
their assistance and participation in this survey, and Liz Brown and Christine
Peters for research assistance. This study is partially supported by the Social
Sciences and Humanities Research Council of Canada.

1. Teaching Profession Act, Revised Statutes of Ontario. 1980 c. 495 (July 1985
s. 1(1)).
2. The School Boards and Teachers Collective Negotiations Act, 1975.
3. Membership figures are obtained from the teachers' unions.

4. In this study, the terms marginal, peripheral, or secondary are used interchangeably to describe the jobs or workers who are employed in substandard employment conditions. Most of these jobs are low-paying, offer little security, and employ low-valued, unskilled, and non-unionized workers with no possibilities for career progression. Education and training do not increase the wages, and most marginal workers are in "dead-end jobs." Core or primary jobs have the opposite characteristics of the marginal or secondary jobs. For more, see Doeringer and Piore (1971); Beechey, and Perkins (1987); Mangum, Mayall, and Nelson (1985).

16 Gender and Career Trajectory: The Case of Part-Time Faculty

Katherina L. P. Lundy and
Barbara D. Warme

Our focus in this paper is on female academics who occupy the part-time track, a career path that is both horizontal and terminal, since it does not provide a bridge to full-time tenured appointments. How did these women get on the part-time track? Once there, what conditions do they confront? How do they experience, and deal with, their marginal role in the university. Finally, to what extent are the answers to these questions related to their gender?

The number of female university teachers has risen even more dramatically than the number of female workers generally. Between 1960 and 1985, they increased by 712 percent (from 736 to 5987) (Canada. Statistics Canada, 1987). Most of this increase was a function of overall expansion in the higher education sector. During the same period, the proportion of full-time female faculty rose only slightly, from 12 percent in 1960 to 17 percent in 1985. Female participation varies inversely with rank; the higher the rank, the lower the proportion of women. Among part-timers, a status in which there are virtually no differences in rank, men and women are represented in equal proportions. One can conclude, then, that academic women are more likely than academic men to occupy part-time university positions.

Data from the United States and Britain show analogous patterns. Bowen and Schuster found that full-time female faculty increased from 17 to 27 percent and part-time female faculty from 23 to 36 percent in the period from 1960/61 to 1982/83. Female faculty were concentrated in the lower academic ranks and in less prestigious institutions, that is to say, in community colleges rather than in research universities. Women

constituted 52 percent of instructors, but only 10 percent of full professors. In Britain, too, there has been an increase in the number of female
academics, though in 1982 they constituted only 13.9 percent of the
professorate but "41 percent of academic-related staff" (Acker, 1984: 29).

Historically, part-time teaching in North American institutions of
higher learning has largely been viewed as an apprenticeship to a full-
time position. Currently, the availability of full-time positions has been
eroded by the confluence of several factors. The rapid expansion of the
higher education sector that occurred in the 1960s produced more graduates, and especially more female ones. However, as political priorities
have shifted and government funding has not kept pace with inflation,
universities have responded by curtailing the creation of tenure-stream
positions. One result has been an increase of part-time faculty, many of
whom become locked into part-time status because of their inability to
find full-time positions.

BACKGROUND

The literature suggests that full-time and part-time faculty occupy
different worlds. In two major studies of the American professorate
(Bowen and Schuster, 1986; Clark 1987), part-timers were not accorded
systematic attention even though "in the mid–1980s part-timers constitute at least one-third of the academic labor force" (Clark, 1987: 200). In
their report on Canadian universities, Symons and Page (1984) do not
specifically discuss part-time faculty, except in a brief note relating to
female academics. Clearly, part-time faculty are treated as peripheral in
analyses of the professorate and of the university system. However, as
the number of part-timers has grown and as their use has become entrenched, a literature dealing with their situation has evolved. As already
noted, relative to their proportion of full-time faculty, women are over-
represented among part-timers. There is considerable overlap between
the "problems" of women and those of part-timers. Accordingly, the
problems of part-time female academics have been touched on in a
number of studies (Abel, 1984; Breslauer, 1985; Spender, 1984; Theodore,
1986).

Universities do not submit data on part-timers to Statistics Canada
regarding their numbers, location, rank, or field. Hence, discussion of
female faculty is largely confined to those who are full time. Breslauer
suggests that the absence of data that would permit the drawing of an
accurate profile of female academics, including part-timers, makes it
difficult to "prove" that women are indeed disadvantaged and that re-
medial action is imperative (1985: 86).

Tuckman and Tuckman (1981) used data from a national survey conducted by the American Association of University Professors (AAUP)

in 1977 to draw up a taxonomy of part-time faculty. They noted that among those who wanted to teach full time, "women were more active in seeking full-time academic positions than men; they were also less successful in obtaining offers" (1981: 675). In part, these differences may be accounted for by the greater geographic mobility of men, by the slightly higher percentage of males who had doctorates, and by their areas of specialization. Forty-four percent of male "hopefuls" were in the Arts and Humanities compared with 62 percent of female hopefuls.

Especially relevant here is the survey conducted by Katz (1984) of the part-time faculty union, the Canadian Union of Educational Workers (CUEW). Katz found that, among teaching assistants, women were underrepresented in science and engineering (20 percent were female; 59 percent were male) and overrepresented in the humanities (25 percent were female; 9 percent were male) and the social sciences (33 percent female and 23 percent male). Fifty-two percent of males and 17 percent of females reported that they would consider leaving academe if they could not obtain a full-time teaching position. Among part-timers, Katz found that men and women were equally active in applying for tenured positions at other institutions, but "significantly fewer females had applied for tenured positions at their present institution. This may be due to fewer tenured positions becoming available in traditionally female disciplines at their institution and/or females having some prior insight into hiring policies at their institution" (1984: 11).

The Status of Women Committee of the Council of Ontario Universities noted in its 1988 Report that women are frequently subject to systemic discrimination, defined as "indirect, impersonal and unintentional discrimination that is the result of inappropriate standards which have been built into the employment systems over the years." Typically, employing institutions do not make allowances for the "indirect" career paths of women that often result in their being older than men at parallel career points and in their being steered into part-time positions.

One can posit two explanations, not necessarily mutually exclusive, for the recent interest in part-time faculty. On the one hand, it has captured attention as a women's issue. On the other hand, it may be precisely because more men are being deprived of the "normal professional career" referred to by Caplow and McGee (1958: 194) that research effort has been directed toward the problem. Furthermore, institutions must deal with the pragmatic issues that have arisen as a result of the increase in the absolute number of part-timers as well as in their proportion of overall faculty complements. These issues have been addressed in books suggesting appropriate strategies (see, for example, *Part-Time Faculty Management Policies* by G. E. Biles and H. P. Tuckman, 1986).

THE CASE STUDY

In 1983, we began a multi-faceted study at York University, Canada's third largest university, located in Toronto. The various phases encompassed a questionnaire survey and in-depth interviews with part-time faculty; in-depth interviews with full-time faculty, senior administrators, and officials of the unions representing full-time faculty — York University Faculty Association (YUFA) and part-time faculty (Canadian Union of Educational Workers [CUEW]), and a questionnaire survey and in-depth interviews with students. (Baker, 1985; Warme and Lundy, 1986, 1988a and 1988b; Lundy and Warme, 1989). When we concentrated attention on the impact of sex on the career patterns and work behaviors of part-time faculty, we found that the questionnaire was neither specific nor exhaustive enough in these areas. Moreover, the information was five years old. We therefore designed a new questionnaire, which was mailed and completed in 1988.

Numbered questionnaires were sent to the 608 members of Unit 2 of the Canadian Union of Educational Workers (CUEW).[1] The questions were grouped into several categories: social characteristics; career history; history; voluntary or involuntary status; scholarly and disciplinary activities; work-setting experiences; perceived impact of gender on career decisions and academic opportunities; job satisfaction; and the meaning of being a part-timer. Reminder cards and a second questionnaire sent to those who had not responded produced a response rate of 63.6 percent (387). Not all respondents answered each question. The questionnaires were numbered, so that returns could be monitored and selected respondents contacted for interviews.

We calculated frequencies for the sample population as a whole, and for men and women separately. Appropriate cross-tabulations were run, along with a compatible significance test. Based on responses to questions dealing with the effect of gender on academic career decisions and career opportunities, and on completions of the statement "to me, being a part-time faculty member means . . . ", we did a content analysis categorized in terms of:

1. emphasizing the intrinsic or extrinsic rewards, or both, of part-time teaching;
2. being active or passive, that is to say, stressing control over one's life, or reporting feelings of powerlessness, of being at the mercy of external forces;
3. expressing positive, mixed, neutral, or negative attitudes toward part-time teaching.

In selecting respondents for personal interviews, we sought to represent different kinds of viewpoints that were expressed in completions of the statement that, "to me, being a part-time faculty member means . . . "

Ten women and ten men were interviewed. Interviews lasted from 60 to 90 minutes, and explored career satisfaction (willingness to choose the same career again); perceived impact of gender on career choice; perceived advantages and drawbacks of part-time faculty, from the perspective of the respondent, for the university, and for students; extent of professional and social contact with full-time faculty; and suggestions for meliorating negative aspects of part-time status. General comments on the part-time experience were invited.

GENDER AND PART-TIME STATUS

Women constitute 50.4 percent of survey respondents, a percent that has remained virtually unchanged since our 1983 survey. The 1986/87 CUEW figures for Unit 2 show a distribution of 58 percent males and 42 percent females. It would appear, therefore, that women are over-represented among our respondents. In her 1984 study of CUEW members at six Ontario institutions, Katz found that women constituted 38 percent of members but 42 percent of her respondents. In a survey of part-time faculty at McMaster University, women were also overrepresented among respondents.[2] They constituted approximately 50 percent of the sample population (those part-timers who reported no employment outside the university), but 63 percent of respondents. The researchers speculate that women may have been motivated to respond because the survey was carried out by the Status of Women Committee. Given the auspices of the survey, women may also have perceived it as an opportunity to raise their concerns regarding pay and working conditions, and possibly to effect improvements (Zeytinoglu and Ahmed, 1988).

However, even the large percentage of women in our sample, and in the McMaster one, falls far below the 70 percent that women represent of all part-time workers. One reason for this may be that university teaching is a high-prestige occupation relative to other occupations in which women are concentrated, although the part-time factor devalues it within the university setting itself. Men are far more likely than women to work outside the university in addition to their university teaching (86.3 percent versus 69.4 percent), (p = .0001). Of those part-timers who do work elsewhere, 76.5 percent of men and 60.4 percent of women work full time at their outside job (p = .002), and men are significantly more likely to consider this outside employment as their primary work.

Discontinuities in Academic Training

The differences are small, but our findings are consonant with those of other researchers (Abel, 1984; Bernard, 1974; Katz, 1984) that, on

Table 16.1
Reasons for Interrupting Academic Training (Percentages)

	Male	*Female*
Domestic responsibilities	23.5	52.4
Financial need to work	55.9	29.5
Partner's work	1.5	7.6
llness	—	1.9
Other	19.1	8.6
Total (numbers)	(68)	(105)

average, women complete their education at a later age, and that female part-timers are slightly older than their male counterparts. In our sample, 73.5 percent of the females were born before 1951, and 28.5 percent obtained their highest degree before 1976; for males, the percentages were 67 percent born before 1951 and 33.9 percent obtaining their highest degree before 1976. In Zeytinoglu and Ahmed's study (1988), 79 percent of female respondents, but only 36 percent of males, were 36 years or older.

Table 16.1 sets out the differences between males and females in reasons given for interrupting their academic training. In our sample, 61.3 percent of women, compared with 38.7 percent of males (p = .0001), reported that they had to interrupt their academic training. Reasons for these interruptions were differently distributed between men and women. A 40-year-old Ph.D. spoke to this issue:

After finishing military service, I attended law classes, but then I got married [at 20] and decided to take my B.A. in sociology and political science. I completed a teaching diploma and started teaching high school. Taught high school for two years, then took an M.A. in sociology because I wanted to get out of high-school teaching. It took me four years to complete my M.A., because I had my second child. Then we moved to Canada and I went to York for my Ph.D. Though I had also been accepted at the University of Toronto, I chose York because it was close to home, convenient, and I was pregnant with my third child. It took me about six years to complete my Ph.D. I enjoyed it, but my career has always been "small." My family was my first priority; my husband works long hours and I cannot count on him for domestic and child-care tasks.

Earlier studies showed a similar pattern (Simeone, 1987; Taylorson, 1984).

Table 16.2
Perceived Effects of Gender on Career Decisions (Percentages)

	Male	Female
Did not complete dissertation because of domestic responsibilities	2.7	11.6
As sole support parent had to work	—	1.1
Gave priority to partner completing his/her education	1.1	5.3
Partner was transferred	—	5.3
Domestic responsibilities	2.7	8.9
Other	2.7	13.2
Total (numbers)	(184)	(190)

Impact of Gender on Career Decisions

We found that 90.8 percent of men, but only 54.7 percent of women reported that gender had not affected their career decisions ($p > .0001$). Table 16.2 shows the distribution of reasons cited by those who believed gender had affected their career decisions. Some of the explanations given were as follows:

During my last year at high school, I announced at the dinner table that I wanted to be a lawyer. My father said: "it's too bad you're a girl." I am not sure it was always the outside world that held me back. It was also my image of myself. I did well at university in the liberal arts. Got scholarships. When I was at grad school, my best friend was at law school. Her fiancé, also a law grad and a Rhodes scholar, wrote her breaking off the engagement. He said he wanted "someone less ambitious." This made an impression on me. (45-year-old female M.A.)

No, I would not make the same choice again. At "O" levels [the respondent attended school in Britain] I would have picked sciences and then gone on to medical school, but I felt this was going to be a long haul. I did not see the study of languages as a career choice. I didn't really think much about my career. (49-year-old female M.A.)

No [effect on career decisions], except that us males are favored. (49-year-old male M.A.)

Table 16.3
Perceived Effects of Gender on Career Opportunities (Percentages)

	Male	*Female*
Took longer to complete qualifications because of domestic responsibilities	4.4	25.8
Interrupted career to stay with children	—	14.2
Moved because of partner's work	1.1	3.7
Encountered prejudice in hiring	3.3	3.2
Other	6.0	6.8
Total (numbers)	(181)	(190)

I did not think that further education was worth the time and energy, and I did not know what it would give me that I particularly wanted or valued. (45-year-old female M.A.)

One of the interviewees who is active in affirmative action and is herself a psychologist, made the point more generally: "By the time women realize that they might actually spend their lives in careers, they have lost years of incidental learning. Some possibilities become frightening, so women start limiting their goals. In order to make real changes, women have to be taught to establish career patterns and priorities much earlier in their academic cycle." Our findings confirm Simeone's finding (1987) that the norms of the society generally, and those of one's significant others in particular, impinge on aspirations and career decisions. It should be noted that a woman may not view the impact of domestic responsibilities as negative. Several respondents changed the printed option on the questionnaire "I had to interrupt my career to stay home with my children" to: "I chose to . . . ."

Impact of Gender on Career Opportunities

Among men, 85.2 percent believed that gender had not affected their career opportunities; only 46.3 per cent of women held this view (p > .0001). Table 16.3 shows the distribution of responses of those who believed that gender had affected their opportunities.

Explanations for "other" perceived effects of gender included these comments:

I had to move because of my partner's work, and my career opportunities were further affected because I "chose" to stay at home with the children. Beware

Table 16.4
Academic Qualifications (Percentages)

	Male	*Female*
Doctorate	33.3	28.0
Master's degree	48.4	50.8
Baccalaureate	15.6	19.7
Other	2.7	1.6
Total (numbers)	(184)	(191)

vocabulary that implies that normal male career rhythm is the only plausible norm. (42-year-old female Ph.D.)

People are inclined to believe I'm smart because I'm male. (37-year-old male Ph.D.)

During her interview a 42-year-old respondent with a doctorate from an Ivy League university pointed to the complex factors that impinge on women's careers: "Being a female makes it easier for me to be in the position in which I am, but it also put me there. Nobody took me under his wing and told me what to do—as was done for my husband. Being female is a two-edged sword—one may need the money less, but this takes away the spur."

Analogously, several respondents in a study of female Ph.D. students at a major university in England told Taylorson that women have an advantage because "they can be less competitive" (1984: 150). This state of affairs appears not to have changed significantly since Epstein observed nearly 20 years ago that at every stage of an academic or work career a woman can "opt out" without societal censure. For a man it would be deemed a "cop out" (1970).

Academic Qualifications

Table 16.4 shows the sample's distribution of qualifications, one that is virtually the same as that of the 1983 group. The differences between men and women in terms of highest degree obtained are not statistically significant. They are consonant with other findings (Abel, 1984; Bernard, 1974; Theodore, 1986) that women are less likely than men to hold a doctorate. Not surprisingly, reluctant or involuntary part-timers are more likely to have a doctorate than those in the voluntary group (59.5 percent versus 40.5 percent) (p > .0001).

Scholarly Activities

In our overall population, a sizable minority report some publishing activity (for example, 39.4 percent had an article published in a refereed journal and 21.5 percent have authored a book). Zeytinoglu and Ahmed report similar results. Half of their respondents had published papers during their part-time employment at McMaster, 20 percent had published books, and 55 percent had read papers at conferences (1988). Our findings show that differences between men and women are small, but consistently in the direction established by other researchers (Abel, 1984; Bernard, 1974; Simeone, 1987; Theodore, 1986) that, on average, women publish less than men. On the one hand, one can emphasize the slightness of the sex differences. On the other hand, one can focus on their consonance with other findings that, however, refer mainly to full-time faculty.

Overall, a high percentage belong to disciplinary associations (61.8 percent–62.4 percent of males and 61.3 percent of females). Among those who belong, women are slightly more likely to attend meetings, hold office, work on a committee, have presented a paper, or organized a session at a conference. The differences are statistically insignificant and therefore inconclusive.

The relatively large proportion of part-timers who are professionally active, as measured by publications and membership in disciplinary associations, merits comment. In our interviews with full-time faculty and with administrators, the argument was repeatedly advanced that an institution's scholarly activity is depressed by part-timers' lack of productivity. At York, no record was kept of research and publications by part-time faculty. Hence, we cannot draw comparisons with those of full-time faculty. However, Clark's comments on the "paradox of academic work" are instructive: "The greatest paradox of academic work in modern America is that most professors teach most of the time, and large proportions of them teach all the time, but teaching is not the activity most rewarded by the academic profession nor most valued by the system at large. Trustees and administrators in one sector after another praise teaching and reward research. Professors themselves do the one and acclaim the other" (1987: 98–99). The exclusion of research and publishing from the mandate of part-timers leads to the untested presumption that all they do is teach. Because "the prestige hierarchy dictates that the research imperative propel the system" (Clark, 1987: 101), the prestige of an institution with a high proportion of part-time faculty is ipso facto undermined.

One factor curtailing part-timers' active participation in professional pursuits is minimal access to funding. At York, the union (CUEW) negotiated access to some funding several years ago. Yet, among the 89.9 percent of respondents who have not applied for internal research or travel funds, 43.3 percent give as the reason: "did not know that such funds are available." This speaks to the marginality of part-timers within the university, a setting in which knowing where and when to apply for what funding has become vital.

Support Structure

Katz (1984) found that a higher proportion of women lacked access to facilities such as an office, telephone, and secretarial assistance for scholarly activities. We found no such differences. Relatively high percentages of both men and women reported lack of access to an office (40.3 percent), to a telephone (40.4 percent), and to secretarial assistance for scholarly activities (56.1 percent). These are facilities that are simply taken for granted by members of the full-time faculty. One of the "permanent" part-timers stated that it was an aggravation to have to apply every year for a library card. Another notes: "I share an office with some 15 other tutorial leaders. I don't consider that access to an office for any useful purpose."

Minimal access to university facilities not only reduces the possibility of engaging in scholarly activities, but also may hamper effective teaching—and teaching is the one thing that members of the part-time faculty are hired to do. Furthermore, comments derived from the questionnaires and interviews suggest that another effect of these petty deprivations is to erode what one might call the "academic persona" of the part-timer. It is not difficult to see the Catch–22 in play even with respect to institutional minutiae: not having a full-time position in the first place increases the likelihood of never obtaining one.

Departmental Participation

We found no differences between men and women in their opportunity to participate in departmental meetings. Of the total population, 45.8 percent reported no opportunity to participate. Of those who do have the opportunity, slightly more men than women actually choose to participate. In the interviews, some respondents defined non-participation as an advantage of part-time status. One woman stated forcefully: "I hate administration and committee work." Others bitterly resented their exclusion from decisions on curriculum planning and general academic governance.

Bowen and Schuster's comments on the lack of integration they encountered in their national study are pertinent here:

In no instance was it claimed that part-time faculty were integrated into the academic departments to which they were assigned or into campus life. Occasionally, a chair or dean would mention that a few of the part-timers, apparently eager to establish themselves as legitimate candidates for full-time openings, attended faculty meetings, made themselves readily available to students, and generally "behaved like regular faculty members." Nonetheless, the overall conclusion was inescapable: typically, the part-timer is viewed as an expedient, and the part-timer's understandable response is a minimal commitment to the institution (1986: 151).

The experience of being viewed as an "expedient" is poignantly described by a 45-year-old female M.A.:

After 12 years [of part-time teaching], I have come to resent the patronizing attitudes and narrow arrogance of full-timers. I dislike the burden of having to apply for jobs every year and never being able to adequately plan my life. It surprises me that I have no commitment to York at all. I am always aware of the cynicism, hostility, and exhaustion of my peers who have been here for a long time. And as the years go on, we almost never talk about our work and I think this bothers me more than all the rest.

Geographic Mobility and Aspirations for Full-Time Academic Appointment

In view of our finding that men are more likely than women to work for pay outside the university and to view such work as their primary job, it comes as no surprise that fewer men report they would want a tenure-stream position now (33.7 percent of males; 40.1 percent of females) or next year (40.8 percent of males; 42.8 percent of females). However, a significantly higher proportion of men than women (50.9 percent versus 39.4 percent) would be willing to commute outside Toronto in order to obtain such an appointment. Geographic immobility may be one reason why Tuckman and Tuckman (1981) found that, among part-time academics who sought full-time positions, men were more successful than women.

Women are not only geographically less mobile; they may also have to give up full-time employment because of a spouse's transfer. In our sample population, 29.2 percent reported one or more work interruptions, and of these, 54.1 percent were women. Only women gave as the reason: "Partner's work took us to another location." Similar findings are reported in other studies, for example:

Table 16.5
Satisfaction with Part-Time Teaching and Status (Percentages)

| | Teaching | | Status | |
	Male	Female	Male	Female
Satisfied	84.9	74.6	47.0	38.0
Neither	11.9	15.3	24.3	23.5
Dissatisfied	3.2	10.1	28.7	38.5
Total (numbers)	(185)	(189)	(181)	(179)

Like myself and many other married women our age, she had dutifully pulled up stakes to follow her husband from job to job in order to keep the family together and to ensure the husband's advancement. This situation has been repeated hundreds of times in the business and industrial communities as well as in the academic community and has unfortunately resulted in the displacement of women. . . . Such women then must accept what they can find in the new area. A whole new exploitable class has been created through this practice (Miller, 1984: 85).

Perceptions of the Part-Time Experience

Women report lower satisfaction with part-time teaching and with part-time status, but for both sexes the striking difference is that between satisfaction with part-time teaching and with part-time status.[3] Indeed, as Table 16.5 shows, many respondents reported themselves satisfied with the former and dissatisfied with the latter. Respondents were eloquent in expressing their resentment at the perceived inequities of part-time status, both in terms of material rewards and in terms of exclusion from the collegium. As one woman said: "I'm a 48-year-old female Ph.D. experiencing insecurity, overwork, and resentment at being so blatantly exploited. I propose changing the terminology to the more accurate 'part-pay faculty.' On the other hand, I love teaching. This seems to be the only way I can do what I want." Another female Ph.D., in her forties, said: "Being marginal and exploited, I continue because I love to teach. Fortunately, I do not have to depend on my teaching as my sole source of income, so what bothers me most is the way most full-timers treat me and other part-timers as if we were a lower form of life. They display the shameless arrogance of the aristocracy of the ancien régime, especially those who talk most loudly of their sympathy for the oppressed." While gender does not significantly affect satisfaction with part-time teaching or with part-time status, being a voluntary or involuntary part-

Table 16.6
Satisfaction of Voluntary and Involuntary Part-Timers (Percentages)

| | Part-time teaching | | Part-time Status | |
	Involuntary part-time	Voluntary part-time	Involuntary part-time	Voluntary part-time
Satisfied	72.3	85.3	20.6	57.8
Neither	21.2	8.3	21.3	25.5
Dissatisfied	6.6	6.4	58.1	16.7
Total (numbers)	(137)	(217)	(136)	(204)
	P = 0.0014		P = 0.0014	

timer has a strong impact on both of these variables (see Table 16.6). Differences in satisfaction with part-time status are especially striking.

As noted previously, women, and those holding doctorates, are over-represented among involuntary part-timers. This category is most likely to regard full-time faculty as a reference group and to experience relative deprivation. Runciman (1966) argues that "to feel relatively deprived of X, a person must also see it as feasible that he should have X."[4] Expectations of social justice are not as strongly violated for those who lack the requisite qualifications for a full-time academic appointment—even though they may still be aware that part-timers are treated unjustly.

Our findings are consistent with those reported by Yang and Zak (1981) from their major study of job satisfaction among part-time academics. Yang and Zak's hypothesis was supported, that "the differences between that segment who choose part-time academic employment and those unwillingly confined to it are immense and far reaching" (48). Those who aspired to full-time academic jobs were likely to be less satisfied, and women were less satisfied than men. Part-timers most likely to be satisfied were those who held outside jobs and those who taught in business or education.

In the interviews, respondents commented on the use of part-time faculty as having negative aspects both for students and for the university. They expressed concern that, because of work overload, some part-time faculty may not be able to devote sufficient time to course preparation and to interaction with students outside of classroom hours.[5] Respondents mentioned the presence of an "alienated" group, low morale, lack of commitment to an institution that relegates them to second-class citizenship, and lack of integration into the university community. The latter is borne out by reports of minimal social and professional contact with full-time colleagues. One respondent noted: "I just couldn't make the departmental luncheon. I was too tied up with my outside work." Another pointed out that the newsletter of the department in which he teaches solicits news of scholarly activities by "full-time faculty." The message is clear—part-timers are not "really" members of the department.

In previous phases of our research, acknowledgment that extensive use of part-time faculty may have negative consequences for the various constituencies did not obscure awareness of the benefits derived from part-timers, both by the university and by students. Respondents from all settings noted that, from the university's viewpoint, part-timers provide economy, flexibility, and the ability to mount specialized programs without long-term commitment, and they inject "new blood" into the system. Students were seen to gain by contact with those who are out in the "real" world, because it enhanced the credibility of the material taught and strengthened the ties between the university and the community. Importantly, part-timers were perceived to be good teachers, both because they must love teaching ("the money is certainly no incentive") and because student evaluations are more fateful for them than for full-timers.

What Does It "Mean" to Be a Part-Timer?

Questionnaire respondents were invited to complete the sentence, "To me, being a part-timer means. . . ." This strategy yielded a rich variety of comments. There were many expressions of frustration and bitterness, exemplified by the following:

A general sense of powerlessness and hopelessness—and the only opportunity I have to do work I love and value. (42-year-old female Ph.D.)

Being an outsider, crippled and disabled. (41-year-old male Ph.D.)

Women were more than twice as likely as men (45 versus 22) to voice negative feelings about their part-time experience, and to see themselves as powerless to change this position. This finding may be related to the greater geographic immobility of women. Being able to accept a full-time position regardless of where it is located certainly enhances the likelihood of getting one. However, we do not have sufficient information to reach any conclusions.

Dissatisfaction need not entail passivity. For example: "Being an outsider looking in, being underutilized and underpaid, having low status at work and among friends who think I'm a helper-teacher, not a real teacher! I'm looking elsewhere for employment now." (40-year-old female M.A.) It is worth noting that, for this respondent, earnings from part-time teaching represent only 3 percent of household income. Therefore, she can afford to search for work that is intrinsically satisfying and does not violate her expectations of fair compensation.

Negative views are by no means the norm. For some respondents, part-time teaching is not central. They reported that part-time teaching means "just that," or "not that much." Young, well-qualified individuals are most likely to view their experience in the traditional sense, as a gateway to a full-time position:

Bridging the gap between graduate school and permanent academic employment. (35-year-old female Ph.D.)

A step to a full-time career and an enriching teaching experience. (34-year-old male Ph.D.)

Their optimism appears realistic in the light of forecasts that, in the 1990s, the pendulum will swing once again, and that there will be a shortage of university teachers.[6]

Respondents with full-time outside employment are most likely to view part-time teaching as the best of all possible worlds. They point to personal rewards and to the contribution they can make to education in general:

Challenge, stimulation, financial benefits. (48-year-old male B.A.)

Being able to teach subjects of my choice without "political" pressures of a full-time job. (35-year-old female Ph.D.)

Challenge, opportunity to teach adults and shape curriculum. Encourage excellence and enthusiasm in teachers. It also pays well. (40-year-old female M.A.)

Whether respondents stressed the intrinsic or extrinsic rewards of part-time teaching appears to be related to its economic salience for the individual. Some mentioned both intrinsic and extrinsic factors, while a number of responses permitted no inference regarding the relative importance of such factors:

Being able to share my knowledge and experience with other teachers, and to benefit personally from the positive interaction of people and content in my course. (48-year-old male M.A. for whom teaching accounted for 7 percent of household income.)

Having freedom and solitude for writing part of the time and the intellectual stimulation of interaction with students part of the time. (50-year-old female Ph.D. for whom teaching accounted for 12 percent of household income.)

Being exploited to the fullest. It means doing the same amount of work (if not more) for half the salary. (35-year-old female M.A. for whom teaching accounted for 33 percent of household income.)

Table 16.7
Gender and Meaning of Being a Part-Time Faculty Member (Percentages)

	Male	*Female*
Intrinsic rewards cited	60.0	61.3
Mixed	30.4	24.0
Extrinsic rewards cited	9.6	14.7
Total (numbers)	(135)	(150)

Putting food on the table. (35-year-old female M.A. for whom teaching accounted for 100 percent of household income.)

The findings that a majority of both men and women mention the intrinsic rewards of teaching are in line with the emphasis that is placed on such rewards in the course of professional socialization. This is especially true for academics, since their material rewards lag far behind those of other professionals, such as physicians or lawyers. What is interesting is the lack of significant differences in the orientations of men and women. On the one hand, this accords with the Marxian and the Durkheimian views that similar work engenders similar values and beliefs. On the other hand, women have traditionally accepted that their main rewards would come from providing service, whether at home or in the work place.

Table 16.7 compares the distribution of rewards cited by males and females. In our sample, women are more likely than men to refer to extrinsic rewards; that is to say, pay and benefits—or to their absence. Again, the numbers are too small to allow confidence in inferences. However, women may now pay attention to material rewards precisely because they have been consistently shortchanged in the past. As one respondent put it: "I am tired of being in the wives' pool, and of not having my work recognized and fairly rewarded." Other factors are the high rates of marriage breakdown in society at large, and the statistically poor chances for women over 35 of remarrying. In the light of this situation, women may regard their earnings as crucial.

CONCLUSIONS

A significantly higher percentage of women than men believe that gender has affected their career decisions and career opportunities. A web of individual and structural variables has brought about these effects. Many female respondents were socialized to regard their careers as secondary to family responsibilities and acted according to these priorities, some more willingly than others. Discontinuities in training and work have led to "indirect career paths," but universities have made few accommodations to these discontinuities, basing the reward system on what can be characterized as a male career model.

Once in the part-time cadre, membership does not differ significantly for men and women, and does not evoke significantly different behaviors and attitudes. The differences that we did find support other research findings that, on average, men publish more and report higher job satisfaction. The willingness or reluctance to teach part time supersedes gender differences in work behavior and attitudes. The 60 percent of our respondents who report themselves to be voluntary part-timers express mainly positive attitudes.

Gender influences who chooses, or is assigned to, part-time teaching. However, the caste-like characteristics of this segment of the academic labor force inhere in its status within the university hierarchy. The status is not only low, but for many it also becomes inescapable. Especially for those part-timers who consider themselves trapped, and who teach in settings where they are on sufferance, the indignities of part-time status are reinforced by the cavalier disrespect they encounter. In settings in which part-timers are perceived as a valuable resource, as in professional faculties, negative aspects of part-time status may scarcely be noticed.[7]

Our findings are congruent with those from our earlier study, and those of other researchers (Gappa, 1984; Leslie, Kellams, and Gunne, 1982; Tuckman and Tuckman, 1981; Wallace, 1984) that part-time faculty constitute a heterogeneous group of individuals in terms of academic qualifications, career aspirations and expectations, willingness or reluctance to teach part-time, job behavior, and how they experience the job.

Our study reveals the anguish of those who see themselves as underutilized and who are stymied in their attempts to pursue a full-scale academic career. The negative features of part-time status, and their destructive consequences, affect both men and women. However, as we have shown, women are more likely than men to be steered into part-time teaching. It is vital that universities restructure such teaching positions according to "new concept" part-time work (Kahne, 1985), if valuable potential contributions to scholarship are not to be lost. This would provide prorated rewards, a flexible work-schedule option, and a bridge to a full-time appointment if and when the individual is qualified and ready to assume it.

NOTES

A version of this chapter was presented at the 1988 Conference of the Society for Research in Higher Education at the University of Surrey, England, (December). This paper originally appeared in *Studies in Higher Education*, 1990, 15 (2): 207–222. Reprinted with permission of the publisher, Carfax Publishing Company, London, the United Kingdom.

We gratefully acknowledge funding for this research by York University and by Local 3 of the Canadian Union of Educational Workers.

1. Local 3 of the Canadian Union of Educational Workers (CUEW) has two units. Unit 1 consists of graduate students who are teaching assistants. Unit 2 is comprised of members of the part-time faculty. We surveyed only Unit 2 members, both in 1983 and 1988.

2. McMaster University is a large university, located in Hamilton, a medium-sized city approximately 50 miles southwest of Toronto.

3. A colleague with whom we discussed this finding suggested that women might be less satisfied because they were overburdened, in that many would also have to cope with domestic responsibilities. This is speculative. However, it would be interesting to incorporate this dimension into a study comparing the job satisfaction of men and women in specified occupations and settings.

4. Somewhat analogously, Brinton remarked in his analysis of political revolutions that "Revolutions seem more likely when social classes are fairly close together than when they are far apart. 'Untouchables' very rarely revolt against a god-given aristocracy" (1952: 265). In our example, full-time and part-time faculty are close in qualifications and in their career aspirations and expectations. What separates them is often an accident of timing—not being at the right place at the right time.

5. In our 1986 survey of students, part-time faculty were not seen as less effective teachers. However, a majority of students believed that outside of classroom hours part-timers were less readily available than full-timers (Lundy and Warme, 1989).

6. This situation has already occurred in the Canadian school system. Hundreds of teachers were dismissed in the late 1970s and early 1980s, and many found jobs outside education. Now, school boards are once again recruiting teachers.

7. We have explored earlier the question of "fit" between faculty context and the academic aspirations of part-timers (Warme and Lundy, 1988). In professional faculties such as Education and Fine Arts, part-timers form an indispensable and explicit link between theory and praxis. The successful practitioner who teaches part-time is a role model for students, and may also facilitate access to job networks.

17 The Crisis in Hospital Nursing and the Retreat to Part-Time Work

Jerry Patrick White

The purpose of this chapter is to assess the context for the current crisis in hospital nursing. In it, we argue that the increasing availability of part-time work, and the increasing numbers of nurses who opt for it, as well as the prevalence of strikes and high turnover among nurses, are linked indications of a serious malaise in Canadian hospitals. Our study is based on data gathered from a range of sources: interviews with full- and part-time nurses and their union representatives, government studies, commissioned reports, union archives, and newspaper articles. The Civic Hospitals in Hamilton, Ontario, provide representative statistics for the more general case. We found that nurses are taking collective action—that is, striking—to force change; individually they are seeking respite from the steadily intensifying and distorting labor process by quitting or by opting for part-time work.

Nurses in the latter part of the nineteenth century, led by Florence Nightingale, were defined by their character; they were obedient to doctors and selflessly devoted to patients (Ehrenreich, 1973: 22). Nurses continue to express commitment and to seek personal satisfaction by providing service. In the late 1980s, nurses report choosing their career because it "provides the opportunity to care and help people and to work with people" (Ontario Nurses Association, 1988: 15).

Such a strong service ethic ought to provide a solid base both for job satisfaction and for a positive set of industrial relations. In the nursing profession, we find quite the opposite: a shift to shorter hours, strikes, and outright resignations. Why is commitment no longer keeping things "glued together"?

THE FOUNDATION OF THE CRISIS

Nurses, like other workers, want to be adequately paid for the work they do. As well, they want some say in how and when the work is done, and respect from those who work with them. Yet, these demands occur in a rapidly changing environment. Certain social factors both militate against their achieving job satisfaction and intensify their demands for job reform. The key social changes that have affected nurses include:

1. the fiscal crisis in Canada (White, 1990);
2. a general democratization of society that has not proceeded as quickly in the medical world (Registered Nurses Association of Ontario, 1981: 13–17);
3. the feminist movement, which has sparked a change in women's attitudes about what they want and deserve.[1]

The influence of the feminist movement on the nursing profession is a large and important topic in its own right. Suffice it to say for purposes of this paper that the social changes women are demanding and the concomitant resistance to change in hospitals has produced, among nurses, resistance to hospital work as it is organized today (Registered Nurses Association of Ontario, 1981: 3–5). Semi-feudal social relations in medicine and increasing feminist awareness have influenced the forms of this resistance. However, we will concentrate here on the material basis of the changes in the hospitals—the fiscal crisis.

THE FISCAL CRISIS

A fiscal crisis occurs when government revenues are outstripped by escalating expenditures. The resulting deficits lead government to take many measures that affect society in general and the work place in particular. Relevant to our purpose, the fiscal crisis faced by government in Canada has affected the provision of health care and, in particular, nursing practice in the hospitals. The economy of the early 1970s was marked by high inflation and expanding deficits. Government expenditures were outstripping government revenues. As early as 1969, Finance Minister Mitchell Sharp warned Prime Minister Pierre Trudeau that the federal government could not sustain this contradiction indefinitely. The Canadian government was interested in assisting the expansion of industrial production in certain sectors. However, federal monies were committed to programs, such as health care, that could not be easily cut. As the Auditor General would say in 1975, "Health care is now a social good. Canadians have come to expect that the government is responsible for providing an ever improving health-care system."

The provinces, not the federal government, are responsible for providing health care programs. The federal government, however, did have substantial fiscal responsibility. Through cost-sharing agreements, it paid more than 50 cents of every dollar spent by the provinces. Sharp argued that the federal government had to divest itself of ongoing responsibility for expanding high-cost programs like health care. The federal government began making cost sharing less predictable by adding regulations, disallowing some claims, canceling small but key programs, and slowing payments (Carter, 1977: 542; Saskatchewan Social Services Department, 1976). At the same time, when the government launched its proposal for restructuring transfer payments, the Established Program Financing Act was negotiated. This Act, it was claimed, would provide maintenance of standards, increased planning potential, greater autonomy, and more democratic federal–provincial relations. In reality, in exchange for some tax points and a no-strings cash transfer, it made the provinces responsible for provision of and payment for major established programs in the health field. The federal government banked on the hope that the provinces would not threaten their own legitimacy by cutting back on health care.

The provinces' response to the impending funding squeeze was to look for ways to tighten up monies allocated to these programs. During the period when the cost-sharing programs for health care were being negotiated, Ontario commissioned Maxwell Henderson to do a complete program review. The *Special Program Review* (1975) provided the guidelines for a more tight-fisted approach to health-care financing. Even then it was clear that deficits were going to rise markedly in the late 1970s and 1980s, and that, in the early 1980s, there would be a decline in the rate of increase of the gross national product due to economic slowdown. Inevitably, economic downturns generated pressure on social, health, and unemployment services. The program review proposed that:

1. there must be a "greater productivity from hospital staff";
2. the province should phase out as many beds as possible without jeopardizing service;
3. the hospitals should be encouraged to use part-time staff;
4. through a thorough review of operating costs in the hospitals, all possible ways of reducing the total paid hours for hospital staff should be found (Henderson, 1975: 143–152).

There can be little doubt that the recommendations were acted on: "In the eight-year period between 1973 and 1981, full-time hospital staff declined by nearly 5,000 positions, while part-time increased about 13,000. The growth in part-time workers did not balance out the full-time since total paid hours of work declined 150,000 hours" (Sykes, 1982:

127). In 1979, the Ontario Economic Council commented: "Since the early 1970s the Ministry of Health has resorted to severe measures to control costs. Many of them focused on the largest institutions . . . [like] hospitals. Hospitals have been closed down, a large number of beds closed, departments emptied . . . mergers of hospitals, staff lay-offs, capital spending down, etc." (Ontario Economic Council, 1979). For nurses, the effect was devastating. The fiscal crisis created a management push for greater productivity, encouraged part-time work, reduced the paid hours of staff per patient, and closed beds. While this was occurring, nurses were demanding greater respect, desiring greater democracy, and seeking rewards commensurate with their work. Problems were inevitable.

WHERE ARE THE NURSES?

The major symptom of trouble in hospital nursing is the apparent scarcity of nurses. Some, such as Meltz (1988), argue that there is a genuine shortage. Using a labor market supply and demand model, he concludes that supply is the key cause of the shortage since it has not increased at the same pace as demand, particularly due to reductions in college spaces for nursing (Meltz, 1988: 44, 65). This supply shortfall has generated the present problem and the "shortage will be solved by the market," according to Meltz (1988: 65). Our investigation indicates that more nurses are trained than are needed and that no actual shortage exists. The problem is more accurately described as a very high turnover rate.

What Shortage? The Supply-Side Argument. Large numbers of nursing graduates are not working. The number of employed nurses who were registered with the College of Nurses of Ontario increased by 18.6 percent over the five-year period from 1981 to 1986. In the same five years, the general population increased by only 4.8 percent (College of Nurses of Ontario, Registration Data, 1981; 1986). General population increases and the consequent "natural" growth of health services do not account for the shortfall in nurses.

Ontario, the province with the greatest reported "shortage," has a residual group of voluntarily unemployed nurses approaching 30 percent of the total nursing work force. Reports vary on the extent of the shortage. However, Ministry of Health officials interviewed report that, as of the middle of 1988, Ontario was short 1143 nurses (see "The Reasons behind the Nursing Shortage," *Toronto Star*, January 11, 1988: A1). The registration data indicate that it is not a supply-side problem in the usual sense. Rather, the "shortage" is a problem of inactivity (McArthur, 1988: A2). Even the new graduates are oversupplying new demand and could service residual demand except for the shortfalls created by those who voluntarily withdraw. This situation is aggravated by the shift to part-time work, creating a need for more personnel to cover the hours of care. Data from the Ontario jurisdiction support the claim that the fundamental "shortage" problem is, in fact, the turnover rate.

The problem of high turnover is not new. Summarizing the research up to 1982, Jenny found that the high turnover of nurses dates back to the mid–1970s (1982: 35). At that time, it was accepted that people would leave, and strategies were developed to fill the hours not covered. "As long as staff attrition could be offset by a fresh supply of nurses coming through the door, traditional responses centered on recruitment were sufficient" (Jenny, 1982). However, in the later 1980s this strategy began to unravel. The recession of 1980–82 worked its way through the system and had many consequences. The cost containment necessary from the mid–1970s aggravated turnover and inactivity (White, 1980). The turnover rate for nursing staff in Ontario between March 1980 and April 1981 was 28.8 percent (Ontario Nurses Association, 1982). Similar findings are reported by Wolf (1981), and officers of the Ontario Nurses Association (ONA) claim that this rate has, at the very least, continued. The *Report of the Task Force on Nursing Turnover at the Toronto General Hospital*, indicates that it has probably even increased.

Turnover and inactivity in the post–1982 period follow the same pattern. The task force of the Registered Nurses Association of Ontario (RNAO) on nursing shortages noted that the shortages are not so much due to the actual lack of nurses but rather to a lack of nurses who are willing to work under the present set of circumstances (ONA, 1988b). The *Report on Nursing Manpower* (1987) indicates that there are adequate numbers of nurses to fill the needs in the province. Administrations, the report urges, must improve the work environment through more sensitive employment relations.

The Goldfarb Corporation's major survey of nurses for the Ontario Nurses Association (ONA, 1988) led to the conclusion that problems in the organization and the wider process of work are forcing people to leave the profession and to stay out. Commenting on their commissioned study, the ONA says, "The problem is not that too few nurses are available for vacant positions; it is that too few nurses are choosing to work in these positions" (ONA, 1988: 1). Working conditions, then, are a major cause of the current nursing "shortage." A related issue is the pressure to professionalize.

THE MOVE TO PROFESSIONALIZE: MORE PRESSURE ON NURSES

There are two pressures on the nursing profession. The first is the decision to move wholly to university-trained nursing staff by the year 2000; the second is the elimination of the Registered Nursing Assistants

(RNAs) and the transfer of their duties to nurses. Although in the midst of staffing difficulties, hospitals have also attempted to alter the composition of the work force by relying more heavily on Registered Nurses (RNs). The most important shift is away from the RNAs to the RNs, a shift justified on the basis that:

1. It is cost efficient.
2. RNAs do not have the skills to meet patient care needs (Woods Gordon, 1985: 21; White, 1988: 19–20). More accurately, the shift is fueled by the contradiction between increasing demand for patient care on the one hand and the perceived need to cut costs on the other. Our examination of the situation in the Hamilton Civic Hospitals suggests that financial considerations are the prime motive for the shift in personnel (see also Meltz, 1988: 18–20, 61). The Hamilton Civic Hospitals are typical in terms of the shift to RN staff. The shift from RNAs to RNs shown in Table 17.1 is dramatic. Clearly, the crisis in funding and the increases in the variety and volume of care have prompted a major change in the composition of the work force, and, as we shall see, in the labor process as well. These changes in turn are responsible for critical declines in labor participation.

STRIKES AND JOB ACTIONS

Strikes and job actions are not normally thought of as characteristic of nurses in hospitals. Many things mitigate against strike action—the illegality of the strike (in many jurisdictions), the "Florence Nightingalism" and professionalism of nurses, and finally, the preconception that women are less likely to strike.[2] However, there has been a growing number of job actions, up to and including strikes, over the past few years. In 1988 alone, the Alberta nurses and Saskatchewan nurses struck. In 1989, British Columbia and Quebec nurses struck. Ontario nurses have been speaking out as a union, criticizing the health-care system. As well, in Ontario and other jurisdictions self-organized groups, such as "Health Professionals for Improving Health-care," have called for public pressure to improve lagging standards in our hospitals.

The changing nature of work (labor process), resulting in actual or perceived workload increases and deterioration of job satisfaction, has created the need for nurses to strike in order to complain about, slow down, or reverse the process. The desire to gain control of their work, its performance, when it is done, and at what level of quality, is at the "eye of the storm." A nurse in Saskatoon sums it up: "I'll tell you what the issues are. We cannot do the job we are trained to do. There are too few of us, patients in the hospitals are older and more ill than they used to be, management are cutting every corner because the province does not give them the funds. I speak for a lot of others when I say the stress

Table 17.1
Complements of Registered Nurses and Registered Nursing Assistants in the Hamilton Civic Hospitals

Year	Registered Nurses		Registered Nursing Assistants
	Part-time	Full-time	
1977	194	516	239
1978	240	497	231
1979	268	485	241
1980	302	504	217
1981	313	534	208
1982	322	610	187
1983	361	603	180
1984	459	591	170
1985	517	637	173
1986	504	646	148
1987	561	643	139

Source: J. White, Brief to the Board of Governors Concerning the Elimination of Registered Nursing Assistants from Active Treatment at the Hamilton Civic Hospitals. Hamilton: Canadian Union of Public Employees, 1988.

is burning me out." The crisis in funding and the increases in the demand for patient care have prompted a shift of work to the RNs. This, in microcosm, is the contradiction. Financial questions push work-force composition changes and labor-process changes that in turn cause critical declines in the participation of labor.

THE GROWTH IN PART-TIME WORK

More nurses in the Canadian hospital system are opting for part-time work. Table 17.1 displays changes in the numbers of full- and part-time nurses over the last decade in our case study hospitals. Table 17.2 provides similar information for the Canadian jurisdiction. In the Hamilton Civic Hospitals, the nurses working full-time decreased from 72.6 per-

Table 17.2
Registered Nurses Working in Canada (Percentage)

Year	Total Number	Part-time	Full-time
1974	128,675	74	26
1975	140,388	72	28
1976	137,858	69	31
1977	139,989	68	32
1978	161,125	67	33
1979	148,954	66	34
1980	155,309	64.7	35.3
1981	161,269	64	36
1982	164,231	62.6	37.3
1983	176,768	62.0[†]	38.0
1984	188,074	55.8	44.2
1985	194,519	63.7[†]	36.3
1986	184,067	63.2	36.8

[†]The data include a sizable "not stated" category; In 1983 (22,776), 1984 (7,363), 1985 and 1986 (20,512). These are largely in the Province of Quebec. The percentage was calculated by dropping, i.e., subtracting the "not stated" from the totals. This biases the data toward full-time employment because a larger percentage of nurses in Quebec are part-time. Armstrong (1986: 19) reports that fully 60 percent of Quebec nurses are part-time.
Sources: A variety of sources were used to compile this table. Table 2, Section A, Countdown, Canadian Nurses Association; 1975–85. Table 13.4, Health Personnel, Health and Welfare Canada; 1987, 1986. Table 2, Nursing in Canada, Statistics Canada (83–226).

cent of all nurses in 1977 to 53 percent in 1987. In 1977, there were 516 full-time nurses and by 1986 there were 643, a modest increase of 25 percent. On the other hand, there were only 194 part-time nurses in 1977 and this had increased to 561 by 1987, an increase of 189 percent. The Canadian data in Table 17.4 indicate that there was a decrease from 74 percent of nurses working full-time in 1974 to a low of 55.8 percent in 1984, and that there was a complementary increase from 26 percent

Table 17.3
Employment in Canada, Age 15 Years and Over

Year	Total Employment	Part-time Male	Part-time Female	Full-time Male	Full-time Female	Part-time as Percent of Total
1975	9,284	301	687	5,602	2,694	10.6
1980	10,708	381	1,011	6,078	3,238	13.0
1981	11,001	413	1,074	6,144	3,372	13.5
1982	10,618	428	1,100	5,808	3,282	14.4
1983	10,675	470	1,169	5,733	3,303	15.4
1984	10,932	482	1,187	5,826	3,438	15.3
1985	11,221	486	1,251	5,941	3,543	15.5
1986	11,531	514	1,274	6,053	3,689	15.5
1987	11,861	510	1,294	6,199	3,858	15.2
1988	12,245	527	1,355	6,350	4,013	15.4
1989	12,486	536	1,352	6,441	4,156	15.1

Source: Statistics Canada, Historical Labour Force Statistics. (Cat. 71–201, 1990), various
   tables.

of nurses working part-time in 1974 to a high of 44.2 percent in 1984. This shift is more pronounced than the shifts that have taken place in the labor force in general.

Part-time employment in Canada generally has increased much more slowly than part-time employment in nursing. As a percentage of total employment, the former has increased from 10.5 percent in 1975 to 15.1 percent in 1987. Over almost the same period and the same number of years, part-time nurses as a percentage of total nurses have increased from 26 percent in 1974 to 36.8 percent in 1986. We can see, then, that there is a sizable shift to part-time work. The magnitude of this increase is significant, for it can be argued that the change to part-time nursing represents yet another way in which nurses are retreating from the profession. In support of this view, a recent study by the Ontario Nursing Association (ONA) of part-time and job-sharing nurses found that the movement to part-time working reflects dissatisfaction with the current labor process (that is, how work is done, its speed, content, form, and intensity), and with the organization of nursing in hospitals. For purposes of this paper, the dissatisfaction raises three related questions: Why are nurses dissatisfied? What do nurses hope to gain, in particular by opting for part-time work? Is the shift procuring for them the results they seek?

PART-TIME WORK AND THE CAUSES OF THE CRISIS IN NURSING

Several structural factors have laid the foundation for the intensification of the labor process and for changes in the hospitals generally. The principal one is the action taken in response to the funding shortfall. Cost-cutting measures such as support-staff reductions (orderlies and RNAs), technological innovations, and more casual staff in the team mix were only some of the changes. Two other concurrent changes exacerbated the problems: first, increasing acuity on the ward because more very ill patients were being placed there; and second, a quicker patient "turnaround" time, especially after surgery, because it was expected that recuperation would take place at home (Jenny, 1982: 15; White, 1990). As a result, patients on the ward are altogether more ill. The effect of these new policies are twofold. The first is summed up by a nurse with 19 years of experience in Ontario hospitals: "What we mean by increasing acuity is a sicker patient and that means the nurse makes more frequent interventions. The increasing acuity also means that people in the wards today would have been in intensive care units 10 years ago" (Lee, 1988: B1).

The earlier release of patients lowers nurses' job satisfaction, for they lose the opportunity to see the results of their work. A nurse with 11 years of experience noted: "As a person recovers from surgery they are interested in yacking and it's part of the job to do it, an enjoyable part. It seems we get a lot less of that now. Patients are gone before you get to know them . . . some of the best parts of my work are gone." We find that the increase in the number of acutely ill patients to be looked after has not been accompanied by an increase in staff, although additional staff are needed. The administrations felt they could not afford the added personnel. We can identify three categories of frustrations experienced by nurses: issues related to the labor-process (such as workload), non–labor-process problems (such as restricted promotion), and time and hours (a category that overlaps the other two).

LABOR-PROCESS SOURCES OF FRUSTRATION

Goldfarb's survey for the Ontario Nurses Association found that "the key sources of frustrations are the workload and the lack of staff to deal with the quantity of work" and the lack of time to "give direct quality patient care" (1988: 43–46). Asked what their major frustrations are, 65 percent complained of understaffing, heavy workload, and no time for patients (ONA, 1988: 44–46). This view is substantiated by the bargaining surveys conducted by the Ontario Nurses Association (ONA). It polls its members prior to bargaining. According to the 1985 report, workload increases led to short-staffing, danger to patients, substandard care, no orientation of new staff to a ward, the assignment of people to areas they do not know and cannot handle, undertrained relief (part-time) staff in specialist areas such as chronic-care units, low staff morale, and forced overtime or overtime with no pay (ONA, 1985: 5–7).

In our case study of hospitals, a similar picture unfolds. The minutes of a meeting of head nurses at the Hamilton General (December 1986) indicated the following problems as sources of absenteeism and dissatisfaction:

1. increased work-load;
2. high turnover of patients;
3. increased age of patients;
4. scheduling confusion;
5. inexperienced staff;
6. lack of resource people;
7. lack of enough orientation to the ward;
8. declining commitment;
9. lack of support staff, therefore increased work-load.

Interviews supported this list. One nurse commented: "There are times when dressings cannot be changed. We have no support staff so we have to do everything and we cannot." Analysis of problems related to the labor process requires an examination of many interrelated factors. Labor-process changes alter how work is done, its speed, content, form, and intensity. When people engage in a process of labor, they form social relations and develop an identity. The outcome is conditioned by the expectations that they bring to the job. When changes in labor process take place, the organization, social interactions and the actors themselves change. Nurses seem to experience the changes in their labor process as a profound alteration in their professional identities. Their attachment to nursing is broken as they are forced to work in a way that challenges their understanding of what is necessary. They are reacting to these changes by resigning, striking, and moving to part time.

NON–LABOR-PROCESS RELATED PROBLEMS

What we have called non–labor-process issues also induce nurses to opt for part-time work or to leave entirely. Four categories can be identified:

1. *Rewards from work.* Nurses report that the flat promotion ladder, inadequate pay, and decrease of in-service training are frustrating in the context of intensified work (Jenny, 1982; ONA, 1988a). Many full-time nurses report want-

ing to cash out their benefits and pensions—some shift to part time in order to do so (Meltz, 1988: 57). The lack of respect from co-workers, particularly doctors, and the low level of autonomy are repeatedly reported as sources of discontent (ONA, 1988: 19; RNAO, 1981).

2. *Interface between home and work.* The vast majority of nurses are women, approximately 98 percent in most jurisdictions (Jenny, 1982). Nurses, as women, seek control over their lives, which include work and socially defined family obligations. Nurses try to fulfill the socially imposed family roles. However, women lack the social supports that men have, i.e., they lack wives (see White, 1990: chapter 3). Goldfarb (ONA, 1988: 38) corroborates this when he reports that "shift work, family responsibilities, and lack of accommodation for mothers are in the top three problems."

3. *Subjugation to males.* Nurses note that doctors and administrators are usually male and when nurses seek access to the loci of power in their work world, they necessarily confront gendered relations.

4. *Hours of work.* In this regard, nurses report two complaints. Staff shortages, or the increasing workload in general, have two consequences. There is too much overtime, forced and requested, and there are few choices in shifts (ONA, 1988). Long and inconvenient hours were seen as unacceptable. A representative comment in interview was that "overtime is the norm now"; other investigators have found the same thing, even in excess: "I've seen people working 24 hours" (Lee, 1988: B1).

These labor process and non labor-process related problems have led nurses to strike, to quit, and to switch to part-time work. However, the effects of these options are very different. Strikes have led to some improvements, but resignations have had no salutary effect. What about the move to part-time work?

PART-TIME WORK: SOLUTION, SYMPTOM, OR PROBLEM?

Gray (1987) points out that part-time work allows nurses to juggle family and work responsibilities. Part-time work is also a way to temper the frustrations arising from the nurses' lack of time to perform traditional bedside duties (Gray, 1987). In this sense, it appears to be a partial solution to more than one problem. In fact, many nursing unions have declared the part-time option a right and have called it a way for women to deal with pressures of home and work. It is also used by nurses as an avenue of escape from the problems of the job. Does it provide escape?

Working part time, as a form of resistance to abuse rather than an active strategy for change, is not very effective. Instead of improving the situation, it actually exacerbates the difficulties both for the individual and for the remaining full-time nurses. I would argue that part-time work contributes to the problem of nurses because it lessens their power and weakens their demands for change. Moreover, it allows the intensification of the labor process to proceed unchecked. The increasing numbers of part-time nurses mean more hours and higher intensity work for the remaining full-time personnel.

The attempt to gain control of one's work life is a major impetus for selecting part-time work (Jenny, 1982: 25). Our interviews, and the research of others, suggest that it is not a successful strategy. A part-time nurse in London, Ontario, comments: "I find that my life is often more complicated. With the strange shifts I get [as a part-time nurse] I feel I have less control than before." Another nurse finds her power to bargain curtailed: "Perhaps I was foolish but I did believe I would get more say on when I would work. I have to work now but I can't do without the shifts, so I cannot be as demanding as I hoped." Many full-time nurses who have switched to part-time are dissatisfied with their work schedule, often because it conflicts with family responsibilities. They want more control over when they work. However, the change is less effective than they had hoped. A nurse comments: "At first I felt a level of relief, almost freedom, as I did not have to get ready for the shifts I was so used to. Very soon I found myself feeling . . . even more uptight after the shifts I did work. . . . I found changing wards and having few patterns affected me." (Part-time acute care nurse, Hamilton, 1988.)

Mathera (1985: 33) finds that part-time nurses, in an acute setting, work more hours and receive fewer benefits than their colleagues. In the Goldfarb study (ONA, 1988: 48), the part-time nurses gave responses that were similar to those of the full-time nurses in terms of their dissatisfactions and complaints, despite the fact that they had opted for part-time working in order to alleviate the frustration that they had felt in the full-time positions. The following were typical expressions of disenchantment with part-time nursing:

I may work less hours but at work it seems even more pressure. I use to think it was me . . . not being used to being in harness, but I think our assignments are heavier. (Part-time nurse, London, Ontario, 1988.)

All I have ever wanted to do is have the chance to practice my nursing up to my ability. I do not mean adequate given the time or given the load. I thought part time would give me that chance. I do not know the patients. . . . When you do not come in regularly things change, people change, I think it is harder to be the kind of nurse you want to be. (Part-time nurse, Burlington, Ontario.)

Lack of respect was another reason why nurses left full-time positions for part-time ones. However, a part-time nurse in Hamilton comments: "As a part-timer, I get even less consideration or respect then I did as a staff nurse. Less from doctors for sure, other nurses sometimes give you less respect and even outside the ward. Some treat you like you are on a hobby or getting spending money."

The full-time nurses find that the work place deteriorates as more people opt for part-time status. This was almost universal in my interviews:

More part-timers, more problems. (Nurse, Hamilton, Ontario.)

You just cannot run a ward with all the part-time nurses. You need more full-time people. (Nurse, London, Ontario.)

Part-timers change, they get moved from place to place. When you do not know the person who is coming in and they don't know the routines, the equipment locations, the patients, or whatever, then I get to do too much. (Nurse, Burlington, Ontario.)

The part-timers report to their nurses' unions that they are used to fill in on a variety of units with many requirements, and that they are not given the orientation necessary to do a good job. At stake is job satisfaction, confidence, and competence (British Columbia Nurses, 1983: 8). Even the administrations that had promoted the extension of part-time nursing complained of lack of continuity in care and inconsistency of performance: "If a nurse works two days a week, on the first they are not so efficient and organized but by the second they are improving" (Godfrey, 1980: 69–70).

Furthermore, according to the submissions to the Commission of Inquiry into Part-Time Work (Canada, 1983) the skill levels of part-time nurses decline. Our interviews confirm this assessment. A Hamilton nurse with seven years of experience complained: "They expect us to know the new drug regimes . . . the new equipment . . . Do they train us? NO! Do they make it easy to take courses outside? No way! . . . Friends who go to regular part time so they get time for training, they get nothing . . . it's worse." The position of many colleges of nurses (the professional bodies for nurses) is that by the year 2000, practicing RNs must possess a university degree in nursing, the Bachelor of Nursing Science degree (BScN). This ruling affects the nurses who do not have degrees from universities, many of whom have gone to part-time work in order to have time for degree courses. Yet part-time work does not necessarily provide the time necessary to pursue education. One Hamilton interviewee reports: "I thought I would have time to update and get my degree but it has not worked that way. My husband seems to expect a lot more at home, I have less time and, with heavy work, I have no energy." The home-life question raised here deserves a great deal of comment; however, suffice it to say that the movement to part-time nursing in hospitals does not, according to our interviews, alleviate the problem of reconciling domestic and professional responsibilities.

One can argue that, as the conditions of part-time nursing become increasingly unattractive, women's options are effectively curtailed. Aside from the financial problems that working part time often entails, part-time nurses report that their hours of housework rise dramatically. This outcome is also reported by the Commission of Inquiry into Part-Time Work (Canada, 1983).

CONCLUSION

Strikes, high turnover, and the growth in part-time nursing are linked symptoms of a serious malaise in Canadian hospitals. We argue that the same set of "problems" that pushed nurses to strike or quit also forced people to seek shorter hours. We found that nurses are choosing to work part-time as a flight from the steadily intensifying labor process. The intensification involves both the content of the work and the time when it is done, and it is a distortion that is perceived as threatening the quality of health care. If nurses feel they are not doing what they can and should do to serve and treat patients, then their raison d'etre is distorted and undermined.

The increasing availability of computers and software has reduced both the cost and the complexity of partial scheduling and payroll (Armstrong, 1986). The technical changes, combined with the push by government to cut costs, have encouraged hospital managements to move to on-call and casual personnel as a cost-cutting measure. Many nurses, faced with the tensions created by the intensified labor process, have turned to the part-time option in order to reduce their exposure to such a stressful working environment, and to regain control over the scheduling of hours devoted to paid work. We find that this strategy fails. Individuals who have actually opted for this type of respite find themselves experiencing even more intensification during their hours at work. Further, the shifts are not under the individual's control. Part-time nurses often report being assigned to the "worst" shifts, which defeats part of the reason for engaging in the part-time process in the first place. Lack of familiarity with units, patients, and procedures potentially decreases the possibility of their delivering quality care, while making work more difficult for the full-timers.

We have argued that the part-time option does not eliminate the fundamental problems and in fact creates further problems. There is a paradox that emerges in both our interviews and other interview-based studies. A lack of staff is in itself a major cause of the "shortage." That is, before people will be enticed back there must be more nurses! Therefore switching to part-time work, in fact, intensifies the nursing crisis.

NOTES

1. In 1988, 99.2 percent of nurses were female.

2. When ward aides are eliminated, nurses take increased responsibility for "non-nursing" tasks such as cleaning, portering, and delivering water pitchers. This has been an important issue for job satisfaction in the profession.

V WHAT OF THE FUTURE?

18 Part-Time Work: A Hope and a Peril

Hilda Kahne

Part-time work is at a crossroads. Although it has a long history and its official definition and measurement by the Department of Labor date back to 1947, the concept and labor market context within which part-time work is considered have grown much more complex in recent years. Groups in the labor force potentially affected by its structure—workers, unions, employers—are buffeted in their views and experience by the positive and negative qualities it simultaneously reflects. Its evolution has a rudderless quality that largely ignores lessons of domestic and international experience. However, part-time work is here to stay. If carefully structured, it can offer important work-scheduling efficiency and flexibility benefits to employers and workers. It deserves more attention and innovative experimentation in the work place.

This paper will examine part-time work in the United States today, its concept, context, and viability as a work schedule to meet employee and employer needs, and then will consider some of the lessons of experience that can help in developing a more enlightened policy guiding its use.

WHAT IS PART-TIME WORK? WHAT ARE ITS CHARACTERISTICS?

The concept of part-time work is a simple one: a work schedule that is less than full time. Since what is considered to be "full time" can change both by custom and by legislation,[1] and can be influenced in definition by an individual's current part- or full-time status in contrast to "usual" work hours, a statistical measurement is more complicated. A part-time worker in the United States is considered to be one who works from one to 35 hours in a "reference week" (that is, a week that includes the 12th of the month when data are collected). Those who work 35 hours or more are full-time workers. Part-time workers are further differentiated between those who work part time by choice (voluntary part time) and those whose part-time work relates to factors affecting the demand for labor, such as slack work, materials shortages, or lack of available full-time work (involuntary or economic part time). A new United States Bureau of Labor Statistics series also reports data on part-timers in terms of the numbers who "usually work part time" (Nardone, 1986).[2] Data based on either definition provide a picture of the characteristics and trends of part-time work in the labor force.

Non-agricultural part-time workers numbered about 20 million in 1989, an increase from 15.5 million in 1979. They represent about 18.4 percent of non-agricultural employment today.[3] Nearly one third of non-farm workers held a part-time job at some time during 1986 and about one fifth usually worked part time. About 73 percent of part-time workers are voluntary part-timers (13.9 million in 1987 compared with 5.1 million economic part-timers). It is the economic part-timers whose growth has been the most dramatic in recent years. Between 1979 and 1987, economic part-time workers grew by over 50 percent, compared with a 14 percent increase in voluntary part-time workers (U.S. Department of Labor, 1980; 1988; unpublished data). Between 1980 and 1988 part-time jobs increased overall by 21 percent, compared with a 14 percent rise in the total labor force. The importance of part-time work has grown over time, but more because of the increase in involuntary, rather than voluntary, part-time work.

Part-time workers are characteristically women (two thirds of all part-time workers in 1988), older workers (18 percent are aged 55 or older), or teenagers (21 percent are aged 16 to 19) (U.S. Department of Labor, 1988). They are concentrated in wholesale and retail trade and in service industries; more than three fourths of non-agricultural voluntary part-time workers work here. About one fourth of trade workers and one fifth of those in services work part time voluntarily, in contrast to manufacturing where about three percent of workers are on voluntary part-time schedules. Occupational distribution of part-time work, more segregated than full-time work (Holden and Hansen in Brown and Pechman, 1987), reflects this industrial concentration. Three fifths of voluntary part-time workers work in clerical, services, and sales occupations. Although part-time work encompasses a wide range of working hours, over one half of all voluntary part-time workers work between 15 and 29 hours weekly.

A brief comment about the earnings and benefits of part-time work explains its low status as a work form. Much part-time work follows a traditional model, with low earnings and no benefits. In 1987, median hourly earnings for part-time workers were $4.42, about 60 percent of the $7.43 hourly rate for full-time workers. Twenty-eight percent of all part-time jobs pay the minimum wage or less, compared with 5 percent of full-time jobs. Two thirds of all minimum-wage earners work part time. Women working part time were about 45 percent of all low-wage workers in 1984; male part-timers comprised about 21 percent of the group (Mellon and Haugen, 1986: 24; Levitan and Conway, 1988: 12–13). Low earnings partly reflect the fact that such jobs are located in the low-pay sectors of the economy (retail trade, food service), and partly they are due to the lower hourly rate paid to part-time than to full-time workers for equivalent work (Plewes, 1983). A similar finding has been reported in a British study that found that 10 percent of establishments surveyed paid lower basic rates for part-time than for full-time equivalent jobs (Blyton, 1985: 110).[4] The absence of benefits reduces even further the economic status of these jobs.

Life insurance and vacation benefits are rare among part-time workers, and only 27.5 percent of part-time workers employed less than 20 hours a week are covered by pension plans. One half of full-time workers are covered. Eighty-four percent of all part-time workers have no direct health benefits through their employment, and 42 percent have neither direct nor spouse-related, employer-provided health coverage (Chollet, 1984). In contrast, about 78 percent of full-time workers receive health insurance as a benefit (Tilly, 1990).

With low earnings, often an amount that approximates the welfare level, few or no benefits, and little job security, it is not surprising that part-time job seekers are often only marginally attached to the labor force. Many work sporadically, often in the underground economy, or intermittently elect welfare over some poorly paid and temporary work (*New York Times*, 1987: September 27). Unemployment insurance eligibility is often lacking for them because of their failure to meet minimum earnings requirements. In all but six states, applicants for unemployment benefits are disqualified if they seek only part-time work (AARP News, February 1990).

However, not all part-time work conforms to this dismal image. Beginning in the late 1960s and continuing into the early to mid–1980s, a number of part-time work arrangements, which we will call New Concept part time, were introduced into the private and public sectors (Kahne, 1985: Chapter 3). New Concept forms fit the definition of part-time work—weekly hours below 35 a week. Each has distinctive qualities as well. Sometimes they are permanent part-time jobs; at other times they take the form of job sharing (two part-time workers filling an equivalent full-time position), work sharing (often reflecting reduced hours in the face of necessary production cutbacks), or phased retirement (gradually reduced hours in a regular job, providing a transition to retirement).

Most important, all share the characteristics of a regular job attachment, wages prorated to that of equivalent full-time work, and payment of at least some benefits. A nationwide survey in the early 1980s of more than 400 public and private sector organizations (Paul, 1983) found one fourth of the organizations with some job sharing, one fourth with phased retirement arrangements, and about two thirds with some permanent part-time employment. Of all reduced-hour employees covered by the survey, temporary and permanent, 11.5 percent received the same benefits as full-time workers and 46 percent received some of the full-time benefits. Another survey of 310 firms, also in the early 1980s (Olmsted, 1983), found that 80 percent of respondents offered fringe benefits, often prorated, to permanent part-time employees, although employees often had to work 20 hours a week to qualify.

With this slowly growing pool of New Concept part-time work arrangements, it seemed as if part-time work was finally taking off. However, in the mid–1980s intervening trends increased the complexity of the circumstances of the labor market and raised questions about problems accompanying the extension of part-time work. Let us look at some of these issues.

IS THERE AN INTEREST IN PART-TIME WORK?

The Labor Market Context: Supply of Labor

This section looks at the composition of the labor force and its projected growth in relation to the possible extension of New Concept part-time work. First, a comment about the special applicability that part-time work has had for the lives of working women since World War II. Throughout this period, there have been successive sharp increases in the labor-force participation rates of specific female groups: married women with grown children (immediate post–World War II), mothers of school-age children (1950s), women with preschool children (1960s and 1970s), and most recently, mothers of preschool children one year of age or younger (1980s). In 1950, women constituted less than one third of the labor force. Only about one fifth of married women worked for pay and fewer than 12 percent of married women with children under six years of age did so. In 1989, women comprised 46 percent of the labor force. Marital status and presence of children now make little difference in women's work status. The proportion of women at work is 50 percent or more, whether or not they are married and whether or not they have children. In 1988, one half of married mothers and 45 percent of single-parent mothers with children one year old or younger were in the labor force. That figure for married mothers had been about one third ten years earlier, an indication of the dramatic change that has occurred in attitude and social roles.

A number of reasons explain this social phenomenon. Economic need and a desire for a higher standard of living play a large role in women's paid work, but so, too, do rising educational levels and women's changing aspirations. Moreover, life patterns no longer always conform to that of a single earner or to that of one lifelong marriage. Two-earner families, with the advantage of two incomes and the disadvantage of severe time constraints for family activities, have grown dramatically, rising from 40 to 52 percent of married-couple families between 1970 and 1988. So, too, has the frequency of divorce as well as the numbers of children born outside of marriage. As a result, there has been a tremendous growth in the number of single female heads of families. Such families, 16 percent of all families in 1989 (compared to 9 percent in 1950), and the fastest-growing family form today, reinforce the need of women for a regular income.

Because of the time pressures involved in combining work and family responsibilities, the proportion of women who work part time exceeds that of men. About 26 percent of employed women work reduced schedules compared with 10 percent of men. About three fourths of all part-time women workers work part time by choice; only about one half of men do so. Sixty percent of women part-timers are married and living with their husbands and 30 percent have never been married. Whereas part-time work for men takes place in youth or just prior to or following retirement, for women, interest in part-time work can occur at periods throughout the working life. In the United States, although the proportion of women working part time has been relatively stable over the past 20 years (Shank, 1988: 60), the number of part-time working women has risen along with the number of women in the labor force. Part-time work, although not ideal, has provided a way for women, especially those with a second income in the family, to care for families without sacrificing labor-market attachment or severely compromising skill and career progression. It has permitted them to retain some income, and to acquire training and education while attending to family matters. Present patterns of voluntary part-time work tell us something about women's work-time preferences. If New Concept part-time jobs become more available across the entire range of occupations and industries, preference for part-time work may be even greater.

A study of role strain experienced by two-earner parents in 224 families, three fifths of whom were in non-professional occupations, provides partial confirmation of the potential for an increased interest in part-time work to reduce work/family strain (Moen and Dempster-

McClain, 1987). In almost one half of the surveyed families, one or both parents worked more than 40 hours a week. Respondents to the inquiry were asked whether they would like to spend less time working so that they could spend more time with husband (or wife) and child(ren), even if it meant earning less money. They were also asked about their preference for spouse's work time. The results showed that over one half of the mothers (53 percent) and almost two fifths (38 percent) of fathers preferred fewer hours for themselves, while 46 percent of fathers and 30 percent of mothers preferred fewer work hours for spouses. One fifth of employed parents preferred fewer hours for both self and spouse, and well over one half wanted both family members, or at least one, to work fewer hours. This is a particularly important finding since parents with a clear priority of family over work, as evidenced by no more than minimal labor-force attachment, were excluded from the sample. A sizable proportion of parents expressed the desire for fewer work hours in order "to spend more time with their spouse and children." The findings of the study provide support for the view that interest in New Concept reduced-hour jobs is far greater than the present configuration of part-time work indicates. The limited availability of desirable options severely hinders the implementation of expressed preferences of working parents.

Women's interest in reduced-hour schedules is particularly important in view of labor-force projections. The labor force is projected to grow at a slower rate. A 1.2 percent rate of annual growth has been projected for the years from 1988 to 2000; however, this is only half the actual rate for the years from 1972 to 1986. Moreover, the projected continuation of a decline in the men's labor-force participation rate (76.2 percent in 1988; 75.9 percent in 2000) and the slowly increasing rate in women's participation (56.6 percent in 1988; 62.6 percent in 2000) suggest that women's importance in the labor force will continue to grow. The proportion of women in the labor force, about 45.0 percent in 1988, may rise to 47.3 percent by 2000. It is estimated that 68 percent of women in the work force will be of child-bearing age by the year 2000 (Fullerton, 1987; 25; 1989: 3–12). Demographic studies suggest that 90 percent of women entering child-bearing years in the last decade of the century can be expected to have children over their life span (U.S. Bureau of Labor Statistics, Correspondence, 1988: October). An increasing awareness of these facts helps in understanding why job sharing and other part-time work forms, along with family-oriented benefits, will inevitably become more important in the future.

In sum, part-time work is certainly not well-paid, secure work in a broad range of occupations and industries. It may not be the answer to the needs of all women for some phase of their lives, such as the period of raising young children or caring for elders. Nor is it necessarily the form that best suits some working women, such as middle-class women, for the entire span of their attachment to the labor market. Part-time employment can provide a critically important work-schedule option for many women at particular periods of time. Unlike men, for whom part-time work is still largely associated with education during youth, or with work around the age of retirement, women's interest in part-time work can occur at any stage throughout their lives. Such work schedules provide a viable option to leaving the labor force entirely when alternative ways of reducing the time pressures associated with dual work and family roles are not yet widespread. Affordable child care for working women has only recently entered our social policy agenda (O'Connell and Bloom, 1987; U.S. Census, May 1987). Men's contribution to family life, although gradually increasing between 1965 and 1981 from 20 to 30 percent of the amount of time spent in such activities by the couple, still does not result in an equal sharing of family duties (Juster and Stafford, 1985: 320–321; 328–329). Part-time work, then, offers a way of retaining labor market attachment and skills, in periods when the demands of responsibilities, including home and child and elder care, preclude a full-time work commitment.

Just as the pressures of work/family roles will lead to an increased interest in part-time work for two-earner families in the years ahead, there are other reasons for the appeal of part-time work for older Americans and teenagers. For older Americans, part-time work can serve as an income supplement while they are phasing into retirement, relieving work stress while allowing them to retain work connectedness and the use of their talents and skills. Currently almost one fourth of Americans aged 55 and over work part time. Older workers are projected to increase slightly over present levels by 2000, but the increase will be less than the increase in the older population because of the continuing popularity of early retirement among those who can afford it. Should New Concept part-time work spread, older workers could benefit from combining a part-time (phased) early retirement with part-time work in their customary job. Employers and society could benefit from this growth of part-time work as well, both from the productive contribution of older workers who might otherwise retire and from cost savings in the payment of social security and other welfare benefits.

For teenagers, part-time work is often a necessary complement to education and training. Employed young people who are simultaneously in school are more than five times more likely to work part time than are employed young people who are not in school (Nardone, 1986: 16). Currently almost two thirds of employed teenagers work part time. Their interest in part-time work, paralleling their interest in education, is expected to continue to be strong.

Overall, there is little fear that the interest in part-time work will disappear. It will be available not only for groups that have traditionally worked these schedules, but at times, also, for customary full-time workers who are moving to a new career, stopping out with a self-assigned sabbatical, returning to school, or pursuing a leisure-time avocation. If the supply of workers interested in part-time employment is secure, what about the demand for them on the part of employers? Can there be a productive contribution in New Concept part-time work when wage rates are equivalent to those of full-time workers and when benefits are prorated?

The Labor Market Context: The Demand for Labor

Feminization of the labor force, trends in retirement, education, and changing values about the use of time and patterns of productive activities are leading to greater interest in part-time work schedules on the part of suppliers of labor. At the same time, a multi-textured fabric continues to develop on the demand side. Changes in demand, coupled with increasing automation and other technological changes, reinforce a fundamental ongoing transformation from an industrial to a service economy. They result in changing skill and training requirements for work, and in alterations in work-place organization and staffing. Required work-place presence is giving way to a potential for flexibility both in job location and in the blocks of time necessary for doing a job. By the year 2000, almost four out of five of all non-farm wage and salary jobs are projected to be in the service sector, an increase from three out of four in 1988. What this will mean is an increase in numbers of part-time jobs, an increase that will partly be in traditional areas such as retail trade and health and food services, and partly in newly developing service areas. Raising the status of jobs in traditional part-time sectors where low pay and benefit patterns have long prevailed may be more difficult than establishing equitable pay and benefits in occupations that have not previously had a heavy component of low-pay, part-time workers.

A further complication adds to the concern about the future role of part-time work in society. Until recently, the trend of job quality has been toward permanence and stability. This trend has been reversed since the early 1980s, when a sharp and rapid extension began in the use of temporary workers. Referred to as contingent workers, in 1986 they included 10 million freelance, self-employed workers (e.g., photographers, salesmen, writers), 5.6 million contract workers and consultants (in such jobs as data processing, health care, security, engineering, legal services), and an estimated one million temporary workers, in addition to 20 million part-time workers. Temporary workers include clerical workers, but also managerial and administrative work-

ers, and professionals such as college teachers (Belous, 1989). A disproportionate number of contingent workers are women, minorities,
seniors, and youth.

Now numbering almost 37 million and estimated to account for more
than one fourth of the American labor force, their numbers have been
increasing recently at a rate of about 25 percent a year. Growth is made
possible by the kinds of jobs prevailing in a service- and computer-driven
society. Their rise has been attributed to an attempt on the part of
employers to alleviate work overload in a way that avoids payment of
overtime, to cover periods of peak demand for production, and to get
tasks done where permanent jobs are not justified. More fundamentally,
the growth reflects employer uncertainty about the state of the economy
and a desire to meet competition—both domestic and foreign—through
measures that increase flexibility in work staffing while containing labor
costs. What marks the quality of a contingent job is its "loose" attachment to the employing establishment and the fact that employment may
be intermittent and unpredictable, the pay low, and benefits absent.

All part-time workers are included in formal estimates of this newly
emerging category of contingent workers, although not all share the
qualities of a low degree of labor-market attachment or poor compensation. The examples of Old Concept part-time work, at low pay and
few benefits, are numerous enough, and the growth of involuntary part-
time employment has been strong enough in the past few years, to
ensure that the general contingent worker description has some validity
for the part-time worker group. It is an issue for social policy and labor-
management decision as to whether part-time work will become a New
Concept force for favorable, expanding work options. Alternatively, will
it contribute to the creation of a two-tier system of jobs, consisting of a
small core of full-time workers with good wages and benefits and a
complement of temporary help with less job security and low compensation, one that serves as a mechanism for avoiding unions and undermining union standards. The trend is an unsettling one, partly because
of the immediate low level of wages and absence of pensions or health
benefits for many part-time workers. It is also unsettling because contingent work gives rise to a class of marginal workers deprived of a
regular and permanent attachment to the labor market, a market that
in today's world, provides a source for community and status as well
as for economic security.

The immediate problems associated with the growth of contingent
work and part-time work with contingent characteristics must not result
in ignoring the introduction and favorable outcome of a number of other
part-time work arrangements. These innovations point the way to another model, a model that not only rewards workers in a way equivalent
to that of full-time work, but also applies across a broad spectrum of

jobs. Although the growth in the numbers of these New Concept part-time jobs in recent years has not been great, the experience garnered so far indicates that there are a number of cost savings and other benefits associated with the work schedule (Kahne, 1985: Chapter 9). How does the experience of these reduced-hour programs contribute to our understanding of the potential for part-time work?

WHAT IS THE POTENTIAL FOR NEW CONCEPT PART-TIME WORK?

Surprisingly, there have been few general evaluative studies of New Concept part-time work. There is some evidence from a number of sources to indicate a much broader potential for part-time work than its current reputation suggests. Employer benefits complement the increased work flexibility that such programs provide for the suppliers of labor. First, part-time work need not be limited to jobs in the low-pay sales and service sectors where they tend to cluster. Individual examples of New Concept reduced-hour jobs, often among professional librarians, teachers, editors, nurses and others, function well. Some public-sector employing agencies have institutionalized their job search in a way that bypasses the full-time/part-time issue. They identify the goals and tasks of the job and evaluate candidates in terms of their skill, experience, and other qualifications relating to job exigencies. Eligibility is not dependent on being available for a specified amount of time (Nollen, 1982: 197–198). Recent innovators include a utilities company that established 50 pairs of job sharing positions, and a children's hospital that has developed a number of flexible work arrangements including job sharing and a relief pool for nurses interested in working reduced hours. In both cases, part-time work was introduced in an attempt to retain valued employees (*Work Times*, 1988: 6 (2) and 6 (3). An aerospace company has established a "casual employment" category to retain skilled employees for part-time work, while protecting their pension benefits. A part-time employment agency on Wall Street is finding a ready market for part-time, highly skilled consultants to work on specific projects. Some firms are permitting employees to move from full time to part time with part-time benefits, when family needs require. In Sweden's phased (early) retirement program, where partial pensions can supplement reduced hours of work for persons aged 60 to 64 who meet the qualifications for labor market attachment, there appears to be little trouble in adapting a full-time job to a part-time position, except in the case of senior staff positions. In one study of 28 work places, fewer than one percent of requests for part-time work were denied. The program, originally appealing largely to blue-collar workers, has gradually spread to white-collar workers as well (Packard, 1982).

Other evidence that reduced-hour work is feasible across a broad range of occupations comes from our unemployment insurance-supported work sharing programs, now enacted in 12 states, which extend the employment relationship in periods of temporary work retrenchment (Best, 1988). Sometimes referred to as short-time compensation, these programs, although not part time in name, are so in fact because they provide for a temporary reduction of work hours below those of a normal full-time workweek in order to maintain worker attachment to the firm. Partial unemployment benefits are payable according to the proportion of reduced work time. In California, for example, in the period July 1978 to December 1980, 70 percent of employers who participated in a work-week reduction shortened work time by 20 to 30 percent, that is, from one to one-and-a-half days a week (Best, 1988: 60). The duration of unemployment benefits varied widely and quite evenly with the duration of reduced work time. More than one half of participating firms and 80 percent of claimants were in manufacturing, the majority being in manual and operative occupations (Best, 1988: 52, 55). Such a concentration lends support to the view that discrete or repetitive tasks, commonly thought of as a prerequisite of part-time work, are not essential for its scheduling.

Second, the use of part-time workers often has the cost-saving effect of enhancing productivity and reducing absenteeism and labor turnover. Productivity gains can result from an improved job design or from the recruitment or retention of a skilled and responsible work force. It can come from a reduction in fatigue and stress on the job and from less use of work time for personal chores. It can also reflect the increase in motivation or commitment of an energized new work force. A number of American studies (Nollen, 1982 and others in Kahne, 1985: Chapter 9) report positive effects, although the degree of benefit varies among employers and occupations. Corroborative evidence from other countries can be found in reports at a 1982 Organization of Economic Cooperation and Development (OECD) meeting (Hurt, 1984), evaluative comments about the Swedish phased retirement program (Packard, 1982), and results of a survey of Canadian employers about their part-time experience (Hay Management Consultants, 1985). At the same time, some employers report increased administrative and supervisory costs for the part-time group working more varied hours, except when job sharers performed the coordinating functions themselves. What is noteworthy, however, is that it is not unusual for employers to conclude that cost savings in labor performance more than compensate for the additional administrative costs associated with an expanded part-time work force (Swank, 1982).

Third, and more complicated, is the issue of non-wage benefits that increase the costs of the compensation package. They are important because they constitute from 30 to 40 percent of direct labor costs (Kahne,

1985: 137). Here, because of the large expenditures involved and the unpredictability of the major risks of life, the question is not whether part-time workers should receive some form of group protection, but rather how such protection will be provided. Should it be extended through the employment structure as it now is for many full-time workers; alternatively, should (and will) needs be met by government insurance programs, or, in their absence, by welfare programs? Further, how should benefit costs be allocated among individuals, employers, and government agencies? Perhaps no single solution will fit all groups, all work situations, or all benefit needs. The issue must be addressed. Creative approaches already in place in the work environment, combined with existing group insurance experience, can contribute to an evolving pattern.

In the United States, some benefits such as holiday, vacation, and sick leave, are easily prorated and are frequently offered to part-time workers on this basis. Pension and health benefits are more difficult to prorate and more complicated to administer (Kahne, 1985: 137–139). Some employers provide full-time benefits to part-time workers, paying for them in higher productivity or reduced overtime [*Work Times*, 1988: 6 (3)]. Others provide benefits unilaterally or through collective bargaining, with shared employee financing to cover added costs due to the part-time nature of an employment connection. Some employers bypass the issue of benefits entirely by paying a higher wage rate. Others offer "cafeteria" or flexible benefits, equivalent to a given proportion of wages, that employees can use in a variety of ways; such benefits can amount to a substitution for taxable salary dollars (United Nations Association– USA, December 1985: 115–117).

NEXT STEPS

The increasing complexity and problems associated with some part-time jobs does not mean that the baby should be thrown out with the bath water. Not only is the composition of the U.S. labor force increasing the numbers and percentage of women workers who have been traditionally in need of reduced-hour schedules, but their employment will be even more sought after in the future, as the rate of growth of other groups in the labor force slows down. Moreover, experience has shown that part-time work, although not yet in evidence on a large scale, is possible in a broad range of occupations and industries. Occupational and industrial trends will facilitate expansion of such jobs, although expansion of part-time work in traditional areas will also add to problems associated with low pay and lack of benefits. At the same time, some part-time work is caught up in employment practices that are defined as contingent work—impermanent and at low pay. This creates problems for full-time workers as well, with the undermining of prevailing full-time wage and work standards. In forging policies and practices with respect to part-time work, society, labor, and employers must take stock of the totality of this picture.

New Concept part-time work is not a substitute for a full-employment policy. It is not an alternative to a reduction in the number of hours that constitute a full-time workweek—a reduction that trade unionists, here and abroad, see as a long-term goal for improvement in life's quality. However, it could complement such a development. Those who advocate New Concept part-time work seek the availability of jobs at less than full-time hours, at prorated pay and benefits, to accommodate home responsibilities, permit the pursuit of job or non-job interests, or to respond to health needs. Arguments for its extension that respond to the needs of suppliers of labor are reinforced by the fact that part-time work has demonstrated cost-saving aspects for the demanders of labor in the form of increased productivity and decreased absenteeism and turnover. In spite of the favorable aspects of this broad-brush potential for part-time work, only a small beginning has been made in public and private sector policies and in studies of New Concept part-time work options. What are some desirable next steps?

In the United States, there is recognition of the increased burden on social welfare, as well as of increased individual costs when benefit coverage is absent. A bill was introduced in Congress that would provide mandatory prorated pension and medical benefits for an employee working less than 30 hours a week (*Wall Street Journal*, June 6, 1988). The bill would have strengthened earlier legislation that sought to preserve benefit coverage for part-time workers in private plans.[5] Such legislation is in tune with that of OECD countries, where governments are developing legislation to protect the rights of part-time workers (Hurt, 1984). For example, the West German Promotion Act of 1985, effective in May 1987, guarantees the same legal protection to part-timers as to full-time workers. Job sharers are protected from layoff if a partner resigns, and employees working flex-time hours are protected against arbitrary short notice changes in scheduling [*Work Times*, 1987: 5 (4)].

Whatever the legislative support for part-time, the bottom line for progress in the United States depends on actions taken within the private sector, where there are still more questions than information or structures to provide answers. Although New Concept part-time work exists in a number of settings, information about enterprise experience that can inform the development of other company policies (Lee, 1987 in *Work Times*, Winter 1988: 1),[6] and about the pitfalls and benefits of its functioning (New Ways to Work, London Office, 1987/88), is sparse. At best, many unions remain skeptical of the advantages of part-time work, despite its potential as an organizing tool appealing to the growing number of women workers. Several public agencies in the United States have achieved both cost saving and employee support for voluntary reduced-time schedules (V-time programs) that offer reductions in work time to full-time employees for limited periods of time while maintaining employee benefits (Olmsted, 1985). In Canada, where union policies are beginning to include regular part-time workers in collective bargaining negotiations, particularly in public and quasi-public sectors, unions have won prorated benefits and higher wages for part-time workers. They have also reduced the wage discrepancy and, hence, competitiveness between part-time and full-time wages for similar jobs, and have negotiated a limit to the number of part-time workers when their employment would result in the laying off of full-time workers (Zeytinoglu, May 1987; December 1986). Unions as well as individuals have benefited from union involvement with part-time workers.

Although research often follows rather than precedes policy formulation, it is nonetheless important. In the United States, we still have only minimal knowledge on which to plan policy and build programs. We need to know more about the patterns of Old Concept and especially of New Concept part-time jobs, their industrial and occupational location, their characteristics and meshing with full-time work, their costs and benefits, and the problems they entail. More information is needed on general guidelines about the methods and costs of benefit financing (Catalyst, 1986/87; Association of Part-Time Professionals, 2nd Edition, 1987; *Work Times*, Winter 1988).

The intensity of future preference for part-time work cannot be known until its evolving character becomes clearer. However, its extension in some form is inevitable, given our labor-force trends, increasingly intertwined work and family roles, and expanded life interests. If the American work place can combine a baseline of federal standards, New Concept part-time jobs jointly developed by labor and management, and thoughtful evaluation of experience, we should be able to forge arrangements in which hope becomes a reality and the peril of losing the advantage of more flexible work scheduling evaporates.

NOTES

With thanks to John Gildea, Barney Olmsted, Joseph Pleck, and Isik Zeytinoglu for a critical reading of an early draft of this chapter and to Alice K. Smith for permission to use phrasing of her book title in the title of this paper.

1. The typical length of the full-time workweek, 60 hours in 1900, was gradually reduced over time, and by the Depression of the 1930s was about 40 hours. In 1940, an amendment to the Fair Labor Standards Act established 40 hours as the base after which penalty overtime of time-and-a-half was paid. This baseline is in effect today.

2. Part-time workers do not include full-time workers who work a partial year. About 20 percent of women work part year as well as part time. This is about twice the proportion for men.

3. International comparisons are difficult to make because of differing cutoff hours defining part-time. For example, Canada, France, and the United Kingdom normally use 30 hours as the cutoff for part time, compared with 35 hours in the United States. About one fourth of American part-time workers work 30 to 34 hours per week. Canada and the United States, but not all countries, include seasonal and casual workers in their computations. In general, it appears that the importance of part-time work in the United States, although less than in the Nordic countries, is still considerable (Blyton, 1985; Hurt, 1984).

4. For a discussion of wage differences among part-time adult women, see Blank, 1986.

5. The Tax Equity and Fiscal Responsibility Act of 1982 discourages employers from denying pension coverage for part-time workers. Provisions of a New Hampshire law, now under consideration in other states as well, prohibit insurance companies from excluding part-time workers from group health plan coverage (see Levitan and Conway in this volume).

6. New Ways to Work in San Francisco is currently sponsoring a project that is designed to create employer awareness of the advantages of flexible work schedules that are equitable.

19 Work Sharing and Job Sharing: Whose Priorities Prevail?

Vivienne Monty

Work sharing and job sharing are two alternative forms of reduced-hour work schedules. Although each form represents tradeoffs in the priorities of both employers and employees, they differ markedly from each other in terms of purpose, participation, and duration. Work sharing is an across-the-board, temporary reduction in the work hours of full-time employees, a rationing device usually serving as an alternative to layoffs in times of economic recession or slow economic recovery. Job sharing is a permanent arrangement in which two (and, on rare occasions, more than two) persons share the responsibilities, pay, and benefits of a full-time position. Work-sharing schemes, dating from a West German initiative in 1927, essentially create involuntary part-time workers, who are enabled to retain some degree of job security and compensation, thus "riding out" periods of employment retrenchment. Job sharing, on the other hand, is a form of voluntary, permanent part-time work which, since its more recent origins in the 1970s, has primarily been employee-driven.[1] Job sharers enjoy more job security, better compensation, more job enrichment, and better opportunities for advancement than occupants of other types of part-time jobs.

WORK SHARING

Under work-sharing schemes, employees work according to a pattern of reduced total hours, while retaining some income and either full or prorated fringe benefits. Under schemes in which government participates, the reduced earnings of employees are buttressed by a partial, prorated unemployment benefit (Morantz, 1983; Nemirow, 1984). This policy initiative, which combines work sharing and partial unemployment insurance, is often called short-term compensation. Usually, the unemployment benefit replaces approximately one half of the workers' lost wages, providing up to 90 percent of previous total earnings, although this varies with different laws and with different unemployment schemes (Grais, 1983).[2] The average duration of instances of work sharing in the United States is approximately six weeks (Bednarzik, 1980). Work sharing has been used as a policy tool by governments to ease the burden of structural change that results in changes in output, production, employment, and unemployment. Under good economic conditions, there is usually scant interest, in the labor market, in structural change (Bureau of Labour Market Research, 1987). Interest heightens in bad times, however, and governments are pressured into action to soften the impact on workers, especially younger ones, who are by tradition and seniority the last hired and first fired:

Whereas for a long time companies had an interest in greater stability in employment, and needed a permanent supply of trained staff, this is nowadays not always quite the position. The new logic dictates that the work force must never be in a non-productive state, and can be laid off when there is a falling off in orders . . . the new forms of work have arisen under the pressure of these demands of companies; labour law has changed. (European Foundation for the Improvement of Living and Working Conditions, 1988: 30.)

The American and Canadian experiences with work sharing have been relatively similar. Work sharing has been used instead of layoffs in some companies. In 13 American states, legislation was enacted in the late 1970s and early 1980s to permit short-time compensation and the experience has generally been positive.[3] In Canada, the federal government began investigating work sharing as an alternative to temporary layoffs in the 1970s (Coates, 1988: 4). The first experimental program was established in 1977 by a temporary modification of the federal unemployment insurance program applied in Saskatchewan, under terms similar to those for unemployment benefits (Posyniak, 1986; Reid, 1982). The Canadian government was impressed by the West German scheme and saw this plan as a potential way to remodel the much criticized unemployment insurance program. Also, under this plan, workers would be reported in the Labour Force Survey as part-time rather than unemployed workers, which would greatly improve the statistical picture (Sandlier-Brown, 1978). The federal experiment operated until 1979 and was reactivated in 1981. Under the program, employees receive wages for days worked, and unemployment benefits for days not worked.[4] In 1983, it was linked to the National Training Program, permitting employees to upgrade their skills on the job or at training institutions and community colleges.

Interest abated in North America in the mid–1980s, not just because the economies were recovering but also because it was found that work sharing had done little to reduce layoffs and had a negative impact on unemployment insurance schemes (Kerachsky, 1986). Hence, governments began to search for better means of coping with unemployment or gave little attention to the issue. Short-term data had pointed to the fact that the administrative costs of work sharing were higher than for layoffs (Best, 1988a). Nevertheless, in response to a surge in demand, the federal government set a 1990 ceiling on allocations to work sharing under the unemployment insurance plan that was the highest since the recession of the early 1980s (*Globe and Mail*, September 19, 1990).

In the United Kingdom, work sharing as a major approach to relieving unemployment (Horn, 1983), achieved its greatest popularity between 1979 and 1982 (Richards, 1987), particularly in the manufacturing sector. Its decline after 1982 can partially be explained by the fact that, being based on a relatively short time scale, it came to be seen as inadequate to meet the problems posed by deepening recession. Another explanation is that fewer companies were able to remain economically viable while continuing to reduce work time. Also government policy, under the Temporary Short Time Working Compensation Scheme (TSTWCS), allowed particular jobs to be rescued only once, meaning that employers could run out of potentially redundant workers on whom the enterprise's bid for government support rested (Blyton, 1985: 93–94).

Another approach to unemployment in Britain, distinguishable from schemes like the TSTWCS, is the job-splitting program. The Department of Employment, in 1983, initiated the Job Splitting Scheme, now called JOBSHARE, giving a grant of £750 (later raised to £840) to every company that split one job into two part-time ones. Those hired for the part-time jobs had to fall into one of the following categories: unemployed and receiving unemployment insurance compensation; an employee at the same establishment under formal notice of redundancy; the incumbent of the full-time job being split; or, another worker at the same establishment whose own job would then be filled by someone from one of the first two categories (New Ways to Work, 1988: 29). Additionally, the job had to provide at least 15 hours of work weekly.[5] The job also had to remain split for one year. Labor in Great Britain argues that the U.K. scheme has encouraged employers to split existing full-time jobs in order to take advantage of government incentives. Some argue that the United Kingdom has actually created unemployment through the application of the scheme (Grais, 1983), that it has masked unemployment (Best, 1989), and that it has served to finance unemployment (Bell, 1986). Evans and Palmer (1985: 63) report that "the initial reaction of employers to job sharing in general, and the government's Job Splitting Scheme in particular, has been cautious, if not unenthusiastic."

There are those who advocate work sharing as one component of a full employment policy (McNeff, 1978). In contrast, many believe that work-sharing proposals represent the refusal or the reluctance of governments to pursue the goal of full employment. In this view, work sharing provides an easy way of avoiding the problems of stimulating the economy without increasing inflation (Zalusky, 1986). Others have also claimed that work sharing is not a practical solution to cyclical unemployment. They argue that fear of unemployment should not lead to inflationary programs that will in turn lead to more serious economic problems throughout society (Garraty, 1978). Some critics claim that where work sharing has been encouraged, in countries such as the United States, Canada, and the United Kingdom, productivity is lowered and subsidies must be provided at considerable cost (List, 1983). In Scandinavia, for instance, varied approaches other than work-sharing schemes have been used in an attempt to create full employment (Zippo, 1982).

Arguments in favor of work sharing are sometimes based on the principle of equity: "The equity aspects of the issue are of equal importance. To accommodate these, it might be desirable to assist groups which are particularly disadvantaged, and government policy may need to be formulated with this objective in mind." (Bureau of Labour Market Research, 1987: 1.) In the United States, it was found that blacks, women, the unskilled, and the young were disproportionately represented in the involuntary shortened work schedules (Swartz, 1983). In general, minority groups tend to be disproportionately laid off (Spiegelman, 1976). One of the reasons that companies, especially in the United States, were amenable to work sharing was because of a stronger government policy on "equal rights" in the work place. Thus, since women and blacks were disproportionately laid off, work sharing became a way of avoiding human rights problems for the employer (Morris, 1980/81). Also, employers had to be careful not to be seen to lay off older workers, a practice that could be viewed as discrimination in terms of age (MaCoy and Morand, 1984).

In the 1930s, when work sharing was first proposed in Europe, unions were strongly opposed, claiming it was a way to "share the misery." The controversies have not abated, despite widespread use of the practice: "According to European unions [such schemes have been used to] wipe out a good proportion of the social advances which have been obtained during the last forty years." (European Foundation for the Improvement of Living and Working Conditions, 1988.) While unions have been more receptive in recent years toward work sharing, and, as in California, have agreed to plans for short-time compensation in order to save employees' jobs, they still harbor concerns. Labor's priority is to achieve the shorter workweek (32 hours) with the same pay, while stemming the tide of part-time work (Benimadhu, 1986). In view of the fact that part-time workers are most often denied equitable pay and benefits relative to full-time employees, and thus constitute a cheap source of labor, unions have historically opposed all forms of part-time employment that are created at the expense of full-time positions (The Job Sharing Equation, 1986). Unions are also deeply concerned about the maintenance of seniority systems, which are undermined by schemes such as work sharing (Sandlier-Brown, 1978). Despite the apprehensions, and even where work sharing is not sanctioned by legislation, unions and management have come to arrangements similar to work sharing so that valued employees may be retained and so that younger ones, who do not have seniority, may continue to earn some salary in times of retrenchment. These are direct agreements between unions and individual companies, and do not involve government (Forbes, 1985; for examples, see Levitan and Belous, 1977: 67–69). The garment industry has had a long history of work sharing.

There have been recent instances, particularly in the United States, where older workers with substantial seniority have voluntarily offered to work share in order to help younger workers keep their jobs.[6] These redistributive schemes, however, have not been funded by any unemployment insurance plan or government policy. Usually, all employees undertake a part-time schedule and receive no compensation for time lost. Many of these arrangements have been for extended periods of time. Management, of course, also needs to support such an arrangement. The reasons many older workers have given for suggesting the scheme are that they have more savings, generally earn a higher salary, and have fewer overheads, such as mortgages, than young workers do. All this means that they can "weather a storm" more easily.

For individual companies, work sharing is more expensive in the short run than regular layoffs because full fringe benefits must be maintained by the employer (Schiff, 1986). Further, it is argued that the unemployment insurance tax increases in most work-sharing situations (Watford, 1986), compounding other increased administrative costs (Meltz, 1981). The only immediate, direct saving that a company has from work sharing is from not having to make severance payments. In a layoff situation, companies have few to no obligations, and little to no administrative maintenance (Campenella, 1987/88). On the other hand, work sharing brings benefits to employers. Work sharing costs nothing to install; no technological changes are required; there is no need to restructure the organization; and a qualified work force is maintained (Lammers, 1987). No less important is the fact that the organization avoids the costs of recruiting, screening, and training new workers when the economic situation improves.[7] Also, there is no lost productivity (Best, 1988).

Work sharing, instituted on a short-term basis, can be seen as one important tool to deal with technological change and structural adjustments (Hall, 1987). The advantages to society, employers, employees, and unions are clearly spelled out by MaCoy and Morand (1984; see also Levitan and Belous, 1977). Proponents of work sharing argue that benefits to society accrue from a reduction in welfare expenditures for the unemployed, from taxes paid by workers who would otherwise be laid off, and from its role in keeping consumption levels from fluctuating widely. That it has not been widely used in North America, but has been considered effective when it has been used, suggests that existing applications of the concept merit more thorough study.

JOB SHARING

> For many people, work no longer holds its traditional meaning of remunerated, full-time, on-site employment. (Piotet, 1987)

In a Canadian survey conducted in the mid–1980s, 31 percent of the respondents stated that they would be willing to take a cut in pay in order to have more time off (Kelly, 1986). The nature of most part-time jobs may discourage such a decision. Job sharing is one of the flexible work patterns that offers permanent part-time employment in a way that challenges the tradition of low status and low pay characteristic of part-time work.

The most common model of job sharing is the sharing of one full-time permanent position by two workers, with the salary, paid leave, pension rights, and fringe benefits divided between them. These two "equally qualified" individuals manage and share the responsibilities of a single position (Kay, 1982). Some refer to this type of permanent part-time employment as "modified full-time" employment (California Hearings, 1986). Although job sharing is usually a work arrangement permitted as a response to individual initiative (Smith, 1981), there has been a move in recent years toward the development of organization-wide policies to promote it (New Ways to Work, 1988).[8] A shared job may require equal or unequal abilities, and the performance of either similar or complementary tasks. The portions may be paid at the same or at different rates, and the working schedule may be split into equal or unequal time blocks (Kushner, 1985). Fringe benefits are often prorated, although this is more characteristic of shared jobs that have been created in recent years (Kahne, 1986: 34).

Job sharing originated as an arrangement to provide access to jobs customarily regarded as full time for people who were career oriented but who either did not wish to work full time or were unable to do so (Nollen et al., 1978). Individuals may be attracted to sharing for a great variety of reasons. People who share jobs may do so because they wish to have more time to pursue an avocation, to upgrade their skills, further their education, or simply enjoy more leisure (Kumar, 1978). Disabled persons who cannot sustain full-time work may find a better job through job sharing than through working in a regular part-time job and this will enhance their self-sufficiency. Older workers may choose job sharing as a transition to retirement (Paul, 1988). Mothers of young children are frequently cited as the group most likely to be attracted to this form of work. In this way, they are enabled to earn some income while maintaining a more interesting level of job and keeping their skills from atrophying. As Ronen observes, this connection "eliminates the trauma of reentry into the work force in later years" (1984: 191). Often a full-time job on a shared basis can be more interesting than a job created for part-time purposes that has built-in limits of responsibility (Meier, 1978).

Job sharing has also helped people to cope with plateauing and burn-out (California Hearings, 1986). The arrangements are sometimes short-term, but they can continue for indefinite periods of time. Short-term arrangements work better for those who envisage returning to a full-time position or for those easing into retirement. Longer-term or permanent arrangements for job sharing are better when an employee wants only part-time work as a career or is disabled and cannot cope with longer hours.

Other reasons often cited for choosing to job share are the following: opportunity for a more balanced life; more time for family life;[9] a mental break from children; more flexibility for arranging days off; a way to develop team skills; an opportunity to keep a foot in the door; more time for continuing education; an opportunity for working with a more experienced person (on-the-job training); personal enrichment and psychological support as a result of close contact with a job partner; a way to maintain one's link to professional networks and to stay in the running for other jobs (Canada. Commission of Inquiry into Part-Time Work, 1983: 178–179).

The way job sharers are treated by their full-time colleagues is often cited as a source of dissatisfaction (Harriman, 1983; Pritchard, 1988); the latter tend to regard them as less serious about their careers, are prone to blame them for problems arising in their absence, and may exclude them from "insider" networks. Time may continue to be a problem for those who have chosen job sharing as a way of having more non-work time. Ronen (1984: 189) notes that it is not unusual for job sharers to find themselves actually working two-thirds time, given the pressure of shorter formal hours and the necessity of communicating closely with a job partner. Other complaints are that with reduced-hours work there is limited opportunity for career advancement, less opportunity for in-service training, less feeling of personal achievement, more feeling of alienation, and more difficulty in changing jobs.

Job sharing brings numerous benefits to employers. Essentially, organizations gain two set of skills, knowledge, and ideas for the price of one (Syrret, 1982). Through job sharing, they are able to retain the valuable skills, experience, and commitment of workers they might otherwise lose (Post, 1986). Many British companies that have already instituted "career break" schemes for employees (especially women) are now linking job sharing to their policy for returnees, since they have found that a substantial number of those taking a career break prefer to return on a part-time basis (New Ways to Work, 1989: 5).[10] A survey of local authorities in Great Britain found that the use of job sharing to further equal opportunities in employment was one of the two most frequently mentioned advantages (New Ways to Work, 1987).

In organizations that permit substantial job sharing, there is evidence of higher morale, less employee turnover, less absenteeism, less lateness, less employee time taken off for medical appointments, less need for overtime, and less time spent in finding relief staff (Olmsted, 1987). Because job sharers can fill in for each other, there is greater continuity in the work. In addition, employers gain greater flexibility in the scheduling of work. Where a job is shared between an older worker and a young trainee, the arrangement provides an effective method of training young people (Evans and Palmer, 1985). In a Canadian survey (Canada. Commission of Inquiry into Part-Time Work, 1983), employers reported that job sharers were more productive than their full-time colleagues, and that they were more innovative (Harvey, 1983). It has also been argued that the job sharer has the ability to work harder for shorter periods of time (Frease, 1979).

Given what organizations stand to gain from using job sharers, it is perhaps surprising that the option has been adopted to date on such a limited basis. What deters its adoption? The costs involved in job sharing, and the complexities (real or imagined) of instituting it, cause most employers to favor standard part-time jobs when they require a flexible work force (Kumar, 1978; Posyniak, 1986). The principal disadvantage of job sharing to employers can be the increased cost of benefits. Other disadvantages often raised are: higher costs of payroll administration; difficulties in recruiting job sharers; possible personality conflicts between sharers; workspace problems if schedules overlap; increased workload for supervisors (or increased costs of supervision); problems of accountability if responsibility is divided; and, the necessity of developing coordinating mechanisms (Ronen, 1984; Wallace, 1986; Evans and Palmer, 1985). Coordination is an important issue, especially in rigidly structured hierarchies. It can, however, be achieved. At the Prudential Company, there is a half-hour overlap between shifts to allow for continuing and good communications. Supervisors vary their hours in order to provide managerial support to all employees (Schroeer, 1983).

In the California hearings on job sharing, one sharer testified that she and her partner spent a great deal of their own time communicating, leaving notes about files and daily happenings to assure continuity. In jobs that require continuity, poor communication can cause clients to suffer from too little, or too much, attention (Meier, 1978). It has been argued that if more emphasis were placed on redesigning jobs to accommodate job sharing, rather than merely placing sharers in currently existing full-time positions, then many of the disadvantages could be eliminated (California Hearings, 1986).

The adoption of the job-sharing option so far has been most successful in the public sector (Smith, 1981) and in service-oriented jobs (Little, 1986). New Ways to Work (1978) found that job sharers were most heavily concentrated in the "human services" industries such as schools, state and local governments, and health services. In a recent survey of job sharers in the United Kingdom, Pritchard (1988) found that 78 percent were working in the public sector, 16 percent were in the voluntary sector, and only 6 percent were in the private sector.

It is not surprising that professionals figure so largely among job sharers (Meier, 1979; Little, 1986). Whether they want to or have to work part time, they are likely to maintain the challenge offered by a full-time job. They are also likely to be in a better position to make a suitable proposal to management, and tend to be seen by the latter as self-driven and highly disciplined. The Hansard Society Commission on Women at the Top (Hansard Society, 1990) has recommended job sharing as an effective way to ensure that women have the opportunity to reach the top rungs of the organizational ladder. Indeed, in the late 1980s, two women shared the presidency of the National Union of Journalists in Britain. However, Nollen (1982: 53) claims that job sharing is found preponderantly in non-managerial or low-level white collar jobs. Job sharing has also been adopted with success in blue-collar operative work (Kahne, 1986: 131). Jobs that already involve shift work, or those that are repetitive or easily divisible into discrete components, are often as amenable to job sharing as are jobs that require initiative and independence.[11] In the former case, job sharing may well provide a solution to absenteeism and high turnover.

To be successful, a job sharing program should be voluntary and the expectations of both employer and employee should be clear from the outset (Olmsted, 1983). Also, direct supervisory personnel must be supportive of the program. There are few clear-cut rules for the restructuring of a full-time job into two part-time ones. Any job sharing proposal, however, should include:

1. needed changes in job qualifications,
2. an evaluation process,
3. clearly defined wages and benefits for each sharer,
4. an implementation plan,
5. an explanation of how any new employee might be hired in case a sharer leaves (Collins, 1984).

Two other elements to be considered are team formation and the division of time, tasks, and earnings (Olmsted, 1979). In team formation, the skills and expertise of the job sharers must relate both to each other and to the job (O'Toole, 1985). Well-written job descriptions are crucial in job sharing, as are the setting of goals and objectives and a system of performance appraisal (Lee, 1984). Lastly, legal and other related employment standards issues should be addressed. Matters such as the continuity of employment, availability of government legislated benefits to part-time employees, availability of private benefit plans, and what type of job security will be offered all require consideration (Leighton, 1987). It cannot be presumed that existing plans will always fit sharers' requirements without changes.

SUMMARY

Increasingly, economic and social forces are prompting a search for alternatives to the traditional employment patterns of full-time work and short-term part-time jobs. Employers, employees, governments, and unions are caught in this quest, though for many different reasons. Work sharing and job sharing are two forms of reduced hours that have been successfully applied on a limited basis. They represent two fundamentally different sets of priorities.

Job sharing is a privilege that only those with clout can negotiate while work sharing is a management right that can be imposed on those without power in the interest of cost cutting at the expense of job security. When an organization's structure is based on scientific management principles, job sharing increases coordination costs or reduces accountability. Work sharing, initiated at the discretion of employers, is a rationing device imposed on full-time workers as an alternative to layoffs where employers are temporarily unable or unwilling to provide full-time work. Job sharing, negotiated between employers and (usually) pairs of individuals, is a mechanism for accommodating the preferences of those who are unable or unwilling to work full time but who seek a more permanent and satisfying arrangement than that provided by standard part-time jobs. Both models provide workers with employment security and prorated pay and benefits. At the same time, both permit employers to retain valued skills and experience that they would otherwise lose. In addition, these alternatives have the potential to promote equity. Work sharing can be especially beneficial to women and minorities, who usually have the least seniority and thus are the most vulnerable in a layoff situation. Likewise, job sharing can be of advantage to persons with disabilities that prevent them from sustaining a full work load, and women who, because of family responsibilities, find it difficult to work on a full-time basis.

NOTES

1. It is considered one of the most desirable options in the new wave of alternative and flexible work patterns (California hearings, 1986; Ronen, 1984; Work in America Institute, 1981).

2. Regular partial unemployment compensation programs, in fact, serve as a disincentive to working, because of stringent provisions that dictate loss of benefits with minimal earnings (Kahne, 1986: 101).

3. For a discussion of State Short-Time Compensation (STC) programs, see Kahne (1986: 102–104). The California Shared Work Program was enacted in 1978 in anticipation of widespread layoffs in the public sector. Although this retrenchment did not eventuate, the program has been rather widely applied in the private sector.

4. In the 1986/87 fiscal year, 910 work sharing applications were approved, representing 9,333 employees. This meant that 4,030 workers were rescued from layoffs, at a total cost of $4.7 million (Coates, 1988: 4).

5. By setting the minimum number of hours at 15, the scheme leaves workers vulnerable to unfair dismissal, since those working hours are not covered by the Employment Protection Act (New Ways to Work, 1988: 30).

6. For example, certain textile firms in Texas have developed such arrangements.

7. As Kahne (1986: 36–37) observes, the saving is not equal for all occupations; it is greater in manufacturing than in construction or mining, for example, because the training costs are higher in the former.

8. There are exceptional instances of companies with long-established formal policies. In the United Kingdom, Barclay's Bank has a program that dates from the early 1940s.

9. Evans and Attew (1986) claim that this reason was the main stimulus (in particular, from women) for job sharing in the United Kingdom.

10. Rajan and van Eupen (1990: 29) point out that this practice also enhances the image of the company as a "good employer," one that encourages the labor market participation of women while recognizing their family responsibilities.

11. For British, Canadian, and American examples of job sharing, which give some indication of its applicability across a broad range of occupations and organizational settings, see: Evans and Palmer, 1985; Hansard Society, 1990; New Ways to Work, 1987; Rajan and van Eupen, 1990; Ronen, 1984; Wallace, 1983.

Bibliography

Abel, Emily K.
  1984 Terminal Degrees: The Job Crisis in Higher Education. New York: Praeger.
  1985 "Organizing Part-Time Faculty." Women's Studies Quarterly 13 (September): 16–17.

Acker, S.
  1984 Women in Higher Education: What is the Problem? In S. Acker and D. W. Piper (eds.) Is Higher Education Fair to Women? University of Surrey: Society for Research into Higher Education and NFER—Nelson: Guildford, Surrey.

Ainsberg, N., and M. Harrington
  1988 Women of Academe: Outsiders in the Sacred Grove. Amherst: University of Massachussets Press.

Akyeampong, Ernest B.
  1986 "Involuntary Part-time Employment in Canada, 1975–1985." In The Labour Force Survey. Cat. 71–001, Ottawa: Statistics Canada.
  1987a "Involuntary Part-Time Employment in Canada, 1975–1986." Canadian Social Trends (Autumn): 26–29.
  1987b "Older Workers in the Canadian Labour Market." The Labour Force (November). Ottawa: Minister of Supply and Service.

American Association of Retired Persons
  1986 Workers 45+: Today and Tomorrow. Washington, DC: American Association of Retired Persons.

American Management Association (AMA)
  1988 Responsible Reductions in Force. AMA Research Report on Downsizing and Replacement. New York: AMA.

Armstrong, Jane
    1988 "Talks Continue as Union Drops Threat to Shut TTC for a Day." The Toronto Star (September 3): A6.

Armstrong, Pat.
    1984 Labor Pains: Women's Work in Crisis. Toronto: The Women's Press.
    1988 "Where Have All the Nurses Gone?" Healthsharing 9 (3): 17–19.

Armstrong, Pat, and Hugh Armstrong
    1983 A Working Majority—What Women Must Do for Pay. Canadian Advisory Committee on the Status of Women. Ottawa.
    1984 The Double Ghetto: Canadian Women and Their Segregated Work (second edition). Toronto: McClelland and Stewart.
    1986 More for the Money: Redefining and Intensifying Work in Canada. Unpublished manuscript. Montreal.
    1988 "Women, Family and Economy." In Nancy Mandell and Ann Duffy (eds.), Reconstructing the Canadian Family: Feminist Perspectives. Toronto: Butterworths.
    1990 Theorizing Women's Work. Toronto: Garamond Press.

Ashbaugh, D. L., and C. H. Fay
    1987 "The Threshold for Aging in the Workplace." Research on Aging 9: 417–427.

Ashton, David
    1988a "Sources of Variation in Labour Market Segmentation: A Comparison of Youth Labour Markets in Canada and Britain." Work, Employment and Society 2: 1–24.
    1988b "Educational Institutions, Youth and the Labour Market." In D. Gallie (ed.), Employment in Britain. Oxford: Blackwell.

Ashton, David, and Michael Maguire
    1983 The Vanishing Youth Labour Market. London: Youth Aid.
    1986 Young Adults in the Labour Market. Department of Employment Research. Paper No. 55. London: Department of Employment.

Ashton, David, Michael Maguire, and Valerie Garland
    1982 Youth in the Labour Market. Department of Employment Research. Paper No.34. London: Department of Employment.

Association of Part-Time Professionals
    1987 Employee Benefits for Part-Timers. Second edition. McLean, VA: Association of Part-Time Professionals.

Australia. Bureau of Labour Market Research. Department of Employment and Industrial Relations
    1987 Structural Change and the Labour Market. Research Report No. 11. Canberra, Australia: Government Publishing Service.

Baillargeon, R.
    1982 "Determinants of Early Retirement." Canada's Mental Health 303: 20–22.

Baillargeon, R., and L. Bélanger
  1981 Travailleurs âgés et prise de retraite nâtive. Québec: Laboratoire de gérontologie sociale, Université Laval.

Baker, Maureen
  1985 "Teacher or Scholar? The Part-Time Academic." Society/Société 9 (1): 3–7.
  1987 Part-time Work. Current Issue Review. Ottawa: Library of Parliament, Research Branch.

Baker, Maureen, and Mary-Anne Robeson
  1986 "Trade Union Reactions to Women Workers and Their Concerns." In Katherina L. P. Lundy and Barbara D. Warme (eds.), Work in the Canadian Context: Continuity Despite Change (second edition). Toronto: Butterworths.

Baker, Patricia
  1990 "Organized Labour and the Transformation of Women's Work in Canadian Banks." Presented at the Canadian Sociology and Anthropology Association Meetings, Victoria, British Columbia, May.

Ballard, Barbara
  1984. "Women Part-time Workers: Evidence from the 1980 Women and Employment Survey." Employment Gazette 92 (9): 409–416.

Bank Book Collective
  1979 An Account to Settle: The Story of the United Bank Workers (SOR-WUC). Vancouver: Press Gang.

Bednarzik, Robert W.
  1980 "Worksharing in the U.S.: Its Prevalence and Duration." Monthly Labor Review 103 (7): 3–12.

Beechey, Veronica
  1987 Unequal Work. Thetford, Norfolk: Thetford Press.

Beechey, Veronica, and Tessa Perkins
  1987 A Matter of Hours: Women, Part-Time Work and the Labor Market. Minneapolis: University of Minnesota Press and Cambridge: Polity.

Bell, Daniel
  1973 The Coming of Post-Industrial Society. New York: Basic Books.
  1986 "Job Start or False Start." Personnel Management 18 (1): 5.

Belous, Richard S.
  1989 The Contingent Economy: The Growth of the Contempory, Part-Time and Subcontracted Workforce. Washington, D.C.: National Planning Association.

Belous, Richard S., and Eileen Appelbaum
  1988 "Human Resource Flexibility and Older Workers: Management and Labor Views." Unpublished paper, December.

Benimadhu, Prem
    1986 "Labour Resists Tide Toward Part-Time Work." Canadian Business
    Review 13 (1): 21–23.

Bernard, Jessie
    1974 Academic Women. New York: Meridian (First published in 1964).

Best, Fred
    1985 "Short-Time Compensation in North America: Trends and Prospects."
    Personnel 62 (1): 34–41.
    1988 Reducing Workweeks to Prevent Layoffs: The Economic and Social
    Impacts of Unemployment Insurance-Supported Work Sharing. Philadel-
    phia: Temple University Press.

Biles, G.E., and Howard P. Tuckman
    1986 Part-Time Faculty Management Policies. New York: American Council
    on Education/Macmillan.

Blanchflower, D. G.
    1989 Fear, Unemployment and Pay Flexibility. Discussion Paper No. 344,
    Centre for Labour Economics. London: London School of Economics.

Blanchflower, D. G., and B. A. Corry
    1987 Part-time Employment in Great Britain: An Analysis Using Establish-
    ment Data. Department of Employment Research Paper No. 57. London:
    Her Majesty's Stationery Office.

Blanchflower, D. G., Neil Millward and A. J. Oswald
    1988 Unionisation and Employment Behaviour. Discussion Paper No. 339,
    Centre for Labour Economics. London: London School of Economics.

Blanchflower, D. G., and A. J. Oswald
    1988 "The Economic Effects of Britain's Trade Unions." Discussion Paper
    No. 324, Centre for Labour Economics. London: London School of Eco-
    nomics.

Blanchflower, D. G., A. J. Oswald and M. D. Garrett
    1990 "Insider Power in Wage Determination." Economica. 57 (226): 143–
    170.

Blank, Rebecca M.
    1986 "Part-time Work and Wages among Adult Women." Proceedings of
    the 39th Annual Meeting of the Industrial Relations Research Association.
    (December).

Bluestone, Barry, Patricia Hanna, Sarah Kuhn, and Laura Moore
    1981 The Retail Revolution: Market Transformation, Investment, and Labor
    in the Modern Department Store. Boston, MA: Auburn House.

Bluestone, Barry, and Bennett Harrison
    1986 The Great American Job Machine: The Proliferation of Low Wage
    Employment in the U.S. Economy. United States Joint Economic Committee.
    Washington, DC: Government Printing Office.

Blyton, Paul
1985 Changes in Working Time: An International Review. New York: St. Martin's Press.

Boaz, R. F.
1987 "Work as a Response to Low and Decreasing Real Income During Retirement." Research on Aging 9: 428–440.

Borman, Kathryn M., and Mary Carol Hopkins
1987 "Leaving School for Work." Research in the Sociology of Education 7: 131–159.

Borus, Michael E.
1982 "Willingness to Work among Youth." Journal of Human Resources 17: 581–593.

Bossen, Marianne
1975 Part-Time Work in the Canadian Economy. Ottawa: Department of Labour, Economics and Research Branch.

Bourdieu, Pierre, and Jean-Claude Passeron
1977 Reproduction in Education, Society and Culture. London: Sage.

Bowen, H. R., and J. H. Schuster
1986 American Professors: A National Resource Imperilled. New York: Oxford University Press.

Breen, Richard
1986 "Does Experience of Work Help School Leavers to Get Jobs?" Sociology 20: 207–227.

Breslauer, H.
1985 The Professoriate—Occupation in Crisis. Toronto: Higher Education Group, Ontario Institute for Studies in Education (OISE).

Breugel, Irene
1979 "Women as a Reserve Army of Labour: A Note on Recent British Experience." Feminist Review 3 (16): 12–23.

Briar, Celia Jane
1987 Part-Time Work: Whose Flexibility? Paper given at the conference on Part-Time Work at the West Yorkshire Centre for Research on Women. University of Bradford.

Brinton, Crane
1952 The Anatomy of Revolution (revised edition). New York: Random House.

Briskin, Linda
1983 "Women's Challenge to Organized Labour." In Linda Briskin and Linda Yanz (eds.), Union Sisters: Women in the Labour Movement. Toronto: The Women's Press.

Bureau of National Affairs
 1984 Collective Bargaining Negotiations and Contracts. Washington, DC: Government Printing Office.
 1987 The Changing Workplace: New Directions in Staffing and Scheduling. Washington, DC: Government Printing Office.

Burke, Mary Anne
 1986 "The Growth of Part-Time Work." Canadian Social Trends (Autumn): 9–14.

California. Legislature. Senate Subcommittee on Women in the Workforce.
 1986 Interim Hearing on Flextime, Reduced Worktime and Job Sharing. Sacramento: Joint Publications: 31 (August 24).

Campenella, Carolyn J.
 1987 "Developing Employment Security Through Alternatives to Layoffs." Employment Relations Today 14 (4): 347–353.

Canada
 1970 Report of the Royal Commission on the Status of Women, 1970. Ottawa: Information Canada.

Canada. Commission of Inquiry into Part-Time Work.
 1983 Part-Time Work in Canada: Report of the Commission. Ottawa: Labour Canada.

Canada. Health and Welfare.
 1977 Retirement in Canada: Summary Report. Ottawa: Minister of Health and Welfare.
 1982 Canadian Government Report on Aging. Ottawa: Minister of Supply and Services.

Canada. Labour Canada
 1985 A Survey of Part-Time Employment in Federally Regulated Industries. Vol. 1. Ottawa: Labour Canada.
 1986. A Survey of Part-Time Employment in Federally Regulated Industries. Vol. 2. Ottawa: Labour Canada.
 1987 Women in the Labor Force, 1986–1987 Edition. Ottawa: Labour Canada.

Canada. National Council of Welfare
 1988 Poverty Profile, 1988. Ottawa: Minister of Supply and Services.
 1990 Women and Poverty Revisited. Ottawa: Minister of Supply and Services.

Canada. Statistics Canada.
 1976 Census of Canada. Labour Force Activity, Vol. 5. Ottawa: Minister of Supply and Services.
 1982a Pension Plans in Canada 1980. (Cat. 74–401). Ottawa: Minister of Supply and Services.
 1982b Women in Canada: A Statistical Report. Ottawa: Minister of Supply and Services.

1985 Women in Canada: A Statistical Report. (Cat. 89–503E). Ottawa: Minister of Supply and Services.

1986a "Results from the Annual Work Patterns Survey 1984 and 1985." The Labour Force. (Cat. 71–001). March: 85–98.

1986b "A Note on Persons Working Few Hours Per Week." The Labour Force. (Cat. 71–001). January: 85–92.

1987 Corporations and Labour Unions Returns Act, Report for 1985, Part II: Labour Unions. Ottawa: Minister of Supply and Services.

1987 The Labour Force. (Cat. 71–001). Ottawa: Minister of Supply and Services.

1988 Historical Labour Force Statistics. (Cat. 71–201). Ottawa: Minister of Supply and Services.

1989 Historical Labour Force Statistics—Actual Data, Seasonal Factors, Seasonally Adjusted Data (Annual). Ottawa: Minister of Supply and Services.

1989 Focus on the Future (1986 Census Data Service). March.

1989 Labour Force Annual Averages 1981–1988. March. Ottawa: Minister of Supply and Services.

1990 Teachers in Universities, 1986–87. Cat. 81–241. Ottawa: Minister of Supply and Services.

1990 The Labour Force. (Cat. 71–001). Ottawa: Minister of Supply and Services.

Canadian Institute of Public Opinion.
1984 "Half Plan Retirement Before Age Sixty-Five." (February) The Gallop Report. 2: 1–2.

Caplow, Theodore, and R. J. McGee
1958 The Academic Marketplace. New York: Basic Books.

Carter, G.E.
1977 "Financial Health and Post Secondary Education: A New and Complete Fiscal Arrangement." Canadian Tax Journal 25 (5).

Catalyst
1987 "Flexible Benefits: How to Set Up a Plan When Your Employees Are Complaining, Your Costs are Rising and You're Too Busy to Think About It." (1986–1987) New York: Catalyst.

Charles, Nicola
1986 "Women and Trade Unions." In Feminist Review (ed.), Waged Work: A Reader. London: Virago Press.

Cheney, Peter
1988 "The Economic Underclass: Left Behind By the Boom." The Toronto Star (June 9): L1, L4.

Chollet, Deborah J.
1984 Employer-Provided Health Benefits, Coverage Provisions and Policy Issues. Washington, DC: Employee Benefits Research Institute.

Christensen, Kathleen
1987 "Women and Contingent Work." Social Policy 17 (4): 15–18.

Christensen, Kathleen
1988 "Flexible Work Arrangements and Older Workers." Unpublished report, May.

Ciffin, S., and J. Martin
1977 Retirement in Canada: When and Why People Retire. Staff Working Paper SWP–7804. Ottawa: Health and Welfare Canada.

Clark, B.R.
1987 The Academic Life: Small Worlds, Different Worlds. Princeton: The Carnegie Foundation for the Advancement of Teaching.

Clark, G.
1982 Working Patterns: Part-Time Work, Job Sharing and Self-Employment. Sheffield: Manpower Intelligence and Planning, Manpower Services Commission.

Clark, George
1982 "Recent Developments in Working Patterns." Employment Gazette (July): 258.

Clarke, Tom
1977 "Introduction: The Raison D'Etre of Trade Unionism." In T. Clarke and L. Clements (eds.), Trade Unions Under Capitalism. London: Fontana.

Clemenson, Heather A.
1987 "Unemployment Rates for the Full-Time and Part-Time Labor Forces." Canadian Social Trends (Autumn): 30–33.

Coates, Mary-Lou
1988 Part-Time Employment: Labour Market Flexibility and Equity Issues. Research and Current Issues Series No. 50. Kingston, ON: Queen's University, Industrial Relations Centre.

Cockburn, Cynthia
1983 Brothers: Male Dominence and Technological Change. London: Pluto.
1987 Two Track Training: Sex Inequalities and the YTS. Basingstoke: Macmillan.

Cohen, Gary L.
1989 "Youth for Hire." Perspectives on Labour and Income (Summer): 7–14.

Collins, Joanne, and Anne-Marie Krause
1984 "Improving Productivity Through Job Sharing." Business Forum 1 (3): 4–7.

Confederation of British Industry
1987 The Structure and Processes of Pay Determination in the Private Sector, 1979–1986. London: Confederation of British Industry.

Conference Board of Canada
1980 Mandatory Retirement Policy: A Human Rights Dilemma. Ottawa: Conference Board of Canada.

Copeland, Jeff B.
    1987 "Back to the Basics: Businesses are Moving to Close the Literacy Gap."
    Newsweek. September 21, 110 (12): 54–55.

Coplan, Jennifer
    1986 "Beyond Retirement: Characteristics of Older Workers and the Impli-
    cations for Employment Policy." Unpublished paper, Florence Heller Grad-
    uate School, Brandeis University.

Coté, Michel
    1990 "The Labour Force: Into the '90s." Perspectives on Labour and Income
    (Spring): 8–16.

Council of Ontario Universities
    1988 Employment Equity for Women: A University Handbook. Toronto:
    The Committee on the Status of Women.

Council of the European Communities
    1982 Proposal for a Council Directive on Voluntary Part-Time Work. Lux-
    embourg: Council of the European Communities.

Cuneo, Carl
    1979 "State, Class and Reserve Labour: The Case of the 1941 Canadian
    Unemployment Insurance Act." Canadian Review of Sociology and An-
    thropology 16 (2): 147–170.
    1990 Pay Equity: The Labour Feminist Challenge. Toronto: Oxford Univer-
    sity Press.

Currie, Carol, and Gerri Sheedy
    1987 "Organizing Eaton's." In Robert Argue, Charlene Gannage, and D.
    W. Livingstone (eds.), Working People and Hard Times. Toronto: Gara-
    mond Press.

Dale, Angela
    1987 "Occupational Inequality, Gender and Life-cycle." Work, Employment
    and Society 1 (3): 326–351.

Dale, Angela, and J. Glover
    1987 A Comparative Analysis of Women's Employment Patterns in the
    United Kingdom, France and the United States of America. Report to the
    Department of Employment. London.

D'Amico, Ronald
    1984a "Does Employment During High School Impair Academic Progress?"
    Sociology of Education 57 (July): 152–164.
    1984b "The Time-Use Behavior of Young Adults." In Michael E. Burns (ed.),
    Youth in the Labor Market. Kalamazoo, MI: W. E. Upjohn Institute for
    Employment Research.

Daniel, W. W., and Neil Millward
    1983 Workplace Industrial Relations in Britain: The DE/PSI/ESRC Survey.
    London: Heinemann Educational.

DeHaney, William T.
1988 "Work Satisfaction and Mental Health of Part-Time Female Employees: The Relative Influence of Job Characteristics and Life Cycle Events." Paper presented at the Canadian Sociology and Anthropology Association Annual Meetings, Windsor, June.

de Neubourg, Chris
1985 "Part-Time Work: An International Quantitative Comparison." International Labour Review 124 (5): 559–576.

Derber, Charles
1978 "Unemployment and the Entitled Worker: Job Entitlement and Radical Political Attitudes among the Youthful Unemployed." Social Problems 26: 26–37.

Deutermann, William V., and Scott Campbell Brown
1978 "Voluntary Part-Time Workers: A Growing Part of the Labor Force." Monthly Labor Review 101 (6): 3–10.

Dex, Shirley
1984 Women's Work Histories: An Analysis of the Women and Employment Survey. Department of Employment Research Paper, No. 46. London: Department of Employment.
1987 Women's Occupational Mobility: A Lifetime Perspective. London: Macmillan.
1988 Women's Attitudes Towards Work. London: Macmillan.

Dex, Shirley, and Lois Shaw
1986 British and American Women at Work. Basingstoke: Macmillan.

Disney, R., and E. Szyszczak
1984 "Protective Legislation and Part-Time Employment in Britain." British Journal of Industrial Relations 22 (1): 78–100.

Dixon, Sylvia
1987 "Union Policies and the Structure of Part-Time Employment: The Case of Registered Nursing." New Zealand Journal of Industrial Relations 12: 61–70.

Doering, M., S. R. Rhodes, and M. Schuster
1983 The Aging Worker. Beverly Hills, CA: Sage Publications.

Doeringer, Peter, and Michael Piore
1971 Internal Labor Markets and Manpower Analysis. Armonk, NY: M. E. Sharpe.

Dombois, Rainer, and Martin Osterland
1987 "New Forms of Flexible Utilization of Labour: Part-Time and Contract Work." In Roger Tarling (ed.), Flexibility in Labour Markets. London: Academic Press.

Duffy, Ann, and Norene Pupo
1986 "Women and Part-Time Work: Looking for Balance Between Home

and 'Work'." Paper presented at the Canadian Sociology and Anthropology Association Annual Meetings, Winnipeg, June.
Forthcoming, The Part-Time Puzzle: Connecting Gender, Work and Family. Toronto: McClelland and Stewart.

Duffy, Ann, and Wendy Weeks
1981 "Women Part-Time Workers and the Needs of Capital." Atlantis 7 (1): 23–35.

Dun and Bradstreet Corporation
1987 The Dun's 5000 Survey on Part-Time and Temporary Employment: 1986 and 1987 Results. New York: Dun and Bradstreet Corporation.

Dunn, S. and J. Gennard
1984 The Closed Shop in British Industry. London: Macmillan.

Earnshaw, Jill
1985 Sex Discrimination and Dismissal: A Review of Recent Case Law. University of Manchester Occasional Papers No. 8505.

Echenberg, Haui
1990 "Safety Net Becoming a Trap?" The Globe and Mail, June 7: A7.

Economic Council of Canada
1979 One in Three: Pensions for Canadians to 2030. Ottawa: Minister of Supply and Services.
1989 Legacies: Twenty-Sixth Annual Review. Ottawa: Minister of Supply and Services.
1990 Good Jobs, Bad Jobs: Employment in the Service Economy: A Statement. Ottawa: Minister of Supply and Services.

Elias, P., and B. Main
1982 Women's Working Lives. Evidence From the National Training Survey. Coventry: Institute for Employment Research, University of Warwick.

England, Geoffrey
1987 Part-Time, Casual and Other Atypical Workers: A Legal View. Research and Current Issues Series No. 48. Kingston, ON: Queen's University Industrial Relations Centre.

Epstein, C. F.
1970 Woman's Place: Options and Limits in Professional Careers. Berkeley: University of California Press.

Equal Opportunities Commission
1986 Women and Men in Britain: A Statistical Profile 1985. London: Her Majesty's Stationery Office.

Esping-Andersen, Gosta
1989 "The Three Political Economies of the Welfare State." Canadian Review of Sociology and Anthropology 1989, 26 (1).

European Foundation for the Improvement of Living and Working Conditions
1988 New Forms of Work: Labour Law and Social Security Aspects in the European Community. Dublin: The Foundation.

Eurostat
1981 Employment and Unemployment 1974–1980. Brussels: Statistical Office of the European Community.
1985 Labour Force Survey. Brussels: Statistical Office of the European Community.
1988 Employment and Unemployment. Brussels: Statistical Office of the European Community.

Evans, Alastair, and Jenny Bell
1986 "Emerging Themes in Flexible Work Patterns." In Chris Curson (ed.), Flexible Patterns of Work. London: Institute of Personnel Management.

Evans, Alastair, and Stephen Palmer
1985 Negotiating Shorter Working Hours. London: Macmillan.

Finch, Michael D., and Jeylan T. Mortimer
1985 "Adolescent Work Hours and the Process of Achievement." In Alan C. Kerchoff (ed.), Research in the Sociology of Education and Socialization. Greenwich, CT: JAI Press.

Fine, Sean
1988 "Local, TTC Swap Threats Over Part-Time Dispute." The Globe and Mail, August 31: E11.
1990 "Women 46 Per Cent of Working Poor in 1986." The Globe and Mail, June 6: A10.

Finn, Dan
1987 Training Without Jobs: New Deals and Broken Promises. Basingstoke: Macmillan.

Foot, D. K.
1987 Population Aging and the Canadian Labour Force. Discussion paper on the Demographic Review. Ottawa: The Institute for Research on Public Policy.

Forbes, Daniel
1985 "The No-Layoff Payoff." Dun's Business Month 126 (1): 64–66.

Fox, Bonnie J., and John Fox
1986 "Women in the Labour Market 1931–81: Exclusion and Competition." Canadian Review of Sociology and Anthropology 23 (1): 1–21.

Frager, Ruth
1983 "Women Workers and the Canadian Labour Movement." In Linda Briskin and Linda Yanz (eds.), Union Sisters: Women in the Labour Movement. Toronto: The Women's Press.

Franklin, Phyllis, David Laurence, and Robert D. Denham
1988 "When Solutions Become Problems: Taking a Stand on Part-Time Employment." Academe 74 (3): 15–19.

Frease, Michael, and Robert A. Zawacki
    1979 "Job Sharing: An Answer to Productivity Problems?" Personnel Administrator 24 (10): 35–38, 56.

Freeman, Richard Barry, and Daved A. Wise (eds.)
    1982 The Youth Labor Market Problem: Its Nature, Causes, and Consequences. Chicago: University of Chicago Press.

Fuchs, Victor
    1983 How We Live. Cambridge, MA: Harvard University Press.
    1978 "Fear of Unemployment Must Not Become the Body of Modern Times." Across the Board 15 (9):37–43.

Fullerton, Howard N., Jr.
    1987 "Labor Force Projections, 1986–2000." Monthly Labor Review 110 (9): 19–29.

Gade, E., and L. Peterson
    1980 "A Comparison of Working and Nonworking High School Students on School Performance, Socioeconomic Status, and Self-Esteem." Vocational Guidance Quarterly 29: 65–69.

Galt, Virginia
    1990 "Labor Calls Aid for Dependents 'Critical Issue'." The Globe and Mail (July 4).

Gappa, J. M.
    1984 Part-Time Faculty: Higher Education at a Crossroads. ASHE—ERIC: Higher Education Report No. 3. Washington, DC: Association for the Study of Higher Education.

Gardiner, Jean
    1976 "Women and Employment." Red Rag (10).

Garraty, John A., and David A. Harvey
    1983 "Job Sharing: What's in It for the Employer?" Chief Executive (May): 9–10.

Garson, Barbara
    1988 The Electronic Sweatshop. New York: Simon and Schuster.

Godfrey, N.
    1980 "The Part-Time Question and the Hospital Answer." Nursing 80, Part 2 (November).

Golden, Lonnie
    1990 "The Insensitive Workweek: Trends and Determinants of Adjustment in Average Hours." Journal of Post Keynesian Economics 13 (1): 79–110.

Golden, Lonnie and Eileen Appelbaum
    1990 "What is Driving the Boom in Temporary Employment?" Unpublished paper.

Goldstein, Bernard, and Jack Oldham
1979 Children and Work: A Study in Socialization. New Brunswick, NJ: Transaction Books.

Gordon, Pamela, and B. J. Meadows
1986 "Sharing a Principal Ship: When Two Heads are Better Than One." Principal 66 (1): 26–29.

Gottfredson, Denise C.
1985 "Youth Employment, Crime, and Schooling: A Longitudinal Study of a National Sample." Development Psychology 21: 419–432.

Gower, David
1988 "The Labour Market in the 80's, Canada and the United States." Canadian Economic Observer (August): 3.11–3.17.

Grais, Bernard
1983 Lay-offs and Short-Time Working in Selected OECD Countries. Paris: Organization for Economic Cooperation and Development.

Grasso, J. T., and J. R. Shea
1979 Vocational Education and Training: Impact on Youth. Berkeley. A technical report for the Carnegie Council on Policy Studies in Higher Education. Berkeley, CA: CCPSHE.

Green, Gary, and Sue Norvill Jaquess
1987 "The Effect of Part-Time Employment on Academic Achievement." Journal of Educational Research 80: 326–329.

Greenberger, Ellen, and Laurence Steinberg
1983 "Sex Differences in Early Labor Force Experience: Harbinger of Things to Come." Social Forces 62: 467–487.
1986 When Teenagers Work: The Psychological and Social Costs of Adolescent Employment. New York: Basic Books.

Greenberger, Ellen, Laurence D. Steinberg, Alan Vaux, and Sharon McAuliffe
1980. "Adolescents Who Work: Effects of Part-Time Employment on Family and Peer Relations." Journal of Youth and Adolescence 9: 189–202.

Gunderson, Morley, and Leon Muszynski
1990 Women and Labour Market Poverty. Ottawa: Canadian Advisory Council on the Status of Women.

Gunderson, Morley, and J. Pesando
1980 "Eliminating Mandatory Retirement: Economics and Human Rights." Canadian Public Policy 6: 352–360.

Gustman, Alan, and Thomas Steinmeier
1983 "Minimum-Hours Constraints and Retirement Behavior." Contemporary Policy Issues: 77–91.

Hall, Kenneth
1987 "Creating Jobs for the People." Management Decision 25 (1): 43–47.

Handy, Charles
    1985 The Future of Work. New York: Basil Blackwell.

Harriman, Ann
    1982 The Work/Leisure Trade Off: Reduced Work Time for Managers and Professionals. New York: Praeger.

Heberlein, T. A., and R. Baumgartner
    1978 "Factors Affecting Response Rates to Mailed Questionnaires: A Quantitative Analysis of the Published Literature." American Sociological Review 43: 447–462.

Henderson, Maxwell
    1975 Special Program Review. Government of Ontario, Treasury. Toronto.

Herz, Diane and Philip Rones
    1989 "Institutional Barriers to Employment of Older Workers." Monthly Labor Review 112 (4): 14–21.

Hills, Stephen M., and Beatrice G. Reubens
    1983 "Youth Employment in the United States." In Beatrice G. Reubens (ed.), Youth at Work: An International Survey. Totowa, NJ: Rowman and Allanheld.

Hodson, R.
    1978 "Labour in the Monopoly, Competitive, and State Sectors of Production." Politics and Society 8: 429–480.

Hogarth, Jeanne M.
    1988 "Accepting an Early Retirement Bonus: An Empirical Study." Journal of Human Resources 23 (1): 21–33.

Holden, Karen C., and W. Lee Hansen
    1987 "Part-Time Work, Full-Time Work, and Occupational Segregation." In Clair Brown and Joseph A. Pechman (eds.), Gender in the Workplace. Washington, DC: The Brookings Institution.

Horn, C. A.
    1983 "A Synopsis of Work and It's Future: A Foretaste of Crisis." Management Services 27 (8): 14–18.
    1986 "The Job Sharing Equation." Modern Office 25 (2): 14–16.

Hoskins, Martin, Johnny Sung, and David Ashton
    1989 "Job Competition and the Entry to Work." University of Leicester, Department of Economics, Discussion paper no. 11.

Hotchkiss, Lawrence
    1986 "Work and Schools—Complements or Competitors?" In Kathryn M. Borman and Jane Reisman (eds.), Becoming a Worker. Norwood, NJ: Ablex Publishing.

Humphries, Judith
    1985 Part Time Work. London: Kogan Page.

Hunt, Audrey
    1968 A Survey of Women's Employment. London: Her Majesty's Stationery
    Office.

Hurt, R. A.
    1984 Shorter Working Time: A Dilemma for Collective Bargaining. Paris:
    Organization of Economic Cooperation and Development (OECD).

Ichniowski, Bernard, and Anne E. Preston
    1985 "New Trends in Part-Time Employment." Proceedings of the 38th
    Annual Meeting of the Industrial Relations Research Association.

International Labour Office
    1987 World Labour Report vol. 1–2. Oxford: Oxford University Press.

International Labour Organization (ILO)
    1963 "An International Survey of Part-Time Employment." International
    Labour Review 88 (4): 380–407.
    1989 Conditions of Work Digest 8 (1): 1–132.

Jenny, J.
    1982 Issues Affecting Nurses' Hospital Employment in the 80's. Canadian
    Hospital Association.

Johnson, Lloyd, Jerald Bachman, and Patrick O'Malley
    1982 Monitoring the Future: Questionnaire Responses from the Nation's
    High School Seniors, 1981. Ann Arbor, MI: Institute for Social Research.

Joshi, Heather
    1987 The Cash Opportunity Costs of Childbearing: An Approach to Esti-
    mation Using British Data. Discussion Paper no. 208. London: Centre for
    Economic Policy Research.

Jostman, Susan
    1990 "Ontario Human Rights Commission Officer." Presentation to Brock
    University Labour Studies Programme. February 5.

Juster, F. Thomas, and Frank P. Stafford
    1985 Time, Goods, and Well Being. Ann Arbor, MI: Survey Research Center,
    Institute for Social Research, University of Michigan.

Kahne, Hilda
    1985 Reconceiving Part-Time Work: New Perspectives for Older Workers
    and Women. Totowa, NJ: Rowman and Allanheld.

Kamerman, S. B., and A. J. Kahn
    1987 The Responsive Workplace: Employers and a Changing Labor Force.
    New York: Columbia University Press.

Kapsalis, C.
    1979 Pensions and the Work Decision. Paper presented at the Annual Meet-
    ing of the Canadian Economic Association, May.

Karabel, Jerome, and A. H. Halsey (eds.)
1977 Power and Ideology in Education. New York: Oxford University Press.

Katz, S.
1984 The Status of Women in CUEW—A Survey. Toronto. Canadian Union of Educational Workers. Research Report No. 2.

Kay, Jeanne
1982 "Job Sharing in Geography." Transition 12 (2): 19–24.

Kelly, Sheila, and David Brattan
1986 "Attitudes Toward Working Patterns Are Changing/Moving Away from Nine to Five." Canadian Business Review 13 (1): 14–17.

Keon, Dan
1988 "Union Organizing Activity in Ontario, 1970–1986." Research Essay Series No. 16. Kingston, ON: Industrial Relations Centre, Queen's University.

Kerachsky, Stuart, et al.
1986 "Work Sharing Programs: An Evaluation of Their Use." Monthly Labor Review 109 (5): 31–33.

Kett, Joseph F.
1971 "Adolescence and Youth in Nineteenth Century America." In Theodore K. Rabb and Robert Rotberg (eds.), The Family in History. New York: Harper and Row.

King, Suzanne
1987 "Temporary Workers in Britain: Findings from the 1986 Labour Force Survey." Employment Gazette (April): 238–247.

Klein, Alice, and Wayne Roberts
1974 "Besieged Innocence: The 'Problem' and Problems of Working Women—Toronto, 1896—1914." In Janice Acton, Penny Goldsmith, and Bonnie Shepard (eds.), Women at Work: Ontario, 1850–1930. Toronto: The Canadian Women's Educational Press.

Klein, Viola
1965 Britain's Married Women Workers. London: Routledge Kegan Paul.

Kluegel, James R., and Eliot Smith
1986 Beliefs About Inequality. New York: Aldine.

Krahn, Harvey
1988 A Study of the Transition from School to Work in Three Canadian Cities: Research Design, Response Rates and Descriptive Results. Population Research Laboratory, University of Alberta.

Krahn, Harvey, and Graham S. Lowe
1988 Work, Industry and Canadian Society. Scarborough: Nelson Canada.
1989 "Young Workers in the Service Economy." Background paper prepared for the Economic Council of Canada's project on Employment and the Service Economy. Ottawa: Economic Council of Canada.

1990 "Transitions to Work: Findings from a Longitudinal Study of High School and University Graduates in Three Canadian Cities." In D. Ashton and G. S. Lowe (eds.), Making Their Way: A Comparative Analysis of the Relationship Between Education, Training and the Labour Market in Canada and Britain. London and Toronto: Open University Press/University of Toronto Press.

Kumar, Krishna
1978 Job Sharing Through Part-Time Contracts: A Consideration in the Context of Declining School Enrollments in Ontario. Toronto: ON Institute for Studies in Education.

Kushner, Sherrill
1985 "Job Sharing: An Alternative to a Traditional Law Practice." Legal Economics 11 (6): 24–28.

Lammers, John C.
1987 "Socialization of Employers' Costs During Economic Recessions: The Use of Shared Work Unemployment Insurance to Keep Skilled Workers." International Journal of Sociology and Social Policy 7 (4): 19–30.

Land, Hilary
1981 Parity Begins at Home: Women's and Men's Work in the Home and its Effects on Their Paid Employment. Manchester: Equal Opportunities Commission/Social Sciences Research Fund.

Lee, B.
1988 "Nurses say ICU is a Real Pressure Cooker." Hamilton Spectator (April 26): B1.

Lee, Patricia
1984 "Job Sharing—A Concept Whose Time Has Come." Office Administration and Automation 45 (4): 28–30, 88.

Lee, R. A.
1988 "Controlling Hours of Work." Work Times 6 (2).

Leighton, Patricia
1986 "Job Sharing—Opportunities or Headaches?" Employee Relations (U.K.) 8 (2): 27–31.
1987 "Responses to Vulnerability: The Example of Job Sharing." Employee Relations (U.K.) 9 (5): 49–59.

Leslie, D. W., S. E. Kellams, and G. M. Gunne
1982 Part-Time Faculty in American Higher Education. New York: Praeger.

Levanoni, Eliahu, and Carol A. Sales
1988 "Differences in Job Attitudes Between Full-Time and Part-Time Employees: A Test in a Canadian Context." Unpublished paper, Brock University, ON.

Lévesque, Jean Marc
1987 "The Growth of Part-Time Work in a Changing Industrial Environ-

ment." Monthly Labor Force Survey, Cat. 71–001 (May) Ottawa: Statistics Canada.

Levitan, Sar A. and R. S. Belous
1977 "Work-Sharing Initiatives at Home and Abroad." Monthly Labor Review 100 (9): 16–20.

Levitan, Sar A. and Elizabeth A. Conway
1988 "Part-Timers: Living on Half Rations." Challenge 31 (3): 9–16.

Lewenhak, Sheila
1977 Women and Trade Unions. London: Benn.

Lewin-Epstein, Noah
1981 Youth Employment During High School. Washington, DC: National Center for Educational Statistics.

List, Wilfrid.
1983 "Jury Still Out on Work Sharing Programs." Industrial Management 7 (7): 15, 44.

Little, T. D.
1986 "Part-Time Work: Crisis or Opportunity?" Canadian Business Review 13 (1): 18–20.

Lowe, Graham S., and Harvey Krahn
1985 "Where Wives Work: The Relative Effects of Situational and Attitudinal Factors." Canadian Journal of Sociology 10 (1): 1–22.

Lundy, Katherina L. P., and Barbara D. Warme.
1989 "Part-Time Faculty: Student Perceptions and Experiences." The Canadian Journal of Higher Education 19 (2): 73–85.

Lush, Patricia, John Heinzl, and Chethan Lakshman
1990 "165,000 Factory Jobs Vanished in Past Year, Statscan Report Says." The Globe and Mail, June 9: A1, A2.

Luxton, Meg
1987 "Time for Myself: Women's Work and the 'Fight for Shorter Hours'." In H. J. Maroney and M. Luxton (eds.), Feminism and Political Economy. Toronto: Methuen.

Lynch, Lisa M.
1987 "Individual Differences in the Youth Labour Market: A Cross-sectional Analysis of London Youth." In P. N. Junankar (ed.), From School to Unemployment: The Labour Market for Young People. London: Macmillan.

McCallum, Margaret E.
1986 "Keeping Women in Their Place: The Minimum Wage in Canada, 1910–25." Labour/Le Travail 17 (Spring): 29–56.

MaCoy, Ramelle, and Martin Morand (eds.)
1984 Short-Time Compensation: A Formula for Work Sharing. New York: Pergamon Press.

McDonald, P. Lynn, and Richard A. Wanner
1982 "Work Past Age 65 in Canada: A Socioeconomic Analysis." Aging and Work 5: 169–180.
1984 "Socioeconomic Determinants of Early Retirement in Canada." Canadian Journal on Aging 3: 105–116.
1987 "Retirement in a Dual Economy: The Canadian Case." In Victor W. Marshall (ed.), Aging in Canada (second edition). Markham, ON: Fitzhenry and Whiteside.
1989 Retirement in Canada. Toronto: Butterworths.

McFarland, Joan
1985 "Women in the Pottery Industry: A Case of Lost Potential." Atlantis 11 (1): 23–35.

McKay-Rispoli, Kathleen
1988 "Small Children: No Small Problem." Management World 17 (March-April): 15.

Mackie, Lynn, and Polly Patullo
1977 Women at Work. London: Tavistock.

MacLeod, Jay
1987 Ain't No Making It. Boulder, CO: Westview.

McNeil, Linda.
1978 "Alternatives to Employee Lay-offs: Work Sharing and Prelayoff Consultation." Personnel 55 (1): 60–64.

McNeff, Nancy, et al.
1984 Lowering Expectations: The Impact of Student Employment on Classroom Knowledge. Madison, WI: Wisconsin Center for Educational Research.

McPherson, B. D.
1983 Aging as a Social Process. Toronto: Butterworths.

Maguire, Malcolm, and Mark Spilsbury
1985 Marginal Workers in the U.K. Extract from Vulnerable Workers: A Pilot Report on the Situation in the United Kingdom. Delivered to the International Labour Office (December).

Mangum, Garth, Donald Mayall, and Kristin Nelson
1985 "The Temporary Help Industry: A Response to the Dual Internal Labour Market." Industrial and Labor Relations Review 38 (4): 599–611.

Maroney, Heather Jon
1987 "Feminism at Work." In Heather Jon Maroney and Meg Luxton (eds.), Feminism and Political Economy. Toronto: Methuen.

Martin, Jean, and Ceridwen Roberts
1984 Women and Employment: A Lifetime Perspective. The Report of the 1980 Women and Employment Survey of the Office of Population Censuses and Surveys. Department of Labour. London: Her Majesty's Stationery Office.

Mathera. D.
1985 "Nursing Pay: How Part-Timers are Doing." R. N. (December): 33.

Meier, Elizabeth
1988 Report. Washington, DC: American Association of Retired Persons.

Meier, Gretl S.
1979 Job Sharing. A New pattern for Quality of Work and Life. Kalamazoo, MI: W. E. Upjohn Institute for Employment Research.

Mellon, Earl F., and Steven E. Haugen
1986 "Hourly Paid Workers: Why They Are and What They Earn." Monthly Labor Review 109 (2): 20–26.

Meltz, Noah
1988 Sorry No Care Available Due to Nursing Shortage. Toronto. Registered Nurses Association of Ontario.

Meltz, Noah, and Jill Marzetti
1988 The Shortage of Registered Nurses. Toronto: Registered Nurses Association of Ontario.

Meltz, Noah, Frank Reid, and Gerald Swartz.
1981 Sharing the Work: An Analysis of the Issues in Work Sharing and Job Sharing. Toronto: University of Toronto Press.

Metcalf, D.
1988 "Trade Unions and Economic Performance: The British Evidence." Discussion Paper No. 320, Centre for Labour Economics, London School of Economics.

Méthot, S.
1987 "Employment Patterns of Elderly Canadians." Canadian Social Trends (Autumn): 7–11.

Meyer, Robert H., and David A. Wise
1982 "High School Preparation and Early Labour Force Experience." In Richard B. Freeman and David A. Wise (eds.), The Youth Labor Market Problem: Its Nature, Causes, and Consequences. Chicago: University of Chicago Press.

Meyers, Jim
1986 "All Work and No Play—or Studies?" USA Today (October 3): 1–2A.

Michelson, William
1985 From Sun to Sun: Daily Obligations and Community Structure in the Lives of Employed Women and Their Families. Totowa, NJ: Rowman and Allanheld.

Milkman, Ruth
1976 "Women's Work and the Economic Crisis." Review of Radical Political Economy 8 (1).

344   Bibliography

Miller, Beatrice J.
    1988 "Unmasking the Labour Board: The Big Chill Organizing Part-Timers."
    Our Times 7 (1): 28–31.

Miller, E. W.
    1984 Demotion and Displacement: Career Paths for Women in Academe.
    In M. E. Wallace (ed.), Part-Time Academic Employment in the Humanities.
    New York: Modern Language Association of America.

Millward, N., and M. Stevens
    1986 British Workplace Industrial Relations, 1980–1984. The DE/ESRC/PSI/
    ACAS Surveys. Aldershot: Gower.

Moen, Phyllis, and Donna Dempster-McClain
    1987 "Employed Parents: Role Strain, Work Time, and Preferences for Work-
    ing Less." Journal of Marriage and the Family 49 (August): 579–590.

Morantz, Alan
    1983 "Work Sharing Averts Layoffs." Worklife 3 (3): 9–10.

Morris, Frank C., Jr., and Sandra King
    1980 "Layoffs, Bonafide Seniority Systems, and EEOC Bootstrap Threats."
    EEO Today 7 (4): 269–276.

Morrison, Malcom
    1983 "The Aging of the U.S. Population: Human Resource Implications."
    Monthly Labor Review, 106 (5): 13–19.

Mortimer, Jeylan T., and Michael D. Finch
    1986 "The Effects of Part-Time Work on Adolescent Self-Concept and
    Achievement." In Kathryn M. Borman and Jane Reisman (eds.), Becoming
    A Worker. Norwood, NJ: Ablex Publishing.

Myles, J. F.
    1984 Old Age in the Welfare State: The Political Economy of Public Pensions.
    Toronto: Little, Brown.

Myles, J., G. Picot, and T. Wannell
    1988 Wages and Jobs in the 1990s: Changing Youth Wages and the Declining
    Middle. Research Paper No. 17, Analytical Studies Branch, Social and Eco-
    nomic Studies Division, Statistics Canada. Ottawa: Minister of Supply and
    Services.

Nardone, Thomas J.
    1986 "Part-Time Workers—Who are They?" Monthly Labor Review 109 (1):
    13–19.

National Council on Aging
    1981 Aging in the Eighties: America in Transition: A Survey. Conducted for
    NCOA by Louis Harris and Associates, Inc. Washington, DC: National
    Council on Aging.

Neill, Shirley
    1988 "Unionization in Canada." Canadian Social Trends (Spring): 12–15.

1990 "Unionization in Canada." In Craig McKie and Keith Thompson (eds.), Canadian Social Trends. Toronto: Thompson Educational Publishing Inc.

Nemirow, Martin
1984 "Work Sharing Approaches: Past and Present." Monthly Labour Review 107 (9): 34–39.

New Earnings Survey
1988 New Earnings Survey 1988. London: Her Majesty's Stationery Office.

New Ways to Work
1987 Job Sharing: Putting Policy into Practice: The Local Authority Experience. London: New Ways to Work.
1988 Job Sharing: An Introductory Guide. London: New Ways to Work.
1988 The Equiflex Project: Promoting Equitable Flexibility in the Workplace. London: New Ways to Work.
1989 Job Sharing and Companies. London: New Ways to Work.

Nilsen, Diane M.
1984 "The Youngest Workers: 14- and 15-Year-Olds." Journal of Early Adolescence 4: 189–97.

Nine to Five, National Association of Working Women
1986 "Working at the Margins: Part-Time and Temporary Workers in the United States." New York (September).
1987 "Social Insecurity: The Economic Marginalization of Older Workers." New York.
1988 "Clerical Displacement in the Service Sector in Ohio." New York (January).

Nishio, H. K., and H. Lank
1987 "Patterns of Labour Participation of Older Female Workers." In Victor W. Marshall (ed.), Aging in Canada (second edition). Markham, ON: Fitzhenry and Whiteside.

Nollen, Stanley D.
1982 New Work Schedules in Practice: Managing Time in a Changing Society. New York: Van Nostrand Reinhold.

Nollen, Stanley D., Brenda B. Eddy, and Virginia H. Martin
1978 Permanent Part-Time Employment: The Manager's Perspective. New York: Praeger.

Norwood, Janet
1986 "Labor Market Contrasts: United States and Europe." Industrial Relations Research Association Proceedings.

Novek, Joel
1988 "Peripheralizing Core Labour Markets? The Case of the Canadian Meat Packing Industry." Unpublished manuscript. University of Winnipeg.

O'Connell, Martin and David E. Bloom
1987 Juggling Jobs and Babies: Americas Child Care Challenge. Population Reference Bureau No. 12 (February).

Olmsted, Barney
    1979 "Job Sharing: An Emergency Work Style." International Labour Review
    118 (3): 283–297.
    1983 "Changing Times: The Use of Reduced Work Time Options in the
    United States." International Labour Review 122 (4): 479–493.
    1985 "V Time: Changing the Nature of Part-Time Work." World of Work
    Report.
    1987 "(Flex) Time is Money." Management Review 7 (11): 47–51.

Ontario Economic Council
    1979 Issues and Alternatives: Update. Monograph. Toronto.

Ontario Ministry of Colleges and Universities
    1988 USIS 1001011112 (Special Tabulation) Rounded.

Ontario Ministry of Education
    1987 Directory of Education 1987/1988. Toronto: Queen's Printer for Ontario.

Ontario Nurses Association
    1982 Brief to the Commission of Inquiry into Part-Time Work in Canada.
    Toronto: The Association.
    1988 The Nursing Shortage in Ontario. Toronto: The Goldfarb Corporation.

Organization of Economic Cooperation and Development (OECD)
    1982 Employment Outlook. Paris: OECD.
    1983 Employment Outlook. Paris: OECD.
    1985 "Note A, Technical Annex." Employment Outlook. Paris: OECD.
    1986a Labor Force Statistics Annual. 1965–1985. Paris: OECD.
    1986b La Flexibilité du Marché du Travail. Paris: OECD.
    1988 Quarterly Labor Force Statistics. Paris: OECD, Department of Econom-
    ics and Statistics (1).

Osterman, Paul
    1982 "Employment Structures Within Firms." British Journal of Industrial
    Relations 20 (3): 349–361.
    1987 "Choice of Employment Systems in Internal Labor Markets." Industrial
    Relations 26 (1): 46–67.
    1988 Employment Futures: Reorganization, Dislocation, and Public Policy.
    New York: Oxford University Press.

O'Toole, James
    1985 "Slow Motorola Got to be Number One." New Management 3 (2): 6–
    13.

Owen, John D.
    1978 "Why Part-Time Workers Tend to be in Low-Wage Jobs." Monthly
    Labor Review 101 (6): 11–14.
    1979 Working Hours: An Economic Analysis. Lexington, MA: Lexington
    Books.
    1988 "Work-Time Reduction in the U.S. and Western Europe." Monthly
    Labor Review 111 (12): 41–45.

Packard, Michael D.
1982 "Retirement Options Under Swedish National Pension System." Social Security Bulletin 45 (11): 12–22.

Palmore, E., B. M. Burchett, G. G. Fillenbaum, L. K. George, and L. M. Wallman
1985 Retirement: Causes and Consequences. New York: Springer.

Pampel, F. C., and J. A. Weiss
1983 "Economic Development, Pension Policies, and the Labour Force Participation of Aged Males: A Cross-National, Longitudinal Approach." American Journal of Sociology 89: 350–372.

Panitch, Leo
1977 "The Role and Nature of the Canadian State." In Leo Panitch (ed.), The Canadian State. Toronto: University of Toronto Press.

Parnes, Herbert, and Steven Sandell
1988 "Introduction and Overview." In The Older Worker, M. Borus, H. Parnes, S. Sandell and B. Seidman (eds.), Madison, WI: Industrial Relations Research Association.

Paul, Carolyn E.
1983 Expanding Part-Time Work Options for Older Americans: A Feasibility Study. Los Angeles: Ethel Percy Andrus Gerontology Center.
1988 "Work Options—A Challenge to the Decision to Retire." ILR Report 25 (2): 18–21.

Personick, Valerie
1987 "Industry Output and Employment Through the End of the Century." Monthly Labor Review 110 (9): 30–45.

Phillips, Paul, and Erin Phillips
1983 Women and Work: Inequality in the Labor Market. Toronto: James Lorimer.

Pilkington, W., and J. Wood
1986 "Job Satisifaction, Role Conflict and Role Ambiguity—A Study of Hospital Nurses." Australian Journal of Advanced Nursing 3 (3): 3–14.

Piotet, François
1987 The Changing Face of Work: Researching and Debating Issues. Dublin: European Foundation for the Improvement of Living and Working Conditions.

Plewes, Thomas
1983 Profile of the Part-Time Worker. Conference of Association of Part-Time Professionals. (October).

Plowden, B. H.
1968 Children and Their Primary Schools. A Report of the Central Advisory Council for Education (England). Vol. 1. London: Her Majesty's Stationery Office.

Podgursky, Michael, and Paul Swaim
   1986 "Labor Market Adjustment and Job Displacement: Evidence from the January 1984 Displaced Worker Survey." U.S. Department of Labor, January.

Pollack, I. C.
   1981 "Elements of a Policy on Part-Time Employment." Report to the Minister of Employment and Immigration. March 13.

Popa, Mary
   1983 "Employers Made Early Retirement More Attractive: Fourth of Surveyed Companies Offer Incentives." Employee Benefit Review Plan, February.

Post, Linda C.
   1986 "Labor of Love." Communication World 3 (7): 16–19, 37.

Posyniak, Len
   1986 "Let's Take a Fresh Look at Alternative Work Time." Canadian Business Review 13 (3): 37–38.

Pritchard, Mary M.
   1988 "A Survey of Job Sharing: An Exploration of the Present Status of Job Sharing, Individual Career Patterns, Trends over Time, and some Organizational Issues." Unpublished Masters Degree Thesis, Birkbeck College, London University.

Progressive Grocer
   1988 "Annual Report of the Grocery Industry." (April).

Pupo, Norene
   1989 "Balancing Responsibilities: The Part-Time Option." In Ann Duffy, Nancy Mandell, and Norene Pupo, Few Choices: Women, Work and Family. Toronto: Garamond Press.

Pupo, Norene and Ann Doris Duffy
   1988 "The Ontario Labor Relations Board and the Part-Time Worker." Relations Industrielle/Industrial Relations 43 (3): 660–684.

Radwanski, George
   1986 Ontario Study of the Service Sector. Toronto: Ontario, Ministry of Treasury and Economics.

Raffe, David
   1988 "The Story so Far: Research on Education, Training and the Labour Market from the Scottish Surveys." In David Raffe (ed.), Education and the Youth Labour Market. London: The Falmer Press.

Rajan, Amin, and Penny van Eupen
   1990 Good Practices in the Employment of Women Returners. Falmer, Brighton: Institute of Manpower Studies.

Rebitzer, James, and Lowell Taylor
1988 "A Model of Dual Labor Markets with Uncertain Product Demand."
Mimeographed, Department of Economics, University of Texas at Austin.
1990 Women in Canada (second edition). Ottawa: Minister of Supply and
Services.

Registered Nurses Association of Ontario
1981 Background Paper Regarding Rights and Responsibilities of Nurses.
Toronto: Registered Nurses Association of Ontario.
1985 The Utilization of the RNA. Toronto: Woods Gordon Consultants.

Reich, Robert
1983 The Next American Frontier. New York: Times Books.

Renwick, Patricia A., and Edward E. Lawler III
1978 "What Do You Really Want From Your Job?" Psychology Today 11:
53–65.

Reubens, Beatrice G. (ed.)
1983. Youth at Work: An International Survey. Totowa, NJ: Rowman and
Allanheld.

Richards, J.
1987 "The Industrial Distribution of the Temporary Short-Time Working
Compensation Scheme." Applied Economics 19 (1): 111–125.

Rinehart, James W.
1987 The Tyranny of Work (second edition). Don Mills, ON: Harcourt Brace
Jovanovich.

Robb, Roberta E., and Morley Gunderson
1987 "Women and Overtime." Report prepared for the Ontario Task Force
on Hours of Work and Overtime (September).

Roberts, Kenneth
1984 School Leavers and Their Prospects: Youth and the Labour Market in
the 1980's. Milton Keynes: Open University Press.

Roberts, Kenneth, Sally Dench, and Deborah Richardson
1987 The Changing Structure of the Youth Labour Market. Department of
Employment Research Paper No. 59 London: Department of Employment.

Robinson, D.
1979 "Part-Time Employment in the European Community." International
Labour Review 118 (3).
1982 "Soon We'll Need the Older Worker." Los Angeles Times (April 6).

Robinson, Olive
1988 "The Changing Labour Market: Growth of Part-Time Employment and
Labour Market Segmentation in Britain." In Sylvia Walby (ed.), Gender
Segregation at Work. Milton Keynes: Open University Press.

Robinson, Olive, and John Wallace
    1984a "Growth and Utilisation of Part-Time Labour in Great Britain." Employment Gazette 92 (9): 391–397.
    1984b Part-Time Employment and Sex Discrimination in Great Britain. Paper No. 43. London: Department of Employment.

Ronen, Simcha
    1984 Alternative Work Schedules: Selecting, Implementing and Evaluating. Homewood, IL: Dow-Jones Irwin.

Rones, Philip
    1983 "Labor Market Problems of Older Workers." Monthly Labor Review 106 (5): 3–12.
    1988 "Employment, Earnings and Unemployment." In M. Borus, H. Parnes, S. Sandell, and B. Seidman (eds.), The Older Worker. Madison, WI: Industrial Relations Research Association.

Root, Lawrence, and Laura Zarrugh
    1985 "Personnel Practices for an Aging Work Force: Private Sector Examples." National Older Worker Information Survey, for the U.S. Senate Select Committee on Aging.

Rosen, B., and T. H. Jerdee
    1985 Older Employees: New Roles for Valid Resources. Homewood, IL: Dow Jones-Irwin.

Rosenbaum, James E.
    1976 Making Inequality. New York: Wiley.

Rosow, Jerome, and Robert Zager
    1983 "Punch Out the Time Clocks." Harvard Business Review 61 (2): 12–30.
    1987 "Recent Labour Market Trends." Employment Outlook. Paris: OECD.

Rotchford N. L., and K. Roberts
    1982 "Part-time Workers as Missing Persons in Organization Research." Academy of Management Review 7: 228–234.

Rubery, Jill (ed.)
    1988 Women and Recession. London: Routledge and Kegan Paul.

Ruggiero, Mary, Ellen Greenberger, and Lawrence D. Steinberg
    1982 "Occupational Deviance Among Adolescent Workers." Youth and Society 13: 423–448.

Runciman, C.
    1966 Relative Deprivation and Social Justice. Los Angeles: University of California Press.

Sacks, Karen
    1988 Caring by the Hour: Women, Work, and Organizing at Duke Medical Center. Urbana: University of Illinois Press.

Sandlier-Brown, Peter
1978 Work Sharing in Canada. Ottawa: C. D. Howe Research Institute.

Saskatchewan, Department of Social Services
1976 Federal-Provincial Briefing Notes re Extended Program Financing. Regina: Saskatchewan Social Services.

Schiff, Frank
1986 "Short-Time Compensation: Assessing the Issues." Monthly Labor Review 109 (5): 28–30.

Schroeer, Susan G.
1983 "Alternative Workstyles: A solution to Productivity Problems?" Supervisory Management 28 (7): 24–30.

Shalla, Vivian
1990 "Flexible Labour: The Part-Time Work Experience of Airline Passenger Agents." Presented at the Canadian Sociology and Anthropology Association Meetings, Victoria, British Columbia, May.

Shank, Susan
1986 "Preferred Hours of Work and Corresponding Earnings." Monthly Labor Review 109 (11): 40–44.
1988 "Women and the Labor Market: The Link Grows Stronger." Monthly Labor Review 111 (3): 3–8.

Shaw, Lois
1988 Special Problems of Older Women Workers." In The Older Worker, M. Borus, H. Parnes, S. Sandell and B. Seidman (eds.), Madison, WI: Industrial Relations Research Association.

Shifrin, Leonard
1990 "Fudging Jobless Numbers." The Toronto Star (July 23): A21.

Simeone, A.
1987 Academic Women: Working Towards Equality. Hadley, MA: Bergin and Garvey.

Slotnick, Lorne
1988 "No Clear Victor in Deal Imposed on Post Office." The Globe and Mail, July 7: A1, A2.

Smigel, Erwin O., and H. Laurence Ross
1970 Crimes Against Bureaucracy. New York: Van Nostrand.

Smith, Jerald R.
1981 "Alternative Work Patterns: Job Sharing." Manage 33 (2): 31–32.

Speck, Dave
1988 "Part-Time Work: Opportunity or Exploitation?" Presentation to Brock University Labour Studies Programme, November 16.

Spencer, Dee Ann
1988 "Public Schoolteaching: A Suitable Job for a Woman?" In Anne Sta-

tham, Eleanor M. Miller, and Hans O. Mauksch (eds.), The Worth of Women's Work, A Qualitative Synthesis. Albany, NY: State University of New York Press.

Spender, D.
1984 "Sexism in Teacher Education." In S. Acker and D. W. Piper (eds.), Is Higher Education Fair to Women? University of Surrey: SRHE and NFER—Nelson.

Spiegelman, Paul J.
1976 "Bona Fide Seniority Systems and Relief From Last Hired, First Fired Layoffs Under Title VII." Employee Relations Law Journal 2 (2): 141–154.

Spilerman, S.
1977 "Careers, Labour Market Structure, and Socioeconomic Achievement." American Journal of Sociology 83: 551–593.

Standing, Guy
1986 Unemployment and Labor Flexibility: The United Kingdom. Geneva: International Labor Organization.

Steinberg, Laurence D.
1982 "Jumping Off the Work Experience Bandwagon." Journal of Youth and Adolescence 11: 183–205.

Stephenson, Stanley P., Jr.
1979 "From School to Work: A Transition with Job Search Implications." Youth and Society 11: 114–132.

Stinson, Jane
1984 "Bargaining Challenge: Part-Time Work." The Facts (December—January, 1984–85): 5–6.

Stinson, John F.
1986 "Moonlighting by Women Jumped to Record Highs." Monthly Labor Review 109 (11): 22–25.

Strong-Boag, Veronica
1979 "The Girl of the New Day: Canadian Working Women in the 1920's." Labour/Le Travaileur 4 (4): 131–164.

Stryckman, J.
1987 "Work Sharing and the Older Worker in a Unionized Setting." In Victor Marshall (ed.), Aging in Canada (second edition). Markham, ON: Fitzhenry and Whiteside.

Summerfield, Penny
1984 Women Workers in the Second World War. London: Croom Helm.

Sundstrom, M.
1982 "Part-Time Work and Trade Union Activities Among Women." Economic and Industrial Democracy 3 (4): 561–567.

Swank, Constance
   1982 Phased Retirement: The European Experience. Washington, DC: National Council for Alternative Work Patterns.

Swartz, Gerald S.
   1983 Worksharing, Jobsharing and Skill Development Leave. Background Paper 27. Ottawa: Department of Employment and Immigration.

Sykes, R.
   1982 "The Squeeze Is On in Ottawa." Proceedings of the Conference on Medicare: The Decisive Year. Montreal: Center for Policy Alternatives.

Symons, T.H.B., and J. E. Page
   1984 Some Questions of Balance: Human Resources and Canadian Studies. Volume III of To Know Ourselves: The Report of the Commission on Canadian Studies. Ottawa: Association of Universities and Colleges of Canada.

Syrett, Michel
   1982 "How to Make Job Sharing Work." Personnel Management (UK) 14 (10): 44–47.

Tanimura, Clinton T.
   1981 Job Sharing Pilot Project in the Department of Education: Final Evaluation. A Report to the Legislature of the State of Hawaii. (81–10) Honolulu, HI: Hawaii State Legislature, Senate.

Taylorson, D.
   1984 The Professional Socialization, Integration and Identity of Women Ph.D. Candidates. In S. Acker and D. W. Piper (eds.), Is Higher Education Fair to Women? University of Surrey: SHRE and NFER—Nelson.

Theodore, Athena
   1986 The Campus Troublemakers: Academic Women in Protest. Houston: Cap and Gown Press.

Thomas, Edward G.
   1987 "Workers Who Set Their Own Time Clocks." Business and Society Review 61 (Spring): 49–51.

Thurman, Joseph E., and Gabriele Trah
   1990 "Part-time Work in International Perspective." International Labour Review 129 (1): 23–40.

Tilly, Chris
   1990 Short Hours Short Shrift: Causes and Consequences of Growing Part-Time Work. Washington, DC: Employment Research Institute.

Tooley, Jo Ann
   1989 "Hardworking High-Schoolers." U.S. News and World Report (June 26): 74.

Torrence, William D., and George Rejda
   1987 "Short-Time Compensation As a New Employee Benefit." Benefits Quarterly 3 (3): 7–16.

Tuckman, Barbara H., and Howard P. Tuckman
    1980 "Part-Timers, Sex Discrimination, and Career Choice at 2-Year Institutions: Further Findings from the AAUP Survey." Academe: Bulletin of the AAUP 66 (March): 71–76.
    1981 "Women as Part-Time Faculty Members." Higher Education: The International Journal of Higher Education and Educational Planning 10 (2): 169–179.

United Kingdom. Central Statistical Office
    1976 British Labour Force Statistics, Yearbook 1976. London: Her Majesty's Stationery Office.
    1988 Annual Abstract of Statistics. London: Her Majesty's Stationery Office.
    1990 Annual Abstract of Statistics. London: Her Majesty's Stationery Office.

United Kingdom. Department of Education and Science
    1985 Statistical Bulletin 5/85 (February).
    1986 Statistical Bulletin 4/86 (February).

United Kingdon. Department of Employment
    1985 Employment Statistics Historical Supplement No. 1—Employment Gazette (April).
    1988a "Definitions." Employment Gazette (April): S67.
    1988b "Membership of Trade Unions in 1986." Employment Gazette (May): 275–278.
    1988c "Employment Statistics: Revised Presentation." Employment Gazette (August): S6.

United Kingdom. House of Lords
    1982 Minutes of Evidence of the Select Committee on Part-Time Work. Her Majesty's Stationery Office (July).

United Kingdom. Parliament
    1942 Manpower in Banking and Allied Business and in Ordinary Insurance and in Industrial Assurance. Cmd. 6402.
    1946/7 Economic Survey for 1947. Cmd. 7046.
    1955/6 Employment for Older Men and Women. National Advisory Committee. Cmd. 9628 October 20, 1955.
    1974 Expenditure Committee, Session 1972–73. Government Observations on the Reports of Youth Employment Services, Employment of Women and Employment Services and Training. Cmd. 5536.
    1986 Building Businesses—Not Barriers. Department of Employment. Cmd 9794.

United Nations Association of the United States of America. Economic Policy Council
    1985 Work and Family in the United States: A Policy Initiative. (December).

United States. Bureau of the Census
    1987 "Who's Minding the Kids?" Current Population Reports, Household Economic Studies. Child Care Arrangements. (Winter 1984–85, Series P–70 (9) May).

1988 Statistical Abstract of the United States. Washington, DC: Government Printing Office.

United States. Department of Labor, Secretary's Commission on Achieving Necessary Skills
1991 What Work Requires of School.

United States. Department of Labor, Bureau of Labor Statistics
1980 Employment and Earnings 27 (1).
1985 Handbook of Labor Statistics.
1988 Employment and Earnings 35 (1).

Vanfossen, Beth E., James D. Jones, and Joan Z. Spade
1987 "Curriculum Tracking and Status Maintenance." Sociology of Education 60: 104–122.

Walby, Sylvia
1985 "Approaches to the Study of Gender Relations in Employment and Unemployment." In B. Roberts, R. Finnegan, and D. Gallie (eds.), New Approaches to Economic Life. London: Manchester University Press.
1987 Flexibility and the Sexual Division of Labour. Paper given at the conference on Part-Time Work at the West Yorkshire Centre for Research on Women. University of Bradford.

Walker, Alan
1983 "Care for Elderly People: A Conflict Between Women and the State." In Janet Finch, and Dulcie Groves (eds.), A Labour of Love. London: Routledge and Kegan Paul.

Wallace, M. E. (ed.)
1984 Part-Time Academic Employment in the Humanities. New York: Modern Language Association of America.

Wanner, Richard A., and P. Lynn McDonald
1987 "Retirement, Public Pension Policy, and Industrial Development: A Time Series Analysis." Paper presented at the annual meeting of the Canadian Sociology and Anthropology Association, Hamilton, ON.

Warme, Barbara D., and Katherina L. P. Lundy
1986 "Part-Time Faculty: Institutional Needs and Career Dilemmas." In Katherina L. P. Lundy and Barbara D. Warme (eds.), Work in the Canadian Context: Continuity Despite Change (second edition). Toronto: Butterworths.
1988a "Erosion of an Ideal: The 'Presence' of Part-time Faculty." Studies in Higher Education 13 (2): 201–213.
1988b "Gender and Academic Caste: The Case of Part-Time Faculty." Presented at the 23rd Annual Meeting of the Canadian Sociology and Anthropology Association, Windsor, June.

Watford, Kim
1986 "Shorter Workweeks: An Alternative to Layoffs." Business Week, Industrial/Technology Edition, No. 2941 (April 14): 77–78.

Way, Philip
1988 "New Developments in Employment Flexibility." Labor Law Journal, August: 552–557.

Weeks, Wendy
1978 "Collective Bargaining and Part-Time Work in Ontario." Relations Industrielles/Industrial Relations 33 (1): 80–92.
1980a "Part-Time Work: The Business View on Second-Class Jobs for House-wives and Mothers." Atlantis 5 (2): 69–88.
1980b "The Extent and Nature of Part-Time Work in Hamilton, Survey Results of Selected Hamilton Businesses—1978." Prepared for the Community Permanent Part-Time Work Committee. Hamilton, ON (September).
1984 "Part-Time Work: The Business View on Second-Class Jobs for House-wives and Mothers." In Graham S. Lowe and Harvey A. Krahn (eds.), Working Canadians: Readings in the Sociology of Work and Industry. Toronto: Methuen.

Wetzel, Kurt, Daniel G. Gallagher, and June M. Bold
1987 "Organizational and Union Commitment of Part-Time Workers." Proceedings of the 24th Annual Meeting of the Canadian Industrial Relations Association. Hamilton, June 4–6: 653–667.

White, Jerry Patrick
1988 Brief to the Board of Governors Concerning the Elimination of Registered Nursing Assistants from Active Treatment at the Hamilton Civic Hospitals. Hamilton: Canadian Union of Public Employees.
1990 Hospital Strike: Women, Unions, and Conflict in the Public Sector. Toronto: Thompson Educational Publishing.

White, Julie
1980 Women and Unions. Ottawa: Minister of Supply and Services.
1983 Women and Part-time Work. Canadian Advisory Council on the Status of Women. Ottawa: Minister of Supply and Services.
1990 Mail and Female: Women and The Canadian Union of Postal Workers. Toronto: Thompson Educational Publishing.

White, Michael
1987 Working Hours. Geneva: International Labour Organization.

Wijting, Jan P., Carole R. Arnold, and Kelley A. Conrad
1977 "Relationships Between Work Values, Socio-Educational and Work Experiences, and Vocational Aspirations of 6th, 9th, 10th and 12th Graders." Journal of Vocational Behavior 11: 51–65.

Williams, Terry, and William Kornblum
1985 Growing Up Poor. Lexington, MA: D. C. Heath.

Wood, William D.
1984 An Overview of the Canadian Industrial Relations Scene. Kingston, ON: Industrial Relations Centre.

Work in America Institute
1981 New Work Schedules for a Changing Society. Scarsdale, NY: Work in America Institute.

Yalnizyan, Armine, and David A. Wolfe
1989 Target on Training: Meeting Workers' Needs in a Changing Economy. Toronto: Social Planning Council of Metropolitan Toronto.

Yamada, Narumi
1985 "Working Time in Japan: Recent Trends and Issues." International Labor Review 124 (November-December): 699–718.

Yang, S. W., and M. W. Zak
1981 Part-Time Faculty Employment in Ohio: A Statewide Study. Kent, OH: Kent State University.

Zalusky, John
1986 "Short-Time Compensation: The AFL-CIO Perspective." Monthly Labor Review 109 (5): 33–34.

Zeytinoglu, Isik Urla
1987a "Part-Time Workers: Unionization and Collective Bargaining in Canada." Industrial Relations Research Association Proceedings (December).
1987b Part-Time Workers and Collective Bargaining in Internal Labour Markets. Working Paper No. 277. (May), Faculty of Business, McMaster University, ON.
1987c "Part-Time Workers: Unionization and Collective Bargaining in Canada." Proceedings of the Thirty-Ninth Annual Meeting (New Orleans, December 28–30, 1986), IRRA series, Madison, WI: Industrial Relations Research Association.

Zeytinoglu, Isik Urla, and Maroussia Ahmed
1988 "Results of a Survey on Part-Time Faculty at McMaster University." Paper presented at the CAUT Status of Women Workshop in Vancouver, British Coumbia, 1988.

Zippo, Mary
1982 "Alternative Work Patterns Sweep Western Europe." Personnel 59 (1): 34–37.

Index

About the Contributors

DAVID G. BLANCHFLOWER teaches economics at Dartmouth College. He is Research Associate at the National Bureau of Economic Research and a senior member of the Centre for Labour Economics at the London School of Economics. He has published widely in the areas of labor economics and industrial relations. He is currently writing a book on international wage determination with his colleague Andrew Oswald that will be published by MIT Press in 1992.

CELIA J. BRIAR teaches Social Policy at Massey University, New Zealand. She has written and done research in the area of women's employment and social policy, women's occupational mobility, and women as a "flexible" work force. She is the author of *Women's Work and Unemployment*, coauthor of *Unemployment in New Zealand*, and is currently editing a text on women and social policy in New Zealand.

ELIZABETH A. CONWAY is currently a policy analyst at the Blue Cross and Blue Shield Association in Washington, D.C. As a former research associate at the Center for Social Policy Studies at The George Washington University, she has written articles about the part-time and temporary work force, health policy, and family issues. While at the Center, she coauthored a special report for the Bureau of National Affairs on *The Family in Flux* and also *American Child Care: Problems and Solutions*.

ANGELA M. DALE is Deputy Director of the Social Statistics Research Unit and Reader in Social Statistics at City University in London. She has published in the areas of stratification, employment, and labor market and is joint author of *Doing Secondary Analysis* (1988). She is currently responsible for academic access to the OPCS Longitudinal Study.

SHIRLEY DEX teaches economics at the University of Keele. Formerly, she held posts in sociology and economics at the universities of Exeter and Ashton. Her writings include a number of books on women's employment: *The Sexual Division of Work, British and American Women at Work* with Lois B. Shaw, *Women's Occupational Mobility,* and *Women's Attitudes Towards Work.*

ROBERT J. DRUMMOND teaches political Science at York University in Toronto. He has published essays on voting behavior, public opinion, and public policy and is currently serving as Associate Dean of Arts at York.

ANN DUFFY teaches sociology and labor studies at Brock University in St. Catharines. Her recent work includes an edited collection of feminist articles on the Canadian family, *Reconstructing the Canadian Family,* and a coauthored examination of women's efforts to manage the demands of domestic work and paid employment, *Few Choices: Women, Work and Family.* She is currently collaborating with Norene Pupo on a book that investigates women's part-time employment in Canada, *The Part-Time Puzzle: Connecting Gender, Work and Family.*

LONNIE GOLDEN is currently a Visiting Professor of Economics at Temple University. His research activity is in the economic analysis of labor market behavior and he has investigated such issues as the rapid rise in temporary jobs and the lack of flexibility in working hours. He spent a year as Director of Economic Research of 9to5, National Association of Working Women, where he investigated the economics of aging and the employment impact of new technology.

HILDA KAHNE teaches economics at Wheaton College, Norton, Massachusetts. She held the A. Howard Meneely Professorship, 1982–84. Her publications span areas of economics of aging and social welfare, flexible work structures, and work and family issues both in the United States and cross-culturally. She is author of *Reconceiving Part-Time Work: New Perspectives for Older Workers and Women.* Currently she is coediting, with Janet Giele, *Women's Work and Women's Lives in Modernizing and Industrial Countries: Common Themes and Contrasts* (forthcoming).

HARVEY KRAHN is Director of the Population Research Laboratory and teaches sociology at the University of Alberta. His main research interests are in the sociology of work, where his recent publications include *Work, Industry and Canadian Society* (1988, with G. S. Lowe).

SAR A. LEVITAN is research professor of economics and director of the Center for Social Policy Studies at The George Washington University. His career has combined research and teaching with government service in the fields of labor, economics, and social policy. He has served as an arbitrator and consultant to government and private organizations. Among the books he has authored are *Working But Poor: America's Contradiction* and *Protecting American Workers*.

GRAHAM S. LOWE is a sociologist at the University of Alberta specializing in the study of work. His recent books include *Women in the Administrative Revolution: The Feminization of Clerical Work*; *Work, Industry and Canadian Society* (coauthored with Harvey Krahn), and *Making Their Way: A Comparative Analysis of the Relationship Between Education, Training and the Labour Market in Canada and Britain* (coedited with David Ashton). He is Editor of the Canadian Journal of Sociology.

KATHERINA L. P. LUNDY was, at the time of her death, a sociologist at Atkinson College of York University and also at Erindale College at the University of Toronto. Most of her research was in occupational sociology and has been widely reported at conferences and in journal articles. She co-authored this and four other books with Barbara Warme.

LARRY A. LUNDY develops computer-assisted modes of analysis of social service data for the provincial Ministry of Community and Social Services in Ontario. His research and teaching have been in anthropology, social work, and sociology.

P. LYNN McDONALD teaches in the Faculty of Social Work at the University of Calgary. Her current areas of research include the social-structural aspects of retirement, elder abuse, and alcohol abuse among elderly persons. She is coauthor of *Retirement in Canada*.

CRAIG McKIE is Chief of Social Reporting in the Housing, Family, and Social Statistics Division of Statistics Canada in Ottawa. He is Editor of *Canadian Social Trends*, Statistics Canada's quarterly social statistics journal. He is also an Adjunct Research Professor in the Department of Sociology and Anthropology at Carleton University in Ottawa.

VIVIENNE MONTY is Head of the Government and Business Library at York University in Toronto. She was President of the Canadian Library Association in 1989. She is the author of the *Canadian Small Business Handbook* and has written articles on the subject of management. She owns and operates a small business.

NORENE PUPO teaches in the Faculty of Social Work at York University. She is coauthor of *Few Choices: Women, Work and Family*. She is also writing a book on Canadian women's part-time work experience, with Ann Duffy. She is interested in the impact of social policy on women's lives and the direction of union policy and activity in the 1990s.

ROBERT A. ROTHMAN teaches sociology at the University of Delaware. His research focuses on the sociological dimensions of occupations and organizations. He is the author of *Working: Sociological Perspectives* and *Inequality and Stratification*.

CHRIS TILLY teaches economics at the University of Lowell in Massachusetts. In recent research, he has focused on part-time work, income inequality, and poverty. He is the author of *Short Hours Short Shrift: Causes and Consequences of Growing Part-Time Work*.

RICHARD A. WANNER teaches sociology at the University of Calgary. His current research projects focus on retirement among displaced workers, part-time employment among older workers, and trends in occupational mobility in Canada. He is the author of *Retirement in Canada* with Lynn McDonald.

BARBARA D. WARME, a sociologist, is currently doing research in the Netherlands. At York University, she has taught in the areas of public policy and the sociology of work, and was the Director of the Writing Workshop for six years. She collaborated with Kitty Lundy on *Work in the Canadian Context: Continuity Despite Change* and *Sociology: A Window on the World*.

JERRY PATRICK WHITE teaches in the Centre for Administrative and Information Studies, Social Sciences, University of Western Ontario. His most recent publication is *Hospital Strike: Women, Unions, and Conflict in the Public Sector*. He is currently conducting a Canada-wide study of the participation of women in unions.

ISIK URLA ZEYTINOGLU teaches industrial relations in the Faculty of Business at McMaster University in Hamilton. Her research interests include international and comparative industrial relations, women in management and in unions, and collective bargaining. Her research has appeared in journals and books in Canada and the United States. She is also coauthor of *The Political, Economic and Labor Climate in Turkey*.